Bangkok

"All you've got to do is decide to go
and the hardest part is over.

So go!"

Contents

(left) **Wat Phra Kaew p58** Join the pilgrims at the Emerald Buddha.

....

(above) **Chinatown p95** Explore bustling streets and markets.

....

(right) **Noodle soup p214** Sample Thai delicacies.

....

Greater Bangkok p145

Thewet & Dusit p88

Banglamphu p76

Ko Ratanakosin & Thonburi p56

Chinatown p95

Siam Square, Pratunam, Ploenchit & Ratchathewi p103

Sukhumvit p133

Riverside, Silom & Lumphini p118

Welcome to Bangkok

Same same, but different. This Thailish T-shirt philosophy sums up Bangkok, a city where the familiar and the exotic collide like the flavours on a plate of pàt tai.

Full-on Food

Until you've eaten on a Bangkok street, your noodles mingling with your sweat amid a cloud of exhaust fumes, you haven't actually eaten Thai food. It can be an overwhelming mix: the underlying flavours – spicy, sour, sweet and salty – aren't exactly meat and potatoes. But for adventurous foodies who don't need white tablecloths, there's probably no better dining destination in the world. And with immigration bringing every regional Thai and international cuisine to the capital, it's also a truly diverse experience.

Fun Folks

The language barrier may seem huge, but it's never prevented anybody from loving the Thai people. The capital's cultural underpinnings are evident in virtually all facets of everyday life, and most enjoyably through its residents' sense of *sà·nùk* (fun). In Bangkok, anything worth doing should have an element of *sà·nùk*. Ordering food, changing money and haggling at markets will usually involve a sense of playfulness – a dash of flirtation, perhaps, and a smile. It's a language that doesn't require words, and one that's easy to learn.

Urban Exploration

With so much of life conducted on the street, there are few cities in the world that reward exploration as handsomely as Bangkok. Cap off an extended boat trip with a visit to a hidden market. A stroll off Banglamphu's beaten track can wind up in a conversation with a monk. Get lost in the tiny lanes of Chinatown and stumble upon a live Chinese opera performance. After dark, let the BTS (Skytrain) escort you to Sukhumvit, where the local nightlife scene reveals a sophisticated and dynamic city.

Contrasts

It's the contradictions that give the City of Angels its rich, multifaceted personality. Here climate-controlled megamalls sit beside 200-year-old village homes; gold-spired Buddhist temples share space with neon-lit strips of sleaze; slow-moving rivers of traffic are bypassed by long-tail boats plying the royal river; and streets lined with food carts are overlooked by restaurants on top of skyscrapers serving exotic cocktails. As Bangkok races towards the future, these contrasts will never stop supplying the city with its never-ending Thai-ness.

Why I Love Bangkok

By Austin Bush, Author

Admittedly, there are some things – the hot weather, the pollution, the political instability – that make Bangkok a less-than-ideal city. But there's so much more that makes it amazing. I love the food. What other city has such a full-flavoured, no-holds-barred, insatiable, fanatical approach to eating? I love old Bangkok. Districts such as Banglamphu and Chinatown still carry the grit and character of the city that used to be. And I'd be lying if I didn't also say that I love new Bangkok – don't we all have a soft spot for megamalls and air-con?

For more about our author, see p272.

Top: Traditional dancer at Erawan Shrine (p106)

Bangkok's
Top 10

Open-air Dining *(p24)*

1 Bangkok's reputation as a polluted city belies its forte as an outdoor-dining capital. Despite the modern conveniences of air-conditioning and contemporary cafes, some of the most memorable meals in the city also called the 'Big Mango' are had at the open-air markets and food stalls. Forget about three square meals: in Bangkok, locals snack throughout the day, packing away at least four meals before sunset. It would be rude not to join them.

BELOW: STREET EATS IN CHINATOWN (P101)

✕ *Eating*

Jim Thompson House *(p105)*

2 The late American entrepreneur Jim Thompson used his traditional Thai-style home as a repository for Thai traditions and artwork. Thompson mysteriously disappeared in 1967, and today his former home is a museum – one that every visitor secretly wishes to live in for a day or more. Why? Rooms are adorned with his exquisite art collection and personal possessions, including rare Chinese porcelain pieces and Burmese, Cambodian and Thai artefacts, and the garden is a jungle of tropical plants and lotus ponds, converging in the epitome of the traditional Thai house.

◉ *Siam Square, Pratunam, Ploenchit & Ratchathewi*

KIMBERLEY COOLEY / GETTY IMAGES ©

Banglamphu (p76)

3 Easily Bangkok's most charming neighbourhood, Banglamphu is the city's former aristocratic centre, once filled with minor royalty and riverside mansions. Today the old quarter is dominated by antique shophouses, backpackers seeking R&R on famous Th Khao San, civil servants sauntering between offices and lunch spots, and Bangkok's predominant enclave of bohemian artists and students. Vendor carts and classic restaurants make a patchwork quilt of Banglamphu, offering ample options for a roving stomach. The area is also home to some of the city's best bars.

TOP LEFT: TH KHAO SAN (P82)

⊙ *Banglamphu*

Chatuchak Weekend Market (p147)

4 In a city obsessed with commerce, Chatuchak Weekend Market takes the prize as Bangkok's biggest and baddest market. Silks, sneakers, fighting cocks and fighting fish, fluffy puppies and souvenirs for the insatiable *fa·ràng* (Westerner) – if it can be sold in Thailand, you'll find it here. From everyday to clubby, clothes dominate much of the market, but this being Thailand, food and drink also have a strong and refreshing presence, making Chatuchak as much about entertainment as it is about shopping.

⊙ *Greater Bangkok*

Wat Pho (p63)

5 The grounds of Wat Pho claim a 16th-century birthday, predating Bangkok itself. In addition to being the country's biggest temple, Wat Pho is home to a school of traditional Thai medicine, where on-site massage pavilions facilitate that elusive convergence of sightseeing and relaxation. Still not impressed? Let us not forget Wat Pho's primary Buddha – a reclining figure that nearly dwarfs its sizeable shelter. Symbolic of Buddha's death and passage into nirvana, the reclining Buddha measures 46m and is gilded with gold leaf, making it truly larger than life.

⊙ *Ko Ratanakosin & Thonburi*

Shopping *(p43)*

6 Even avowed anticonsumerists weaken in Bangkok. One minute they're touting the virtues of a life without material possessions, the next they're admiring the fake Rolex watches and mapping out the route to MBK Center (p113). Bangkok's malls, however, are just a warm-up for the markets, the cardio workout of shopping. In this city, footpaths are for additional retail space, not for pedestrians. In addition to Chatuchak Weekend Market – one of the world's largest markets – Bangkok is an established destination for bespoke tailoring, and has its own emerging fashion scene.

BELOW: MBK CENTER

🛍 *Shopping*

Chinatown *(p95)*

7 Forgive us for positing that Bangkok's Chinatown is something of an Asian El Dorado. The neighbourhood's main artery, Th Yaowarat, is crowded with gold shops – sealed glass-front buildings that look more like Chinese altars than downtown jewellers. Likewise, the Buddha statue at Wat Traimit has more gold than you've likely ever seen in one place, and the pencil-thin lanes that branch off Talat Mai are decked with gold-leaf-coated goods. Throw in the blazing neon signs and smoky, open-air kitchens and you have an urban explorer's fantasy.

RIGHT: WAT TRAIMIT (P97)

👁 *Chinatown*

Mae Nam Chao Phraya *(p125)*

8 Mae Nam Chao Phraya (Chao Phraya River) is always teeming with activity: hulking freighter boats trail behind dedicated tugs, river-crossing ferries skip across the wake, and children practise cannonballs into the muddy water. You can witness this from the shore (ideally from Ko Ratanakosin or Thonburi), from a chartered long-tail boat or while on the deck of a river taxi. Regardless of your vantage point, as the blinding sun slips below the horizon of an evening in serene streaks of reds and golds, sooty Bangkok suddenly looks beautiful.

LEFT: WAT ARUN (P67)

◉ *Ko Ratanakosin & Thonburi*

Thai Cookery Schools (p50)

9 Why let a plump tummy be the only sign of your visit to Thailand? Instead, spice up your life – and your dinner-party menus – a little by learning to create the kingdom's zesty dishes in your own kitchen. Cooking schools in Bangkok range from formal affairs for amateur chefs to home cooking for the recipe-phobic. Everyone always has a grand time, visiting a wet market, fumbling with ingredients, tasting the fruits of their labour and trotting home with new cooking techniques.

🏃 *Sports & Activities*

Songkran (p20)

10 If the idea of no-holds-barred water-based warfare appeals to you, make a point of being in Bangkok during April. With origins in an ancient religious practice of Buddha images being 'bathed', in recent decades the celebration of the Thai lunar New Year has evolved into a citywide water fight. Foreigners, especially well-dressed ones, are obvious targets, and the majority of the mayhem occurs on Th Khao San. In addition to water-throwing, festivities include open-air concerts and visits to Buddhist temples.

🎆 *Month by Month*

What's New

Hotels on Ko Ratanakosin

Formerly home to lots of atmosphere and many attractions (not to mention great river views) yet a dearth of accommodation, over the last couple of years several new hotels and guesthouses have sprung up in the heart of Bangkok's historical district. The sexiest of these are Inn A Day and Sala Rattanakosin, but there are also several handsome and good-value options, such as Royal Tha Tien Village, Chetuphon Gate and Arom D Hostel. (p180)

Asiatique

A unique riverside location and heaps of hip vendors, restaurants and photo-ops have made this Bangkok's most-talked-about market. (p130)

Samsara

Finally, a reason to eat in Chinatown that isn't hawker-based. (p101)

Badmotel

A fun new bar taking its hints from Thailand's past. (p140)

Opposite Mess Hall

This new, lauded opening is the latest to follow the trend of eclectic, international-style dining. (p139)

Loy La Long

Tiny, trendy, retro-themed boutique hotel elevated over Mae Nam Chao Phraya. (p187)

Never Ending Summer

Achingly hip Thai restaurant that could turn heads in London or New York City. (p122)

Terminal 21

New mall where shopping comes second to taking selfies. (p143)

Maggie Choo's

Bangkok's new speakeasy that everybody knows about. (p128)

Nuer Koo

Street-stall influences and fine-dining flavours in a mall address. (p109)

For more recommendations and reviews, see **lonelyplanet.com/bangkok**

Need to Know

For more information, see Survival Guide (p223)

Currency
Thai baht (B)

Language
Thai

Visas
International air arrivals receive 30-day visa; 60-day visas available from a Thai consulate before leaving home.

Money
ATMs widespread; 150B foreign-account fee. Upmarket places accept Visa and MasterCard.

Mobile Phones
GSM and 3G networks available through inexpensive pre-paid SIM cards.

Time
Asia/Bangkok (GMT/UTC +7 hours)

Tourist Information
Tourism Authority of Thailand (TAT; ✆1672; www.tourismthailand.org) National tourism department.

Bangkok Information Center (✆0 2225 7612-4; www.bangkoktourist.com) City-specific tourism office; staffed booths throughout the city.

Daily Costs

Budget: less than 1500B
➡ Dorm bed/basic guesthouse room 250–600B

➡ Street-stall meals 200–500B

➡ One or two of the big-hitter sights 500–600B

➡ Get around town on public transport 20–100B

Midrange: 1500B to 3000B
➡ Flashpacker guesthouse or midrange hotel room 800–1500B

➡ Restaurant meals 500–1000B

➡ Most, if not all, of the big sights 500–1000B

➡ Get around town on public transport and occasional taxis 100–300B

Top End: more than 3000B
➡ Boutique hotel room 3000B

➡ Fine dining 1500–3000B

➡ Private tours from 850B

➡ Get around town in taxis 300–800B

Advance Planning

Three months before Book a room at a smaller boutique hotel, especially if visiting during December/January.

One month before Make reservations at nahm (p127); if you plan to stay in Thailand longer than 30 days, apply for a visa at the Thai embassy or consulate in your home country.

One week before Buy clothes appropriate for hot weather; book lessons at a Thai cooking school.

Useful Websites

➡ **Lonely Planet** (www.lonelyplanet.com) Destination information, hotel bookings, traveller forum and more.

➡ **BK** (www.bk.asia-city.com) Online version of Bangkok's best listings magazine.

➡ **Bangkok 101** (www.bangkok101.com) Tourist-friendly listings mag.

➡ **Bangkok Post** (www.bangkokpost.com) English-language daily.

WHEN TO GO

Late December/
early January is the
coolest time of year
and peak tourist sea-
son. Go in November
or February for (rela-
tively) cool weather
and fewer people.

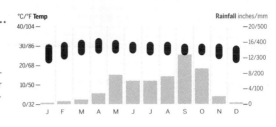

Arriving in Bangkok

Suvarnabhumi International Airport The Airport Rail Link runs a local service (45B, 30 minutes) to Phaya Thai station and an express service (90B, 17 minutes) to Makkasan or Phaya Thai stations; both run from 6am to midnight. Meter taxis run 24 hours and cost approxi-mately 200B to 300B plus 50B airport surcharge and tolls.

Don Muang International Airport There are two bus lines from Bangkok's de facto budget airport: bus A1 makes stops at BTS Mo Chit, while bus A2 makes stops at BTS Mo Chit and BTS Victory Monument (30B, hourly from 9am to midnight). Meter taxis from Don Muang also charge a 50B airport sur-charge, and trips to town start at approximately 200B.

For much more on **arrival,** see p224

Getting Around

➡ **BTS** The elevated Skytrain runs from 6am to midnight. Tickets 15B to 52B.

➡ **MRT** The metro runs from 6am to midnight. Tickets 16B to 40B.

➡ **Taxi** Outside of rush hours, Bangkok taxis are a great bargain. Flag fall 35B.

➡ **Chao Phraya Express** River boats run from 6am to 10pm, charging from 10B to 40B.

➡ **Klorng boat** Bangkok's canal boats run from 5.30am to 8.30pm. Tickets from 10B to 20B.

➡ **Bus** Cheap but slow and confusing way to get around Bangkok. Tickets 5B to 30B.

For much more on **getting around,** see p226

Sleeping

Travellers are spoilt for accommodation options in Bangkok, with the added benefit that much of what's available is excellent value. If you're on a budget, dorm beds can be had for as little as 250B, while cheap rooms start at about 600B. There's a wide choice of midrange hotels and an astonishing number of top-end places. Be sure to book ahead if you're arriving during peak tourist season (from ap-proximately November to February) and are keen on the smaller, boutique-type hotel.

Useful Websites

➡ **Travelfish** (www.travelfish. org) Independent reviews of budget and midrange places, with lots of reader feedback.

➡ **Airbnb** (www.airbnb.com) Yep, Bangkok is covered here.

➡ **Lonely Planet's Hotels & Hostels** (www.lonelyplanet. com/hotels) Find reviews and make bookings.

➡ **Trip Advisor** (www. tripadvisor.com) An overabundance of Bangkok listings.

For much more on **sleeping,** see p177

ENGLISH IN BANGKOK

Don't know a lick of Thai? Don't worry: Bangkok is well stocked with English speakers. Street-stall vendors, shop owners and taxi drivers generally speak enough English to conduct a basic transaction. If there is a communica-tion problem, though, Thais will find someone to sort things out. Thais are patient with (and honoured by) at-tempts to speak their language; with just a few phrases, you'll be rewarded with big grins and heaps of praise.

Top Itineraries

Day One

Ko Ratanakosin & Thonburi (p56)

 Get up as early as you can and take the Chao Phraya Express Boat north to Tha Chang to explore one of Ko Ratanakoson's museums such as the **Museum of Siam**, as well as one of its must-see temples, such as **Wat Pho**.

 Lunch Plunge into authentic Bangkok-style street food at Pa Aew (p73).

Riverside, Silom & Lumphini (p118)

 Refresh with a spa treatment at **Health Land** or soothe those overworked legs with a traditional Thai massage at **Ruen-Nuad Massage Studio**. After freshening up, get a new perspective on Bangkok with rooftop cocktails at **Moon Bar**.

 Dinner nahm (p127) serves what is arguably the best Thai food in Bangkok.

Riverside, Silom & Lumphini (p118)

 If you've still got it in you, get dancing at **Tapas Room** or head over to **Telephone Pub** or any of the other bars in Bangkok's lively gaybourhood. For a night that doesn't end until the sun comes up, bang on the door at **Wong's Place**.

Day Two

Siam Square, Pratunam, Ploenchit & Ratchathewi (p103)

 Take the BTS (Skytrain) to National Stadium and start your day with a visit to the popular and worthwhile museum that is **Jim Thompson House**. Follow this by exploring nearby **Baan Krua** or by making a wish at the **Erawan Shrine**.

 Lunch The MBK Food Island (p110) is an ideal introduction to Thai food.

Siam Square, Pratunam, Ploenchit & Ratchathewi (p103)

 Walk, or let the BTS escort you, through Bangkok's ultramodern commercial district, stopping off at linked shopping centres including **MBK Center**, **Siam Paragon** and **Siam Square**. Make time for a sweet snack at **Gourmet Gallery** or an afternoon cuppa at the **Erawan Tea Room**.

 Dinner Try Thai food with a modern twist at Sra Bua (p111).

Greater Bangkok (p145)

 If it's Tuesday, Friday or Saturday, consider catching a Thai boxing match at **Lumpinee Boxing Stadium**, or make a point of schlepping over to eastern Bangkok's RCA (Royal City Avenue) to check out fun clubs such as **Cosmic Café** or **Slim/Flix**.

Ancient City (Muang Boran; p150)

Day Three

Ko Ratanakosin & Thonburi (p56)

 Take the Chao Phraya Express Boat to Tha Chang and set off on a **longtail boat tour** of Thonburi's canals. Alternatively, combine canals and the culinary arts with a visit to **Amita Thai Cooking Class**.

 Lunch Enjoy the air-con and spicy noodles at Coconut Palm (p74).

Banglamphu (p76)

 Spend the afternoon shopping at the **Th Khao San Market** and visiting the surrounding sights such as the **Golden Mount** and **Wat Suthat**. Or, if you've got energy to spare, book an afternoon or night bike tour of the area with **Velo Thailand** or **Grasshopper Adventures**.

Dinner Take a temporary break from Thai food at Nasir Al-Masri (p138).

Thanon Sukhumvit (p133)

End the night with a Thai-themed cocktail at a cosy local such as **WTF** or **Badmotel**, or a street-side Singha at **Cheap Charlie's**. If it's still too early for you to turn in, extend the night with a visit to nightclubs **Grease** or **Arena 10**.

Day Four

Greater Bangkok (p145)

 If it's a weekend, take the BTS north for a half-day of shopping at the **Chatuchak Weekend Market**. Otherwise, consider a half-day excursion outside the city to the provincial-feeling **Nonthaburi Market**, the man-made island of **Ko Kret** or the recreated ruins at **Ancient City** (Muang Boran).

 Lunch Chatuchak Weekend Market (p147) has cheap and tasty food stalls.

Chinatown (p95)

Recover from the market in the relative cool of the late afternoon before taking the MRT (metro) to Chinatown to visit the home of the Golden Buddha, **Wat Traimit**, and the Chinese-style **Wat Mangkon Kamalawat**. Consider popping over to **Phahurat** to sample that neighbourhood's South Asian feel, or if you're there after dark, the flower market at **Pak Khlong Talat**.

Dinner Follow our walking tour (p100) of Chinatown's best street eats.

Banglamphu (p76)

Make the brief taxi ride to Banglamphu and begin the evening with drinks at **Madame Musur**, followed by a rowdy live music show at **Brick Bar** or dancing at **Club**. If bedtime is irrelevant, head for the shishas (water pipes) and dance floor of **Triple-D**.

If You Like...

Temples

Wat Phra Kaew The granddaddy of Thai temples – not to mention the home of a certain Emerald Buddha. (p58)

Wat Pho If you haven't seen the ginormous reclining Buddha here, you haven't seen Bangkok. (p63)

Wat Suthat One of Thailand's biggest Buddhas and equally impressive floor-to-ceiling temple murals await visitors here. (p79)

Wat Arun Predating Bangkok, this temple makes the best of a unique riverside location. (p67)

Wat Mangkon Kamalawat The epitome of the hectic, smoky, noisy Chinese-style Buddhist temple. (p98)

Sri Mariamman Temple The main Hindu temple in Bangkok practically leaps from the street, taking all comers. (p120)

Museums

National Museum An occasionally dusty but wholly worthwhile survey of Thai history. (p69)

Museum of Siam A fun summary of the Thai people and their culture. (p68)

Bangkokian Museum A preserved house that's a time-warp back to the Bangkok of the early-to-middle 20th century. (p120)

Songkran Niyomsane Forensic Medicine Museum & Parasite Museum Not for the faint of

Bhuddhaiswan Chapel, National Museum (p69)

heart: a queasy look at the more graphic side of death. (p69)

Architecture

Riverside Architecture Ramble Follow our walking tour, which takes in some of Bangkok's most notable secular structures. (p123)

Jim Thompson House Beautiful former home that brings together Thailand's past and present. (p105)

Ban Kamthieng A perfectly preserved northern-style Thai home – right in the middle of modern Bangkok. (p135)

Ancient City (Muang Boran) See models of Thailand's most famous structures without having to leave the greater Bangkok area. (p150)

Eating Like a Local

Likhit Kai Yang Where locals fuel up before the big *moo-ay tai* (Thai boxing; also spelt *muay thai*) match. (p93)

MBK Food Island Do the local thing by forgetting about ambiance and focusing on the food at this mall-based food court. (p110)

A Taste of Chinatown Take our food-based walking tour and you'll see why Thais are willing to cross town for a bowl of noodles. (p100)

Pa Aew An open-air curry stall that excels in the flavours of Bangkok and Central Thailand. (p73)

Boats

Chao Phraya Express Boat The slow but steady – not to mention scenic – way to get around Bangkok. (p227)

Long-tail boat tour of Thonburi canals Race through the narrow, wooden-house-lined canals of Thonburi, James Bond–style. (p68)

Chao Phraya Cruise Dinner on the deck of a cruise ship is an admittedly cheesy, yet obligatory Bangkok experience. (p125)

Royal Barges National Museum A riverside museum that's home to some of the most ornate boats in the world. (p70)

Hipster Haunts

Never Ending Summer The Thai restaurant that's almost too cool to eat at. (p122)

Opposite Mess Hall This restaurant has international cred to match its cuisine. (p139)

Grease New nightclub where celebs and wannabes mix and bump. (p140)

Badmotel Modern lines and Thai kitsch draw Bangkok's 'in' crowd to this bar. (p140)

Talat Rot Fai Witness every Thai youth subculture at this open-air market. (p150)

Urban Exploration

Talat Mai Blaze your own path in this web-like riverside neighbourhood. (p98)

For more top Bangkok spots, see the following:

➡ Eating (p24)

➡ Drinking & Nightlife (p33)

➡ Entertainment (p39)

➡ Shopping (p43)

➡ Sports & Activities (p48)

Sampeng Lane Explore the narrow lanes that spread from this market alley in the heart of Bangkok's Chinatown. (p99)

Amulet Market One of Bangkok's most bizarre markets is also a great destination for aimless wandering. (p68)

Church of Santa Cruz Get lost in the winding, elevated lanes surrounding this Thonburi church. (p99)

Art

Jim Thompson House Antique Thai-style house crammed with beautiful works of art from across Southeast Asia. (p105)

100 Tonson Gallery Housed in a villa, 101 Tonson is regarded as one of Bangkok's top commercial galleries. (p107)

Bangkok Art & Culture Centre Contemporary art meets commerce in the centre of Bangkok. (p106)

Tang Gallery Private gallery featuring the work of contemporary Thai and Chinese artists. (p121)

Month by Month

January

The weather is still relatively cool in Bangkok, and the number of foreign tourists remains quite high.

✵ Chinese New Year

Some time from late January to late February, Bangkok's large Thai-Chinese population celebrate their lunar new year, called *drùd jeen* in Thai, with a week full of house cleaning, lion dances and fireworks. The most impressive festivities, not surprisingly, take place in Chinatown.

February

With relatively comfortable (although increasingly warm) temperatures and few tourists, February is a clever time to visit Bangkok.

☆ Kite Flying Season

During the windy season, from the middle of February to early April, colourful kites battle it out over the skies of Sanam Luang and Lumphini Park.

✵ Makha Bucha

Makha Bucha is held on the full moon of the third lunar month (late February to early March) to commemorate the Buddha preaching to 1250 monks who came to hear him 'without prior summons'. It culminates with a candlelit walk around the main chapel at every wát.

April

This is the height of Bangkok's hot season, so it should come as no surprise that the Thais have a festival that revolves around splashing water on each other.

✵ Songkran

Songkran is the Thai New Year, and although it has origins in a religious practice of 'bathing' Buddha images, today's celebrations resemble a citywide water fight. The most intense battles are fought on Th Khao San – don't carry anything you don't want to get wet.

May

May and June mean the beginning of the rainy season in most parts of Thailand, and some of the festivals during these months have origins in this significant occasion.

✵ Royal Ploughing Ceremony

To kick off the official rice-planting season in early May, the crown prince presides over this ancient Brahman ritual held at Sanam Luang. It culminates in sacred white oxen ploughing the earth and priests declaring it a good or bad year for farmers.

✵ Visakha Bucha

Visakha Bucha, on the full moon of the sixth lunar month (May or June), is considered the date of the Buddha's birth, enlightenment and *parinibbana* (passing away). Activities are centred on the local wát, with candlelit processions, chanting and sermonising.

July

Thailand's rainy season is well under way during this time, and tourist numbers are correspondingly low. The most significant event of the season is a Buddhist holiday ushering in the rains.

✺ Asanha Bucha & Khao Phansa

Held on the full moon of the eighth lunar month (July or August), Asanha Bucha commemorates the Buddha's first post-enlightenment sermon. The following day, young men traditionally enter the monkhood and monks sequester themselves in a monastery for three months (known as Khao Phansa).

September

September is the wettest month in and around Bangkok, and as a result most festivals alternate between being held indoors or taking place directly on water.

☆ Thailand International Swan Boat Races

In late September, more than 20 international teams race traditional Thai-style long boats in various classes (the largest has 55 paddlers) along Mae Nam Chao Phraya in Ayuthaya.

✗ Vegetarian Festival

During the first nine days of the ninth lunar month

(September or October), this Chinese-Buddhist festival, called *têt·sà·gahn gin jair*, sees street-side vendors serving meatless meals to help cleanse the body. Most of the action is in Chinatown: look for the yellow banners and white clothes.

October

Bangkok is wet during October, so festivals are few on the ground.

☆ World Film Festival of Bangkok

More than 80 films are shown at this increasingly popular film festival (www.worldfilmbkk.com), which has an emphasis on Asian cinema. For popular films, book ahead.

November

The rain's (mostly) stopped, the weather's (relatively) cool, the crowds are low, and the festivals are plentiful: November is one of the best months to visit Bangkok.

✺ Loi Krathong

On the night of the full moon of the 12th lunar month, *grà·tong* (boats made of a section of banana trunk) are floated on Mae Nam Chao Phraya. The ceremony is both an offering to the water spirits and a symbolic cleansing of bad luck.

◉ Wat Saket Fair

The grandest of Bangkok's temple fairs (*ngahn wát*)

is held at Wat Saket and the Golden Mount around Loi Krathong. The temple grounds turn into a colourful, noisy fair selling flowers, incense, bells, saffron cloth and tonnes of Thai food.

December

The coolest month of the year sees a handful of outdoor festivals and events. Tourist numbers are at their peak, but this is arguably the most pleasant month to visit Bangkok.

✺ King's Birthday/ Father's Day

Celebrating King Bhumibol's birthday (5 December), the city is festooned with lights and large portraits of the king. In the afternoon, Sanam Luang is packed for a fireworks display that segues appropriately into a noisy concert with popular Thai musicians.

☆ Phra Nakhon Si Ayuthaya World Heritage Fair

A series of cultural performances and evening sound-and-light shows among the ruins of the World Heritage Site in the former Thai capital, Ayuthaya. Late December.

☆ Concert in the Park

Free concerts from the Bangkok Symphony Orchestra are performed Sunday evenings (from 5.30pm to 7.30pm) between mid-December and mid-February at Lumphini Park.

With Kids

There aren't a whole lot of attractions in Bangkok meant to appeal directly to the little ones, but there's no lack of locals willing to provide attention. This means kids are welcome almost anywhere and you'll rarely experience the sort of eye-rolling annoyance often seen in the West.

Snake handling, Dusit Zoo (p92)

Parks & Playgrounds

Lumphini Park

Central Bangkok's biggest park (p122) is a trusty ally in the cool hours of the morning and afternoon for kite flying (in season – February to April), boat rentals and fish feeding, as well as stretching of the legs and lungs. Nearby, kids can view lethal snakes become reluctant altruists at the antivenin-producing Snake Farm (p121).

Animals

In addition to the animals, Dusit Zoo (p92) has shady grounds, plus a lake in the centre with paddle boats for hire and a small children's playground.

It's not exactly a zoo, but kids can join the novice monks and Thai children at **Tha Thewet** (Map p257; Th Samsen; ⊙7am-7pm; bus 32, 315, ⊜Tha Thewet) as they throw food (bought on the pier) to thousands of flapping fish.

Play Centres & Amusement Parks

For kid-specific play centres, consider Funarium (p144), central Bangkok's largest, or the new and impressive KidZania (p117). Alternatively, Siam Park City (p154), Safari World (p154) or Dream World (p154) are all vast amusement parks found north of the city.

Rainy-Day Fun

If you're visiting during the rainy season (approximately from June to October), the brief-but-daily downpours will inevitably complicate things, so you'll need a few indoor options in your back pocket.

Megamalls

MBK Center (p113) and Siam Paragon (p111) both have bowling alleys to keep the older ones occupied. The latter also has an IMAX theatre and Siam Ocean World (p106), a basement-level aquarium. All of these malls and most others in Bangkok have amusement centres with video games, small rides and playgrounds (they're often located near the food courts).

NEED TO KNOW

Bambi (www.bambiweb.org) A useful resource for parents in Bangkok.

Thorn Tree Kids To Go forum (www.lonelyplanet.com/thorntree) Questions and answers from other travellers with children on Lonely Planet's community forum.

Bangkok.com (www.bangkok.com/kids) This website lists a dizzying array of things to do for kids.

Bangkok Doll Factory & Museum

This somewhat hard-to-find museum (p107) houses a colourful selection of traditional Thai dolls, both new and antique.

Kid Friendly Museums

Museum of Siam

Although not specifically targeted towards children, the Museum of Siam (p68) has lots of interactive exhibits that will appeal to kids.

Madame Tussaud's

Siam Discovery Center has a branch of this famous wax museum (p116).

Ancient City (Muang Boran)

Outside of town, this open-air museum (p150) recreates Thailand's most famous monuments. They're linked by bicycle paths and were practically built for being climbed on.

Practicalities

Many hotels offer family deals, adjoining rooms and (in midrange and top-end hotels) cots, so enquire specifically. Car seats, on the other hand, are almost impossible to find, and even if you bring your own most taxis have no seatbelt in the back. Taxi drivers generally won't temper their speed because you're travelling with a child, so if need be don't hesitate to tell them to *cháh cháh* ('slow down').

For moving by foot, slings are often more useful than prams, as Bangkok sidewalks are infamously uneven.

Infants

Nappies (diapers), international brands of milk formula and other infant requirements are widely available. For something more specific you'll find the Central Chidlom (p117) as well stocked as anywhere on earth (there's an entire floor devoted to kids). In general, Thai women don't breastfeed in public, though in department stores they'll often find a changing room.

Eating

Dining with children in Thailand, particularly with infants, is a liberating experience, as Thai people are so fond of kids. Take it for granted that your babies will be fawned over, played with – and even carried around – by restaurant waitstaff. Consider this a much-deserved break, not to mention a bit of free cultural exposure.

For the widest choice of food, child-friendly surroundings and noise levels that will drown out even the loudest child, you may find the food courts of Bangkok's many megamalls to be the most comfortable family dining options. Highchairs are rare outside expensive restaurants.

Because much of Thai food is so spicy, there is an entire art devoted to ordering 'safe' dishes for children, and the vast majority of Thai kitchens are more than willing to oblige. Many a child in Thailand has grown up on a diet of little more than *gaang jèut,* a bland, Chinese-influenced soup containing ground pork, soft tofu and a handful of noodles, or variations on *kôw pàt,* fried rice. Other mild options include *kôw man gài,* Hainanese chicken rice, and *jóhk,* rice gruel. For something bland, big hotels usually sell their baked goods for half price after 6pm.

Amphawa Floating Market (p16)

Eating

Nowhere else is the Thai reverence for food more evident than in Bangkok. To the outsider, the life of a Bangkokian appears to be a string of meals and snacks punctuated by the odd stab at work, not the other way around. If you can adjust your mental clock to this schedule, your visit will be a delicious one indeed.

stall, Chatuchak Weekend Market (p147)

Bangkok's Dining Scene

During the last couple of decades, Thai food has become internationally famous, and Bangkok is, not surprisingly, the best place in the world to eat it. From roadside stalls to restaurants with Michelin stars in their eyes, the whole spectrum of Thai food is available here. Bangkok is home to its own unique cuisine, and because of its position as a cultural and literal crossroads, just about every regional Thai cuisine is available in the city as well. More recent immigration to the city has resulted in a dining scene whose options range from Korean to French, touching on just about everything in between.

If you're new to Thai cuisine, check out our crash course on Thai food (p212) before digging in.

Where to Eat & Drink

Prepared food is available just about everywhere in Bangkok, and it shouldn't come as a surprise that the locals do much of their eating outside the home. In this regard, as a visitor, you'll fit right in.

Open-air markets and food stalls are among the most popular dining spots for Thais. In the mornings, stalls selling coffee and Chinese-style doughnuts spring up along busy commuter corridors. At lunchtime, diners might grab a plastic chair at yet another stall for a simple stir-fry, or pick up a foam box of noodles to scarf down at the office. In Bangkok's suburbs, night markets often spring up in the middle of town with a cluster of food vendors, metal tables

and chairs, and some shopping as an after-dinner mint.

For impromptu drinking and snacking, Bangkok also has an overabundance of modern cafes – including branches of several international chains. Most serve passable takes on Western-style coffee drinks, cakes and sweets.

There are, of course, restaurants *(ráhn ah·hăhn)* in Bangkok. Lunchtime is the right time to point and eat at the *ráhn kôw gaang* (rice and curry shops), which sell a selection of pre-made dishes. The more generic *ráhn ah·hăhn dahm sàng* (made-to-order restaurant) can often be recognised by a display of raw ingredients – Chinese

PLAN YOUR TRIP EATING

NEED TO KNOW

Price Ranges

Prices are for the cost of a meal (a main dish and a drink), as indicated in eating reviews.

$	less than 150B
$$	150B to 300B
$$$	more than 300B

Opening Hours

Restaurants serving Thai food are generally open from 10am to 8pm or 9pm. Foreign-cuisine restaurants tend to keep only lunch and dinner hours (ie 11am to 2pm and 6pm to 10pm).

Bangkok has passed a citywide ordinance banning street vendors from setting up shop on Mondays.

Reservations

If you have a lot of friends in tow or will be attending a formal restaurant (including hotel restaurants), reservations are recommended. Bookings are also recommended for Sunday brunches and dinner cruises. Otherwise, you shouldn't have a problem scoring a table at the vast majority of restaurants in Bangkok.

Tipping

You shouldn't be surprised to learn that tipping is not obligatory in Thailand. Some people leave roughly 10% at any sit-down restaurant where someone fills their glass every time they take a sip. Others don't. Most upmarket restaurants will apply a 10% service charge to the bill.

(Above) *Pàt tai*, a traditional dish of thin rice noodles stir-fried with shrimp, bean sprouts, tofu, egg and seasonings.

(Left) Seafood *dôm yam*, a spicy-and-sour soup.

Eating by Neighbourhood

Thewet & Dusit
Breezy
riverfront dining
(p93)

Greater Bangkok
Regional Thai
cuisine and
vibrant markets
(p152)

Banglamphu
Classic, old-school
Bangkok-style eateries
(p81)

**Siam Square, Pratunam,
Ploenchit & Ratchathewi**
Mall-based food courts
(p109)

Chinatown
Thai-Chinese
street eats
(p101)

Sukhumvit
Cuisine from
every country
(p136)

Mae Nam Chao Phraya

**Riverside, Silom
& Lumphini**
Everything from hotel
restaurants to street carts
(p122)

kale, tomatoes, chopped pork, fresh or dried fish, noodles, eggplant, spring onions – and offer a standard repertoire of Thai and Chinese-Thai dishes. As the name implies, the cooks will attempt to prepare any dish you can name – a potentially difficult operation if you can't speak Thai.

The most common type of restaurant in Bangkok – and arguably the most delicious – is the shophouse restaurant. The cooks at these places have most likely been serving the same dish, or a limited repertoire of dishes, for several decades, and really know what they're doing. The food may cost slightly more than on the street, but the setting is usually more comfortable and hygienic, not to mention the fact that you're eating a piece of history. While such restaurants rarely have English-language menus, you can usually point to a picture or dish. If that fails, turn to the language chapter (p236) and practise your Thai.

Bangkok is of course also home to dozens of upscale restaurants, many of which are attached to hotels. For the most part, those serving Thai cuisine have adjusted their recipes to suit foreign palates – for more authentic food you're much better off eating at the cheaper shophouse-style restaurants. On the other hand, upscale and hotel restaurants are probably the best places in Bangkok for authentic Western-style food. If this is outside your price range, you'll be happy to know that there's also a huge spread of midrange foreign restaurants in today's Bangkok, many of them quite good.

Local Specialities

In Bangkok, geography, the influence of the royal palace and the country's main minorities Chinese and Muslims – have all served to shape the local cuisine.

BANGKOK'S BEST BITES

David Thompson is a Michelin-starred chef and a best-selling author; he's also head chef at Bangkok restaurant nahm (p127).

Classic Bangkok-Style Dishes

I like some of the dishes in Chinatown, whether it be the oyster place I adore, Nai Mong Hoi Thod (p100), or whether it be noodles with fish dumplings or with roast duck; *boo pat pong gàrìi* (crab fried with curry powder), when done well, is bloody delicious and accessible. And *pàt tai* – well, you can't really escape from the cliché, however delicious it might be.

Best Food 'Hood

It depends on what I'm looking for. Chinatown, for smoked duck or noodles. But if you want to eat Thai food, you need to go to the markets. Bangkok still has some remnants of the city or villages that it was. For Muslim food you can go down near the Oriental Hotel (Haroon village), or for Portuguese cakes, you can go to Santa Cruz.

Favourite Restaurant

It changes all the time. I like Krua Apsorn (p83). It's local. It's good. It's unreformed. It's not too precious. They cook for Thais, they feed Thais and it is Thai.

Best Market

Of course, Or Tor Kor Market (p151). Even though it's sanitised, its soul has not been expunged from it as it's modernised. There's some great stuff there.

Best Eating Advice for a First-Time Visitor

Just bloody well eat it – don't think about it – just eat it. It's so unlikely you'll get sick, but you will kick yourself for not actually just diving in. Go to places that look busiest, because they're busy for a reason. And a bit of food poisoning, well that adds local colour, doesn't it?

CENTRAL THAI CUISINE

The people of central Thailand are fond of sweet/savoury flavours, and many dishes include freshwater fish, pork, coconut milk and palm sugar – common ingredients in the central Thai plains. Because of the region's proximity to the Gulf of Thailand, central Thai eateries, particularly those in Bangkok, also serve a wide variety of seafood. Chinese labourers and vendors introduced a huge variety of noodle and wok-fried dishes to central Thailand as many as 200 years ago.

Must-eat central Thai and Bangkok dishes include the following:

Pàt tai Thin rice noodles stir-fried with dried and/or fresh shrimp, bean sprouts, tofu, egg and seasonings, traditionally served with lime halves and a few stalks of Chinese chives and a sliced banana flower. **Thip Samai** (p81), in Banglamphu, is probably Bangkok's most lauded destination for the dish.

Yam blah dùk foo Fried shredded catfish, chilli and peanuts served with a sweet/tart mango dressing. Try it at **Kimleng** (p83), in Bangkok's Banglamphu district.

Đôm yam Lemon grass, kaffir lime leaf and lime juice give this soup its characteristic tang; fresh chillies or an oily chilli paste provide it with its legendary sting. Available just about everywhere, but it's hard to beat the version at **Krua Apsorn** (p83).

Yen đah foh Combining a slightly sweet crimson-coloured broth with a variety of meat balls, cubes of blood and crispy greens, *yen đah foh* is probably both the most intimidating and popular noodle dish in Bangkok. Available at **Soi 10 Food Centres** (p124) and many street stalls.

Gaang sôm Central Thailand's famous 'sour soup' often includes freshwater fish, vegetables and/or herbs, and a thick, tart broth. Available at **Poj Spa Kar** (p83).

Gŏo-ay đĕe-o reu-a Known as boat noodles because they were previously served from small boats along the canals of central Thailand, these intense pork- or beef-based bowls are among the most full-flavoured of Thai noodle dishes. Try a bowl at **Bharani** (p136).

ROYAL THAI CUISINE

Another significant influence on the city's kitchens has come from the Bangkok-based royal court, which has been producing sophisticated and refined takes on central Thai dishes for nearly 300 years. Although originally only available within the palace walls, these so-called 'royal' Thai dishes are now available across the city.

Máh hór With origins in the palace, this is a Thai appetiser that combines chunks of mandarin, orange or pineapple and a sweet/savoury/peppery topping that includes pork, chicken, peanuts, sugar, peppercorns and coriander root. Available as part of the set meal at **nahm** (p127).

Ъlah hâang Dried fish combined with sugar and crispy deep-fried shallots, served on top of slices of watermelon – this ancient and refreshing palace recipe is available at **Mangkud Cafe** (p74).

Kà·nŏm bêu·ang The old-school version of these taco-like snacks comes in two varieties: sweet and savoury.

Mèe gròrp Crispy noodles made the traditional way, with a sweet/sour flavour (a former palace recipe), are a dying breed. Banglamphu restaurant **Chote Chitr** (p82) serves an excellent version of the dish.

THAI-CHINESE CUISINE

Immigrants from southern China have been influencing Thai cuisine for centuries, and it was most likely Chinese labourers and vendors who introduced the wok and several varieties of noodle dishes to Thailand. They also influenced Bangkok's cuisine in other ways: beef is not widely eaten in Bangkok due to a Chinese-Buddhist teaching that forbids eating 'large' animals.

Thai-Chinese dishes you're likely to run across in Bangkok include the following:

Kôw kăh mŏo Braised pork leg served over rice, often with sides of greens and a hard-boiled egg, is the epitome of the Thai-Chinese one-dish meal. Available at the **Soi 10 Food Centres** (p124) and other street markets.

Kôw man gài Chicken rice, originally from the Chinese island of Hainan, is now found in just about every corner of Bangkok. We particularly like the version served at **Boon Tong Kiat Singapore Hainanese Chicken Rice** (p136).

Bà·mèe Chinese-style wheat and egg noodles typically served with slices of barbecued pork,

PLAN YOUR TRIP EATING

…d stall, Chatuchak Weekend Market (p147)

a handful of greens and/or wontons. **Mangkorn Khǎo** (p100), a street stall in Chinatown, does one of Bangkok's better bowls.

Sǎh·lah·ʿbow Chinese-style steamed buns, served with sweet or savoury fillings, are a favourite snack in Bangkok.

Gǒo·ay dĕe·o kôo·a gài Wide rice noodles fried with little more than egg, chicken, salted squid and garlic oil is a popular dish in Bangkok's Chinatown.

Or sòo·an Another Bangkok Chinatown staple, this dish combines a sticky, eggy batter topped with oysters. **Nai Mong Hoi Thod** (p100) does what is arguably Bangkok's best take on this dish.

Gǒo·ay jáp This dish consists of an intensely peppery broth and pork offal; look for it on our food-based walking tour of Chinatown (p100).

THAI-MUSLIM CUISINE

Muslims are thought to have first visited Thailand during the late 14th century. Along with the Quran, they brought with them a meat- and dried-spice-based cuisine from their homelands in India and the Middle East. Nearly 700 years later, the impact of this culinary commerce can still be felt in Bangkok.

While some Muslim dishes such as *roh·dee,* a fried bread similar to the Indian paratha, have changed little, if at all, others such as *gaang mát·sà·màn* are a unique blend of Thai and Indian/Middle Eastern cooking styles and ingredients.

Common Thai-Muslim dishes include the following:

Kôw mòk Biryani, a dish found across the Muslim world, also has a foothold in Bangkok. Here the dish is typically made with chicken and is served with a sweet-and-sour dipping sauce and a bowl of chicken broth. We love the version served at **Naaz** (p122).

Sà·dé (satay) These grilled skewers of meat probably came to Thailand via Malaysia. The savoury peanut-based dipping sauce is often mistakenly associated with Thai cooking. Typically available at street markets such as **Soi 38 Night Market** (p136).

Má·dà·bà Known as murtabak in Malaysia and Indonesia, these are *roh·dee* that have been stuffed with a savoury or sometimes sweet filling and fried until crispy. Available at **Roti-Mataba** (p83).

Súp hǎhng woo·a Oxtail soup, possibly another Malay contribution, is even richer and often more

Top: *Gaang mát·sà·màn* ('Muslim curry')
Middle: Soups at a street stall
Bottom: Fried seafood snacks

sour than the 'Buddhist' Thai *đôm yam*. Try the dish at **Muslim Restaurant** (p122).

Sà·làt kàak Literally 'Muslim salad' (*kàak* is a somewhat derogatory word used to describe people or things of Indian and/or Muslim origin), this dish combines iceberg lettuce, chunks of firm tofu, cucumber, hard-boiled egg and tomato, all topped with a sweet peanut sauce.

Gaang mát·sà·màn 'Muslim curry' is a rich coconut-milk-based dish, which, unlike most Thai curries, gets much of its flavour from dried spices. As with many Thai-Muslim dishes, there is an emphasis on the sweet. Longstanding **Muslim Restaurant** (p122) does a good take on the dish.

Roh·đee This crispy fried pancake, drizzled with condensed milk and sugar, is the perfect street dessert. Get yours on the street or at **Roti-Mataba** (p83).

Cooking Courses

Bangkok has a number of great cooking courses (p50) that are geared towards visitors wanting to recreate the cuisine at home.

Food Markets

If you take pleasure in seeing food in its raw form, Bangkok is home to dozens of traditional-style wet markets (p28), ranging from the grungy to the flashy.

Lonely Planet's Top Choices

nahm (p127) Upscale Thai that's worth every baht.

Eat Me (p126) Modern, international dining in a gallery setting.

Krua Apsorn (p83) Rich central Thai fare in a homely setting.

Jay Fai (p83) Decades-old shophouse serving flash-fried masterpieces.

MBK Food Island (p110) Cheap, cheerful and tasty: Bangkok's best food court.

Best by Budget

$

Pa Aew (p73)

Nai Mong Hoi Thod (p100)

Nuer Koo (p109)

Muslim Restaurant (p122)

Likhit Kai Yang (p93)

Chennai Kitchen (p124)

$$

Kai Thort Jay Kee (p126)

Shoshana (p83)

Samsara (p101)

Crystal Jade La Mian Xiao Long Bao (p109)

Thanon Phadungdao Seafood Stalls (p101)

Taling Pling (p125)

$$$

Little Beast (p138)

Quince (p138)

Le Normandie (p124)

D'Sens (p126)

Bo.lan (p139)

nahm (p127)

Best for Old-School Thai Dining

Muslim Restaurant (p122)

Ngwanlee Lung Suan (p126)

Sanguan Sri (p109)

Roti-Mataba (p83)

Ming Lee (p74)

Best Foreign Cuisine Restaurants

Jidori-Ya Kenzou (p138)

Little Beast (p138)

Nasir Al-Masri (p138)

Myeong Ga (p139)

Appia (p138)

Best for Vegetarian

Baan Suan Pai (p152)

Saras (p136)

Arawy Vegetarian Food (p81)

Chennai Kitchen (p124)

Best for Regional Thai Cuisine

Likhit Kai Yang (p93)

Supanniga Eating Room (p137)

Mallika Restaurant (p111)

Jay So (p124)

Best for Bangkok-Style Food

Pa Aew (p73)

Poj Spa Kar (p83)

Thip Samai (p81)

Kimleng (p83)

Nang Loeng Market (p93)

Best for Dessert

Eat Me (p126)

Old Siam Plaza (p101)

Gourmet Paradise (p110)

Nang Loeng Market (p93)

Little Beast (p138)

Best Riverside Views

Sala Rattanakosin (p74)

Mangkud Cafe (p74)

Steve Café & Cuisine (p94)

Samsara (p101)

Lord Jim's (p124)

Best Buffets

Four Seasons Sunday Brunch (p110)

Rang Mahal (p136)

Marriott Café (p136)

Sunday Jazzy Brunch (p136)

Lord Jim's (p124)

Chocolate Buffet (p128)

Best Food Markets

Or Tor Kor Market (p151)

Nonthaburi Market (p150)

Talat Mai (p98)

Nang Loeng Market (p93)

AUSTIN BUSH / GETTY IMAGES ©

Cheap Charlie's (p140)

🍷 Drinking & Nightlife

Despite what your dodgy uncle told you, having a good time in Bangkok does not necessarily have to involve ping-pong balls or the word 'go-go'. As in any big international city, the drinking and partying scene in Bangkok ranges from classy to trashy and hits just about everything in between.

The Scene

Bangkok is a party animal – even when on a tight leash. Back in 2001, the Thaksin administration started enforcing closing times and curtailing other excesses that made the city's nightlife famous. Since his 2006 ousting, the laws have been conveniently circumvented or inconsistently enforced; several years on, the post-coup party scene has shown signs of restoring Bangkok to its old position as Southeast Asia's fun master – a role uptight Singapore almost usurped. But it's not uncommon for the men in brown to switch on the lights in clubs and bars way before most folks' bedtime, or at least before dawn.

Bars

Bangkok's watering holes cover the spectrum from English-style pubs where you can comfortably sit with a pint and the paper to chic dens where the fair and beautiful go to be seen more than imbibe. Bangkok is one of the few big cities in the world where nobody seems to mind if you slap a bar on top of a

NEED TO KNOW

Opening Hours

Since 2004, authorities have ordered most of Bangkok's bars and clubs to close by 1am. A complicated zoning system sees venues in designated 'entertainment areas', including RCA, Th Silom, and parts of Th Sukhumvit, open until 2am (sometimes as late as 4am), but even these 'later' licences are subject to police whimsy.

Smoking

Smoking has been outlawed at all indoor (and some quasi-outdoor) entertainment places since 2008.

Dress Code

Most rooftop bars enforce a dress code – no shorts or sandals. This is also the case with many of Bangkok's dance clubs.

ID

The drinking age in Thailand is 20, although it's only usually dance clubs that ask for ID.

Wine Whinge

Imported wine is subject to a litany of taxes, making Thailand among the most expensive places in the world to drink wine. A bottle typically costs 400% of its price back home, up to 600% in upmarket restaurants. Even domestic wines are subject to many of the same taxes, making them only marginally cheaper.

Other Resources

To keep crowds interested, clubs host weekly theme parties and visiting DJs that ebb and flow in popularity. To find out what's on, check out **Dude Sweet** (www.dudesweet.org), **Club Soma** (www.facebook.com/clubsomaparty) or **Paradise Bangkok** (www.zudrangmarecords.com), all organisers of hugely popular monthly parties, or local listings rags such as *BK* and the *Bangkok Post*'s Friday supplement, Guru.

skyscraper (although it's worth noting that most rooftop bars enforce a dress code – no shorts or sandals).

But many visitors associate Bangkok with the kind of bars that don't have an address – found just about everywhere in the city. Think streetside seating, plastic chairs, auto exhaust, and tasty dishes absentmindedly nibbled between toasts.

Bangkok bars don't have cover charges, but they do generally enforce closing time at 1am, and sometimes earlier if they suspect trouble from the cops.

If you want to drink your way through Bangkok's best nightlife zone, take our Banglamphu pub crawl (p85).

Nightclubs

Bangkok's club scene is as fickle as a ripe mango, and venues that were pulling in thousands a night just last year are often only vague memories today. Clubs here also tend to burn strong and bright on certain nights – a visit from a foreign DJ or the music flavour of the month – then hibernate every other night.

What used to be a rotating cast of hot spots has slowed to a few standards on the sois off Th Sukhumvit, Th Silom, Th Ratchadapisek and Royal City Ave (RCA) – the city's 'entertainment zones' – which qualify for the 2am closing time. Most places don't begin filling up until midnight. Cover charges can run as high as 600B and usually include a drink or two. You'll need ID to prove you're legal (20 years old); they'll card even the grey-haired.

If you find 2am too early to call it a night, don't worry – Thais have found curiously creative methods of flouting closing times. Speakeasies have sprung up all over the city, so follow the crowds – no one is heading home. Some places just remove the tables and let people drink on the floor (somehow this is an exemption), while other places serve beer in teapots. If it seems strange...welcome to Bangkok.

For live music, traditional performances and Bangkok's infamous 'adult' entertainment, see our Entertainment chapter (p39).

Drinks

Bangkok is justifiably renowned for its food and nightlife, but markedly less so for its beverages. Yet drinks are the glue that fuse these elements, and without them, that cabaret show would be markedly less entertaining.

BEER

Advertised with such slogans as *'ฅrà·têht row, bee·a row'* ('our land, our beer'), the Singha label is considered the quintessential Thai beer by *fa·ràng* (Westerners) and locals alike. Pronounced *sĭng*, this pilsner claims about half the domestic market. The alcohol content for Singha beer is a heady 6%. It is sold in brown glass bottles (330mL, 500mL and 630mL) with a shiny gold lion on the label, as well as in cans (330mL). It's also available on tap as *bee·a sòt* (draught beer) – slightly tastier than either bottled or canned brew – in many Bangkok pubs and restaurants.

Singha's biggest rival, Beer Chang, pumps the alcohol content up to 7%. Beer Chang has managed to gain an impressive following mainly because it retails at a significantly lower price than Singha and thus offers more bang per baht. Boon Rawd (the maker of Singha) responded with its own cheaper brand, Leo. Sporting a black-and-red leopard label, Leo costs only slightly more than Beer Chang but is similarly high in alcohol.

Dutch-licensed but Thailand-brewed Heineken comes third after Singha and Chang in sales rankings. Similar 'domestic imports' include Asahi and San Miguel. Other Thai-brewed beers, all at the lower end of the price spectrum, include Cheers and Beer Thai. More variation in Thai beer brands is likely in the coming years as manufacturers scramble to command market share by offering a variety of flavours and prices.

To the surprise of many foreigners, most Thais drink their beer with ice. Before you rule this supposed blasphemy out completely, there are a few reasons why the Thais actually prefer beer on the rocks. Thai beer does not possess the most sophisticated bouquet in the world and is best drunk as cold as possible. The weather in Thailand is often extremely hot, so it makes sense to maintain your beer at maximum chill. And lastly, domestic brews are generally quite high in alcohol and the ice helps to dilute this, preventing dehydration and one of those infamous Beer Chang hangovers the next day. Taking these theories to the extreme, some places serve *bee·a wún,* or

'jelly beer' – beer that has been semi-frozen until it reaches a deliciously slushy and refreshing consistency.

SPIRITS

Thai rice whisky has a sharp, sweet taste – not unlike rum – with an alcohol content of 35%. The most famous brand for many years was Mekong (pronounced *mâa kŏng*), but currently the most popular brand is the slightly more expensive Sang Som (actually a rum). Both come in 750mL bottles called *glom,* or in 375mL flask-shaped bottles called *baan.*

There are also more expensive barley-based whiskies produced in Thailand, which appeal to the can't-afford-Johnnie-Walker-yet set. Brands include Blue Eagle, 100 Pipers and Spey Royal, each with a 40% alcohol content.

Thais normally buy whisky by the bottle and drink it with ice, plenty of soda water and a splash of Coke. If you don't finish your bottle, simply tell your waiter, who will write your name and the date on the bottle and keep it for your next visit.

Drinking & Nightlife by Neighbourhood

→ **Ko Ratanakosin & Thonburi** Romantic riverside drinking.

→ **Banglamphu** Rowdy Th Khao San is one of the city's best areas for a night out.

→ **Siam Square, Pratunam, Ploenchit & Ratchathewi** Bangkok's most central zone is home to a scant handful of bars.

→ **Riverside, Silom & Lumphini** Bangkok's gaybourhood has fun bars and dance clubs for all comers.

→ **Sukhumvit** This long street is home to Bangkok's most sophisticated bars and clubs.

→ **Greater Bangkok** Suburban RCA is the city's best clubbing strip; good live-music venues dot other regions.

Lonely Planet's Top Choices

WTF (p139) A sophisticated yet friendly local boozer.

Hippie de Bar (p84) Retro-themed bar in the middle of Th Khao San.

Moon Bar (p128) Bangkok's best rooftop bar.

DJ Station (p127) Gay nightclub that's fun for all.

Slim/Flix (p153) The epitome of the club alley that is RCA.

Bangkok's Best Nightclubs

Tapas Room (p128)

Club (p84)

Grease (p140)

Funky Villa (p140)

Nung-Len (p140)

Q Bar (p141)

Best Bars for Relaxed Chilling

Rolling Bar (p86)

Taksura (p86)

Tuba (p140)

Shades of Retro (p140)

Best Bars for Thai-Style Drinking

Co-Co Walk (p111)

Bangkok Bar (p140)

Nung-Len (p140)

Telephone Pub (p127)

To-Sit (p112)

Best Cocktails

Hyde & Seek (p112)

Soul Food Mahanakorn (p139)

Opposite Mess Hall (p139)

Alchemist (p141)

Diplomat Bar (p112)

Best Bars with Views

Roof (p75)

Long Table (p141)

Viva & Aviv (p128)

River Vibe (p101)

Best Bars with Food

Viva & Aviv (p128)

Wine Pub (p113)

Madame Musur (p84)

Phra Nakorn Bar & Gallery (p84)

Badmotel (p140)

Above 11 (p141)

Best Bars & Clubs for Late-Night Fun

Wong's Place (p128)

Triple-d (p84)

Narz (p141)

Levels (p141)

Best Bars & Nightclubs in Which to Be Seen

Badmotel (p140)

Maggie Choo's (p128)

Grease (p140)

Demo (p140)

Route 66 (p153)

Best Rooftop Bars

Sky Bar (p128)

River Vibe (p101)

Phra Nakorn Bar & Gallery (p84)

Red Sky (p112)

Roof (p112)

Sky Train Jazz Club (p113)

Gay & Lesbian Bangkok

Bangkok has a notoriously pink vibe to it. From kinky male-underwear shops mushrooming at street corners to lesbian-only nightclubs, as a homosexual you could eat, shop and play here for weeks without ever leaving the comfort of gay-friendly venues. Unlike elsewhere in Southeast Asia, homosexuality is not criminalised in Thailand and the general attitude remains extremely laissez-faire.

Gay Men

Gay people are out and ubiquitous in Bangkok. Yet gay male (and lesbian) couples, like straight couples, do not show public affection, unless they are purposefully flouting social mores.

Lesbians

Although it would be a stretch to claim that Bangkok's lesbian scene is as vibrant as its male gay scene, lesbians have become more visible in recent years. It's worth noting that, perhaps because Thailand is still a relatively conservative place, lesbians in Bangkok generally adhere to rather strict gender roles. Overtly 'butch' lesbians, called *tom* (from 'tomboy'), typically have short hair, bind their breasts and wear men's clothing. Femme lesbians refer to themselves as *dêe* (from 'lady'). Visiting lesbians who don't fit into one of these categories may find themselves met with confusion.

Transgender People

Bangkok is famous for its open and visible transgender population – known locally as *gà·teu·i* (also spelt *kàthoey*). Some are cross-dressers, while others have had sex reassignment surgery – Thailand is one of the leading countries for this procedure. Foreigners seem to be especially fascinated by Thai transgender males as they often appear very feminine, and *gà·teu·i* cabarets aimed at tourists are popular venues for observing gender-bending.

For more, see our interview with a transgender activist (p112).

Issues

Beneath the party vibe, serious issues remain for Bangkok's vast and visible population of LGBT people. After the government's initial success slowing the progression of HIV among the general population, there are new signs of an epidemic among young gay men. Transgender people are often treated as outcasts, same-sex couples enjoy no legal rights and lesbians have the added burden of negotiating a patriarchal society. In short, Bangkok's LGBT community may party as they please, sleep with whomever they want or even change their sex, but they do so without the protection, respect and rights enjoyed by heterosexuals – particularly heterosexual men.

Gay & Lesbian by Neighbourhood

➡ **Riverside, Silom & Lumphini** Lower Th Silom is Bangkok's unofficial gaybourhood.

➡ **Greater Bangkok** Th Kamphaeng Phet and the Lamsalee Intersection on Th Ramkhamhaeng are suburban Bangkok's gay zones.

NEED TO KNOW

Websites

➤ **Bangkok Lesbian** (www.bangkoklesbian. com) The city's premier website for ladies who love ladies.

➤ **Utopia** (www.utopia-asia.com) Publisher of the *Utopia Guide to Thailand,* covering gay-friendly businesses in 18 Thai cities, including Bangkok. Its website is also a good, if slightly outdated, source of information.

Other Resources

Look for gay-themed entertainment tips in local listings rags such as *BK* (bk.asia-city.com) and the *Bangkok Post's* Friday supplement, Guru (www. bangkokpost.com/guru).

Varying locales play host to weekend-long 'circuit parties'. Visit G Circuit (www.gcircuit. com) to find out when and where the next one is.

Lonely Planet's Top Choices

DJ Station (p127) Quite possibly one of the most legendary gay nightclubs in Asia

Telephone Pub (p127) Long-standing bar right in the middle of Bangkok's pinkest zone.

Best Gay Nightclubs

G Bangkok (p127)

Castro (p153)

Fake Club (p153)

Best Gay & Lesbian Bars

Balcony (p127)

Bearbie (p127)

Duangthawee Plaza (p127)

Best Camp & Drag Shows

Playhouse Theater Cabaret (p113)

Mambo Cabaret (p154)

Balcony (p127)

Calypso Bangkok (p130)

Best Gay- & Lesbian-Friendly Hotels

Babylon (p127)

LUXX XL (p185)

Baan Saladaeng (p186)

Rose Hotel (p186)

PETER STUCKINGS / GETTY IMAGES ©

Dancers at Sala Rim Naam (p130)

 # Entertainment

Although Bangkok's hyper-urban environment caters to the inner philistine in all of us, the city is home to a diverse but low-key art scene. Add to this dance performances, live music, some of the world's best-value cinemas and, yes, the infamous go-go bars, and you have a city whose entertainment scene ranges from – in local parlance – lo-so (low society) to hi-so (high society).

Live Music

As Thailand's media capital, Bangkok is the centre of the Thai music industry, packaging and selling pop, crooners, *lôok tûng* (Thai-style country music) and the recent phenomenon of indie bands. Music is a part of almost every Thai social gathering; the matriarchs and patriarchs like dinner with an easy-listening soundtrack – typically a Filipino band and a synthesiser. Patrons pass their request (on a napkin) up to the stage. An indigenous rock style, *pleng pêu·a chee·wít* ('songs for life'), makes appearances at a dying breed of country-and-western bars decorated with buffalo horns and pictures of Native Americans. Several dedicated bars throughout the city feature blues and rock bands, but are relatively scant on live indie-scene performances. Up-and-coming garage bands occasionally pop up at free concerts where the kids hang out: Santichaiprakan Park (Th Phra Athit), Th Khao San and Siam Square. For more subdued tastes, Bangkok also attracts grade-A jazz musicians to several hotel bars.

NEED TO KNOW

Opening Hours

Live music venues generally close by 1am. A complicated zoning system sees venues in designated 'entertainment areas', including RCA (Royal City Ave), Th Silom and parts of Th Sukhumvit, open until 2am, but even these 'later' licenses are subject to police whimsy.

Bars in the various red-light districts are open until 2am.

Reservations

Reservations are recommended for prominent theatre events. Tickets can often be purchased through **Thai Ticket Major** (www.thaiticketmajor.com).

See p208 for more on the ins and outs of the Thai music scene.

Most bars and clubs close at 1am, but this is subject to police discretion. The drinking age is 20 years old.

Traditional Theatre & Dance

The stage in Thailand typically hosts a *kŏhn* performance, one of the six traditional dramatic forms. Acted only by men, *kŏhn* drama is based upon stories of the *Ramakian,* Thailand's version of India's epic *Ramayana,* and was traditionally staged only for royal audiences. Places to watch *kŏhn* include the National Theatre (p75) and Sala Chalermkrung (p102).

The less formal *lá·kon* dances, of which there are many dying subgenres, usually involve costumed dancers (of both sexes) performing elements of the *Ramakian* and traditional folk tales. If you hear the din of drums and percussion from a temple or shrine, follow the sound to see traditional *lá·kon gâa bon* (shrine dancing). At Lak Meuang (p70) and the Erawan Shrine (p106), worshippers commission costumed troupes to perform dance movements that are similar to classical *lá·kon,* but not as refined.

Another option for viewing Thai classical dance is at a dinner theatre. Most dinner theatres in Bangkok are heavily promoted through hotels to an ever-changing clientele, so standards are poor to fair. The performances at Sala Rim Nam (p130) come recommended.

See p210 for more on traditional Thai dance.

Gà·teu·i Cabaret

In recent years, watching men dressed as women perform tacky show tunes has become a 'must-do' fixture on the Bangkok tourist circuit. Calypso Bangkok (p130), Mambo Cabaret (p154) and Playhouse Theater Cabaret (p113) host choreographed stage shows featuring Broadway high kicks and lip-synched pop tunes.

Cinemas

Hollywood movies are released in Bangkok's theatres in a relatively timely fashion. But as home-grown cinema grows bigger, more and more Thai films, often subtitled in English, fill the roster. Foreign films are sometimes altered by Thailand's film censors before distribution; this usually involves obscuring nude sequences.

The shopping-centre cinemas have plush VIP options. Despite the heat and humidity on the streets, keep in mind that Bangkok's movie theatres pump the air-conditioning with such vigour that a jumper is an absolute necessity. Ticket prices range from 120B to 220B for regular seats, and more than 1000B for VIP seats.

Bangkok also hosts a handful of annual film festivals, including the World Film Festival of Bangkok (www.worldfilmbkk.com) in October.

See p209 for more on Thai film.

Moo·ay tai (Thai Boxing)

Quintessentially Thai, almost anything goes in *moo·ay tai* (also spelt *muay thai*), the martial art more commonly known elsewhere as Thai boxing or kickboxing. If you don't mind the violence, a Thai boxing match is well worth attending for the pure spectacle: the wild musical accompaniment, the ceremonial beginning of each match and the frenzied betting.

The best of the best fight at Bangkok's two boxing stadiums. Built on royal land at the end of WWII, the art deco–style Ratchadamnoen Stadium (p94) is the original and has a relatively formal atmosphere. The other main stage, Lumpinee Boxing Stadium (p154), recently moved to a new modern home north of Bangkok.

Admission fees vary according to seating. Ringside seats (from 2000B to 3000B) are the most expensive and will be filled with subdued VIPs; tourists usually opt for the 2nd-class seats (from 1500B to 2000B); diehard *moo·ay tai* fans bet and cheer from 3rd class (1000B). If you're thinking these prices sound a bit steep for your average fight fan (taxi drivers are big fans and they make about 600B a day), then you're right – foreigners pay several times what the Thais do.

We recommend the 2nd- or 3rd-class seats. Second class is filled with numbers-runners who take bets from fans in rowdy 3rd class, which is fenced off from the rest of the stadium. Akin to a stock-exchange pit, hand signals communicate bets and odds fly between the areas. Most fans in 3rd class follow the match (or their bets) too closely to sit down, and we've seen stress levels rise to near-boiling point. It's all very entertaining.

Most programs have eight to 10 fights of five rounds each. English-speaking 'staff' outside the stadium, who practically tackle you upon arrival, will hand you a fight roster and steer you to the foreigners' ticket windows; they can also be helpful in telling you which fights are the best match-ups (some say that welterweights, between 61.2kg and 66.7kg, are the best). To avoid supporting scalpers, purchase your tickets from the ticket window, not from a person outside the stadium.

See the boxed text on p93 for more on the history of *moo·ay tai*, for the inside scoop on the fighters and upcoming programs, see www.muaythai2000.com.

Go-Go Bars

Although technically illegal, prostitution is fully 'out' in Bangkok, and the influence of organised crime and healthy kickbacks mean that it will be a long while before the existing laws are ever enforced. Yet despite the image presented by much of the Western media, the underlying atmosphere of Bangkok's red-light districts is not one of illicitness and exploitation (although these do inevitably exist), but rather an aura of tackiness and boredom.

Patpong (p130) earned notoriety during the 1980s for its wild sex shows, involving everything from ping-pong balls and razors to midgets on motorbikes. Today it is more of a circus for curious spectators than sexual deviants. Soi Cowboy (p142) and Nana Entertainment Plaza (p142) are the real scenes of sex for hire. Not all of the love-you-long-time business is geared towards Westerners: Th Thaniya, off Th Silom, is filled with massage parlours for Japanese expats and visitors, while the immense massage parlours outside of central Bangkok attract Thai customers.

See the Sex Industry chapter (p219) for background on Thailand's sex industry.

Entertainment by Neighbourhood

➡ **Ko Ratanakosin & Thonburi** The area to visit for Traditional Thai performances, both scheduled and impromptu.

➡ **Banglamphu** Home to some of the city's best live-music venues.

➡ **Thewet & Dusit** This is where you'll find the city's oldest Thai boxing stadium.

➡ **Siam Square, Pratunam, Ploenchit & Ratchathewi** *Gà·teu·i* (transgender) cabaret and Bangkok's best cinemas.

➡ **Riverside, Silom & Lumphini** Traditional Thai dinner theatre.

➡ **Greater Bangkok** Bangkok's 'burbs are where you'll find some of the city's best live music and its other premier Thai boxing stadium.

Lonely Planet's Top Choices

Brick Bar (p86) Tabletop dancing to live Thai pop – right on Th Khao San.

Ratchadamnoen Stadium (p94) The country's premiere venue for Thai boxing.

Living Room (p142) Bangkok's best and classiest locale for live jazz.

Best for Thai-Style Live Music

Raintree (p113)

Tawandang German Brewery (p154)

Parking Toys (p153)

Hollywood (p154)

Best for Western-Style Live Music

Ad Here the 13th (p86)

Titanium (p142)

Saxophone Pub & Restaurant (p113)

Apoteka (p141)

Rock Pub (p113)

Sonic (p142)

Best for a Quirky Night Out

Tawandang German Brewery (p154)

Rock Pub (p113)

Hollywood (p154)

Best for Traditional Performance

National Theatre (p75)

Sala Chalermkrung (p102)

Sala Rim Naam (p130)

Siam Niramit (p154)

Best Cinemas

Paragon Cineplex (p111)

House (p154)

Scala (p111)

Lido (p111)

Best for Moo·ay Tai (Thai Boxing)

Ratchadamnoen Stadium (p94)

Lumpinee Boxing Stadium (p154)

Shopping

Prime your credit card and shine your baht, as shopping is serious business in Bangkok. Hardly a street corner in this city is free from a vendor, hawker or impromptu stall, and it doesn't stop there: Bangkok is also home to one of the world's largest outdoor markets, not to mention some of Southeast Asia's largest malls.

Markets & Malls

Although the tourist brochures tend to tout the upmarket malls, Bangkok still lags slightly behind Singapore and Hong Kong in this area, and the open-air markets are where the best deals and most original items are to be found.

Antiques

Real Thai antiques are rare and costly and reserved primarily for serious collectors. Everything else is designed to look old and most shopkeepers are happy to admit it. Reputable antique dealers will issue an authentication certificate. Contact the **Department of Fine Arts** (Map p257; ☏ 0 2221 4443; www.finearts.go.th; 81/1 Th Si Ayuthaya) to obtain the required license for exporting religious images and fragments, either antique or reproductions.

It's worth noting that trading in bona fide antiquities might not be either ethical or, in your country, legal. For more on this issue and the campaign to preserve Southeast Asia's cultural heritage, see **Heritage Watch** (www.heritagewatchinternational.org).

Gems & Jewellery

Countless tourists are sucked into the prolific and well-rehearsed gem scam, in which they are taken to a store by a helpful stranger and tricked into buying bulk gems that can supposedly be resold in their home country for 100% profit. The expert con artists (part of a well-organised cartel) seem trustworthy and convince tourists that they need a citizen of the country to circumvent tricky customs regulations. Unsurprisingly, the gem world doesn't work like that, and what most tourists end up with are worthless pieces of glass. By the time you sort all this out, the store has closed and changed names, and the police can do little to help.

Tailor-Made Clothes

Many tourists arrive in Bangkok with the notion of getting clothes custom-tailored at a bargain price. While this is entirely possible, there are a few things to be aware of. Prices are almost always lower than what you'd pay at home, but common scams such as commission-hungry túk-túk (pronounced *đúk đúk;* a type of motorised rickshaw) drivers, shoddy workmanship and inferior fabrics make bespoke tailoring in Bangkok a potentially disappointing investment.

The golden rule of custom tailoring is that you get what you pay for. If you sign up for a suit, two pants, two shirts and a tie, with a silk sarong thrown in, for just US$199 (a very popular offer in Bangkok), chances are it will look and fit like a sub-US$200 wardrobe. Although an offer may seem great on the surface, the price may fluctuate significantly depending on the fabric you choose. Supplying your own fabric won't necessarily reduce the price by much, but it should ensure you get exactly the look you're after.

Have a good idea of what you want before walking into a shop. If it's a suit you're after,

NEED TO KNOW

Opening Hours

Most family-run shops are open from 10am to 7pm daily. Malls are open from approximately 10am to 10pm. Street markets are either daytime (from 9am to 5pm) or night-time (from 7pm to midnight). Note that city ordinance forbids street-side vendors from cluttering the pavements on Mondays, but they are present every other day.

Scams

Thais are generally so friendly and laid-back that some visitors are lulled into a false sense of security, forgetting that Bangkok is a big city with the usual untrustworthy characters. While your personal safety is rarely at risk in Thailand, you may be unwittingly charmed out of the contents of your wallet or fall prey to a scam.

Bargaining

At Bangkok's markets and at a handful of its malls, you'll have to bargain for most, if not all, items. In general, if you see a price tag, it means that the price is fixed and bargaining isn't an option.

Counterfeits

Bangkok is ground-zero for the production and sale of counterfeit goods. Although they may seem cheap, keep in mind that counterfeit goods are almost always shoddy.

Shopping Guide

Bangkok's intense urban tangle sometimes makes orientation a challenge, and it can be difficult to find out-of-the-way shops and markets. Like having your own personal guide, **Nancy Chandler's Map of Bangkok** (www.nancychandler.net) tracks all sorts of small, out-of-the-way shopping venues and markets, as well as dissects the innards of the Chatuchak Weekend Market (p147). The colourful map is sold in bookstores throughout the city.

should it be single- or double-breasted? How many buttons? What style trousers? Of course, if you have no idea, the tailor will be more than happy to advise. Alternatively,

bring a favourite garment from home and have it copied.

Set aside a week to get clothes tailored. Shirts and trousers can often be turned around in 48 hours or less with only one fitting, but no matter what a tailor may tell you, it takes more than one and often more than two fittings to create a good suit. Most reliable tailors will ask for two to five fittings. Any tailor that can sew your order in less than 24 hours should be treated with caution.

Counterfeits

One of the most ubiquitous aspects of shopping in Bangkok, and a drawcard for many visitors, is fake merchandise. Counterfeit clothes, watches and bags line sections of Th Sukhumvit and Th Silom, while there are entire malls dedicated to copied DVDs, music CDs and software. Fake IDs are available up and down Th Khao San, and there are even fake Lonely Planet guides, old editions of which are made over with a new cover and 'publication date' to be resold (often before the new editions have even been written!). Fakes are so prominent in Bangkok that there's even a **Museum of Counterfeit Goods** (✆0 2653 5546; www.tillekeandgibbins.com/museum/museum.htm; Tilleke & Gibbins, 26th fl, Supalai Grand Tower, 1011 Th Phra Ram III; admission free; ⊗by appointment only; Ⓜ Khlong Toei exit 1 & taxi) where all the counterfeit booty that has been collected by the law firm Tilleke and Gibbins over the years is on display.

The brashness with which fake goods are peddled in Bangkok gives the impression that black-market goods are fair game, which is and isn't true. Technically, knock-offs are illegal, and periodic crackdowns by the Thai police have led to the closure of shops and the arrest of vendors. The shops typically open again after a few months, however, and the purchasers of fake merchandise are rarely the target of such crackdowns.

The tenacity of Bangkok's counterfeit goods trade is largely due to the fact that tourists aren't the only ones buying the stuff. A poll conducted by Bangkok University's research centre found that 80% of the 1104 people polled in Bangkok admitted to having purchased counterfeit goods (only 48% admitted they felt guilty for having bought fakes).

AN INSIDER'S TIPS ON SHOPPING IN BANGKOK

Nima Chandler of **Nancy Chandler Graphics** (www.nancychandler.net), whose colourful maps are some of the best guides to shopping in Bangkok, shares her Bangkok shopping secrets:

Your favourite Bangkok market? For visitors, Chatuchak Weekend Market (p147) remains my top recommendation, but personally I prefer quirky smaller markets catering to locals, such as the Flashlight Market (p98) just north of Chinatown on Friday and Saturday nights, where collectibles of all kinds are on sale. My most bizarre find there: an antique popcorn machine.

Your favourite Bangkok mall? MBK Center (p113), the market in a mall, as I describe it. It's one of the few that has retained a distinctly Thai atmosphere within, unlike the gleaming malls nearby, which could be anywhere in the world. More importantly, MBK's vendors do carry 'fa·ràng [foreigner]-size' clothing. Highlights for visitors: silly shirts and beachwear in the southern end of the 3rd floor and the cheap food court and crafts on the 6th floor.

Where's a good place to go for Thai handicrafts? Chatuchak Weekend Market (p147) is probably the most popular for arts and crafts, but I find it much easier and fulfilling to shop for crafts at ThaiCraft Fair (p143). ThaiCraft is a self-financed social enterprise dedicated to helping maintain and promote traditional Thai arts and crafts direct from the villages, under fair-trade practices. Favourite finds: yoga-mat-carrying bags with tribal motifs, necklaces made of recycled materials, wonderful woven baskets and silver jewellery.

A good place for quirky souvenirs? Propaganda (Map p270; ☑2664 8574; 2nd fl, Siam Discovery Center; ☺10am-8pm; ⓜNational Stadium or Siam), a Thai brand gone international with cheeky, sometimes naughty, modern design products, such as a 'Help' wine stopper (with a drowning swimmer's hand raised) and an emergency wedding ring, which comes on a credit-card-sized plastic card and can be popped out when needed.

Other than Jim Thompson, what are some high-quality Thai brands visitors should seek out? The 3rd floor of Siam Center (p115) houses several top Thai fashion designer boutiques.

Where's a good place in Bangkok for antiques? River City (p130) is home to several antique galleries, selling both real and reproduction antiques. We recommend serious antique buyers do some research before visiting, however, as several top dealers only offer private appointments.

Any insider tips for approaching Chatuchak Weekend Market? When you see something you know you'll love, buy it, as it can be difficult to retrace your steps back to a shop in this market. Plan to use the restrooms in advance – lines can be long, and in the ladies' room, women often line up by stall rather than in turn. Stop to rest and drink water every hour. Chatuchak can be a draining experience, especially during the hot season. Try to stay until closing, then enjoy an early evening drink at Viva's (p148) while watching the market transform itself into something else after dark.

It's worth pointing out that some companies, including even a few luxury brands, argue that counterfeit goods can be regarded as a net positive. They claim that a preponderance of fake items inspires brand awareness and fosters a demand for 'real' luxury items while also acting as a useful gauge of what's hot. But the argument against fake goods points out that the industry supports organised crime and potentially exploitative and abusive labour conditions, circumvents taxes and takes jobs away from legitimate companies.

If the legal or moral repercussions aren't enough to convince you, keep in mind that in general, with fake stuff, you're getting exactly what you pay for. Consider yourself lucky if, after arriving home, you can actually watch all of season four of the *Simpsons* DVD you bought, if the Von Dutch badge on your new hat hasn't peeled off within a week, and if your 'Rolex' is still ticking after the first rain.

Bargaining

Many of your purchases in Bangkok will involve an ancient skill that has long been abandoned in the West: bargaining. Contrary to what you'll see on a daily basis on Th Khao San, bargaining (in Thai, *gahn dòr rah·kah*) is not a terse exchange of numbers and animosity. Rather, bargaining Thai-style is a generally friendly transaction where two people try to agree on a price that is fair to both of them.

The first rule to bargaining is to have a general idea of the price. Ask around at a few vendors to get a rough notion. When you're ready to buy, it's generally a good strategy to start at 50% of the asking price and work up from there. If you're buying several of an item, you have much more leverage to request and receive a lower price. If the seller immediately agrees to your first price you're probably paying too much, but it's bad form to bargain further at this point. In general, keeping a friendly, flexible demeanour throughout the transaction will almost always work in your favour. And remember: only begin bargaining if you're really planning on buying the item. Most importantly, there's simply no point in getting angry or upset over a few baht – Thai locals, who inevitably have less money than you, never do this.

Tax Refunds

A 7% Value Added Tax (VAT) applies to most purchases in Thailand, but if you spend enough and get the paperwork, the kindly Revenue Department will refund it at the airport when you leave. To qualify to receive a refund, you must not be a Thai citizen, part of an airline air crew or have spent more than 180 days in Thailand during the previous year. Your purchase must have been made at an approved store; look for the blue-and-white VAT Refund sticker.

Minimum purchases must add up to 2000B per store in a single day and to at least 5000B total for the whole trip. Before you leave the store, get a VAT Refund form and tax invoice. Most major malls in Bangkok will direct you to a dedicated VAT Refund desk, which will organise the appropriate paperwork (it takes about five minutes). Note that you won't get a refund on VAT paid in hotels or restaurants.

At the airport, your purchases must be declared at the customs desk in the departure hall, which will give you the appropriate stamp; you can then check them in. Smaller items (such as watches and jewellery) should be carried on your person, as they will need to be reinspected once you've passed immigration. You actually get your money at a **VAT Refund Tourist Office** (☎ 0 2272 8198); at Suvarnabhumi International Airport these are located on Level 4 in both the east and west wings. For how-to info, go to www.rd.go.th/vrt/howwill.html.

Shopping by Neighbourhood

➡ **Ko Ratanakosin & Thonburi** Shopping here is limited to the amulet vendors and traditional Thai medicine shops that line Th Maha Rat.

➡ **Banglamphu** Home to a couple of souvenir shops, not to mention the street-side wares of Th Khao San.

➡ **Chinatown** Street markets with a flea-market feel.

➡ **Siam Square, Pratunam, Ploenchit & Ratchathewi** Simply put: malls, malls and more malls.

➡ **Riverside, Silom & Lumphini** The place to go for antiques and art.

➡ **Sukhumvit** Upscale malls and touristy street markets.

➡ **Greater Bangkok** Bangkok's best fresh and open-air markets lie a fair hike outside the city centre.

Lonely Planet's Top Choices

Chatuchak Weekend Market (p147) One of the world's largest markets and a must-do Bangkok experience.

MBK Center (p113) The Thai market in a mall.

Thanon Khao San Market (p86) Handicrafts, souvenirs and backpacker essentials.

Siam Square (p115) Ground Zero for Thai teen fashion in Bangkok.

Best Markets

Asiatique (p130)

Talat Rot Fai (p150)

Pak Khlong Talat (Flower Market) (p98)

Talat Mai (p98)

Nonthaburi Market (p150)

Best Malls

CentralWorld (p115)

Siam Paragon (p115)

Siam Center (p115)

Siam Discovery Center (p115)

Emporium (p143)

Best Housewares & Handicrafts

ThaiCraft Fair (p143)

Nandakwang (p142)

Doi Tung (p116)

Taekee Taekon (p86)

Tamnan Mingmuang (p131)

Sop Moei Arts (p143)

Best for One-of-a-Kind Souvenirs

Ban Baat (p78)

Flashlight Market (p98)

Thai Nakon (p86)

House Of Chao (p131)

Talat Rot Fai (p150)

Best Thai Fashion Labels

It's Happened To Be A Closet (p116)

Flynow III (p116)

Tango (p116)

Senada Theory (p115)

Best Tailors

Raja's Fashions (p142)

Rajawongse (p142)

July (p131)

Nickermann's (p142)

Pinky Tailors (p116)

Ricky's Fashion House (p142)

Best for Books

Kinokuniya (p115)

Dasa Book Café (p143)

Asia Books (p115)

RimKhobFah Bookstore (p87)

Best Food & Drink

Nittaya Curry Shop (p86)

Chiang Heng (p130)

Or Tor Kor Market (p151)

Maison Des Arts (p131)

Best for Music

ZudRangMa Records (p143)

DJ Siam (p115)

Kitcharoen Dountri (p147)

Best for Cheap Stuff

Sampeng Lane (p99)

Pratunam Market (p115)

Phahurat (p98)

Soi Lalai Sap (p132)

Best for Gadgets

Digital Gateway (p115)

Fortune Town (p155)

Pantip Plaza (p116)

Siam Paragon (p115)

Best for Antiques

River City (p130)

House Of Chao (p131)

Talat Rot Fai (p150)

Flashlight Market (p98)

ZudRangMa Records (p143)

Street massage on Khao San Rd (p82)

Sports & Activities

Seen all the big sights? Eaten enough pàt tai *for a lifetime? When you're done soaking it all in, consider some of Bangkok's more active pursuits. Massage and spa visits are justifiably a huge draw, but the city is also home to some great guided tours and courses, the latter in subjects ranging from Thai cookery to meditation.*

Spas & Massage

According to the teachings of traditional Thai healing, the use of herbs and massage should be part of a regular health-and-beauty regimen, not just an excuse for pampering. You need no excuse to get a massage and it's just as well, because Bangkok could mount a strong claim to being the massage capital of the world. Exactly what type of massage you're after is another question. Variations range from store-front traditional Thai massage to an indulgent 'spa experience' with service and style. And even within the enormous spa category there are many options: there's plenty of pampering going around but some spas now focus more on the medical than the sensory, while plush resort-style spas offer a menu of appealing treatments.

The most common variety is traditional Thai massage (nôo·at pǎan boh·rahn). Although it sounds relaxing, at times it can seem more closely related to Thai boxing than to shiatsu. Thai massage is based on yogic techniques for general health, which involve pulling, stretching, bending and manipulating pressure points. If done well, a traditional massage will leave you sore but revitalised.

Full-body massages usually include scented balms or herbal compresses. Note that 'oil massage' is sometimes taken as code for 'sexy massage'. A foot massage is arguably (and it's a strong argument) the best way to treat the leg-weariness of sightseeing.

Depending on the neighbourhood, prices for massages in small parlours are 200B to 350B for a foot massage and 300B to 500B for a full-body massage. Spa experiences start at about 800B and climb like a Bangkok skyscraper.

Jogging & Cycling

Lumphini Park (p122) and Benjakiti Park (p135) host early-morning and late-evening runners.

For something more social, one of Bangkok's longest-running sports groups is the Hash House Harriers (www.bangkokhhh.com), which puts on weekly runs. Cyclists also have their own hash, with the Bangkok Hash House Bikers (www.bangkokbikehash.org) meeting one Sunday a month for a 40km to 50km mountain-bike ride and post-ride refreshments.

Gyms

Bangkok is well stocked with gyms, ranging in style from long-running, open-air affairs in spaces such as Lumphini Park to ultra-modern megagyms complete with high-tech equipment. Most large hotels have gyms and swimming pools, as do a growing number of small hotels.

Yoga & Pilates

Yoga studios – and enormous accompanying billboards of smiling gurus – have popped up faster than mushrooms at a full-moon party. Expect to pay about 650B for a one-off class.

Golf

Bangkok's outer suburbs are well stocked with golf courses, with green fees ranging from 250B to 5000B, plus the customary 200B tip for caddies. The website Thai Golfer (www.thaigolfer.com) rates every course in Thailand (click through to 'Course Reviews').

Tours
GUIDED TOURS

If you're not travelling with a group but would like a guide, recommended outfits

NEED TO KNOW

Long-term courses like language or meditation should ideally be booked a month or so in advance to ensure vacancies. Shorter courses, including cookery courses, and most guided tours can be arranged a week or a few days in advance. Massage and spa treatments can often be booked on the same day.

include **Tour with Tong** (08 1835 0240; www.tourwithtong.com; day tour from 1500B), whose team of guides conduct tours in and around Bangkok, and **Thai Private Tour Guide** (08 9661 6706, 08 9822 1798; www.thaitourguide.com; day tour from 2000B), where Ms Pu and TJ get good reviews.

WALKING/SPECIALITY TOURS

Although the pollution and heat are significant obstacles, Bangkok is a fascinating city to explore on foot. If you'd rather do it with an expert guide, **Bangkok Private Tours** (www.bangkokprivatetours.com; half-/full-day walking tour 4700/6000B) and Co van Kessel Bangkok Tours (p132) conduct customised walking tours of the city. Foodies will appreciate the offerings at **Bangkok Food Tours** (08 9126 3657; www.bangkokfoodtours.com; tours from 850B), which offers half-day culinary tours of Bangkok's older neighbourhoods.

BICYCLE & SEGWAY TOURS

You might be wondering who the hell would want to get on a bike and subject themselves to the notorious traffic jams and sauna-like conditions of Bangkok's streets. But the fact that they sound so unlikely is part of what makes these trips so cool. The other part is that you discover a whole side of the city that's virtually off-limits to four-wheeled transport. Routes include unusual ways around Chinatown and Ko Ratanakosin, but the pick are journeys across the river to Thonburi and, in particular, to the Phra Pradaeng Peninsula. Better known as Bang Kachao, this exquisite expanse of mangrove, banana and coconut plantations lies just a stone's throw from the frantic city centre, on the opposite side of Chao Phraya. You cycle to the river, take a boat to Bang Kachao and then follow elevated concrete paths that zigzag through the growth to a local village for lunch.

Several companies run regular, well-received tours starting at about 900B for a half-day.

RIVER & CANAL TRIPS

The cheapest and most obvious way to commute between riverside attractions is on the commuter boats run by Chao Phraya Express Boat (p227). The terminus for most northbound boats is Tha Nonthaburi, while for most southbound boats it's Tha Sathon (also called Central Pier), near the Saphan Taksin BTS station (although some boats run as far south as Wat Ratchasingkhon).

For a more personal view, you might consider chartering a long-tail boat along the city's canals. Pandan Tour (p68) offers 'small-boat', full-day private tours of Bangkok's canals. Another option is the dinner cruises that ply Mae Nam Chao Phraya at night.

AYUTHAYA CRUISES

A little faster than the days of sailing ships, river cruises from Bangkok north to the ruins of the former royal capital of Ayuthaya take in all the romance of the river. Normally only one leg of the journey between Bangkok and Ayuthaya is aboard a boat, while the return or departing trip is by bus. Outfits include **Asian Oasis** (Map p260; ☎08 1496 4516, 08 8809 7047; www.asian-oasis.com; 7th fl, Nai Lert Tower, 2/4 Th Witthayu (Wireless Rd); 2-day trip 6050-10,600B; ⏰9am-5pm Mon-Fri; [S]Phloen Chit exit 1) and Manohra Cruises (p155).

Courses

MEDITATION

Although at times Bangkok may seem like the most un-Buddhist place on earth, there are a few places where foreigners can practise Theravada Buddhist meditation. Some courses allow drop-ins on a daily basis, while others require a relatively long-term commitment.

See p206 for background information on Buddhism. Additional sources of information include Dharma Thai (www.dharmathai.com), which has links to a few prominent wát and meditation centres.

THAI BOXING

Training in *moo·ay tai* (also spelt *muay Thai*) for foreigners has increased in popularity in the last decade and many camps all over the country are tailoring their programs for English-speaking fighters of both sexes. Food and accommodation can often be provided for an extra charge. The website for Muay Thai Camps (www.muaythaicampsthailand.com) contains additional information on Thailand's various training centres.

THAI COOKERY

Having consumed everything Bangkok has to offer is one thing, but imagine the points you'll rack up if you can make the same dishes for your friends back at home. A visit to a Thai cooking school has become a must-do for many Bangkok itineraries, and for some visitors it's a highlight of their trip.

Courses range in price and value, but a typical half-day course should include at least a basic introduction to Thai ingredients and flavours and a hands-on chance to both prepare and cook several dishes. Nearly all lessons include a set of printed recipes and end with a communal lunch consisting of your handiwork.

THAI LANGUAGE

Although it generally involves a pretty serious time commitment, Bangkok is home to several schools that specialise in teaching Thai to foreigners.

THAI MASSAGE

There are few places in Bangkok that offer instruction in Thai-style massage, but both Wat Pho Thai Traditional Medical and Massage School (p75) and Pussapa Thai Massage School (p143) have English-language curricula.

Sports & Activities by Neighbourhood

➡ **Ko Ratanakosin & Thonburi** Canal- and river-based boat tours, and Thai massage.

➡ **Banglamphu** Bike tours.

➡ **Siam Square, Pratunam, Ploenchit & Ratchathewi** Spas and language courses.

➡ **Riverside, Silom & Lumphini** Some of Bangkok's best cooking schools and spas are found here.

➡ **Sukhumvit** This street is home to Bangkok's greatest variety of good-quality massage and spas.

➡ **Greater Bangkok** The suburbs are where you'll find Bangkok's most lauded Thai boxing schools.

Lonely Planet's Top Choices

Helping Hands (p143) Cooking school that offers a unique Bangkok experience.

Oriental Spa (p132) Riverside spa that sets the standard for luxury and pampering.

Health Land (p144) Quite possibly one of the best-value massage studios in the world.

Ruen-Nuad Massage Studio (p132) Cosy, reputable massage studio.

Best Spas

Banyan Tree Spa (p132)

Thann Sanctuary (p117)

Divana Massage & Spa (p144)

Eugenia Spa (p144)

Rakuten (p144)

Best for Thai-Style Massage

Asia Herb Association (p144)

Coran (p144)

Lavana (p144)

Wat Pho Thai Traditional Medical and Massage School (p75)

Baan Dalah (p144)

Best Thai Cookery Schools

Amita Thai Cooking Class (p155)

Blue Elephant Thai Cooking School (p132)

Baipai Thai Cooking School (p155)

Silom Thai Cooking School (p132)

Oriental Hotel Thai Cooking School (p132)

Best Bicycle & Segway Tours

ABC Amazing Bangkok Cyclists (p144)

Velo Thailand (p87)

Co van Kessel Bangkok Tours (p132)

Grasshopper Adventures (p87)

Segway Tour Thailand (p75)

Best for Kids

KidZania (p117)

Fun-arium (p144)

Siam Ocean World (p106)

Siam Park City (p154)

Dream World (p154)

SF Strike Bowl (p117)

Best for Moo·ay Tai (Thai Boxing)

MuayThai Institute (p155)

Fairtex Muay Thai (p155)

Sor Vorapin Gym (p87)

Krudam Gym (p144)

Best for Meditation

Meditation Study and Retreat Center (p75)

House of Dhamma (p155)

International Buddhist Meditation Center (p75)

Best for Learning Thai Massage

Pussapa Thai Massage School (p143)

Wat Pho Thai Traditional Medical and Massage School (p75)

Explore Bangkok

BANGKOK'S TOP SIGHTS

Neighbourhoods at a Glance

❶ Ko Ratanakosin & Thonburi p56

The artificial island of Ko Ratanakosin is Bangkok's birthplace, and the Buddhist temples and royal palaces here comprise some of the city's most important and most-visited sights. By contrast, Thonburi, located across Mae Nam Chao Phraya (Chao Phraya River), is a seemingly forgotten yet visit-worthy zone of sleepy residential districts connected by *klorng* (canals, also spelt *khlong*).

❷ Banglamphu p76

Leafy lanes, antique shophouses, buzzing wet markets and golden temples convene in Banglamphu – easily the city's most quintessentially 'Bangkok' neighbourhood. It's a quaint postcard picture of the city that used to be, that is until you stumble upon Th Khao

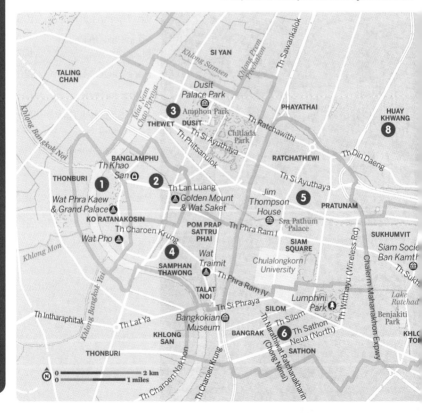

San, arguably the world's most famous backpacker enclave.

neighbourhood, where half the fun is getting completely lost.

❸ Thewet & Dusit p88

With its wide boulevards, manicured parks, imposing palaces and statues dedicated to former kings, Dusit has a knack for making you second-guess what city you're in. The reality check comes in neighbouring Thewet, where the soggy riverside setting, busy wet market and relentless traffic are classic Bangkok.

❹ Chinatown p95

Although many generations removed from the motherland, Bangkok's Chinatown could be a bosom buddy of any Chinese city. The streets are crammed with shark-fin restaurants, gaudy yellow-gold and jade shops, and flashing neon signs in Chinese characters. This is Bangkok's most hectic

❺ Siam Square, Pratunam, Ploenchit & Ratchathewi p103

Multistorey malls, outdoor shopping precincts and never-ending markets leave no doubt that Siam Square, Pratunam and Ploenchit combine to form Bangkok's commercial district. The BTS (Skytrain) interchange at Siam has also made this area the centre of modern Bangkok, while only a few blocks away, scruffy Ratchathewi has a lot more in common with provincial Thai cities.

❻ Riverside, Silom & Lumphini p118

Although you may not see it behind the office blocks, hi-rise condos and hotels, Mae Nam Chao Phraya forms a watery backdrop to these linked neighbourhoods. History is still palpable in the riverside area's crumbling architecture, while heading inland, Silom, Bangkok's de facto financial district, is frenetic and modern, and Th Sathon is the much more subdued embassy zone.

❼ Sukhumvit p133

Japanese enclaves, French restaurants, Middle Eastern nightlife zones, tacky 'sexpat' haunts: it's all here along Th Sukhumvit, Bangkok's unofficial international zone. Where temples and suburban rice fields used to be, today you'll also find shopping centres, nightlife and a host of other amenities that cater to middle-class Thais and resident foreigners.

❽ Greater Bangkok p145

Once ringed by rice fields, modern Bangkok has since expanded in every possible direction with few concessions to agriculture or charm. The sights may be relatively few and far between, but the upside is that Bangkok's 'burbs are a good place to get a taste of provincial Thailand if you don't have the time to go upcountry.

Ko Ratanakosin & Thonburi

Neighbourhood Top Five

1 Trying to stop your jaw from dropping to the floor upon encountering the enormous reclining Buddha at **Wat Pho** (p63) for the first time.

2 Basking in the glow of the Emerald Buddha at **Wat Phra Kaew** (p58).

3 Getting up close with the iconic riverside temple known as **Wat Arun** (p67).

4 Getting lost in the weirdness of commerce that is the **Amulet Market** (p68).

5 Learning about the origins of Thai culture at the **Museum of Siam** (p68).

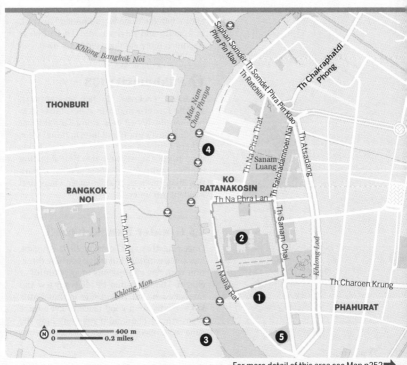

For more detail of this area see Map p252 ➡

Explore: Ko Ratanakosin & Thonburi

The birthplace of Bangkok, the artificial island of Ko Ratanakosin is where it all started more than 200 years ago. The remnants of this history – today Bangkok's biggest sights – draw just about every visitor to the city. The big-hitters, Wat Phra Kaew & Grand Palace and Wat Pho, are a short walk from the Chao Phraya Express boat piers at Tha Chang and Tha Tien, and are within walking distance of each other, although the hot sun may make doing this a more demanding task than it appears. Alternatively, túk-túks (pronounced *đúk đúk*) are a dime a dozen around here. If you're planning on doing our walking tour or visiting several sights, it's a good idea to arrive early in the morning, to avoid the crowds and take advantage of the cool weather. Evening is best for photography, particularly if you're hoping for the classic sunset shot of Wat Arun.

Located across the river, neighbouring Thonburi has significantly less to offer in terms of sights, but is great for those who fancy urban exploration. The cool morning is a wise time to visit the area, which is accessible via the 3B river-crossing ferries at Tha Chang and Tha Tien.

Local Life

➡**Local Life** This is probably Bangkok's most touristy neighbourhood, but hop on any of the 3B river-crossing ferries and you'll be whisked to Thonburi, where regular Thai life carries on uninterrupted.

➡**Dance Floor** Lak Meuang receives daily supplications from Thai worshippers, some of whom commission classical Thai dancers to perform *lákon gâa bon* (shrine dancing) as thanks for granted wishes.

➡**Life Aquatic** Thonburi remains home to several *klorng* (canals; also spelt *khlong*) that once were responsible for Bangkok's former nickname, 'Venice of the East'.

➡**Traditional Healing** Along Th Maha Rat, dozens of handsome shophouses feature family-run herbal medicine and traditional massage shops.

Getting There & Away

➡**River boat** To Ko Ratanakosin: Tha Rajinee, Tha Tien and Tha Chang. To Thonburi: Tha Wang Lang (Siriraj), Thonburi Railway and Tha Saphan Phra Pin Klao. Several cross-river ferries also connect to Bangkok piers.

➡**BTS** To Thonburi: Krung Thonburi and Wong Wian Yai. To Ko Ratanakosin: National Stadium or Phaya Thai and taxi.

➡**Bus** To Ko Ratanakosin: air-con 503, 508 and 511; ordinary 3, 25, 39, 47 and 53. To Thonburi: air-con 507 and 509; ordinary 21, 42 and 82.

➡**Taxi** Best taken outside of rush hours.

Lonely Planet's Top Tip

Anyone standing outside any of the big sights in Ko Ratanakosin who claims that the sight is closed is either a gem tout or con artist – ignore them and proceed inside.

KO RATANAKOSIN & THONBURI

 Best Places to Eat
➡ Pa Aew (p73)
➡ Ming Lee (p74)
➡ Coconut Palm (p74)
➡ Khunkung (p74)
For reviews, see p73.➡

 Best Temples
➡ Wat Phra Kaew (p58)
➡ Wat Pho (p63)
➡ Wat Arun (p67)
For reviews, see p58.➡

 Best Museums
➡ Museum of Siam (p68)
➡ National Museum (p69)
➡ Songkran Niyomsane Forensic Medicine Museum & Parasite Museum (p69)
For reviews, see p68.➡

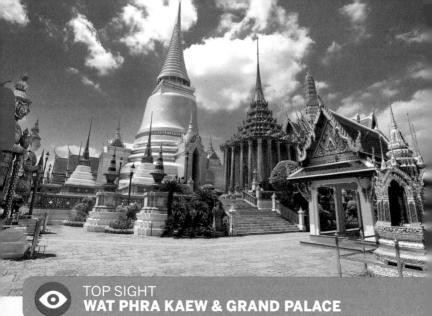

Wat Phra Kaew (Temple of the Emerald Buddha) gleams and glitters with so much colour and glory that its earthly foundations seem barely able to resist the celestial pull. Architecturally fantastic, the temple complex is also the spiritual core of Thai Buddhism and the monarchy, symbolically united in what is the country's most holy image, the Emerald Buddha. Attached to the temple complex is the former royal residence, once a sealed city of intricate ritual and social stratification.

The ground was consecrated in 1782, the first year of Bangkok rule, and is today Bangkok's biggest tourist attraction and a pilgrimage destination for devout Buddhists and nationalists. The 94.5-hectare grounds encompass more than 100 buildings that represent 200 years of royal history and architectural experimentation. Most of the architecture, royal or sacred, can be classified as Ratanako-sin (old-Bangkok style).

Guides can be hired at the ticket kiosk; ignore anyone outside. An audio guide can be rented for 200B for two hours. Wat Phra Kaew and the Grand Palace are best reached either by a short walk south from Banglamphu, via Sanam Luang, or by Chao Phraya Express boat to Tha Chang. From the Siam Sq area (in front of the MBK Center, Th Phra Ram I), take bus 47.

DON'T MISS...

➡ Emerald Buddha
➡ *Ramakian* murals
➡ Grand Palace structures

PRACTICALITIES

➡ วัดพระแก้ว, พระบรม มหาราชวัง
➡ Map p252
➡ Th Na Phra Lan
➡ admission 500B
➡ ◷8.30am-4pm
➡ 🚢Tha Chang

Wat Phra Kaew

Ramakian Murals

Outside the main *bòht* (ordination hall) is a stone statue of the Chinese goddess of mercy, Kuan Im; nearby are two cow figures, representing the year of Rama I's birth. In the 2km-long cloister that defines the perimeter of the complex are 178 murals depicting the

Ramakian (the Thai version of the Indian *Ramayana* epic) in its entirety, beginning at the north gate and moving clockwise around the compound.

The story begins with the hero, Rama (the green-faced character), and his bride, Sita (the beautiful, shirtless maiden). The young couple are banished to the forest, along with Rama's brother. In this pastoral setting, the evil king Ravana (the character with many arms and faces) disguises himself as a hermit in order to kidnap Sita.

Rama joins forces with Hanuman, the monkey king (logically depicted as the white monkey), to attack Ravana and rescue Sita. Although Rama has the pedigree, Hanuman is the unsung hero. He is loyal, fierce and clever. En route to the final fairytale ending, great battles and schemes of trickery ensue until Ravana is finally killed. After withstanding a loyalty test of fire, Sita and Rama are triumphantly reunited.

If the temple grounds seem overrun by tourists, the mural area is usually mercifully quiet and shady.

Emerald Buddha

Upon entering Wat Phra Kaew you'll meet the *yaksha,* brawny guardian deities. Beyond them is a courtyard where the central *bòht* (ordination hall) houses the Emerald Buddha. The spectacular ornamentation inside and out does an excellent job of distracting first-time visitors from paying their respects to the image. Here's why: the Emerald Buddha is only 66cm tall and sits so high above worshippers in the main temple building that the gilded shrine is more striking than the small figure it cradles. No one knows exactly where it comes from or who sculpted it, but it first appeared on record in 15th-century Chiang Rai (in northern Thailand). Stylistically it seems to belong to Thai artistic periods of the 13th to 14th centuries.

Because of its royal status, the Emerald Buddha is ceremoniously draped in monastic robes. There are now three royal robes (for the hot, rainy and cool seasons), which are still solemnly changed at the beginning of each season. This duty has traditionally been performed by the king, though in recent years the crown prince has presided over the ceremony.

Grand Palace

Adjoining Wat Phra Kaew is the Grand Palace (Phra Borom Maharatchawang), a former royal residence that is today only used on ceremonial occasions. Visitors are allowed to survey the Grand Palace grounds and four of the remaining palace buildings, which are interesting for their royal bombast.

DRESS CODE

At Wat Phra Kaew and the Grand Palace grounds, dress rules are strictly enforced. If you're wearing shorts or a sleeveless shirt you will not be allowed into the temple grounds – this applies to both men and women. If you're showing a bit too much calf or ankle, expect to be shown into a dressing room and issued with a sarong (rental is free, but you must provide a 200B deposit). Officially, sandals and flip-flops are not permitted, though the guards are less zealous in enforcing this rule.

Despite the name, the Emerald Buddha is actually carved from a single piece of nephrite (a type of jade).

TICKETS

Enter Wat Phra Kaew and the Grand Palace complex through the clearly marked third gate from the river pier. Tickets are purchased inside the complex; anyone telling you it's closed is a gem tout or con artist. Remember to keep your ticket: it also allows same-day entry to Dusit Palace Park (p90).

Wat Phra Kaew & Grand Palace

EXPLORE BANGKOK'S PREMIER MONUMENTS TO RELIGION AND REGENCY

This tour can be covered in a couple of hours. The first area tourists enter is the Buddhist temple compound generally referred to as Wat Phra Kaew. A covered walkway surrounds the area, the inner walls of which are decorated with the **murals of the *Ramakian*** 1 and 2. Originally painted during the reign of Rama I (r 1782–1809), the murals, which depict the Hindu epic the *Ramayana*, span 178 panels that describe the struggles of Rama to resc his kidnapped wife, Sita.

After taking in the story, pass through one of the gateways guarded by ***yaksha*** 3 to th inner compound. The most important struct here is the ***bòht*, or ordination hall** 4, whic houses the **Emerald Buddha** 5.

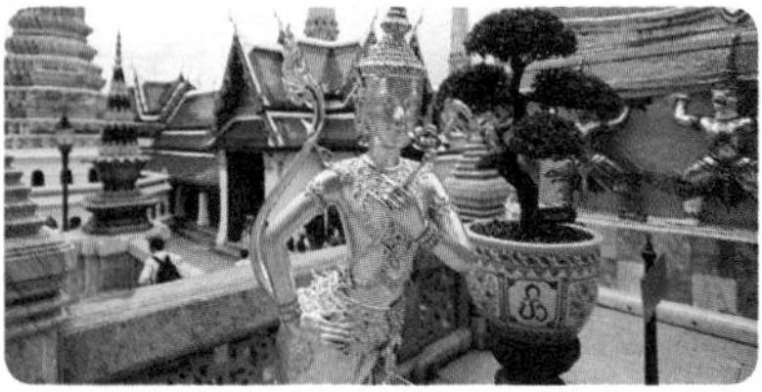

AUSTIN BUSH ©

Kinaree

These graceful half-swan, half-women creatures from Hindu-Buddhist mythology stand outside Prasat Phra Thep Bidon.

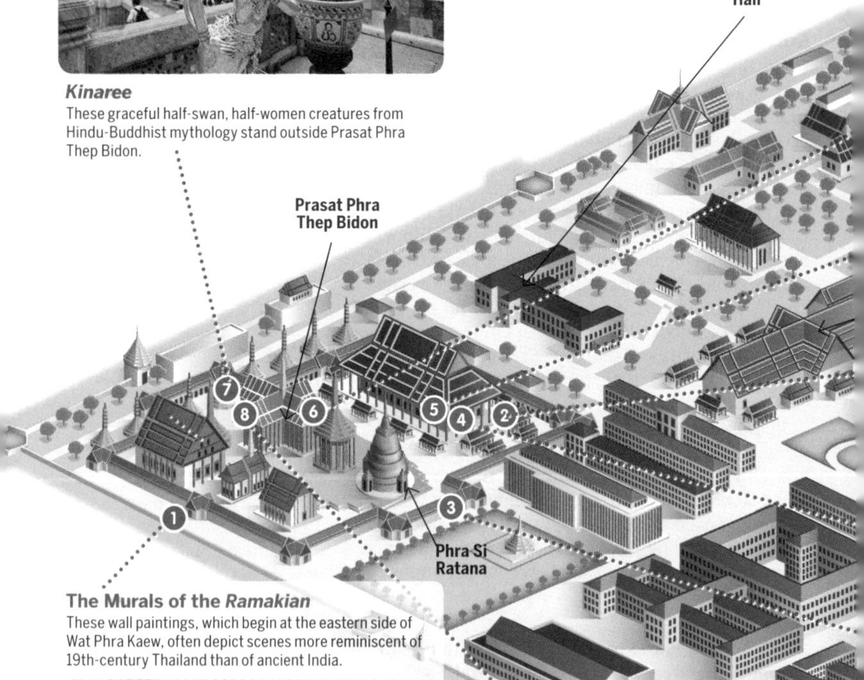
Borombhiman Hall
Prasat Phra Thep Bidon
Phra Si Ratana
1
2
3
4
5
6
7
8

The Murals of the *Ramakian*

These wall paintings, which begin at the eastern side of Wat Phra Kaew, often depict scenes more reminiscent of 19th-century Thailand than of ancient India.

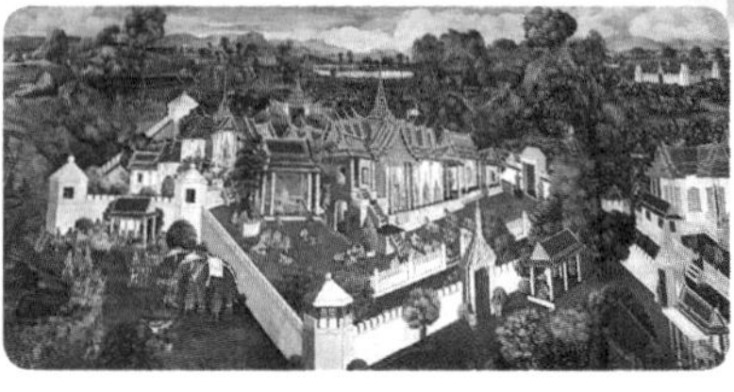

AUSTIN BUSH ©

Hanuman

Rows of these mischievous monkey deities from Hindu mythology appear to support the lower levels of two smal *chedi* near Prasat Phra Thep Bidon.

Head east to the so-called Upper Terrace, an elevated area home to the **spires of the three primary chedi** ⑥. The middle structure, Phra Mondop, is used to house Buddhist manuscripts. This area is also home to several of Wat Phra Kaew's noteworthy mythical beings, including beckoning *kinaree* ⑦ and several grimacing **Hanuman** ⑧.

Proceed through the western gate to the compound known as the Grand Palace. Few of the buildings here are open to the public. The most noteworthy structure is **Chakri Mahaprasat** ⑨. Built in 1882, the exterior of the hall is a unique blend of Western and traditional Thai architecture.

The Three Spires
he elaborate seven-tiered
oof of Phra Mondop, the
hmer-style peak of Prasat
hra Thep Bidon, and the
ilded Phra Si Ratana *chedi* are
he tallest structures in the
ompound.

Emerald Buddha
Despite the name, this diminutive statue (it's only 66cm tall) is actually carved from nephrite, a type of jade.

Amarindra Hall

The Death of Thotsakan
The panels progress clockwise, culminating at the western edge of the compound with the death of Thotsakan, Sita's kidnapper, and his elaborate funeral procession.

Chakri Mahaprasat
This structure is sometimes referred to as *fa·ràng sài chá·dah* (Westerner in a Thai crown) because each wing is topped by a *mon·dòp*: a spire representing a Thai adaptation of a Hindu shrine.

Dusit Hall

Bòht (Ordination Hall)
This structure is an early example of the Ratanakosin school of architecture, which combines traditional stylistic holdovers from Ayuthaya along with more modern touches from China and the West.

Yaksha
Each entrance to the Wat Phra Kaew compound is watched over by a pair of vigilant and enormous *yaksha*, ogres or giants from Hindu mythology.

THE TRAVELS OF THE EMERALD BUDDHA

Some time in the 15th century, the Emerald Buddha is said to have been covered with plaster and gold leaf and placed in Chiang Rai's own Wat Phra Kaew. Many valuable Buddha images were masked in this way to deter potential thieves and marauders during unstable times. Often the true identity of the image was forgotten over the years until a 'divine accident' exposed its precious core. The Emerald Buddha experienced such a divine revelation while it was being transported to a new location. In a fall, the plaster covering broke off, revealing the brilliant green inside. But while this was seen as a divine revelation, the return of the Phra Kaew would prove anything but peaceful for the people of Siam and Laos.

During territorial clashes with Laos, the Emerald Buddha was seized and taken to Vientiane in the mid-16th century. Some 200 years later, after the fall of Ayuthaya and the ascension of the Bangkok-based kingdom, the Thai army marched up to Vientiane, razed the city and hauled off the Emerald Buddha. The Buddha was enshrined in the then capital, Thonburi, before the general who led the sacking of Vientiane assumed the throne and had it moved to its current location.

At the eastern end, **Borombhiman Hall** is a French-inspired structure that served as a residence for Rama VI (King Vajiravudh; r 1910–25). Today it can only be viewed through its iron gates, but in April 1981 General San Chitpatima used it as the headquarters for an attempted coup. **Amarindra Hall**, to the west, was originally a hall of justice but is used (very rarely indeed) for coronation ceremonies; the golden, boat-shaped throne looks considerably more ornate than comfortable.

The largest of the palace buildings is the triple-winged **Chakri Mahaprasat** (Grand Palace Hall). Completed in 1882 following a plan by British architects, the exterior shows a peculiar blend of Italian Renaissance and Thai architecture. It is believed the original plan called for the palace to be topped with a dome, but Rama V (King Chulalongkorn; r 1868–1910) was persuaded to go for a Thai-style roof instead. The tallest of the *mon·dòp* (the layered, heavily ornamented spire), in the centre, contains the ashes of Chakri kings; the flanking *mon·dòp* enshrine the ashes of the many Chakri princes who failed to inherit the throne.

The last building to the west is the Ratanakosin-style **Dusit Hall**, which initially served as a venue for royal audiences and, later, as a royal funerary hall.

Until Rama VI decided one wife was enough for any man, even a king, Thai kings housed their huge harems in the inner palace area (not open to the public), which was guarded by combat-trained female sentries. The intrigue and rituals that occurred within the walls of this cloistered community live on in the fictionalised epic *Four Reigns,* by Kukrit Pramoj, which follows a young girl named Phloi growing up within the Royal City.

TOP SIGHT
WAT PHO

Of all Bangkok's temples, Wat Pho is arguably the one most worth visiting, for both its remarkable Reclining Buddha image and its sprawling, stupa-studded grounds. The temple boasts a long list of credits: the oldest and largest wát in Bangkok; the longest Reclining Buddha and the largest collection of Buddha images in Thailand; and the country's first public education institution. For all that, it sees (slightly) fewer visitors than neighbouring Wat Phra Kaew and feels less commercial.

Narrow Th Chetuphon divides the grounds in two, and it's well worth entering Wat Pho from either this quiet lane or Th Sanam Chai to avoid the touts and tour groups of the main entrance on Th Thai Wang. You'll come into the northern compound (the southern part is closed to the public), where Phra Ubosot, the main ordination hall or *bòht,* is constructed in Ayuthaya style and is strikingly more subdued than Wat Phra Kaew. A temple has stood on this site since the 16th century, but in 1781 Rama I (King Phraphutthayotfa; r 1782–1809) ordered the original Wat Photharam to be completely rebuilt as part of his new capital. Rama I's remains are interred in the base of the presiding Buddha figure in Phra Ubosot.

The images on display in the four *wíhǎhn* (sanctuaries) surrounding Phra Ubosot are worth investigation. Particularly beautiful are the Phra Chinnarat and Phra Chinnasri Buddhas in the western and southern chapels, both rescued from Sukhothai by relatives of Rama I.

Encircling Phra Ubosot is a low marble wall with 152 bas-reliefs depicting scenes from the Ramakian. You'll recognise some of these figures when you exit the temple past the hawkers with mass-produced rubbings for sale: these are made from cement casts based on Wat Pho's reliefs.

DON'T MISS...

➡ Reclining Buddha
➡ Granite statues
➡ Massage pavilions

PRACTICALITIES

➡ วัดโพธิ์ (วัดพระเชตุพน), Wat Phra Chetuphon
➡ Map p252
➡ Th Sanam Chai
➡ admission 100B
➡ ⏱8.30am-6.30pm
➡ 🚢Tha Tien

Wat Pho

A WALK THROUGH THE BIG BUDDHAS OF WAT PHO

The logical starting place is the main *wi·hǎhn* (sanctuary), home to Wat Pho's centrepiece, the immense **Reclining Buddha ❶**. Apart from its huge size, note the **mother-of-pearl inlays ❷** on the soles of the statue's feet. The interior walls of the *wi·hǎhn* are covered with murals depicting previous lives of the

Buddha, and along the south side of the structure are 108 bronze monk bowls; for 20B you can buy 108 coins, each of which i dropped in a bowl for good luck.

Exit the *wi·hǎhn* and head east via the t**stone giants ❸** who guard the gateway to the rest of the compound. Directly south o these are the four towering **royal *chedi* ❹**

Continue east, passing through two consecutive **galleries of Buddha**

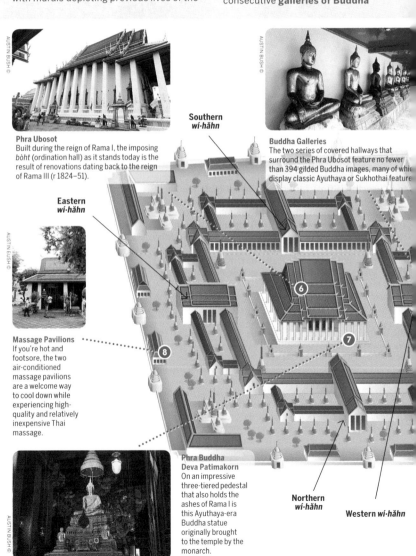

Southern *wi·hǎhn*

Phra Ubosot
Built during the reign of Rama I, the imposing *bòht* (ordination hall) as it stands today is the result of renovations dating back to the reign of Rama III (r 1824–51).

Buddha Galleries
The two series of covered hallways that surround the Phra Ubosot feature no fewer than 394 gilded Buddha images, many of whic display classic Ayuthaya or Sukhothai feature

Eastern *wi·hǎhn*

Massage Pavilions
If you're hot and footsore, the two air-conditioned massage pavilions are a welcome way to cool down while experiencing high-quality and relatively inexpensive Thai massage.

Phra Buddha Deva Patimakorn
On an impressive three-tiered pedestal that also holds the ashes of Rama I is this Ayuthaya-era Buddha statue originally brought to the temple by the monarch.

Northern *wi·hǎhn*

Western *wi·hǎhn*

statues [5] linking four *wí·hăhn*, two of which contain notable Sukhothai-era Buddha statues; these comprise the exterior of **Phra Ubosot** [6], the immense ordination hall that is Wat Pho's second-most noteworthy structure. The base of the building is surrounded by bas-relief inscriptions, and inside is the notable Buddha statue, **Phra Buddha Deva Patimakorn** [7].

Wat Pho is often referred to as Thailand's first university, a tradition that continues today in an associated traditional Thai medicine school and, at the compound's eastern extent, two **massage pavilions** [8].

Interspersed throughout the eastern half of the compound are several additional minor *chedi* and rock gardens.

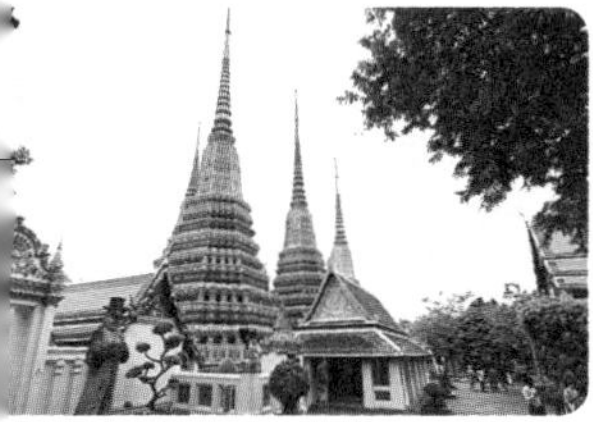

AUSTIN BUSH ©

Royal Chedi
Decorated in coloured tiles in a classic example of Ratanakosin style, these four *chedi* are meant to represent the first four kings of the Chakri dynasty.

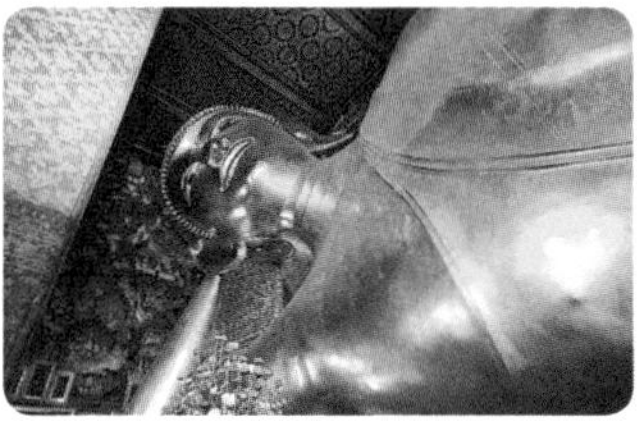

AUSTIN BUSH ©

Reclining Buddha
Modelled around a brick core 46m long and 15m high and finished in plaster and gold leaf, Wat Pho's Reclining Buddha is an imposing reminder of the Buddha's passing into nirvana (the Buddha's death).

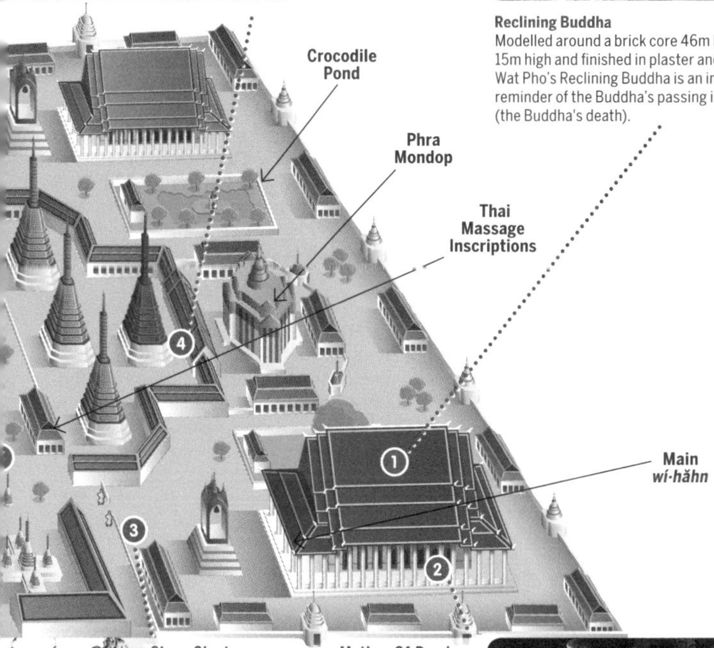

Crocodile Pond
Phra Mondop
Thai Massage Inscriptions
Main *wí·hăhn*
1
2
3
4

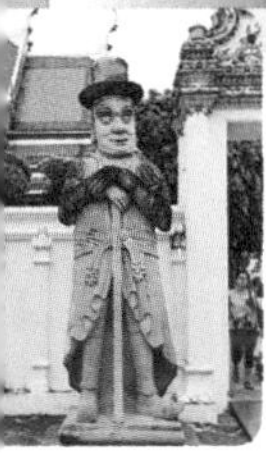

AUSTIN BUSH ©

Stone Giants
These huge granite figures – depictions range from Chinese opera characters to Marco Polo – originally arrived in Thailand in the 19th century as ballast aboard Chinese junks.

Mother-Of-Pearl Inlay
The 108 auspicious *lák·sà·nà*, physical characteristics of the Buddha, are depicted on the soles of the feet of the Reclining Buddha.

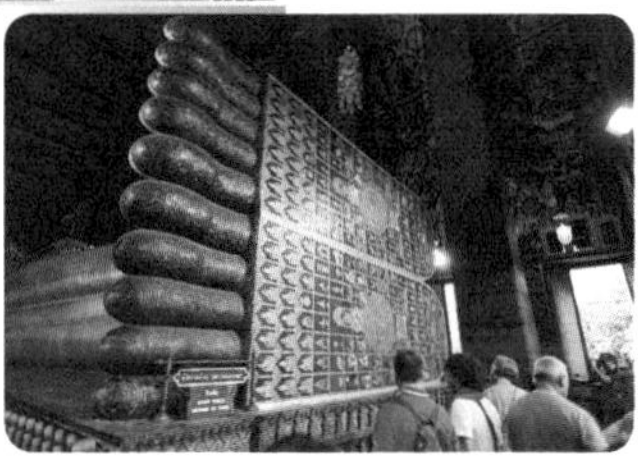

AUSTIN BUSH ©

WAT PHO'S GRANITE STATUES

Aside from monks and sightseers, Wat Pho is filled with an altogether stiffer crowd: dozens of giants and figurines carved from granite. The rock giants first arrived in Thailand as ballast aboard Chinese junks and were put to work in Wat Pho (and other wát, including Wat Suthat), guarding the entrances of temple gates and courtyards. Look closely and you'll see an array of Chinese characters. The giants with bulging eyes and Chinese opera costumes were inspired by warrior noblemen and are called Lan Than. The figure in a straw hat is a farmer, forever interrupted during his day's work cultivating the fields. And can you recognise the guy in the fedora-like hat with a trimmed beard and moustache? Marco Polo, of course, who introduced such European styles to the Chinese court.

What other holy site in the world includes massage? The air-conditioned massage pavilions near Wat Pho's east gate provide a unique opportunity to combine relaxation with sightseeing.

On the western side of the grounds a collection of four towering tiled *chedi* (stupa) commemorates the first four Chakri kings. The surrounding wall was built on the orders of Rama IV (King Mongkut; r 1851–68), who for reasons we can only speculate about decided he didn't want any future kings joining the memorial. Note the square bell shape with distinct corners, a signature of Ratanakosin style. Among the compound's additional 91 smaller *chedi* are clusters containing the ashes of lesser royal descendants.

Small Chinese-style rock gardens and hill islands interrupt the tiled courtyards providing shade, greenery and quirky decorations depicting daily life. Keep an eye out for the distinctive rockery festooned with figures of the hermit Khao Mor – who is credited with inventing yoga – in various healing positions. According to the tradition, a few good arm stretches should cure idleness.

Massage Pavilions

A small pavilion west of Phra Ubosot has Unesco-awarded inscriptions detailing the tenets of traditional Thai massage. These and other similar inscriptions led Wat Pho to be regarded as Thailand's first university. Today it maintains that tradition as the national headquarters for the teaching and preservation of traditional Thai medicine, including Thai massage. The famous traditional Thai medicine school has two **massage pavilions** (Map p252; Thai massage per hr 420B; ☺8.30am-6.30pm) located within the temple area and additional rooms within the training facility (p75) outside the temple.

Reclining Buddha, Stupas & Gardens

In the northwest corner of the site you'll find Wat Pho's main attraction, the enormous Reclining Buddha. The figure was originally commissioned by Rama III (King Phranangklao; r 1824–51), and illustrates the passing of the Buddha into nirvana. It is made of plaster around a brick core and finished in gold leaf, which gives it a serene luminescence that keeps you looking, and looking again, from different angles.

TOP SIGHT
WAT ARUN

The missile-shaped temple that rises from the banks of Mae Nam Chao Phraya is known as Temple of Dawn, and was named after the Indian god of dawn, Aruna. It was here that, in the wake of the destruction of Ayuthaya, King Taksin stumbled upon a small local shrine and interpreted the discovery as such an auspicious sign that this should be the site of the new capital of Siam.

King Taksin built a palace beside the shrine, which is now part of Navy Headquarters, as well as a royal temple that housed the Emerald Buddha for 15 years until Taksin was assassinated and the capital moved across the royal river to Bangkok.

The Spire

Today, the central feature of Wat Arun is the 82m-high Khmer-style *brahng* (spire), constructed during the first half of the 19th century by Rama II (King Phraphutthaloetla Naphalai; r 1809–24). From the river it is not apparent that this corn-cob-shaped steeple is adorned with colourful floral murals made of glazed porcelain, a common temple ornamentation in the early Ratanakosin period, when Chinese ships calling at Bangkok used porcelain as ballast.

At time of research, it had been announced that the *brahng* would be closed for as many as three years due to renovation. Visitors can enter the compound, but cannot, as in previous years, climb the tower.

Buddhist Murals

Also worth a look is the interior of the *bòht*. The main Buddha image is said to have been designed by Rama II himself, whose ashes are interred beneath. The murals date to the reign of Rama V. Particularly impressive is one depicting Prince Siddhartha (the Buddha) encountering examples of birth, old age, sickness and death outside his palace walls, an experience that led him to abandon the worldly life.

Exploring the Neighbourhood

Wat Arun is directly across from Wat Pho, on the Thonburi side of the river. A lot of people visit the wát on long-tail boat tours, but it's easier and more rewarding to just jump on the 3B cross-river ferry from Tha Tien. For our money, visiting Wat Arun in the late afternoon is best, with the sun shining from the west lighting up the *brahng* and the river behind it. If you come earlier, consider taking a stroll away from the river on Th Wang Doem, a quiet tiled street of wooden shophouses.

Sunset Cocktails

Sunset views of the temple compound can be caught from across the river at the riverfront warehouses that line Th Maha Rat – although be forewarned that locals may ask for a 20B 'fee'. Other great viewpoints include Roof (p75) or Amorosa (p75), rooftop bars located directly across from the temple.

DON'T MISS...

➡ A close-up look of the tile-coated Khmer-style *brahng* (spire)

➡ Buddhist murals inside the main *bòht*

➡ Exploring the surrounding neighbourhood

➡ A sunset cocktail and photo op at Roof or Amorosa

PRACTICALITIES

➡ วัดอรุณฯ

➡ Map p252

➡ www.watarun.net

➡ off Th Arun Amarin

➡ admission 50B

➡ ⊙8am-6pm

➡ 🚢cross-river ferry from Tha Tien

⊙ SIGHTS

WAT PHRA KAEW & GRAND PALACE
BUDDHIST TEMPLE, HISTORICAL SITE
See p58.

WAT PHO   BUDDHIST TEMPLE
See p63.

WAT ARUN   BUDDHIST TEMPLE
See p67.

AMULET MARKET   MARKET
Map p252 (ตลาดพระเครื่องวัดมหาธาตุ; Th Maha
Rat; ⊙7am-5pm; 🚢Tha Chang) This arcane
and fascinating market claims both the
footpaths along Th Maha Rat and Th Phra
Chan, as well as a dense network of covered
market stalls near Tha Phra Chan. The
trade is based around small talismans carefully prized by collectors, monks, taxi drivers and people in dangerous professions.

Potential buyers, often already sporting
many amulets, can be seen bargaining and
flipping through magazines dedicated to
the amulets, some of which command astronomical prices. While money changes
hands between vendor and customer,
both use the euphemism of 'renting' to get
around the prohibition of selling Buddhas.

This is a great place to just wander and
watch men (because it's rarely women)
looking through magnifying glasses at the
tiny amulets, seeking hidden meaning and,
if they're lucky, hidden value. The market
stretches all the way to the riverside, where
a narrow alley leads north to wooden kitchens overhanging the water. Each humble
kitchen garners a view of the river; students
from nearby Thammasat University con-
gregate here for cheap eats before heading
off to class. It's an ideal stop for a lunch of
classic Thai comforts and Western adapta-
tions popular with students.

Also along this strip are handsome shophouses overflowing with family-run herbal
medicine and traditional massage shops.

MUSEUM OF SIAM   MUSEUM
Map p252 (สถาบันพิพิธภัณฑ์การเรียนรู้แห่งชาติ;
www.museumsiam.com; Th Maha Rat; admission
300B; ⊙10am-6pm Tue-Sun; 🚢Tha Tien) This
fun museum employs a variety of media to
explore the origins of the Thai people and
their culture. Housed in a European-style
19th-century building that was once the
Ministry of Commerce, the exhibits are presented in an engaging, interactive fashion
not often found in Thailand. They are also
refreshingly balanced and entertaining,
with galleries dealing with a range of questions about the origins of the nation and its
people.

Each room has an informative narrated
video started by a sensory detector, keeping
waiting to a minimum. An Ayuthaya-era

LOCAL KNOWLEDGE

ROLLIN' ON THE... CANAL

For an up-close view of Thonburi's famed canals, long-tail boats are available for
charter at Ko Ratanakosin piers Tha Chang and Tha Tien. Prices at these piers are
slightly higher than elsewhere and allow little room for negotiation, but you stand the
least chance of being taken for a ride or being hit up for tips and other unexpected
fees.

Trips explore the canals **Khlong Bangkok Noi** and **Khlong Mon**, taking in the
Royal Barges National Museum, Wat Arun and a riverside temple with fish feeding.
Longer trips diverge into **Khlong Bangkok Yai**, further south, which offers more
typical canal scenery, including orchid farms. On weekends, you have the option of
visiting the Taling Chan Floating Market (p174). However, it's worth pointing out that
to actually disembark and explore any of these sights, the most common tour of one
hour (1000B, up to eight people) is simply not enough time – you'll most likely need
1½ (1300B) or two hours (1500B). Most operators have set tour routes, but if you
have a specific destination in mind, you can request it.

If you'd prefer something longer or more personal, **Pandan Tour** (📞0 2689 1232,
08 7109 8873; www.thaicanaltour.com; tours from 1995B) conducts a variety of mostly
full-day tours.

A cheaper alternative is to take the **commuter long-tail boat** (Map p252; 25B;
⊙4.30am-7.30pm) from Tha Chang to Bang Yai, at the distant northern end of Khlong
Bangkok Noi.

LOCAL KNOWLEDGE

BANGKOK STREET SMARTS

Keep the following in mind to survive the traffic and avoid joining the list of tourists sucked in by Bangkok's numerous scam artists:

➡ Good jewellery, gems and tailor shops aren't found through a túk-túk driver.

➡ Skip the 10B túk-túk ride unless you have the time and willpower to resist a heavy sales pitch in a tailor or gem store.

➡ Ignore 'helpful' locals who tell you that tourist attractions and public transport are closed for a holiday or cleaning; it's the beginning of a con, most likely a gem scam.

➡ Don't expect any pedestrian rights; put a Bangkokian between you and any oncoming traffic, and yield to anything with more metal than you.

➡ Walk away from the tourist strip to hail a taxi that will use the meter – tell the driver 'meter'. If the driver refuses to put the meter on, get out.

battle game, a room full of traditional Thai toys and a street vending cart where you can be photographed pretending to whip up a pan of *pàt tai* (fried noodles) will help keep kids interested for at least an hour, adults for longer. Check out the attached shop for some innovative gift ideas.

NATIONAL MUSEUM MUSEUM

Map p252 (พิพิธภัณฑสถานแห่งชาติ; 4 Th Na Phra That; admission 200B; ⊙9am-4pm Wed-Sun; ⚑Tha Chang) Thailand's National Museum is the largest museum in Southeast Asia and covers a broad range of subjects, from historical surveys to religious sculpture displays. The buildings were originally constructed in 1782 as the palace of Rama I's viceroy, Prince Wang Na. Rama V turned it into a museum in 1884.

The **history wing** presents a succinct chronology of events and figures from the prehistoric, Sukhothai, Ayuthaya and Bangkok eras. Despite the corny dioramas, there are some real treasures here: look for King Ramkhamhaeng's inscribed stone pillar (allegedly the oldest record of Thai writing, although this has been contested), King Taksin's throne and the Rama V section.

The other parts of the museum aren't as well presented, but this might be part of the charm. Dimly lit rooms, ranging in temperature from lukewarm to boiling, offer an attic-like collection of Thai art and handicrafts.

In the **decorative arts and ethnology exhibit**, there are collections of traditional musical instruments from Thailand, Laos, Cambodia and Indonesia, as well as ceramics, clothing and textiles, woodcarving, royal regalia, and Chinese art and weaponry.

The **archaeology and art history wing** covers every Southeast Asian art period and style, from Dvaravati to Ratanakosin.

The museum grounds also contain the restored **Bhuddhaisawan Chapel**. The chapel, built in 1795, is home to some well-preserved original murals and one of the country's most revered Buddha images, Phra Phuttha Sihing. Legend claims the image came from Sri Lanka (legend claims a lot of Buddha images came from Sri Lanka), but art historians attribute it to the 13th-century Sukhothai period.

The museum also runs guided **tours** (free with museum admission; ⊙9.30am Wed & Thu).

SONGKRAN NIYOMSANE FORENSIC MEDICINE MUSEUM & PARASITE MUSEUM MUSEUM

Map p252 (พิพิธภัณฑ์นิติเวชศาสตร์สงกรานต์นิยม เสน; 2nd fl, Adulyadejvikrom Bldg, Siriraj Hospital; admission 40B; ⊙9am-4pm Mon-Sat; ⚑Tha Wang Lang, Siriraj) Pickled body parts, ingenious murder weapons and other crime-scene evidence are on display at this medical museum, the intent of which is ostensibly to educate rather than nauseate. Next door, the **Parasite Museum** continues the queasy theme.

The best way to get here is by express ferry or cross-river ferry to Tha Wang Lang (Siriraj) in Thonburi; turn right (north) into the hospital and follow the green 'Museum' signs.

Among the grisly displays is a bloodied T-shirt from a victim stabbed to death with a dildo, and the preserved but rather withered cadaver of Si Ouey, one of Thailand's most prolific and notorious serial killers who murdered – and then ate – more than

30 children in the 1950s. Despite being well and truly dead (he was executed), today his name is still used to scare misbehaving children into submission: 'Behave yourself or Si Ouey will come for you'.

NATIONAL GALLERY ART GALLERY

Map p252 (พิพิธภัณฑ์สถานแห่งชาติหอศิลป์ (หอ ศิลป์เจ้าฟ้า); ngbangkok.wordpress.com; 4 Th Chao Fa; admission 200B; ☺9am-4pm Wed-Sun; 🚢Tha Phra Athit, Banglamphu) Housed in a weathered colonial building that was the Royal Mint during the reign of Rama V, the National Gallery's permanent exhibition is admittedly a rather dusty and dated affair. More interesting are the rotating exhibits held in the spacious rear galleries; take a look at the posters out front to see what's on.

Secular art is a relatively new concept in Thailand and most of the country's best examples of fine art reside in the temples for which they were created (much as historic Western art is often found in European cathedrals). As such, most of the permanent collection here documents Thailand's homage to modern styles.

ROYAL BARGES
NATIONAL MUSEUM MUSEUM

Map p252 (พิพิธภัณฑสถานแห่งชาติ เรือพระราช พิธี (เรือพระที่นั่ง); Khlong Bangkok Noi or 80/1 Th Arun Amarin; admission 100B, camera/video 100/200B; ☺9am-5pm; 🚢Tha Saphan Phra Pin Klao) Every foreign country has its famous religious monuments and museums, but how many have their own fleet of royal boats on display? The royal barges were once used daily by the royal family to get about their realm, but are now used only for grand ceremonies.

The most convenient way to get to the museum is by taking a motorcycle taxi (ask the driver to go to *reu·a prá têe nâng*) from Tha Saphan Phra Pin Klao. The museum is also an optional stop on long-tail boat trips through Thonburi's canals.

These are not those wide, lumbering barges you'll see hauling sand and produce up and down Mae Nam Chao Phraya. These barges are slender like their mainstream cousins, the long-tail boats, and fantastically ornamented with religious symbolism. The largest is more than 45m long and requires a rowing crew of 50 men, plus seven umbrella bearers, two helmsmen and two navigators, as well as a flag bearer, rhythm keeper and chanter.

Suphannahong (Golden Swan) is the king's personal barge. Built on the orders of Rama I after an earlier version had been destroyed in the sacking of Ayuthaya, *Suphannahong* is made from a single piece of timber, making it the largest dugout in the world. Appropriately, a huge swan's head is carved into the prow. More recent barges feature bows carved into other Hindu-Buddhist mythological shapes, such as the seven-headed *naga* (sea dragon) and *garuda* (Vishnu's bird mount).

To mark auspicious Buddhist calendar years, the royal barges in all their finery set sail during the royal *gà·tǐn*, the cloth-giving ceremony that falls in the month following the end of the Buddhist retreat in October or November. During this ceremony, a barge procession travels to the temples to offer new robes to the monastic contingent, and countless Bangkokians descend on the river to watch.

LAK MEUANG MONUMENT

Map p252 (ศาลหลักเมือง; cnr Th Sanam Chai & Th Lak Meuang; ☺6.30am-6.30pm; 🚢Tha Chang) What would otherwise be an uninteresting mileage marker has both religious and historical significance in Thailand. Lak Meuang is the city shrine, a wooden pillar erected by Rama I in 1782 to represent the founding of the new Bangkok capital. Distances are measured to all other city shrines in the country from this point. But its importance doesn't stop there. The pillar is endowed with a spirit, Phra Sayam Thewathirat (Venerable Siam Deity of the State), and is considered the city's guardian.

Like the sacred banyan trees and the holy temples, Lak Meuang receives daily invocations from Thai worshippers in the form of commissioned *lákon gâa bon* (shrine dancing) as thanks for granted wishes. Offerings also include those cute yet macabre pigs' head with sticks of incense sprouting from their foreheads.

SANAM LUANG PARK

Map p252 (สนามหลวง; bounded by Th Na Phra That, Th Ratchadamnoen Nai & Th Na Phra Lan; 🚢Tha Chang) On a hot day, Sanam Luang (Royal Field) is far from charming – a shadeless expanse of dying grass and concrete pavement ringed by flocks of pigeons and homeless people. Despite its shabby appearance, it has been at the centre of both royal ceremony and political upheaval since Bangkok was founded.

Neighbourhood Walk
Ko Ratanakosin Stroll

START THA CHANG
END WAT ARUN
LENGTH APPROXIMATELY 4KM; THREE TO FIVE HOURS

The bulk of Bangkok's 'must-see' destinations are in the former royal district, Ko Ratanakosin. Start early to beat the heat and get in before the hordes descend. Remember to dress modestly to gain entry to the temples and ignore any strangers who approach you with advice on sightseeing or shopping.

Start at Tha Chang and follow Th Na Phra Lan east, with a quick diversion to **1 Silpakorn University**, Thailand's premier fine-arts university. If you haven't already been, continue east to the main gate into **2 Wat Phra Kaew & Grand Palace**, two of Bangkok's most famous attractions.

Return to Th Maha Rat and proceed north, through an enclave of herbal apothecaries and sidewalk amulet sellers. Immediately after passing the cat-laden newsstand (you'll know it when you smell it), turn left into **3 Trok Tha Wang**, a narrow alleyway holding a seemingly hidden classic Bangkok neighbourhood. Returning to Th Maha Rat, continue moving north. On your right is **4 Wat Mahathat**, one of Thailand's most respected Buddhist universities.

Across the street, turn left into crowded Trok Mahathat to discover the cramped **5 Amulet Market**. As you continue north alongside the river, amulets soon turn to food vendors. The emergence of white-and-black uniforms is a clue that you are approaching **6 Thammasat University**, known for its law and political science departments.

Exiting at Tha Phra Chan, cross Th Maha Rat and continue east until you reach **7 Sanam Luang**, the 'Royal Field'. Cross the field and continue south along Th Ratchadamnoen Nai until you reach the home of Bangkok's city spirit, **8 Lak Meuang**. Pay your respects and head south along Th Sanam Chai and turn right onto Th Thai Wang, which will lead you to the entrance of **9 Wat Pho**, home of the giant reclining Buddha.

If you've still got the energy, head to adjacent Tha Tien to catch the cross-river ferry to **10 Wat Arun**.

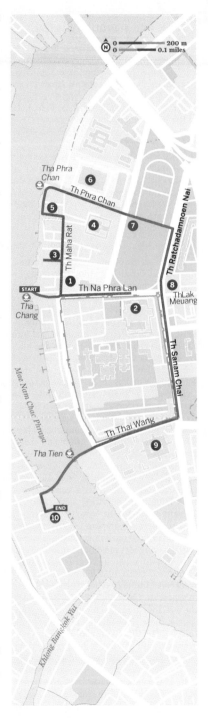

BANGKOK TONGUE-TWISTER

Upon completion of the royal district in 1785, at a three-day consecration ceremony attended by tens of thousands of Siamese, the capital of Siam was given a new name: 'Krungthep mahanakhon amonratanakosin mahintara ayuthaya mahadilok popnopparat ratchathani burirom udomratchaniwet mahasathan amonpiman avatansathit sakkathattiya witsanukamprasit'. This lexical gymnastic feat translates roughly as: 'Great City of Angels, the Repository of Divine Gems, the Great Land Unconquerable, the Grand and Prominent Realm, the Royal and Delightful Capital City full of Nine Noble Gems, the Highest Royal Dwelling and Grand Palace, the Divine Shelter and Living Place of Reincarnated Spirits'.

Understandably, foreign traders continued to call the capital Bang Makok, which eventually truncated itself to 'Bangkok', the name most commonly known to the outside world. These days all Thais understand 'Bangkok' but use a shortened version of the official name, Krung Thep (City of Angels). When referring to greater Bangkok, they talk about Krung Thep Mahanakhon (Metropolis of the City of Angels). Expats living in Bangkok have numerous nicknames for their adopted home, with the Big Mango being the most common.

Less dramatic events staged here include the annual Royal Ploughing Ceremony, in which the king (or more recently, the crown prince) officially initiates the rice-growing season, an appropriate location given that Sanam Luang was used to grow rice for almost 100 years after the royals moved into Ko Ratanakosin. After the rains, the kite-flying season (mid-February to April) sees the air above filled with butterfly-shaped Thai kites. Matches are held between teams flying either a 'male' or 'female' kite in a particular territory; points are won if they can force a competitor into their zone.

Large funeral pyres are constructed here during elaborate, but infrequent, royal cremations, and explain the field's alternate name, Thung Phra Men (Cremation Ground). The most recent cremation was a six-day, 300-million baht ceremony for King Bhumibol Adulyadej's sister, Princess Galyani Vadhana, in November, 2009; it took 11 months to prepare.

In a way the park is suffering a career crisis, having lost most of its full-time employment to other locales or the whims of fashion. Until 1982 Bangkok's famous Weekend Market was regularly held here (it's now at Chatuchak Park). Previously, the wealthy came here for imported leisure sports; these days they head to air-conditioned gyms. Today the cool mornings and evenings still attract a health-conscious crowd of joggers, walkers and groups playing *dà·grôr* (*sepak takraw;* kick volleyball). If you fancy a big-crowd experience, Sanam Luang draws the masses in December for the King's Birthday (5 December), Constitution Day (10 December) and New Year.

Across Th Ratchadamnoen Nai to the east is the statue of Mae Thorani, the earth goddess (borrowed from Hindu mythology's Dharani), which stands in a white pavilion. Erected in the late 19th century by Rama V, the statue was originally attached to a well that provided drinking water to the public.

SILPAKORN UNIVERSITY   UNIVERSITY

Map p252 (มหาวิทยาลัยศิลปากร; www.su.ac.th; 31 Th Na Phra Lan; ⊠Tha Chang) Thailand's universities aren't usually repositories for interesting architecture, but Silpakorn (pronounced *sĭn lá 'bà gorn*), the country's premier art school, breaks the mould. The classical buildings form the charming nucleus of what was an early Thai aristocratic enclave, and the traditional artistic temperament still survives.

The building immediately facing the Th Na Phra Lan gate was once part of a palace and now houses the Silpakorn University Art Centre. To the right of the building is a shady sculpture garden displaying the work of Corrado Feroci (also known as Silpa Bhirasri), the Italian art professor and sculptor who came to Thailand at royal request in the 1920s and later established the university (which is named after him), sculpted parts of the Democracy Monument and, much to his own annoyance, the Victory Monument.

SILPAKORN UNIVERSITY ART CENTRE
ART GALLERY

Map p252 (www.su.ac.th/html_organizations_eng/artcentre.asp; 31 Th Na Phra Lan; ⊙9am-7pm Mon-Fri, to 4pm Sat; ⛴Tha Chang) **FREE** This gallery, located inside Thailand's most prestigious arts school, showcases faculty and student exhibitions. There's also an accompanying courtyard cafe and art shop.

THAMMASAT UNIVERSITY
UNIVERSITY

Map p252 (มหาวิทยาลัยธรรมศาสตร์; www.tu.ac.th; 2 Th Phra Chan; ⛴Tha Phra Chan) Much of the drama that followed Thailand's transition from monarchy to democracy has unfolded on this quiet riverside campus. Thammasat University was established in 1934, two years after the bloodless coup that deposed the absolute monarchy. Its remit was to instruct students in law and political economy, considered to be the intellectual necessities for an educated democracy.

The university was founded by Dr Pridi Phanomyong, whose statue stands in Pridi Court at the centre of the campus. Pridi was the leader of the civilian People's Party that successfully advocated a constitutional monarchy during the 1920s and '30s. He went on to serve in various ministries, organised the Seri Thai movement (a Thai resistance campaign against the Japanese during WWII) and was ultimately forced into exile when the postwar government was seized by a military dictatorship in 1947.

Pridi was unable to counter the dismantling of democratic reforms, but the university he established continued his crusade. Thammasat was a hotbed of pro-democracy activism during the student uprising era of the 1970s. On 14 October 1973, an estimated 10,000 protesters convened on the parade grounds beside the university's Memorial Building demanding the government reinstate the constitution. From the university the protest grew and moved to the Democracy Monument, where the military and police opened fire on the crowd, killing 77 and wounding 857. The massacre prompted the king to revoke his support of the military rulers and for a brief period a civilian government was reinstated. On 6 October 1976, Thammasat itself was the scene of a bloody massacre, when at least 46 students were shot dead while rallying against the return from exile of former dictator Field Marshal Thanom Kittikachorn. Near the southern entrance to the university is the Bodhi Court, where a sign be-

neath the Bodhi tree explains more about the democracy movement that germinated at Thammasat.

Walk north from the Tha Phra Chan pier and you'll go straight through Thammasat, emerging near Th Phra Athit in Banglamphu.

SARANROM ROYAL GARDEN
PARK

Map p252 (สวนสราญรมย์; bounded by Th Ratchini, Th Charoen Krung & Th Sanam Chai; ⊙5am-9pm; ⛴Tha Tien) **FREE** Easily mistaken for a European public garden, this Victorian-era green space was originally designed as a royal residence in the time of Rama IV. After Rama VII (King Prajadhipok; r 1925–35) abdicated in 1935, the palace served as the headquarters of the People's Party, the political organisation that orchestrated the handover of the government. The open space remained and in 1960 was opened to the public.

Today a wander through the garden reveals a Victorian gazebo, paths lined with frangipani and a moat around a marble monument built in honour of one of Rama V's favourite wives, Queen Sunantha, who died in a boating accident in 1880. The queen was on her way to Bang Pa-In Summer Palace in Ayuthaya when her boat began to sink. The custom at the time was that commoners were forbidden to touch royalty, which prevented her attendants from saving her from drowning.

✖ EATING

In stark contrast to the rest of Bangkok, there aren't many restaurants in Ko Ratanakosin, and those that do exist serve only Thai cuisine. For something more international, consider heading to Banglamphu, a short taxi ride away.

PA AEW
THAI **$**

Map p252 (Th Maha Rat, no roman-script sign; mains 20-60B; ⊙10am-5pm; ⛴Tha Tien) Pull up a plastic stool at this deceptively bare-bones open-air curry stall for some rich, seafood-heavy Bangkok-style dishes, such as *pàt chàh lôok chín blah* (freshwater fish dumplings fried with fresh herbs) or a fragrant *gaang mát·sà·màn* (a dried, spice-heavy 'Muslim' curry). Pa Aew is located in front of the Krung Thai Bank near Soi Pratu Nokyung.

MING LEE　　　　　　　　　　THAI **$**

Map p252 (28-30 Th Na Phra Lan, no roman-script sign; mains 70-100B; ⊘11.30am-6pm; ⚓Tha Chang) Seemingly hidden in plain sight across from Wat Phra Kaew is this decades-old shophouse restaurant. The menu spans Western/Chinese dishes (such as stewed tongue) to Thai standards (such as the impossibly tart and garlicky 'beef spicy salad'). Often closed before 6pm, Ming Lee is best approached as a lunchtime option post-sightseeing.

COCONUT PALM　　　　　　THAI **$**

Map p252 (www.coconutpalmrestaurant.com; 392/1-2 Th Maha Rat; mains 40-100B; ⊘11am-6pm; ❄; ⚓Tha Tien) Coconut Palm serves a generous spread of Thai dishes, but most locals come for the Sukhothai-style noodles – thin rice noodles served with pork, ground peanuts and dried chili. Even if you're not hungry, you might want to stop by for the reinvigorating blast of air-con and the refreshing drinks.

RUB AROON CAFE　　　　　　THAI **$**

Map p252 (Th Maha Rat; mains 75-120B; ⊘8am-6pm; ⚓Tha Tien) This traveller-friendly cafe is a pleasant escape from sightseeing in Ko Ratanakosin. The restored shopfront opens directly out to the street with cosy seating and patient service. The dishes are basic and satisfying, served alongside fruit drinks and coffees good for sipping away tropical fatigue.

MANGKUD CAFE　　　　　　THAI **$$**

Map p252 (Club Arts; www.clubartsgallery.com; Soi Wat Rakhang; mains 100-350B; ⊘11am-10pm

Tue-Thu, to 11pm Fri-Sun; ✍; ⚓cross-river ferry from Tha Chang) Combining a warehouse-like art gallery, a minimalist restaurant and an enviable riverfront location, Mangkud is one of the more sophisticated places to eat on this side of Mae Nam Chao Phraya (Chao Phraya River). The river views and breezes are unparalleled, and the upscale-ish, herb-heavy Thai dishes are clever and tasty: try the 'watermelon with dried fish', a traditional sweet-savoury snack. Look for the sign that says 'Club Arts'.

KHUNKUNG　　　　　　　　THAI **$$**

Map p252 (Navy Club; 77 Th Maha Rat; mains 75-720B; ⊘11am-2pm & 6-10pm Mon-Fri, 11am-10pm Sat & Sun; ❄; ⚓Tha Chang) The restaurant of the Royal Navy Association has one of the few coveted riverfront locations along this stretch of Mae Nam Chao Phraya. Locals come for the combination of riverfront views and cheap and tasty seafood-based eats – possibly not for the cafeteria-like atmosphere. The entrance to the restaurant is near the ATM machines at Tha Chang.

SALA RATTANAKOSIN　　　THAI **$$$**

Map p252 (☎0 2622 1388; www.salaresorts.com/rattanakosin; Sala Rattanakosin, 39 Th Maha Rat; mains 240-1100B; ❄; ⚓Tha Tien) Located on an open-air deck next to the river with Wat Arun virtually towering overhead, the Sala Rattanakosin hotel's signature restaurant has nailed the location. The food – largely central and northern Thai dishes with occasional Western twists – doesn't necessarily live up to the scenery, but for upscale dining in this corner of town it's really the only option.

LOCAL KNOWLEDGE

MEDITATIONS ON MEDITATION

Prasuputh Chainikom (Kosalo) is a meditation master at Wat Mahathat.

Why did you become a monk? [So] I can develop my own life and help other people.

Why teach foreigners? I have English skills and experience with meditation – most Thai monks don't have these skills.

Why are so many foreigners interested in meditation? We're all stressed. Meditation teaches us how to relax our minds. If we know how to relax, we can find peace.

Can one study meditation if one is not Buddhist or has no experience? Yes. When we practise meditation, we're not thinking of the Buddha, we're just trying to make our minds empty.

What benefits does meditation provide? 1: It purifies your mind. 2: It gets rid of sorrow and lamentation. 3: It gets rid of physical and mental suffering. 4: It helps us understand the truth of life. 5: You can extinguish suffering and attain Nirvana. Five is difficult, but if you try, you can attain one to four.

🍷 DRINKING & NIGHTLIFE

As with restaurants, bars are a rare sight in Ko Ratanakosin. Luckily, the bars of Banglamphu are only a short taxi ride away.

ROOF BAR
Map p252 (www.salaresorts.com/rattanakosin; Sala Rattanakosin, 39 Th Maha Rat; ⊙5pm-midnight; ⛴Tha Tien) The open-air bar on top of the new Sala Rattanakosin hotel has upped the stakes for sunset views of Wat Arun – if you can see the temple at all through the wall of selfie-snapping tourists.

AMOROSA BAR
Map p252 (www.arunresidence.com; rooftop, Arun Residence, 36-38 Soi Pratu Nokyung; ⊙5pm-midnight Mon-Thu, to 1am Fri-Sun; ⛴Tha Tien) The original venue for a riverside sundowner in Ko Ratanakosin, though the views of Wat Arun are a lot more impressive than the quality of the drinks.

☆ ENTERTAINMENT

NATIONAL THEATRE THEATRE
Map p252 (☎0 2224 1342; 2 Th Ratchini; tickets 60-100B; ⛴Tha Chang) Holds performances of *kŏhn* (masked dance-drama based on stories from the *Ramakian*) at 2pm on the first and second Sundays of the month from January to March and July to September, and *lá·kon,* Thai dance-dramas, at 2pm on the first and second Sundays of the month from April to June and October to December.

🏃 SPORTS & ACTIVITIES

WAT MAHATHAT MEDITATION
Map p252 (3 Th Maha Rat; ⛴Tha Chang) This temple is home to two independently operating meditation centres. The **Interna-**

tional Buddhist Meditation Center (Map p252; ☎0 2222 6011; Section 5, Wat Mahathat, Th Maha Rat; donations accepted; ⊙lessons 7am, 1pm & 6pm; ⛴Tha Chang) offers three hour-long daily meditation classes at 7am, 1pm and 6pm. The **Meditation Study and Retreat Center** (Map p252; ☎0 2623 6326; www.mcu.ac.th/IBMC/; Wat Mahathat, Th Maha Rat; donations accepted; ⛴Tha Chang) offers a regimented daily program of meditation. With both of these programs, longer stays, including accommodation and food, can be arranged, but students are expected to follow a strict regimen of conduct.

WAT PHO THAI TRADITIONAL MEDICAL AND MASSAGE SCHOOL THAI MASSAGE
Map p252 (☎0 2622 3551; www.watpomassage .com; 392/25-28 Soi Phen Phat; lessons from 2500B; ⊙lessons 9am-4pm; ⛴Tha Tien) Associated with the nearby temple of the same name, this pint-sized institute offers basic and advanced courses in traditional massage; basic courses offer 30 hours spread out over five days and cover either general massage or foot massage.

The school is outside the temple compound in a restored Bangkok shophouse at the end of unmarked Soi Phen Phat; look for Coconut Palm restaurant.

The advanced level spans 60 hours, requires the basic course as a prerequisite, and covers therapeutic and healing massage. Other advanced courses include oil massage and aromatherapy, and infant and child massage.

SEGWAY TOUR THAILAND SEGWAY TOUR
Map p252 (☎0 2221 4525; www.segwaytourthai land.com; Maharaj Pier Bldg, Tha Maharaj, off Th Maha Rat; half-day tour 3500B; ⊙8.30am-6.30pm Tue-Sun; ⛴Tha Maharaj) Bicycles are so 20th century – explore Bangkok from the, er, platform of an electronic Segway. This outfit runs half-day and full-day Segway tours in and around Bangkok, including excursions among the ruins in Ayuthaya.

Banglamphu

Neighbourhood Top Five

1 Visiting **Th Khao San**: more than just freaks in dreadlocks and fisherman pants, it is a unique cultural melting pot with something for (almost) everyone (p82).

2 Taking in the panoramic views of old Bangkok from **Golden Mount** (p80).

3 Tasting classic Bangkok-style nosh at old-school restaurants such as **Krua Apsorn** (p83).

4 Dancing on the tables with Thai hipsters at **Brick Bar** (p86).

5 Sitting and gazing at the huge Buddha and sky-high murals in **Wat Suthat** (p79).

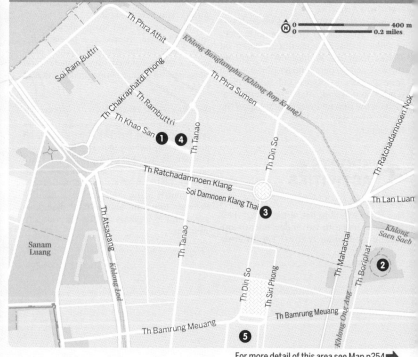

For more detail of this area see Map p254

Explore: Banglamphu

Antique shophouses, classic restaurants, ancient temples... Banglamphu is old Bangkok encapsulated in one leafy, breezy district. If you've come for the sights, arrive early, while the heat is still tolerable and the touts few. It's worth sticking around Banglamphu for lunch, as this is when the majority of the area's street stalls and shophouse restaurants are operating. Come evening, young locals flood the area in search of a cheap meal and a cold Chang, giving the area an entirely different vibe, but there are enough restaurants and bars here that there's no need to consider another destination for the night.

Despite being one of the city's best areas for accommodation, sights, eating and nightlife, Banglamphu is also among Bangkok's most impenetrable 'hoods. During the day, a good strategy is to approach the area from the river ferry pier at Tha Phra Athit (Banglamphu) – most of the sights are within walking distance. At night, most of the action is centered around Th Khao San, which can be accessed via taxi from the BTS stop at National Stadium or the MRT stop at Hua Lamphong.

Local Life

➡ **Local Cuisine** Bangkok's most traditional district is not surprisingly one of the best places to try authentic central Thai- and Bangkok-style food.

➡ **Street-side Shopping** The spectrum of goods available in this district ranges from backpacker staples along Th Khao San to delicious Thai curry pastes and high-quality handicrafts in the more traditional areas nearby.

➡ **Pop & Lock** Most evenings the wide expanse in front of Bangkok's City Hall becomes a gathering place for young kids who meet to practise break-dancing moves.

➡ **Les Champs Élysées de Bangkok** The royal boulevard of Th Ratchadamnoen Klang links the Grand Palace in Ko Ratanakosin with newer palaces in Dusit, and is suitably adorned with billboard-sized pictures of the king, the queen and other royal family members.

➡ **Lucky Number** Because the national lottery office has its office nearby, both sides of Th Ratchadamnoen Klang east of the Democracy Monument (p79) are often clogged with vendors selling lottery tickets.

Getting There & Away

➡ **River boat** Tha Phra Athit (Banglamphu).

➡ **Taxi** From the BTS stops at National Stadium or Phaya Thai, or from the MRT stop at Hua Lamphong.

➡ **Klorng boat** Tha Phan Fah.

➡ **Bus** Air-con 44, 79, 503 and 511; ordinary 2, 15, 49, 59, 60, 69 and 70.

Lonely Planet's Top Tip

Boats – both the Chao Phraya River Express and the *klorng* boats – are a steady, if slow, way to reach Banglamphu, but remember that most only run until about 7pm.

✖ Best Places to Eat

➡ Krua Apsorn (p83)

➡ Jay Fai (p83)

➡ Shoshana (p83)

➡ Thip Samai (p81)

For reviews, see p81.

☕ Best Drinking & Entertainment

➡ Madame Musur (p84)

➡ Brick Bar (p86)

➡ Hippie de Bar (p84)

➡ Phra Nakorn Bar & Gallery (p84)

For reviews, see p84.

🔒 Best Places to Shop

➡ Thanon Khao San Market (p86)

➡ Nittaya Curry Shop (p86)

➡ Taekee Taekon (p86)

For reviews, see p86.

BANGLAMPHU

👁 SIGHTS

BAN BAAT   NEIGHBOURHOOD

Map p254 (บ้านบาตร, Monk's Bowl Village; Soi Ban Baat; ⊙8am-5pm; ☝klorng boat to Tha Phan Fah) **FREE** Ban Baat is the only remaining village of three established in Bangkok by Rama I (King Phraphutthayotfa; r 1782–1809) for the purpose of handcrafting *bàht,* the bowls that monks use to collect alms from the faithful each morning.

The alms bowls are sold for between 600B and 2000B and make great souvenirs. To find the village, walk south on Th Boriphat, south of Th Bamrung Meuang, then follow the signs into narrow Soi Ban Baat.

As cheaper factory-made bowls are now the norm, the artisanal tradition has shrunk to about half a dozen families. You can observe the process of hammering the bowls together from eight separate pieces of steel, said to represent Buddhism's Eightfold Path. The joints are then fused with melted copper wire, and the bowl is beaten, polished and coated with several layers of black lacquer. A typical *bàht*-smith's daily output is one large bowl, more if the bowls are smaller.

WAT RATCHANATDARAM   BUDDHIST TEMPLE

Map p254 (วัดราชนัดดาราม; Th Mahachai; ⊙8am-5pm; ☝klorng boat to Tha Phan Fah) **FREE** Across Th Mahachai from the Golden Mount, this temple is most stunning at night when the 37 spires of the all-metal **Loha Prasat** (Metal Palace) are lit up like a medieval birthday cake. It was built for Rama III (King Phranangklao; r 1824–51) in the 1840s in honour of his granddaughter.

At the back of the compound, behind the formal gardens, is a well-known market selling Buddhist *prá krêu·ang* (amulets) in all sizes, shapes and styles.

Wat Ratchanatdaram's design is said to derive from metal temples built in India and Sri Lanka more than 2000 years ago. The 37 spires represent the 37 virtues that lead to enlightenment. The interior is relatively unadorned by Thai temple standards, but the hallways and square edges contribute to a symmetry reminiscent of the much earlier temples at Angkor, in Cambodia.

SAO CHING-CHA   MONUMENT

Map p254 (เสาชิงช้า, Giant Swing; Th Bamrung Meuang; ⊙24hr; ☝klorng boat to Tha Phan Fah) **FREE** During the second lunar month (usually in January), Brahman beliefs dictate that Shiva comes down to earth for a 10-day residence and should be welcomed by grand ceremonies and, in the past, great degrees of daring. So each year the acrobatic and desperate braved the Giant Swing, a now disused but emblematic red frame made from six giant teak logs. The ceremony saw these men swing in ever-higher arcs in an effort to reach a bag of gold suspended from a 15m bamboo pole.

Whoever grabbed the gold could keep it. But that was no mean feat, and deaths were as common as successes. A black-and-white photo illustrating the risky rite can be seen at the ticket counter at adjacent Wat Suthat.

The Brahmans enjoyed a mystical position within the royal court, primarily in the coronation rituals. But after the 1932 revolution the Brahmans' waning power was effectively terminated and the festival, including the swinging, was discontinued during the reign of Rama VII (King Prajadhipok; r 1925–35). In 2007 the Giant Swing was replaced with the current, newer model. The previous version is kept at the National Museum.

PHRA SUMEN FORT & SANTI-
CHAIPRAKAN PARK   NOTABLE BUILDING, PARK

Map p254 (ป้อมพระสุเมรุ, สวนสันติชัยปราการ; Th Phra Athit; ⊙5am-10pm; ☝Tha Phra Athit, Banglamphu) **FREE** Beside Mae Nam Chao Phraya (Chao Phraya River) stands one of Bangkok's original 18th-century forts.

Alongside the fort and fronting the river is a small, grassy park with an open-air pavilion, river views, cool breezes and a bohemian mix of alternative young Thais and fisherman-pants-wearing, fire-stick-twirling backpackers. It's an interesting place to sit, people-watch and see what are said to be the last two *lam·poo* trees – the tress after which the area was named – in Banglamphu.

Built in 1783 to defend against potential naval invasions and named for the mythical

---

LOCAL KNOWLEDGE

BANGLAMPHU
....

Banglamphu means 'Place of Lamphu', a reference to the *lam·poo* tree (*Duabanga grandiflora*) that was once prevalent in the area.

Phra Sumen (Mt Meru) of Hindu-Buddhist cosmology, the octagonal brick-and-stucco bunker was one of 14 city watchtowers that punctuated the old city wall alongside Khlong Rop Krung (now Khlong Banglamphu but still called Khlong Rop Krung on most signs). Apart from Mahakan Fort, this is the only one still standing.

WAT BOWONNIWET

BUDDHIST TEMPLE

Map p254 (วัดบวรนิเวศวิหาร; www.watbowon .org; Th Phra Sumen; ⊙8.30am-5pm; 🚤Tha Phra Athit, Banglamphu) **FREE** Founded in 1826, Wat Bowonniwet (Wat Bowon) is the national headquarters for the Thammayut monastic sect, a reformed version of Thai Buddhism. The murals in the panels of the *ùbohsòt* (chapel) of this temple are noteworthy, and include Thai depictions of Western life (possibly copied from magazine illustrations) during the early 19th century. Because of its royal status, visitors should be particularly careful to dress properly for admittance to this *wát* – shorts and sleeveless clothing are not allowed.

Rama IV (King Mongkut; r 1851–68), who set out to be a scholar, not a king, founded the sect and began the royal tradition of ordination at this temple. In fact, Mongkut was the abbot of Wat Bowon for several years. Rama IX (King Bhumibol Adulyadej; r 1946–present) and Crown Prince Vajiralongkorn, as well as several other males in the royal family, have been ordained as monks here.

TH BAMRUNG MEUANG RELIGIOUS SHOPS

SHOPPING DISTRICT

Map p254 (ถนนบำรุงเมือง; Th Bamrung Meuang; ⊙9am-6pm; 🚤klorng boat to Tha Phan Fah) The stretch of Th Bamrung Meuang (one of Bangkok's oldest streets and originally an elephant path leading to the Grand Palace) from Th Mahachai to Th Tanao is lined with shops selling all manner of Buddhist religious paraphernalia. You probably don't need a Buddha statue or a creepily lifelike model of a famous monk, but browsing is always fun. Behind the storefronts, back-room workshops produce gigantic bronze Buddha images for *wát* all over Thailand.

DEMOCRACY MONUMENT

MONUMENT

Map p254 (อนุสาวรีย์ประชาธิปไตย; Th Ratchadamnoen Klang; ⊙24hr; 🚤klorng boat to Tha Phan Fah) **FREE** The Democracy Monument is the focal point of the grand, European-

TOP SIGHT
WAT SUTHAT

The main attraction at Wat Suthat is Thailand's biggest *wí·hǎhn* (main chapel) and the imperious yet serene 8m-high **Phra Si Sakayamuni** that resides within. The Buddha image is Thailand's largest surviving Sukhothai-period bronze, cast in the former capital in the 14th century. Today the ashes of Rama VIII (King Ananda Mahidol; r 1935–46) are contained in the base of the image.

Colourful, if now somewhat faded, *jataka* murals depicting scenes from the Buddha's past lives cover every wall and pillar. The deep-relief wooden doors are also impressive and were carved by artisans including Rama II (King Phraphutthaloetla Naphalai; r 1809–24) himself.

Behind the *wí·hǎhn,* the *bòht* (ordination hall) is the largest of its kind in the country. To add to its list of 'largests', Wat Suthat holds the rank of Rachavoramahavihan, the highest royal temple grade. It maintains a special place in the national religion because of its association with the Brahman priests who perform important ceremonies, such as the Royal Ploughing Ceremony in May. These priests also perform religious rites at two Hindu shrines near the *wát* – **Dhevasathan** on Th Din So, and the smaller **Saan Jao Phitsanu** on Th Siri Phong.

DON'T MISS...

➡ Phra Si Sakayamuni

➡ Temple murals

PRACTICALITIES

➡ วัดสุทัศน์

➡ Map p254

➡ Th Bamrung Meuang

➡ admission 20B

➡ ⊙8.30am-8.30pm

➡ 🚤klorng boat to Tha Phan Fah

TOP SIGHT
GOLDEN MOUNT & WAT SAKET

Before glass and steel towers began growing out of Bangkok's flat plain, the massive Golden Mount (Phu Khao Thong) was the only structure to make any significant impression on the horizon.

The Golden Mount was commissioned by Rama III (King Phranangklao; r 1824–51), who ordered that the earth dug out to create Bangkok's expanding *klorng* (canal) network be piled up to build a 100m-high, 500m-wide *chedi* (stupa). As the hill grew, the weight became too much for the soft soil beneath and the project was abandoned until his successor built a small gilded *chedi* on its crest and added trees to stave off erosion. Rama V (King Chulalongkorn; r 1886–1910) later added to the structure and interred a Buddha relic from India in the *chedi*. The concrete walls were added during WWII. At the peak, you'll find a 360-degree view of Bangkok's most photogenic side.

Next door, seemingly peaceful Wat Saket contains murals that are among both the most beautiful and the goriest in the country; proceed to the pillar behind the Buddha statue for explicit depictions of Buddhist hell. In November there's a festival in the grounds that includes a candlelight procession up the Golden Mount.

DON'T MISS...

➡ View from summit of Golden Mount

➡ Temple paintings at Wat Saket

PRACTICALITIES

➡ ภูเขาทอง & วัดสระเกศ

➡ Map p254

➡ Th Boriphat

➡ admission to summit of Golden Mount 10B

➡ ⊘7.30am-5.30pm

➡ 🚤klorng boat to Tha Phan Fah

---

style boulevard that is Th Ratchadamnoen Klang. As the name suggests, it was erected to commemorate Thailand's momentous transformation from absolute to constitutional monarchy. It was designed by Thai architect Mew Aphaiwong and the relief sculptures were created by Italian Corrado Feroci who, as Silpa Bhirasri, gives his name to Silpakorn University. Feroci combined the square-jawed 'heroes of socialism' style popular at the time with Mew Aphaiwong's art deco influences.

There are 75 cannonballs around the base to signify the year BE (Buddhist Era) 2475 (AD 1932); the four wings of the monument stand 24m tall, representing 24 June, the day the constitution was signed; and the central plinth stands 3m high (June was then the third month in the Thai calendar) and supports a chiselled constitution. Each wing has bas-reliefs depicting soldiers, police and civilians who helped usher in the modern Thai state.

During the era of military dictatorships, demonstrators often assembled here to call for a return to democracy, most notably in 1973 and 1992.

OCTOBER 14 MEMORIAL MONUMENT
Map p254 (อนุสรณ์สถาน ๑๔ ตุลา; cnr Th Ratchadamnoen Klang & Th Tanao; ⊘24hr; 🚤klorng boat to Tha Phan Fah) **FREE** A peaceful amphitheatre commemorates the civilian demonstrators who were killed by the military during a pro-democracy rally on 14 October 1973. Over 200,000 people had assembled at the Democracy Monument and along the length of Th Ratchadamnoen to protest against the arrest of political campaigners and continuing military dictatorship. Although some in Thailand continue to deny it, photographs confirm that more than 70 demonstrators were killed when the tanks met the crowd.

The complex is an interesting adaptation of Thai temple architecture for a secular and political purpose. A central *chedi* (stupa) is dedicated to the fallen and a gallery of historic photographs lines the interior wall.

MAHAKAN FORT FORT
Map p254 (ป้อมมหากาฬ; Th Ratchadamnoen Klang; ⊘24hr; 🚤klorng boat to Tha Phan Fah) **FREE** The white-washed Mahakan Fort is one of two surviving citadels that defended the old walled city. The octagonal fort is a

picturesque, if brief and hot, stop en route to Golden Mount, but the neighbouring village is more interesting. This small community of wooden houses has been here for more than 100 years. But since the mid-1990s it has fought the Bangkok municipal government's plan to demolish it and create a 'tourist' park.

The community blocked progress and even proposed the development of another tourist attraction: a *lí·gair* (bawdy dance-drama) museum honouring the dance tradition that traces its creation to a school located here in 1897. Some of the homes were eventually demolished, resulting in the park you see today. But behind the fort many others remain (for now). Visitors are welcome. Climb the ramparts (not for children) running away from the fort and walk to the far end, where stairs lead down and into the village.

QUEEN'S GALLERY   ART GALLERY

Map p254 (หอศิลป์สมเด็จพระนางเจ้าสิริกิติ์; www.queengallery.org; 101 Th Ratchadamnoen Klang; admission 30B; ⏱10am-7pm Thu-Tue; 🚣klorng boat to Tha Pan Fah) This royal-funded museum presents five floors of rotating exhibitions of modern and traditionally influenced art. The building is sleek and contemporary and the artists hail from the upper echelons of the conservative Thai art world. The attached shop is filled with fine-arts books and gifts

KING PRAJADHIPOK MUSEUM   MUSEUM

Map p254 (พิพิธภัณฑ์พระบาทสมเด็จพระปกเกล้าเจ้าอยู่หัว; 2 Th Lan Luang; admission 40B; ⏱9am-4pm Tue-Sun; 🚣klorng boat to Tha Phan Fah) This museum uses modern techniques to relate the rather dramatic life of Rama VII, while neatly documenting Thailand's transition from absolute to constitutional monarchy. The museum occupies a grand neo-colonial-style building constructed on the orders of Rama V for his favourite firm of

Bond St merchants; it was the only foreign business allowed on the royal road linking Bangkok's two palace districts.

The exhibitions reveal that Prajadhipok did not expect to become king, but once on the throne showed considerable diplomacy in dealing with what was, in effect, a revolution fomented by a new intellectual class of Thais. The 1st floor deals with the life of Queen Rambhai Barni, while the upper two floors cover the king's own life. It reveals, for example, that the army-officer-turned-king spent many of his formative years in Europe where he became fond of British democracy. Ironically, those plotting his downfall had themselves learned of democracy during years of European education. A coup, carried out while the king and queen were playing golf, ended Thailand's absolute monarchy in 1932. Prajadhipok's reign eventually ended when he abdicated while in England in 1935; he died there in 1941.

✖ EATING

Banglamphu is famous for its old-school Thai food – the dominant cuisine in this part of town. For something more international, head to Th Khao San, where you'll find a few international fast-food franchises as well as foreign and vegetarian restaurants.

THIP SAMAI   THAI $

Map p254 (313 Th Mahachai; mains 25-120B; ⏱5.30pm-1.30am; 🚣klorng boat to Tha Phan Fah) Brace yourself – you should be aware that the fried noodles sold from carts along Th Khao San have little to do with the dish known as *pàt tai*. Luckily, less than a five-minute túk-túk ride away lies Thip Samai, home to some of the most legendary fried noodles in town. Closed on alternate Wednesdays.

VEGING OUT IN BANGLAMPHU

Due to the strong foreign influence, there's an abundance of vegetarian restaurants in the Banglamphu area. In addition to Hemlock (p83), Seven Spoons (p83) and Shoshana (p83), which have generous vegie sections, the meat-free dining destinations include **Arawy Vegetarian Food** (Map p254; 152 Th Din So; mains 20-40B; ⏱7am-8.30pm; 🍴; 🚣Tha Phan Fah), with heaps of prepared meat-free curries, dips and stir-fries; and **May Kaidee's** (Map p254; www.maykaidee.com; 33 Th Samsen; mains 50-100B; ⏱9am-10pm; ❄ 🍴; 🚣Tha Phra Athit, Banglamphu), a longstanding restaurant that also houses a vegie Thai cooking school.

WHAT'S SO LONELY ABOUT THE KHAO SAN ROAD?

Th Khao San, better known as the Khao San Rd, is genuinely unlike anywhere else on earth. It's an international clearing house of people either entering the liberated state of travelling in Southeast Asia or returning to the coddling bonds of first-world life, all coming together in a neon-lit melting pot in Banglamphu. Its uniqueness is probably best illustrated by a question: apart from airports, where else could you share space with the citizens of dozens of countries at the same time, people ranging from first-time backpackers scoffing banana pancakes to 75-year-old grandparents ordering G&Ts, and everyone in between, including hippies, hipsters, nerds, glamazons, package tourists, global nomads, people on a week's holiday and those taking a gap year, people of every colour and creed looking at you looking at them looking at everyone else?

Th Khao San (*kôw săhn*), meaning 'uncooked rice', is perhaps the most high-profile bastard child of the age of independent travel. Of course, it hasn't always been this way. For its first two centuries or so it was just another unremarkable road in old Bangkok. The first guesthouses appeared in 1982, and as more backpackers arrived through the '80s the old wooden homes were converted one by one into low-rent dosshouses. By the time Alex Garland's novel *The Beach* was published in 1997, with its opening scenes set in the seedier side of Khao San, staying here had become a rite of passage for backpackers coming to Southeast Asia.

The publicity from Garland's book and the movie that followed pushed Khao San into the mainstream, romanticising the seedy, and stereotyping the backpackers it attracted as unwashed and countercultural. It also brought the long-simmering debate about the relative merits of Th Khao San to the top of backpacker conversations across the region. Was it cool to stay on KSR? Was it uncool? Was this 'real travel' or just an international anywhere surviving on the few baht Western backpackers spent before they headed home to start their high-earning careers? Was it really Thailand at all?

Perhaps one of Garland's characters summed it up most memorably when he said: 'You know, Richard, one of these days I'm going to find one of those Lonely Planet writers and I'm going to ask him, what's so fucking lonely about the Khao San Road?'

Today more than ever the answer would have to be: not that much. With the help of all that publicity, Khao San continued to evolve, with bedbug-infested guesthouses replaced by boutique hotels, and downmarket TV bars showing pirated movies transformed into hip design bars peopled by flashpackers in designer threads. But the most interesting change has been in the way Thais see Khao San.

Once written off as home to cheap, dirty *fa·ràng kêe ngók* (stingy foreigners), Banglamphu has become just about the coolest district in Bangkok. Attracted in part by the long-derided independent traveller and their modern ideas, the city's own counterculture kids have moved in and brought with them a tasty selection of small bars, organic cafes and shops. Indeed, Bangkok's indie crowd has proved to be the Thai spice this melting pot always lacked.

Not that Khao San has moved completely away from its backpacker roots. The strip still anticipates every traveller need: meals to soothe homesickness, cafes and bars for swapping travel tales about getting to the Cambodian border, tailors, travel agents, teeth whitening, secondhand books, hair braiding and, of course, the perennial Akha women trying to harass everyone they see into buying wooden frogs. No, it's not very lonely at all...

CHOTE CHITR   THAI **$**

Map p254 (146 Th Phraeng Phuthon; mains 30-200B; ⊙11am-10pm; ⛴klorng boat to Tha Phan Fah) This third-generation shophouse restaurant boasting just six tables is a Bangkok foodie landmark. The kitchen can be inconsistent and the service is consistently grumpy, but when they're on, dishes like *mèe gròrp* (crispy fried noodles) and *yam tòo·a ploo* (wing-bean salad) are in a class of their own.

ROTI-MATABA
MUSLIM-THAI $

Map p254 (136 Th Phra Athit; dishes 17-111B; ☻9am-10pm Tue-Sun; ❋ ✎; ☖Tha Phra Athit, Banglamphu) This classic Bangkok eatery may have become a bit too big for its britches in recent years, but it still serves tasty Thai-Muslim dishes such as roti, *gaang mát-sà-màn* (Muslim curry), a brilliantly sour fish curry, and *má-tà-bà* (a stuffed Muslim-style pancake). An upstairs air-con dining area and outdoor tables provide barely enough seating for its loyal fans.

KIMLENG
THAI $

Map p254 (158-160 Th Tanao; mains 20-60B; ☻10am-10pm Mon-Sat; ❋; ☖klorng boat to Tha Phan Fah) This tiny family-run restaurant specialises in the dishes and flavours of central Thailand. It's a good place to whet your appetite with an authentic *yam* (Thai-style salad) such as *yam 'blah dùk foo*, a mixture of crispy catfish and mango. Located on Th Tanao across from the October 14 Memorial.

PHEN THAI FOOD
THAI $

Map p254 (Th Rambuttri; mains 50-90B; ☻11.30am-10pm; ☖Tha Phra Athit, Banglamphu) If you're looking for authentic Thai but don't want to stray far from the comforts of Th Khao San, this street-side eatery is your best bet. Simply look for the overflowing tray of prepared dishes, point to what you want and Phen will plate it up for you. The clientele is decidedly international, but the flavours wholly domestic.

★KRUA APSORN
THAI $$

Map p254 (www.kruaapsorn.com; Th Din So; mains 65-350B; ☻10.30am-8pm Mon-Sat; ❋; ☖klorng boat to Tha Phan Fah) This homely dining room is a favourite of members of the Thai royal family and restaurant critics alike. Must-eat dishes include mussels fried with fresh herbs, the decadent crab fried in yellow chilli oil and the *tortilla Española*–like crab omelette. There's another branch on Th Samsen.

SHOSHANA
ISRAELI $$

Map p254 (88 Th Chakraphong; mains 70-240B; ☻10am-midnight; ❋ ✎; ☖Tha Phra Athit, Banglamphu) One of Khao San's longest-running Israeli restaurants, Shoshana resembles a typical grandparents' living room, right down to the tacky wall art and plastic placemats. Feel safe ordering anything deep-fried – they do an excellent job

of it – and don't miss the deliciously garlicky eggplant dip.

ESCAPADE BURGERS & SHAKES
AMERICAN $$

Map p254 (112 Th Phra Athit; mains 120-330B; ☻4-10.30pm Mon-Sat; ❋; ☖Tha Phra Athit, Banglamphu) Escapade is proof that, where it concerns American food, the Thais have moved way beyond McDonald's. Squeeze into this tiny shophouse for messy burgers with edgy ingredients such as 'toasted rice mayo' and truly decadent milkshakes.

POJ SPA KAR
THAI $$

Map p254 (443 Th Tanao; mains 65-200B; ☻12.30-8.30pm; ❋; ☖klorng boat to Tha Phan Fah) Pronounced *pôht sà-pah-kahn*, this is allegedly the oldest restaurant in Bangkok, and continues to maintain recipes handed down from a former palace cook. Be sure to order the simple but tasty lemongrass omelette or the deliciously sour-sweet *gaang sôm*, a traditional central Thai soup.

HEMLOCK
THAI $$

Map p254 (56 Th Phra Athit; mains 75-280B; ☻4pm-midnight Mon-Sat; ❋ ✎; ☖Tha Phra Athit, Banglamphu) Taking full advantage of its cosy shophouse location, this perennial favourite has enough style to feel like a special night out but doesn't skimp on flavour or preparation. The eclectic menu reads like an ancient literary work, reviving old dishes from aristocratic kitchens across the country. Try the flavourful *mêe-ang kam* (wild tea leaves wrapped around ginger, shallots, peanuts, lime and shredded coconut) or *yam kà-moy* ('thieves' salad').

★JAY FAI
THAI $$$

Map p254 (327 Th Mahachai; mains from 400B; ☻3pm-2am Tue-Sun; ☖klorng boat to Tha Phan Fah) You wouldn't think so by looking at her bare-bones dining room, but Jay Fai is known far and wide for serving Bangkok's most expensive *pàt kee mow* ('drunkard's noodles' – wide rice noodles fried with seafood and Thai herbs). The price is justified by the copious fresh seafood, as well as Jay Fai's distinct frying style that results in an (almost) oil-free finished product. Jay Fai is in a virtually unmarked shophouse on Th Mahachai, directly across from a 7-Eleven.

SEVEN SPOONS
INTERNATIONAL $$$

Map p257 (✆0 2629 9214, 08 4539 1819; seven spoonsbkk.wordpress.com; 22-24 Th Chakraphatdi

Phong; mains 160-580B; ⊙11am-3pm & 6pm-1am Tue-Sat, 6pm-1am Sun; 🅰️🅰️; 🅰️klorng boat to Tha Phan Fah) Dark woods, smooth concrete, a menu with influences ranging from Montreal to Morocco – one doesn't expect a place this modern and cosmopolitan in such an antiquated corner of Bangkok. And best of all, it delivers. Lots of vegetarian options.

SHEEPSHANK
INTERNATIONAL **$$$**

Map p254 (📞0 2629 5165; www.sheepshankpublichouse.com; 47 Th Phra Athit; mains 320-1150B; ⊙6pm-midnight Tue-Sat; 🅰️Tha Phra Athit, Banglamphu) Seizing upon Bangkok's current desire for anything industrial is this former warehouse–turned gastropub. Pulleys, brick, rivets and glass create the vibe, while comforting dishes such as 'sausages with blue cheese–mashed potatoes', or more adventurous options like 'slow-cooked octopus and creamed corn risotto', make up the menu.

DRINKING & NIGHTLIFE

MADAME MUSUR
BAR

Map p254 (41 Soi Ram Buttri; ⊙8am-1am; 🅰️Tha Phra Athit, Banglamphu) Saving you the trip north to Pai, Madame Musur pulls off that elusive combination of 'northern Thailand meets *The Beach* meets Th Khao San'. It's a fun place to chat, drink and people-watch, and serving a short menu of northern Thai dishes (mains 120B to 200B), it's also not a bad place to eat.

HIPPIE DE BAR
BAR

Map p254 (www.facebook.com/hippie.debar; 46 Th Khao San; ⊙3pm-2am; 🅰️Tha Phra Athit, Banglamphu) Popular with the domestic crowd, Hippie boasts a Thai retro theme and several levels of fun, both indoor and outdoor. There's also food, pool tables and a more sophisticated soundtrack than the average Th Khao San bar.

PHRA NAKORN BAR & GALLERY
BAR

Map p254 (58/2 Soi Damnoen Klang Tai; ⊙5pm-1am; 🅰️klorng boat to Tha Phan Fah) Located an arm's length from the hype of Th Khao San, Phra Nakorn Bar & Gallery is a home away from hovel for students and arty types, with eclectic decor and changing gallery exhibits. Our tip: head directly for the breezy rooftop and order some of the bar's cheap 'n' tasty Thai food.

CLUB
NIGHTCLUB

Map p254 (www.theclubkhaosan.com; 123 Th Khao San; ⊙10pm-3am; 🅰️Tha Phra Athit, Banglamphu) Located right in the middle of Th Khao San, this cavernlike dance hall hosts a good mix of locals and backpackers. Expect a door fee of 100B on Friday and Saturday nights.

TRIPLE-D
BAR

Map p254 (3rd fl, 44 Th Chakraphong; ⊙6pm-late; 🅰️Tha Phra Athit, Banglamphu) This vaguely Middle Eastern–themed bar represents the posh alter ego of Th Khao San. There's live music, lounges for puffing on shisha, and a dark club. The bar's elevated setting appears to lend it some leniency with the city's strict closing times.

STREET TROUBADOURS

Banglamphu is home to Bangkok's greatest concentration of live-music bars. The western stretch of Th Phra Athit in particular is home to half a dozen back-to-back pint-sized music pubs that offer lots of loud Thai pop, but not a whole lot of breathing room.

For something a bit more approachable, head to Th Khao San's chilled-out next door neighbour, Th Rambuttri, where there's an abundance of open-air live-music pubs including the bluesy **Barlamphu** (Map p254; Th Rambuttri; ⊙noon-1am; 🅰️Tha Phra Athit, Banglamphu), or the poppier **Suk Sabai** (Map p254; 96 Th Rambuttri; ⊙24hr; 🅰️Tha Phra Athit) and **Molly Bar** (Map p254; 108 Th Rambuttri; ⊙8pm-1am; 🅰️Tha Phra Athit, Banglamphu).

Elsewhere, Th Khao San is home to one of our favourite places in Bangkok for live music, Brick Bar (p86). Just around the corner is Triple-D (p84), which occasionally hosts indie Thai rock bands, while Ad Here the 13th (p86), a Bangkok blues legend, is only a couple of blocks away.

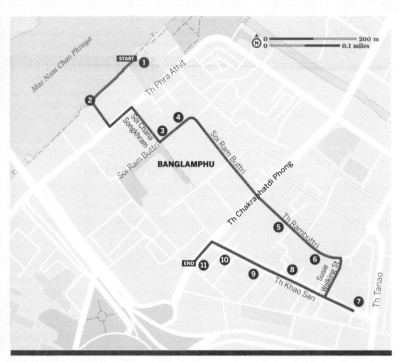

Neighbourhood Walk
Banglamphu Pub Crawl

START SHEEPSHANK
END TRIPLE-D
LENGTH APPROXIMATELY 1.5KM; THREE
TO SIX HOURS

You don't need to go far to find a decent bar in Banglamphu, but why limit yourself to just one? With this in mind, we've assembled a pub crawl that spans river views, people-watching, live music and late-night shenanigans.

Begin your crawl in sophisticated, air-conditioned comfort at **1 Sheepshank** (p84), a new gastropub with an intriguing menu of bar snacks and classic cocktails. If you still have space for tapas, head west along the riverfront promenade until you reach **2 Babble & Rum**, the Riva Surya hotel's open-air restaurant/bar.

From Th Phra Athit, enter Soi Chana Songkhram and take a left at Soi Ram Buttri, where you begin phase two of your crawl: people-watching. **3 Gecko Bar** is a frugal and fun place to gawk at other patrons and passers by, while a few doors

down, **4 Madame Musur** (p84) offers the same perks, but with a bit more sophistication and tasty northern-style eats.

It's time to add some music to the mix, so for phase three, cross Th Chakraphong and head down Th Rambuttri towards one of the open-air live-music bars such as **5 Barlamphu** (p84) or **6 Molly Bar** (p84).

At this point, you should be lubricated enough for the main event, so, crossing via Susie Walking St, proceed to Th Khao San. If you need a bathroom or a blast of air-con, make a pit stop at **7 Mulligans**, a tidy Irish-themed bar in the Buddy Lodge. Otherwise, get a bird's eye view of the human parade from elevated **8 Roof Bar & Restaurant**, or ringside at the noisy and buzzy **9 Center Khao Sarn** (p86).

End the night on a good note by planting yourself at **10 Hippie de Bar** (p84), one of Banglamphu's best pubs. Or if 2am is too early to call it a night, crawl over to **11 Triple-D** (p84), a rooftop lounge and nightclub that stays open until morning.

CENTER KHAO SARN
BAR

Map p254 (Th Khao San; ⊘24hr; ⊜Tha Phra Athit, Banglamphu) Center Khao Sarn offers ringside seats for the human parade on Th Khao San. The upstairs bar here hosts late-night bands.

TAKSURA
BAR

Map p254 (156/1 Th Tanao; ⊘5pm-1am; ⊜klorng boat to Tha Phan Fah) There's little English-language signage to lead you to this 90-year-old mansion in the heart of old Bangkok, which is all the better, according to the overwhelmingly Thai, uni/artsy crowd that frequents the place. Take a seat outside to soak up the breeze and go domestic by ordering some spicy nibbles with your drinks.

ROLLING BAR
BAR

Map p254 (Th Prachathipatai; ⊘5pm-midnight; ⊜klorng boat to Tha Phan Fah) An escape from hectic Th Khao San is a good enough excuse to schlep to this quiet canal-side boozer. Live music and decent bar snacks are good reasons to stay.

ENTERTAINMENT

★ BRICK BAR
LIVE MUSIC

Map p254 (www.brickbarkhaosan.com; basement, Buddy Lodge, 265 Th Khao San; ⊘8pm-2am; ⊜Tha Phra Athit, Banglamphu) This basement pub, one of our fave destinations in Bangkok for live music, hosts a nightly revolving cast of bands for an almost exclusively Thai crowd – most of whom will end the night dancing on the tables. Brick Bar can get infamously packed, so be sure to get there early. Fridays and Saturdays command a 150B entry fee.

LOCAL BOOZERS

Although Th Khao San remains associated with foreign tourists, in recent years it's also become a popular nightlife destination for young locals. Check out the live-music pubs along Th Phra Athit or the low-key bars south of Th Ratchadamnoen Klang for a more local drinking scene.

AD HERE THE 13TH
LIVE MUSIC

Map p254 (13 Th Samsen; ⊘6pm-midnight; ⊜Tha Phra Athit, Banglamphu) Located beside Khlong Banglamphu, this closet-sized blues bar is everything a neighbourhood joint should be: lots of regulars, cold beer and heart-warming tunes delivered by a masterful house band starting at 10pm. Everyone knows each other, so don't be shy about mingling.

SHOPPING

★ THANON KHAO SAN MARKET
SOUVENIRS

Map p254 (Th Khao San; ⊘10am-midnight; ⊜Tha Phra Athit, Banglamphu) The main guesthouse strip in Banglamphu is a day-and-night shopping bazaar. Cheap T-shirts, trendy purses, those croaking wooden frogs, fuzzy puppets, bootleg CDs, hemp clothing, fake student ID cards, knock-off designer wear, souvenirs, corn on the cob, orange juice... You name it, they've got it.

NITTAYA CURRY SHOP
FOOD & DRINK

Map p254 (136-40 Th Chakhraphong; ⊘9am-7pm Mon-Sat; ⊜Tha Phra Athit, Banglamphu) Follow your nose: Nittaya is famous throughout Thailand for her pungent but high-quality curry pastes. Pick up a couple of takeaway canisters for prospective dinner parties or peruse the snack and gift sections, where visitors to Bangkok load up on local specialities for friends back in the provinces.

TAEKEE TAEKON
HANDICRAFTS

Map p254 (118 Th Phra Athit; ⊘9am-6pm Mon-Sat; ⊜Tha Phra Athit, Banglamphu) This atmospheric shop has a decent selection of Thai textiles from the country's main silk-producing areas, especially northern Thailand, as well as interesting postcards not widely available elsewhere.

THAI NAKON
HANDICRAFTS

Map p254 (79 Th Prachathipatai; ⊘10am-6pm Mon-Sat; ⊜klorng boat to Tha Phan Fah) This family-owned enterprise has been in business for 70 years and often fills commissions from the royal family for nielloware and silver ornaments. Silver cases and clutches and ceremonial bowls and tea sets are also among the offerings. If you can navigate the language barrier, ask to go behind the showroom to witness the aged artisans at work.

LOOK, MA – NO HANDS!

Wandering around Bangkok, it's likely you'll encounter a group of men playing a volleyball-like game with a small plastic ball. Characterised by gravity-defying flips and spikes, the sport is known as *dà-grôr* (also spelt takraw, or known as sepak takraw).

Traditionally *dà-grôr* is played by men standing in a circle (the size of which depends on the number of players) and trying to keep the ball airborne by kicking it soccer-style. Points are scored for style, difficulty and variety of kicking manoeuvres. A modern variation of the game incorporates a net and the rules of volleyball, while only allowing contact with the ball using feet, knees and the head. *Dà-grôr* is also popular in several neighbouring countries and is a hotly contested sport in the Southeast Asian Games; at the 2013 games, Thailand won gold in six of the 10 categories.

RIMKHOBFAH BOOKSTORE   BOOKSTORE
Map p254 (78/1 Th Ratchadamnoen Klang; ⊙10am-7pm; ▣klorng boat to Tha Phan Fah) The scholarly publications from the Fine Arts Department on Thai art and architecture are handily slim, so you don't have to commit too much suitcase space to accommodate them.

🏃 SPORTS & ACTIVITIES

VELO THAILAND   BICYCLE TOURS
Map p254 (📞0 2628 8628; www.velothailand. com; 29 Soi 4, Th Samsen; tours from 1000B; ⊙10am-9pm; ▣Tha Phra Athit, Banglamphu) Velo Thailand is a small and personal outfit based out of Banglamphu. Day and night tours to Thonburi and further afield are on offer.

SOR VORAPIN GYM   THAI BOXING
Map p254 (📞0 2282 3551; www.thaiboxings.com; 13 Th Kasab; per session/month 500/9000B; ⊙lessons 7.30-9.30am & 3-5pm; ▣Tha Phra Athit, Banglamphu) Conveniently located steps from Th Khao San, this gym offers training in Thai boxing for foreign students of both genders.

GRASSHOPPER ADVENTURES   BICYCLE TOURS
Map p254 (📞0 2280 0832; www.grasshopper adventures.com; 57 Th Ratchadamnoen Klang; half-/full-day tours from 1100B/1600B; ⊙9am-6pm; ▣klorng boat to Tha Phan Fah) This lauded outfit runs a variety of unique bicycle tours in and around Bangkok, including a night tour and a tour of the city's green zones.

Thewet & Dusit

Neighbourhood Top Five

1 Witnessing Victorian sense and Thai sensibilities merge in the former royal enclave of **Dusit Palace Park** (p90).

2 Cheering on Thai boxing – the sport that makes Steven Seagal look as soft as a pillow – at **Ratchadamnoen Stadium** (p94).

3 Sampling homestyle Thai food good enough for royalty at **Krua Apsorn** (p94).

4 Wondering what country you're in while among the Carrara marble, European-style frescoes and red carpet of **Wat Benchamabophit** (p92).

5 Enjoying the breezy, tasty riverside dining at **Steve Café & Cuisine** or **Kaloang Home Kitchen** (p94).

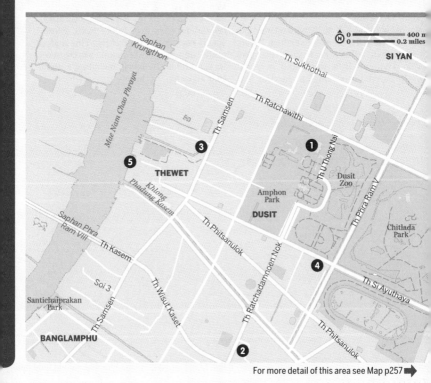

For more detail of this area see Map p257 ➡

Explore: Thewet & Dusit

Thewet, particularly the area near Th Samsen, has the hectic, buzzy feel often associated with Bangkok: relentless traffic, throngs of civil servants and schoolkids, and a soggy market. The adjacent river is the only respite from the action, and it also functions as a good point from which to approach the area, as most sights and restaurants are a short walk from the river ferry pier. Plan to visit this area at lunch or dinner time to best take advantage of the riverside restaurants.

Dusit, on the other hand, is possibly Bangkok's most orderly district, home to the kind of tree-lined avenues and regal monuments you'd expect to find in Paris. Set aside a few hours – ideally in the cool morning – to visit the area's gems: Dusit Palace Park and Wat Benchamabophit.

The two districts are a brief walk from each other, one made more difficult by the harsh Bangkok sun. Dusit's sights are relatively far apart and are best approached by taxi or túk-túk (pronounced *dúk dúk*).

Local Life

→ **Local Hero** Visit the Rama V (King Chulalongkorn; r 1868–1910) Memorial (p92) on any Tuesday (the day of the monarch's birth) to witness worshippers make offerings of candles, flowers, incense and bottles of whisky. An even larger celebration is held on 23 October, the former monarch's birthday.

→ **Boxing Day Dinner** Planning to watch a Thai boxing match at Ratchadamnoen Stadium (p94)? Do as the locals do: before the match, grab a plate of *gài yâhng* (grilled chicken) from the restaurants surrounding the stadium, such as Likhit Kai Yang (p93).

→ **Royal Digs** Dusit is home to Chitlada Palace (p92), the official residence of the royal family. The compound is generally closed to the public, and you're not likely to see any royals – at the time of writing the king was living at Siriraj Hospital in Thonburi – but it's worth taking a peek through one of the gates.

Getting There & Away

→ **River boat** The easiest way to approach the area is via the river ferry stop at Tha Thewet. From here it's a brief walk through shady walkways to the riverside restaurants, or a short túk-túk or taxi ride to Dusit Palace Park and other attractions.

→ **Bus** Air-con 505, 510 and 510; ordinary 3, 16, 18, 32, 53, 70 and 72.

→ **Skytrain** An option best attempted outside of rush hours is to take the BTS to the stop at Phaya Thai before continuing by taxi.

Lonely Planet's Top Tip

If you're keen to see a Thai boxing match at Ratchadamnoen Stadium, go on a Thursday night, when aficionados say the best-matched bouts are on.

✕ Best Places to Eat

→ Krua Apsorn (p94)
→ Likhit Kai Yang (p93)
→ Steve Café & Cuisine (p94)

For reviews, see p93.

▤ Best Drinking & Entertainment

→ River Bar Café (p94)
→ Post Bar (p94)
→ Ratchadamnoen Stadium (p94)

For reviews, see p94.

◉ Best Historical Structures

→ Vimanmek Teak Mansion (p90)
→ Wat Benchamabophit (p92)
→ Abhisek Dusit Throne Hall (p91)
→ Ananta Samakhom Throne Hall (p92)

For reviews, see p92.

THEWET & DUSIT

Following Rama V's first European tour in 1897 (he was the first Thai monarch to visit the continent), he returned home with visions of European castles swimming in his head and set about transforming those styles into a uniquely Thai expression – today's Dusit Palace Park. The royal palace, throne hall and minor palaces for extended family were all moved here from Ko Ratanakosin, and were supplemented with beaux-arts institutions and Victorian manor houses. All of this and the expansive gardens make the compound a worthwhile escape from the chaos of modern Bangkok.

Vimanmek Teak Mansion

The highlight of the park is this structure, said to be the world's largest golden-teak mansion, built with nary a single nail. The mansion was originally constructed on Ko Si Chang in 1868 as a retreat for Rama V; the king had it moved to its present site in 1901. For the following few years it served as Rama V's primary residence, with the 81 rooms accommodating his enormous extended family. The interior of the mansion contains various personal effects of the king and a treasure trove of early Ratanakosin and European art objects and antiques. Compulsory English-language tours of the building start every 30 minutes and last an hour, though it's up to luck as to whether your guide will actually speak decent English or not.

DON'T MISS...

➡ Vimanmek Teak Mansion
➡ Abhisek Dusit Throne Hall
➡ Royal Thai Elephant Museum
➡ Ancient Cloth Museum

PRACTICALITIES

➡ วังสวนดุสิต
➡ Map p257
➡ ☏ 0 2628 6300
➡ bounded by Th Ratchawithi, Th U Thong Nai & Th Ratchasima
➡ adult/child 100/20B or free with Grand Palace ticket
➡ ⊙ 9.30am-4pm Tue-Sun, last entry 3.15pm
➡ 🚤 Tha Thewet, ⓈPhaya Thai exit 2 & taxi

Abhisek Dusit Throne Hall

Visions of Moorish palaces and Victorian mansions must have still been spinning around in King Rama V's head when he commissioned this intricate building of porticoes and fretwork fused with a distinctive Thai character. Built as the throne hall for the palace in 1904, it opens onto a big stretch of lawn and flowerbeds, just like any important European building. Inside, the heavy ornamentation of the white main room is quite extraordinary, especially if you've been visiting a lot of overwhelmingly gold temples or traditional wooden buildings. Look up to just beneath the ceiling to see the line of brightly coloured stained-glass panels in Moorish patterns. The hall displays regional handiwork crafted by members of the Promotion of Supplementary Occupations & Related Techniques (Support), a charity foundation sponsored by Queen Sirikit.

Other Exhibits

Beside the Th U Thong Nai gate, the **Royal Thai Elephant Museum** showcases two large stables that once housed three white elephants (it's more interesting than it sounds). Near the Th Ratchawithi entrance, two residence halls display the **HM King Bhumibol Photography Exhibitions**, a collection of photographs and paintings by the present monarch. The **Ancient Cloth Museum** presents a beautiful collection of traditional silks and cottons that make up the royal cloth collection.

VERSAILLES OF BANGKOK

In 1897, Rama V became the first Thai monarch to visit Europe, a trip that seemingly had a profound impact on the king in more ways than one. Upon returning to Siam, Rama V soon set about building a new royal district comprised of relocated Thai structures and spacious, grand, Western-style buildings surrounded by expansive gardens (Suan Dusit means 'Celestial Gardens') – a significant contrast with the increasingly crowded walled district of Ko Ratanakosin. Having chosen a rural-feeling spot within walking distance of the Grand Palace – the king was allegedly a fan of the new-fangled trend of bicycling – Rama V hired a team of German and Italian architects and imported materials such as marble from Carrara, Italy, for the construction of his new European-style home.

COVER UP!

Because Dusit Palace Park is royal property, visitors should wear long pants (no capri pants) or long skirts and sleeved shirts.

⊙ SIGHTS

DUSIT PALACE PARK MUSEUM, HISTORICAL SITE
See p90.

WAT BENCHAMABOPHIT BUDDHIST TEMPLE
Map p257 (วัดเบญจมบพิตร (วัดเบญจะฯ); cnr Th Si
Ayuthaya & Th Phra Ram V; admission 20B; ⊘8am-
6pm; Ⓢ Phaya Thai exit 3 & taxi) Inside and out,
this temple is one of the most unusual, and
most extravagant, in the kingdom. Built
at the turn of the century on the orders of
Rama V, the *bòht* (ordination hall) is made
of white Carrara marble – hence its alternative name, 'Marble Temple' – imported from
Italy especially for the job.

This structure is a prime example of
modern Thai temple architecture, as is the
interior design, which melds Thai motifs
with European influences: the red carpets,
the gold-on-white motifs painted repeti-
tively on the walls, the walls painted like
stained-glass windows and the royal blue
wall behind the central Buddha image are
strongly reminiscent of a European palace.
It's not all that surprising when you consider how enamoured Rama V (whose ashes
are in the base of said Buddha image) was
with Europe – just walk across the street to
Dusit Park for further evidence.

The courtyard behind the *bòht* has 53
Buddha images (33 originals and 20 copies)
representing every *mudra* (gesture) and
style from Thai history, making this the
ideal place to compare Buddhist iconogra-
phy. If religious details aren't for you, this
temple still offers a pleasant stroll beside
landscaped canals filled with blooming lotus and Chinese-style footbridges.

**ANANTA SAMAKHOM
THRONE HALL** MUSEUM
Map p257 (พระที่นั่งอนันตสมาคม; www.arts
ofthekingdom.com; Th U Thong Nai; admission
150B; ⊘10am-6pm Tue-Sun; Ⓢ Phaya Thai exit 3
& taxi) The domed neoclassical building behind the Rama V Memorial was originally
built as a royal reception hall during the
reign of Rama V, but wasn't completed until 1915, five years after his death. Today the
building houses an exhibit called *Arts of the
Kingdom,* which, like the nearby Abhisek
Dusit Throne Hall, displays the products of
Queen Sirikit's Support foundation.

The hall was designed as a place to host –
and impress – foreign dignitaries, and on
occasion it still serves this purpose, most notably during celebrations of King Bhumibol

Adulyadej's 60th year on the throne, when
royals from around the world converged
here in full regalia (you may encounter a
much-published picture of this meeting
while in Bangkok). The first meeting of the
Thai parliament was held in the building before being moved to a facility nearby.

RAMA V MEMORIAL MONUMENT
Map p257 (พระบรมรูปทรงม้า; Th U Thong Nai;
Ⓢ Phaya Thai exit 3 & taxi) The bronze figure
on horseback is Rama V, the monarch widely credited for steering the country into the
modern age and for preserving Thailand's
independence from European colonialism.
He is also considered a champion of the
common people for his abolition of slav-
ery and corvée (the requirement that every
citizen be available for state labour when
called). The statue is also the site of a huge
celebration on 23 October, the anniversary
of the monarch's death.

DUSIT ZOO ZOO
Map p257 (สวนสัตว์ดุสิต (เขาดิน); Th Ratchawithi;
adult/child 100/50B; ⊘8am-6pm; Ⓢ Phaya Thai
exit 3 & taxi) Originally a private botanic
garden for Rama V, Dusit Zoo (*sŏo·an sàt
dùsìt* or *kŏw din*) was opened in 1938 and
is now one of the premier zoological facilities in Southeast Asia. Squeezed into the 19
hectares are more than 300 mammals, 200
reptiles and 800 birds, including relatively
rare indigenous species. The shady grounds
feature trees labelled in English, plus a lake
in the centre with paddle boats for rent.

CHITLADA PALACE NOTABLE BUILDING
Map p257 (พระราชวังจิตรลดา; cnr Th Ratchawithi
& Th Phra Ram V; ⊘closed to the public; Ⓢ Phaya
Thai exit 3 & taxi) Formerly the current royal
family's official residence (at time of writing the king was in hospital), Chitlada
Palace is also a royally funded agriculture
centre demonstrating the reigning king's
commitment to the progress of the country's major industry. The palace is not open
to the general public and it's pretty difficult
to see from the outside, but you can spot
rice paddies and animal pastures – smack
in the middle of Bangkok – through the perimeter fence.

NATIONAL LIBRARY LIBRARY
Map p257 (Th Samsen; ⊘9am-6.30pm Mon-Fri, to
5pm Sat & Sun; 🚤 Tha Thewet) FREE The country's largest repository of books has few
foreign-language resources, but its strength

KICK BOXING

More formally known as Phahuyut (from the Pali-Sanskrit *bhahu* or 'arm' and *yodha* or 'combat'), Thailand's ancient martial art of *moo·ay tai* (Thai boxing) is one of the kingdom's most striking national icons. Overflowing with colour and ceremony as well as exhilarating moments of clenched-teeth action, the best matches serve up a blend of such skill and tenacity that one is tempted to view the spectacle as emblematic of Thailand's centuries-old devotion to independence in a region where most other countries fell under the European colonial yoke.

Many martial-arts aficionados agree that *moo·ay tai* is the most efficient, effective and generally unbeatable form of ring-centred, hand-to-hand combat practised today. According to legend, it has been for a while. After the Siamese were defeated at Ayuthaya in 1767, several expert *moo·ay boh·rahn* (from which *moo·ay tai* is derived) fighters were among the prisoners hauled off to Burma. A few years later a festival was held; one of the Thai fighters, Nai Khanom Tom, was ordered to take on prominent Burmese boxers for the entertainment of the king and to determine which martial art was most effective. He promptly dispatched nine opponents in a row and, as legend has it, was offered money or beautiful women as a reward; he promptly took two new wives. Today a *moo·ay tai* festival in Ayuthaya is named after Nai Khanom Tom.

Unlike some martial disciplines, such as kung fu or *qi gong, moo·ay tai* doesn't entertain the idea that martial-arts techniques can be passed only from master to disciple in secret. Thus the *moo·ay tai* knowledge base hasn't fossilised – in fact, it remains ever open to innovation, refinement and revision. Thai champion Dieselnoi, for example, created a new approach to knee strikes that was so difficult to defend that he retired at 23 because no one dared to fight him anymore.

Another famous *moo·ay tai* champion is Parinya Kiatbusaba, aka Nong Thoom, a *gà·teu·i* (transgender person) from Chiang Mai who arrived for weigh-ins wearing lipstick and rouge. After a 1998 triumph at Lumphini, Parinya used the prize money to pay for sex-change surgery; in 2003 the movie *Beautiful Boxer* was made about her life.

While Bangkok has long attracted foreign fighters, it wasn't until 1999 that French fighter Mourad Sari became the first non-Thai fighter to take home a weight-class championship belt from a Bangkok stadium. Several Thai *nák moo·ay* (fighters) have gone on to triumph in world championships in international-style boxing. Khaosai Galaxy, one of the greatest Asian boxers of all time, successfully defended his World Boxing Association super-flyweight world title 19 times before retiring in 1991.

is in its astrological books and star charts; the collection also holds recordings by the king, sacred palm-leaf writings and ancient maps.

✖ EATING

Thewet's workaday vibe and Dusit's nearly restaurant-free avenues mean that Thai is virtually the only option in this part of town. For a bit more culinary diversity, head to adjacent Banglamphu.

 LIKHIT KAI YANG NORTHEASTERN THAI **$**

Map p257 (off Th Ratchadamnoen Nok; mains 30-150B; ◷10am-10pm; ✳; ☒klorng boat to Tha Phan Fah) Located just behind Ratchadamoen Stadium (avoid the rather grotty

branch directly next door to the stadium), this decades-old restaurant is where locals come for a quick northeastern Thai–style meal before a Thai boxing match. The friendly English-speaking owner will coach you through the ordering process, but don't miss the deliciously herbal grilled chicken.

NANG LOENG MARKET THAI **$**

Map p257 (btwn Soi 8-10, Th Nakhon Sawan; mains 30-80B; ◷10am-2pm Mon-Sat; ☒klorng boat to Tha Phan Fah, ⓢPhaya Thai exit 3 & taxi) Dating back to 1899, this atmospheric fresh market offers a wonderful glimpse of old Bangkok, not to mention a great place to grab a bite. Nang Loeng is renowned for its Thai sweets, and at lunchtime is also an excellent place to fill up on savouries. Try a bowl of handmade egg noodles at **Rung Rueng**

THEWET & DUSIT EATING

or the wonderful curries across the way at **Ratana**.

KALOANG HOME KITCHEN THAI $

Map p257 (Th Si Ayuthaya; mains 60-170B; 🕒11am-11pm; ⛴Tha Thewet) Don't be alarmed by the peeling paint and dilapidated deck – the owners at Kaloang Home Kitchen certainly aren't. The laid-back atmosphere and seafood-heavy menu will quickly dispel any concerns about sinking into Mae Nam Chao Phraya, and a beer and the breeze will temporarily erase any scarring memories of Bangkok traffic. To reach the restaurant, follow the final windy stretch of Th Si Ayuthaya all the way to the river.

★KRUA APSORN THAI $$

Map p257 (www.kruaapsorn.com; 503-505 Th Samsen; mains 65-350B; 🕒10.30am-7.30pm Mon-Fri, to 6pm Sat; ❄; ⛴Tha Thewet) This is the original branch of this homey, award-winning and royally patronised restaurant. Expect a clientele made up of fussy families and big-haired, middle-aged ladies, and a cuisine revolving around full-flavoured, largely seafood- and vegetable-heavy central Thai dishes. If you have dinner in mind, be sure to note the early closing times.

STEVE CAFÉ & CUISINE THAI $$

Map p257 (www.stevecafeandcuisine.com; 68 Soi 21, Th Si Ayuthaya; mains 160-390B; 🕒11.30am-2.30pm Mon-Fri, 11.30am-11pm Sat & Sun; ⛴Tha Thewet) The cheesy name is seemingly a cover for this sophisticated, house-bound, riverside Thai restaurant. The menu spans a good selection of Thai dishes, with an emphasis on those from the country's south, and service is friendly and efficient, even when the place is mobbed.

To get here, enter Th Si Ayuthaya and walk through Wat Thevaratkunchong until you reach the river; locals will help point the way.

KHINLOM CHOM SA-PHAN THAI $$

Map p257 (☎0 2628 8382; www.khinlom-chomsaphan.com; 11/6 Soi 3, Th Samsen; mains 75-280B; 🕒11am-2am; ⛴Tha Thewet) Locals come here for the combination of riverfront views and tasty, seafood-based eats. It's popular, so be sure to call ahead to book a riverfront table.

🍷 DRINKING & NIGHTLIFE

There's very little – almost nothing, really – in terms of nightlife in this part of town. Luckily, Banglamphu and Th Khao San are a brief taxi ride away. Alternatively, the riverside restaurants also function as open-air bars.

RIVER BAR CAFÉ BAR, RESTAURANT

Map p257 (405/1 Soi Chao Phraya; 🕒5pm-midnight; ⛴Tha Saphan Krung Thon) Sporting a picture-perfect riverside location, good food and live music, River Bar Café combines all the essentials of a perfect Bangkok night out. Grab a table closest to the river to fully take advantage of the breeze, as well as to avoid noise fallout from the sometimes overly enthusiastic bands.

POST BAR BAR

Map p257 (Th Samsen; 🕒5pm-1am; ⛴Tha Thewet) If 'Chinese pawn shop' can be considered a legitimate design theme, Post Bar has nailed it. The walls of this narrow, shophouse-bound bar are decked with retro Thai kitsch; the soundtrack is appropriately classic rock; and the clientele overwhelmingly Thai.

☆ ENTERTAINMENT

RATCHADAMNOEN STADIUM SPORTS

Map p257 (off Th Ratchadamnoen Nok; tickets 3rd-class/2nd-class/ringside 1000/1500/2000B; ⛴klorng boat to Tha Phan Fah, [S]Phaya Thai exit 3 & taxi) Ratchadamnoen Stadium, Bangkok's oldest and most venerable venue for *moo·ay tai* (Thai boxing; also spelt *muay thai*), hosts matches on Monday, Wednesday, Thursday and Sunday from 6pm to around 11pm. Be sure to buy tickets from the official ticket counter, not from the touts and scalpers who hang around outside the entrance.

Chinatown

Neighbourhood Top Five

1 Dining al fresco at decades-old street food stalls such as **Nai Mong Hoi Thod** (p100).

2 Witnessing 5.5 tonnes of solid gold Buddha at **Wat Traimit** (p97).

3 Checking out the oil-stained machine shops, hidden Chinese temples and twisting lanes of **Talat Noi** (p98).

4 Watching chaos and commerce battle it out in **Talat Mai** (p98), China-town's hectic yet photogenic fresh-food market.

5 Enjoying Bollywood-style markets and the city's cheapest and best Indian food in **Phahurat** (p98).

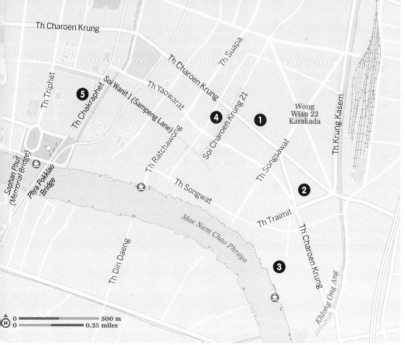

For more detail of this area see Map p258 ➡

Lonely Planet's Top Tip

Most of Bangkok's street-food vendors close up shop on Monday, so don't plan on eating in Chinatown on this day.

✕ Best Places to Eat

➤ Nai Mong Hoi Thod (p100)

➤ Samsara (p101)

➤ Th Phadungdao Seafood Stalls (p101)

➤ Royal India (p101)

For reviews, see p101.

🔒 Best Markets

➤ Talat Mai (p98)

➤ Pak Khlong Talat (Flower Market; p98)

➤ Flashlight Market (p98)

➤ Sampeng Lane (p99)

For reviews, see p102. ➡

⊙ Best Temples & Churches

➤ Wat Traimit (p97)

➤ Wat Mangkon Kamalawat (p98)

➤ Church of Santa Cruz (p99)

➤ Holy Rosary Church (p99)

For reviews, see p98. ➡

Explore: Chinatown

Chinatown embodies everything that's hectic, noisy and polluted about Bangkok, but that's what makes it so fascinating. The big sights – namely Wat Traimit and the street markets – are worth hitting, but be sure to set aside enough time to do some map-free wandering among the neon-lit gold shops, hidden temples, crumbling shopfronts and pencil-thin alleys, especially the tiny winding lanes that extend from Soi Wanit 1 (aka Sampeng Lane).

For ages, Chinatown was home to Bangkok's most infamous traffic jams, but the arrival of the MRT (Metro) in 2005 finally made the area a sane place to visit. Still, the station is about a kilometre from many sights, so you'll have to take a longish walk or a short taxi ride. An alternative is to take the Chao Phraya Express boat to the stop at Tha Ratchawong, from where it's a brief walk to most restaurants and a bit further to most sights.

The whole district is buzzing from dawn until after dusk, but Chinatown is at its best during these two times. The best time to eat is from 7pm to 9pm, as there aren't many interesting lunch options in the area.

Local Life

➤**Street Food** Although it's dominated by restaurants serving shark-fin and bird's nest soup, the true Chinatown meal is what's prepared by the street vendors that line Th Yaowarat after dark. Locals come from all over Bangkok to eat at Chinatown's stalls, and so should you.

➤**Markets** Phahurat (p98) and Chinatown districts have interconnected markets selling fabrics, clothes and household wares, as well as shops for every imaginable bulk item and a few places selling gems and jewellery.

➤**Living on a Prayer** In many Chinatown temples you'll see locals shaking cans of thin sticks called *seeam see*. When a stick falls to the floor, look at its number and find the corresponding paper that gives a no-nonsense appraisal of your future in Thai, Chinese and English.

➤**Nightlife** Or should we say, lack thereof… Other than River Vibe (p101) or Cotton (p102), there's zilch in the realm of non-dodgy nightlife in Bangkok's Chinatown. Instead, fuel up on street eats here first, then head to nearby Banglamphu or Silom for drinks.

Getting There & Away

➤**MRT** Hua Lamphong.

➤**River boat** Tha Marine Department, Tha Ratchawong, Tha Saphan Phut (Memorial Bridge).

➤**Bus** Air-con 507 and 508; ordinary 1, 4, 25, 33, 37, 49 and 53.

TOP SIGHT
WAT TRAIMIT (GOLDEN BUDDHA)

Wat Traimit, also known as the Temple of the Golden Buddha, is home to the world's largest gold statue, a gleaming, 3m-tall, 5.5-tonne Buddha with a mysterious past and a current value of more than US$40 million in gold alone. Sculpted in the graceful Sukhothai style, the image is thought to date from around the late 15th century. But if it is possible for a Buddha to lead a double life, then this priceless piece has most certainly done so.

Possibly sometime in the 17th century, at what is thought to have been a time of great danger to the Siamese kingdom – presumably prior to an invasion from Burma – the Buddha was rendered with a plaster exterior in an attempt to disguise it from the looting hordes. And it worked. After various assaults, the Burmese hauled off vast quantities of Thai treasure, but this most valuable of all Buddha images – indeed, the most valuable in all of Buddhism – remained as shabby-looking and anonymous as intended. It was moved first to Bangkok and later to Wat Traimit, the only temple in the Chinatown area modest enough to take such a world-weary Buddha. And thus it remained, beneath a tin roof, until the mid-1950s, when the temple had collected enough money to build a proper shelter for the image. During the move the Buddha was dropped from a crane, an act of such ill fortune that the workers are said to have downed tools and run. When the abbot inspected the Buddha the following day he found the plaster had cracked and, after centuries of anonymity, the golden Buddha's true identity was finally revealed.

The image remained seated in its modest pavilion until 2009, smiling benevolently down upon an underwhelming and seemingly endless procession of tour groups, which seem to have scared off most of the genuine worshippers. But Wat Traimit's days of poverty are long gone. A new marble hall has been built with a combination of Chinese-style balustrades and a steep, golden Thai-style roof. Surrounding it is a narrow strip of grass watered via mist fountains.

The 2nd floor of the structure is home to the **Phra Buddha Maha Suwanna Patimakorn Exhibition** (admission 100B; ☺8am-5pm Tue-Sun), which has exhibits on how the statue was made, discovered and came to arrive at its current home, while the 3rd floor is home to the **Yaowarat Chinatown Heritage Center** (admission 100B; ☺8am-5pm Tue-Sun), a small but engaging museum with multimedia exhibits on the history of Bangkok's Chinatown and its residents.

DON'T MISS...

➡ The Golden Buddha
➡ Phra Buddha Maha Suwanna Patimakorn Exhibition
➡ Yaowarat Chinatown Heritage Center

PRACTICALITIES

➡ วัดไตรมิตร, Temple of the Golden Buddha
➡ Map p258
➡ Th Mitthaphap (Th Traimit)
➡ admission 40B
➡ ☺8am-5pm
➡ 🚢Tha Ratchawong, Ⓜ Hua Lamphong exit 1

 SIGHTS

WAT TRAIMIT
(GOLDEN BUDDHA)   BUDDHIST TEMPLE
See p97.

TALAT MAI   MARKET
Map p258 (ตลาดใหม่; Soi Charoen Krung 16 (Trok Itsaranuphap), Soi 6, Th Yaowarat; ⏱6am-6pm; 🚤Tha Ratchawong, Ⓜ Hua Lamphong exit 1 & taxi) With nearly two centuries of commerce under its belt, 'New Market' is no longer an entirely accurate name for this strip of commerce. Regardless, this is Bangkok's, if not Thailand's, most Chinese market, and the dried goods, seasonings, spices and sauces will be familiar to anyone who's ever spent time in China. Yet even if you're not interested in food, the hectic atmosphere (be on guard for the motorcycles that squeeze between shoppers) and exotic sights and smells culminate in something of a surreal sensory experience.

While much of the market centres on cooking ingredients, the section north of Th Charoen Krung (equivalent to Soi 21, Th Charoen Krung) is known for selling incense, paper effigies and ceremonial sweets – the essential elements of a traditional Chinese funeral.

TALAT NOI   NEIGHBOURHOOD
Map p258 (ตลาดน้อย; ⏱7am-7pm; 🚤Tha Marine Department) This microcosm of soi life is named after a small (nóy) market (dà-làht) that sets up between Soi 22 and Soi 20, off Th Charoen Krung. Wandering here you'll find streamlike soi turning in on themselves, weaving through people's living rooms, noodle shops and grease-stained machine shops. Opposite the River View Guesthouse, **San Jao Sien Khong** (ศาลเจ้าเซียนโค้ง; Map p258; ⏱6am-6pm) FREE is one of the city's oldest Chinese shrines, and is guarded by a playful rooftop terracotta dragon; it's one of the best places to come during the yearly Vegetarian Festival.

PHAHURAT   NEIGHBOURHOOD
Map p258 (พาหุรัด; Th Chakraphet; ⏱9am-5pm; 🚤Tha Saphan Phut, Memorial Bridge) Heaps of South Asian traders set up shop in this small but bustling Little India, where everything from Bollywood movies to bindis is sold by enthusiastic, small-time traders.

The emphasis is on cloth, and Phahurat proffers boisterously coloured textiles, traditional Thai dance costumes, tiaras, sequins, wigs and other accessories to make you look like a cross-dresser, a mŏr lam (Thai country music) performer, or both. Amid the spectacle of colour there are also good deals on machine-made Thai textiles and children's clothes.

Behind the more obvious storefronts are winding alleys that criss-cross Khlong Ong Ang, where merchants grab a bite to eat or make travel arrangements for trips home. It's a great area to just wander through, stopping for masala chai or lassi as you go.

PAK KHLONG TALAT   MARKET
Map p258 (ปากคลองตลาด, Flower Market; Th Chakraphet; ⏱24hr; 🚤Tha Saphan Phut, Memorial Bridge) This sprawling wholesale flower market has become a tourist attraction in its own right. The endless piles of delicate orchids, rows of roses and stacks of button carnations are a sight to be seen, and the shirtless porters wheeling blazing piles of colour set the place in motion. The best time to come is late at night, when the goods arrive from upcountry.

WAT MANGKON
KAMALAWAT   BUDDHIST TEMPLE
Map p258 (วัดมังกรกมลาวาส; cnr Th Charoen Krung & Th Mangkon; ⏱6am-6pm; 🚤Tha Ratchawong, Ⓜ Hua Lamphong exit 1 & taxi) FREE Explore the cryptlike sermon halls of this busy Chinese temple (also known as Leng Noi Yee) to find Buddhist, Taoist and Confucian shrines. During the annual Vegetarian Festival, religious and culinary activities are centred here. But almost any time of day or night this temple is busy with worshippers lighting incense, filling the ever-burning altar lamps with oil and making offerings to their ancestors.

Offering oil is believed to provide a smooth journey into the afterlife and to fuel the fire of the present life. Surrounding the temple are vendors selling food for the gods – steamed lotus-shaped dumplings and oranges – which are donated to the temple in exchange for merit.

FLASHLIGHT MARKET   MARKET
Map p258 (ตลาดไฟฉาย; cnr Th Phlap Phla Chai & Th Luang; ⏱5am Sat-5pm Sun; 🚤Tha Ratchawong, Ⓜ Hua Lamphong exit 1 & taxi) This street market extends west from the Phlap Phla Chai intersection, forging a trail of antiques, secondhand items and sometimes, well, just plain junk along the area's footpaths. It's at its busiest on Saturday night,

when a flashlight (torch) is needed to see many of the goods for sale.

CHURCH OF SANTA CRUZ CHURCH
Map p258 (โบสถ์สังตาครูส; Soi Kuti Jiin; ☉7am-noon Sat & Sun; ⛴river-crossing ferry from Tha Pak Talat, Atsadang) FREE Centuries before Sukhumvit became Bangkok's international district, the Portuguese claimed *fa·ràng* (Western) supremacy and built the Church of Santa Cruz in the 1700s. The land was a gift from King Taksin in appreciation for the loyalty the Portuguese community had displayed after the fall of Ayuthaya. The surviving church dates to 1913.

Very little activity occurs on the grounds itself, but small and fascinating village streets break off from the main courtyard into the area known as Kuti Jiin, the local name for the church. On Soi Kuti Jiin 3, several houses sell Portuguese-inspired cakes and sweets.

SAMPENG LANE MARKET
Map p258 (สำเพ็ง; Soi Wanit 1 (Sampeng Lane); ☉8am-6pm; ⛴Tha Ratchawong, Ⓜ Hua Lamphong exit 1 & taxi) Sampeng Lane is a narrow artery running parallel to Th Yaowarat and bisecting the commercial areas of Chinatown and Phahurat. The Chinatown portion is lined with wholesale shops of hair accessories, pens, stickers, household wares and beeping, flashing knick-knacks. Near Th Chakrawat, gem and jewellery shops abound. Weekends are horribly crowded, and it takes a gymnast's flexibility to squeeze past the pushcarts, motorcycles and other roadblocks.

SAPHAN PHUT NIGHT BAZAAR MARKET
Map p258 (ตลาดนัดสะพานพุทธ; Th Saphan Phut; ☉8pm-midnight Tue-Sun; ⛴Tha Saphan Phut, Memorial Bridge) On the Bangkok side of Tha Saphan Phut, this night market has bucketloads of cheap clothes, late-night snacking and a lot of people-watching. As Chatuchak Weekend Market (p147) becomes more design-orientated, Saphan Phut has begun filling the closets of fashion-forward, baht-challenged teenagers.

HOLY ROSARY CHURCH CHURCH
Map p258 (วัดแม่พระลูกประคำกาลหว่าร์; Th Yotha; ☉Mass 7.30pm Mon-Sat, 8am, 10am & 7.30pm Sun; ⛴Tha Marine Department) FREE Portuguese seafarers were among the first Europeans to establish diplomatic ties with Siam, and their influence in the kingdom was rewarded with prime riverside estate. When a Portuguese contingent moved across the river to the present-day Talat Noi area of Chinatown in 1787, they were given this piece of land and built the Holy Rosary Church, known in Thai as Wat Kalawan, from the Portuguese 'Calvario'.

Over the years the Portuguese community dispersed and the church fell into disrepair. However, Vietnamese and Cambodian Catholics displaced by the Indochina wars adopted it, and together with Chinese speakers now constitute much of the parish. Of particular note are the splendid Romanesque stained-glass windows, gilded ceilings and a Christ statue that is carried through the streets during Easter celebrations.

HUALAMPHONG
TRAIN STATION HISTORICAL BUILDING
Map p258 (สถานีรถไฟหัวลำโพง; off Th Phra Ram IV; Ⓜ Hua Lamphong exit 2) At the southeastern edge of Chinatown, Bangkok's main train station was built by Dutch architects and engineers between 1910 and 1916.

Above the 14 platforms it was designed in a neoclassical style by Italian architect-and-engineer combination Mario Tamagno and Annibale Rigotti, who were working at the same time on the grand Ananta Samakhom Throne Hall (p92) at Dusit. It also embraces other influences, such as the patterned, two-toned skylights that exemplify nascent De Stijl Dutch modernism – it is through these that it is known as an early example of the shift towards Thai art deco. If you can zone out of the chaos for a moment, look for the vaulted iron roof and neoclassical portico, which were a state-of-the-art engineering feat.

GURDWARA SIRI GURU
SINGH SABHA TEMPLE
Map p258 (พระศาสนสถานคุรุดววารา; off Th Chakraphet; ☉9am-5pm; ⛴Tha Saphan Phut, Memorial Bridge) FREE Just off Th Chakraphet is this gold-domed Sikh temple. Basically it's a large hall, somewhat reminiscent of a mosque interior, devoted to the worship of the Guru Granth Sahib, the 17th-century Sikh holy book, which is itself considered the last of the religion's 10 great gurus.

Prasada (blessed food offered to Hindu or Sikh temple attendees) is distributed among devotees every morning around 9am, and if you arrive on a Sikh festival day you can partake in the *langar* (communal

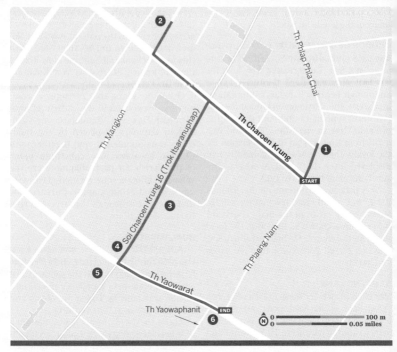

🏃 Neighbourhood Walk
A Taste of Chinatown

START CNR TH PLAENG NAM & TH CHAROEN KRUNG
END CNR TH YAOWAPHANIT & TH YAOWARAT
LENGTH APPROXIMATELY 1KM; TWO TO THREE HOURS

Street food rules in Chinatown, making the area ideal for a culinary adventure. Although many vendors stay open late, the more popular stalls tend to sell out quickly, so the best time to feast in this area is from 7pm to 9pm. Don't try this walk on a Monday, when most of the city's street vendors stay at home. Bringing a friend (or three) and sharing is a good way to ensure that you can try as many dishes as possible.

Start your walk at the intersection of Th Plaeng Nam and Th Charoen Krung. Head north along Th Phlap Phla Chai, staying on the right-hand side for about 50m, until you reach ❶ **Nai Mong Hoi Thod**, a shop-house restaurant renowned for its delicious *or sòo·an* (oysters fried with egg and a sticky batter).

Backtrack to Th Charoen Krung and turn right. On reaching Th Mangkon make a right; on your left-hand side you'll see ❷ **Jek Pui**, a table-less stall famous for its Chinese-style Thai curries.

Cross Th Charoen Krung again, turn left, and continue east until you reach Soi Charoen Krung 16 (Trok Itsaranuphap), also known as ❸ **Talat Mai** (p98), the area's most famous strip of commerce. At the end of the alley you'll see a gentleman making ❹ **gŏo·ay dĕe·o kôo·a gài**, rice noodles fried with chicken, egg and garlic oil.

Upon emerging at Th Yaowarat, cross over to the busy market area directly across the street. The first vendor on the right, ❺ **Nay Leek Uan**, sells *gŏo·ay jáp nám săi*, an intensely peppery broth containing noodles and pork offal.

Returning back to Th Yaowarat, turn right and continue until the next intersection. On the corner of Th Yaowaphanit and Th Yaowarat you'll see ❻ **Mangkorn Khao**, a stall selling *bà·mèe* (Chinese-style wheat noodles) and barbecued pork.

Sikh meal) served in the temple. If you do visit this shrine, be sure to climb to the top for panoramic views of Chinatown. Stores surrounding the temple sell assorted religious paraphernalia.

original – become a culinary train wreck of outdoor barbecues, screaming staff, iced seafood trays and messy sidewalk seating. True, the vast majority of diners are foreign tourists, but this has little impact on the cheerful setting, the fun experience and the cheap bill.

EATING

OLD SIAM PLAZA
THAI SWEETS **$**

Map p258 (cnr Th Phahurat & Th Triphet; mains 30-90B; ◷6am-7pm; ❄; ⛴Tha Saphan Phut, Memorial Bridge) Sugar junkies, be sure to include this stop on your Bangkok eating itinerary. The ground floor of this shopping centre is a candy land of traditional Thai sweets and snacks, most made right before your eyes.

SAMSARA
JAPANESE, THAI **$$**

Map p258 (1612 Th Songwat; mains 110-320B; ◷4pm-midnight Tue-Thu, to 1am Fri-Sun; ✐; ⛴Tha Ratchawong, ⛟Hua Lamphong exit 1 & taxi) Combining Japanese-Thai dishes, Belgian beers and a retro/artsy atmosphere, Samsara is easily Chinatown's most eclectic place to eat. It's also very tasty, and the generous riverside breezes and views simply add to the package. The restaurant is at the end of tiny Soi Khang Wat Pathum Khongkha, just west of the temple of the same name.

THANON PHADUNGDAO
SEAFOOD STALLS
THAI **$$**

Map p258 (cnr Th Phadungdao & Th Yaowarat; mains 100-600B; ◷4pm-midnight Tue-Sun; ⛴Tha Ratchawong, ⛟Hua Lamphong exit 1 & taxi) After sunset, these two opposing open-air restaurants – each of which claims to be the

ROYAL INDIA
INDIAN **$$**

Map p258 (392/1 Th Chakraphet; mains 70-195B; ◷10am-10pm; ❄ ✐; ⛴Tha Saphan Phut, Memorial Bridge) A windowless dining room of 10 tables in a dark alley may not be everybody's ideal lunch destination, but this legendary north Indian place continues to draw foodies despite the lack of aesthetics. Try any of the delicious breads or saucy curries, and finish with a house-made Punjabi sweet.

HUA SENG HONG
CHINESE **$$$**

Map p258 (371-373 Th Yaowarat; mains 100-1050B; ◷9am-1am; ❄; ⛴Tha Ratchawong, ⛟Hua Lamphong exit 1 & taxi) Shark-fin soup may draw heaps of Asian tourists into this place, but Hua Seng Hong's varied menu, which includes dim sum, braised goose feet and noodles, makes it a handy destination for anybody craving Chinese.

 DRINKING & NIGHTLIFE

RIVER VIBE
BAR

Map p258 (8th fl, River View Guest House, 768 Soi Phanurangsi, Th Songwat; ◷7.30-11pm; ⛴Tha Marine Department, ⛟Hua Lamphong exit 1 & taxi) Can't afford the drinks at Bangkok's upscale rooftop bars? The excellent river

LOCAL KNOWLEDGE

CHINATOWN VEGETARIAN FESTIVAL

During the annual Vegetarian Festival in September/October, Bangkok's Chinatown becomes a virtual orgy of nonmeat cuisine. The festivities centre on Chinatown's main street, Th Yaowarat, and the Talat Noi (p98) area, but food shops and stalls all over the city post yellow flags to announce their meat-free status.

Celebrating alongside the ethnic Chinese are Thais who look forward to the special dishes that appear during the festival period. Most restaurants put their normal menus on hold and instead prepare soy-based substitutes for standard Thai dishes like *dôm yam* and *gaang kĕe·o wăhn* (green curry). Even Thai regional cuisines are sold (without the meat, of course). Yellow Hokkien-style noodles often make an appearance in the special festival dishes, usually in stir-fried dishes along with meaty mushrooms and big hunks of vegetables.

Along with abstinence from meat, the 10-day festival is celebrated with special visits to the temple, often requiring worshippers to dress in white.

CHINATOWN'S SHOPPING STREETS

Chinatown is the neighbourhood version of a big-box store divided up into categories of consumerables.

Th Charoen Krung Chinatown's primary thoroughfare is a prestigious address. Starting on the western end of the street, near the intersection of Th Mahachai, is a collection of old record stores. **Talat Khlong Ong Ang** (Map p258; ⊛Tha Ratchawong, ⓂHua Lamphong exit 1 & taxi) consumes the next block, selling all sorts of used and new electronic gadgets. **Nakhon Kasem** (Map p258; ⊘8am-8pm; ⊛Tha Saphan Phut) is the reformed thieves' market where vendors now stock up on nifty gadgets for portable food prep. Further east, near Th Mahachak, is **Talat Khlong Thom** (Map p258; ⊛Tha Ratchawong, ⓂHua Lamphong exit 1 & taxi), a hardware centre. West of Th Ratchawong is everything you'd need to give a Chinese funeral.

Th Yaowarat A hundred years ago this was a poultry farm; now it's gold street, the biggest trading centre of the precious metal in the country. Along Th Yaowarat, gold is sold by the *bàht* (a unit of weight equivalent to 15g) from neon-lit storefronts that look more like shrines than shops. Near the intersection of Th Ratchawong, stores shift to Chinese and Singaporean tourists' tastes: dried fruit and nuts, chintzy talismans and accoutrements for Chinese festivals. The multistorey buildings around here were some of Bangkok's first skyscrapers and a source of wonder for the local people. Bangkok's skyline has grown and grown, but this area retains a few Chinese apothecaries, smelling of wood bark and ancient secrets.

Th Mittraphan (Map p258) Sign-makers branch off Wong Wian 22 Karakada, near Wat Traimit and the Golden Buddha; Thai and Roman letters are typically cut out by a hand-guided lathe placed prominently beside the pavement.

Th Santiphap (Map p258) Car parts and other automotive gear make this the place for kicking tyres.

Sampeng Lane (p99) Plastic cuteness in bulk, from pencil cases to pens, stuffed animals, hair flotsam and enough bling to kit out a rap video – it all hangs out near the eastern end of the alley.

Talat Mai (p98) This ancient produce market splays along the cramped alley between Th Yaowarat and Th Charoen Krung.

views from the top of this guesthouse will hardly feel like a compromise. We suggest getting dinner elsewhere, though.

⭐ ENTERTAINMENT

COTTON   LIVE MUSIC
Map p258 (www.cotton.shanghaimansion.com; 3rd fl, Shanghai Mansion, 479-481 Th Yaowarat; ⊘live music 6.30-10.30pm; ⊛Tha Ratchawong, ⓂHua Lamphong exit 1 & taxi) Walk through a bland restaurant to this cosy Chinatown-themed lounge in the Shanghai Mansion hotel. Virtually the only non-karaoke-based place of

entertainment in Chinatown, it has smooth acoustic jazz and affordable cocktails.

SALA CHALERMKRUNG   THEATRE
Map p258 (⌇0 2222 0434; www.salachalerm krung.com; 66 Th Charoen Krung; tickets 800-1200B; ⊘shows 7.30pm Thu & Fri; ⊛Tha Saphan Phut (Memorial Bridge), ⓂHua Lamphong exit 1 & taxi) This art deco Bangkok landmark, a former cinema dating to 1933, is one of the few remaining places *kŏhn* can be witnessed. The traditional Thai dance-drama is enhanced here by laser graphics, high-tech audio and English subtitles. Concerts and other events are also held; check the website for details.

Siam Square, Pratunam, Ploenchit & Ratchathewi

Neighbourhood Top Five

1 Visiting **Jim Thompson House** (p105) – the teak mansion that put Thai style on the map... before its ex-spy owner disappeared off that map.

2 Shopping at the malls, department stores and shops that surround Siam Square, such as **MBK Center** (p113).

3 Exploring **Baan Krua** (p106), the canal-side Muslim village where Jim Thompson first encountered Thai silk.

4 Making a wish at the crossroads of commerce and faith that is the **Erawan Shrine** (p106).

5 Enjoying the luxury of what must be one of the world's best-value cinemas, **Paragon Cineplex** (p111).

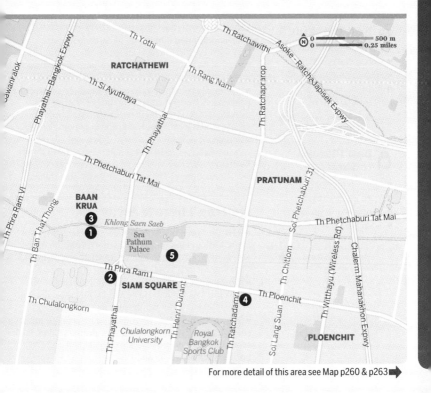

For more detail of this area see Map p260 & p263 ➡

Lonely Planet's Top Tip

Admittedly, they tend to have all the ambience of a hospital cafeteria, but the mall-based food courts that abound in this part of town are among the most user-friendly introductions to Thai food in Bangkok. They're generally clean and convenient, and also have the benefit of having English-language menus, so ordering is a snap.

✗ Best Places to Eat

➡ MBK Food Island (p110)

➡ Nuer Koo (p109)

➡ Crystal Jade La Mian Xiao Long Bao (p109)

➡ Mallika Restaurant (p111)

For reviews, see p109.➡

🍷 Best Drinking & Entertainment

➡ Co-Co Walk (p111)

➡ Hyde & Seek (p112)

➡ Saxophone Pub & Restaurant (p113)

For reviews, see p111.➡

🔒 Best Places to Shop

➡ MBK Center (p113)

➡ Siam Square (p115)

➡ CentralWorld (p115)

➡ Siam Paragon (p115)

➡ Pratunam Market (p115)

For reviews, see p113.➡

SIAM SQUARE, PRATUNAM, PLOENCHIT & RATCHATHEWI

Explore: Siam Square, Pratunam, Ploenchit & Ratchathewi

Siam Square, Pratunam and Ploenchit combine to form the de facto geographical and commercial centre of modern Bangkok. Huge air-conditioned malls, towering hotels, international fast-food chains and open-air shopping centres dominate this area, and if you're serious about shopping, set aside the better part of a day to burn your baht here. Try to arrive around 11am, when the crowds are minimal. Likewise, try to avoid Sundays when much of Bangkok seems to flock to the area's air-conditioned malls. Siam Square is most easily accessed via the BTS (Skytrain), and if you're going to hit all the area's malls, it makes the most sense to start at National Stadium and work your way east, taking advantage of the bridges, mall corridors and elevated walkways that link the various shopping centres.

Ratchathewi has a lot less to offer – unless you have a specific sight in mind or simply want to check out a more workaday side of Bangkok. The attractions in this area can be covered in a couple hours, and most are within walking distance of the BTS stop at Victory Monument.

Local Life

➡**Mall-hopping** On Sunday a significant part of Bangkok's population is drawn to this area's malls to socialise in stylish settings and air-con comfort.

➡**Air-conditioned dining** A mall-based food court may not seem like the most authentic place to eat, but several of Bangkok's most famous restaurants and stalls maintain branches at the various Siam Sq area malls.

➡**Wholesale retail** For local penny-pinchers and visiting wholesalers the ultimate destination is Pratunam district, where a seemingly never-ending clothing bazaar stocks locally made and cheap import clothes.

➡**Keeping it real** For a view of Bangkok without malls, cupcake bakeries, fashionistas and tourists, take the BTS north to the Victory Monument in Ratchathewi, where you'll find ordinary Thais doing ordinary Thai things.

Getting There & Away

➡**BTS** To Siam Square, Pratunam and Ploenchit: Siam, National Stadium, Chit Lom, Phloen Chit and Ratchadamri. To Ratchathewi: Ratchathewi, Phaya Thai and Victory Monument.

➡**Klorng boat** To Siam Square, Pratunam and Ploenchit: Tha Saphan Hua Chang, Tha Pratunam and Tha Witthayu. To Ratchathewi: Tha Pratunam.

➡**Bus** To Siam Square, Pratunam and Ploenchit: air-con 141, 183, 204, 501, 508 and 547; ordinary 15, 16, 25, 47 and 73. To Ratchathewi: air-con 503, 513 and 536; ordinary 29, 36, 54, 59 and 112.

TOP SIGHT
JIM THOMPSON HOUSE

In 1959, 12 years after he single-handedly turned Thai silk into a hugely successful export business, American Jim Thompson bought a piece of land next to Khlong Saen Saeb and built himself a house. It wasn't, however, any old house. Thompson's love of all things Thai saw him buy six traditional wooden homes and reconstruct them in his garden. Although he met a mysterious end in 1967, today Thompson's house remains, both as a museum to these unique structures and as a tribute to the man.

The Man

Born in Delaware, USA, in 1906, Jim Thompson served in a forerunner of the CIA in Thailand during WWII. When in 1947 he spotted some silk in a market and was told it was woven in Baan Krua, he found the only place in Bangkok where silk was still woven by hand.

Thompson's Thai silk eventually attracted the interest of fashion houses in New York, Milan, London and Paris, and he gradually built a worldwide clientele for a craft that had, just a few years before, been in danger of dying out.

By 1967 Thai silk had annual sales of almost US$1.5 million. In March that year Thompson went missing while out for an afternoon walk in the Cameron Highlands of western Malaysia; his success as a businessman, background as a spy and the fact that his sister was also murdered in the same year made it an international mystery. Thompson has never been heard from since, but the conspiracy theories have never stopped. Was it communist spies? Business rivals? A man-eating tiger? Although the mystery has never been solved, evidence revealed by American journalist Joshua Kurlantzick in his profile of Thompson, *The Ideal Man,* suggests that the vocal anti-American stance Thompson took later in his life may have made him a potential target of suppression by the CIA.

The House

Traditional Thai homes were multipurpose affairs, with little space for luxuries like separate living and sleeping rooms. Thompson adapted his six buildings, joining some, to create a larger home in which each room had a more familiar Western function. One room became an air-conditioned study, another a bedroom and the one nearest the *klorng* (canal; also spelt *khlong*) his dining room. Another departure from tradition is the way Thompson arranged each wall with its exterior side facing the house's interior, thus exposing the wall's bracing system.

Thompson's small but splendid Asian art collection is also on display in the main house; photography is not allowed inside any of the buildings. After the tour, be sure to poke around the house's jungle-like gardens, which include ponds filled with exotic fish. Recent additions to the compound include the excellent **Jim Thompson Art Center** FREE, a cafe and a shop flogging Jim Thompson–branded goods.

Beware of well-dressed touts in the soi near the Jim Thompson House who will tell you it is closed and then try to haul you off on a dodgy buying spree.

DON'T MISS...

➡ Thompson's art and antique collection

➡ A walk in the jungle-like garden

➡ Jim Thompson Art Center

PRACTICALITIES

➡ Map p260

➡ www.jimthompson house.com

➡ Soi Kasem San 2

➡ adult/child 100/50B

➡ ⏲9am-5pm, compulsory tours in English & French every 20 min

➡ 🚤klorng boat to Tha Saphan Hua Chang, ⬚National Stadium exit 1

SIGHTS

Siam Square, Pratunam & Ploenchit

JIM THOMPSON HOUSE HISTORICAL BUILDING
See p105.

BAAN KRUA NEIGHBOURHOOD
Map p260 (บ้านครัว; ⛴klorng boat to Tha Saphan Hua Chang, [S]National Stadium exit 1) This canal-side neighbourhood is one of Bangkok's oldest communities. It dates back to the turbulent years at the end of the 18th century, when Cham Muslims from Cambodia and Vietnam fought on the side of the new Thai king and were rewarded with this plot of land east of the new capital. The immigrants brought their silk-weaving traditions with them, and the community grew when the residents built Khlong Saen Saeb to better connect them to the river.

The 1950s and '60s were boom years for Baan Krua after Jim Thompson hired the weavers and began exporting their silks across the globe. The last 50 years, however, haven't been so good. Silk production was moved elsewhere following Thompson's disappearance and the community spent 15 years successfully fighting to stop a freeway being built right through it. Through all this many Muslims moved out of the area; today it is estimated that only about 30% of the population is Muslim, the rest primarily immigrants from northeast Thailand. However, Baan Krua retains its Muslim character, and one of the original families is still weaving silk on old teak looms. The village, which is great for self-guided exploration, consists of old, tightly packed homes threaded by tiny paths barely wide enough for two people to pass. It has been described as a slum, but the house-proud residents are keen to point out that they might not live in high-rise condos, but that doesn't make their old community a slum.

ERAWAN SHRINE MONUMENT
Map p260 (ศาลพระพรหม; cnr Th Ratchadamri & Th Ploenchit; ⏲6am-11pm; [S]Chit Lom exit 8) [FREE] The Erawan Shrine was originally built in 1956 as something of a last-ditch effort to end a string of misfortunes that occurred during the construction of a hotel, at that time known as the Erawan Hotel. After several incidents ranging from injured construction workers to the sinking of a ship carrying marble for the hotel, a Brahmin priest was consulted. Since the hotel was to be named after the elephant escort of Indra in Hindu mythology, the priest determined that Erawan required a passenger, and suggested it be that of Lord Brahma. A statue was built and, lo and behold, the misfortunes miraculously ended.

Although the original Erawan Hotel was demolished in 1987, the shrine still exists, and today remains an important place of pilgrimage for Thais, particularly those in need of some material assistance. Those making a wish from the statue should ideally come between 7am and 8am, or 7pm and 8pm, and should offer a specific list of items that includes candles, incense, sugar cane or bananas, all of which are almost exclusively given in multiples of seven. Particularly popular are teak elephants, the money gained through the purchase of which is donated to a charity run by the current hotel, the Grand Hyatt Erawan. And as the tourist brochures depict, it is also possible to charter a classical Thai dance, often done as a way of giving thanks if a wish has been granted.

BANGKOK ART & CULTURE CENTRE ART GALLERY
Map p260 (BACC; www.bacc.or.th; cnr Th Phayathai & Th Phra Ram I; ⏲10am-9pm Tue-Sat; [S]National Stadium exit 3) [FREE] This large, modern building in the centre of Bangkok is the most recent and promising addition to the city's arts scene. As well as its three floors and 3000 sq metres of gallery space, the centre also contains shops, private galleries and cafes.

SIAM OCEAN WORLD AQUARIUM
Map p260 (สยามโอเชี่ยนเวิร์ล; www.siamoceanworld.com; basement, Siam Paragon, 991/1 Th Phra Ram I; adult/child 900/700B; ⏲10am-9pm; [S]Siam exits 3 & 5) More than 400 species of fish, crustaceans and even penguins populate this vast underground facility. Diving with sharks (for a fee) is also an option if you have your diving licence, though you'll have almost as much fun timing your trip to coincide with the shark and penguin feedings; the former are usually at 1pm and 4pm, the latter at 12.30pm and 4.30pm; check the website for details.

JAMJUREE ART GALLERY ART GALLERY
Map p260 (Jamjuree Bldg, Chulalongkorn University, Th Phayathai; ⏲10am-7pm Mon-Fri, noon-

TOP SIGHT
SUAN PAKKAD PALACE MUSEUM

Everyone loves Jim Thompson's House, but few have even heard of Suan Pakkad Palace Museum (Lettuce Farm Palace), another noteworthy traditional Thai house-museum. Once the residence of Princess Chumbon of Nakhon Sawan (and before that a lettuce farm – hence the name), the museum is a collection of five traditional wooden Thai houses linked by elevated walkways containing varied displays of art, antiques and furnishings. The landscaped grounds are a peaceful oasis complete with ducks, swans and a semi-enclosed, Japanese-style garden.

The diminutive **Lacquer Pavilion** at the back of the complex dates from the Ayuthaya period (the building originally sat in a monastery compound on the banks of Mae Nam Chao Phraya, just south of Ayuthaya) and features gold-leaf *Jataka* and *Ramayana* murals as well as scenes from daily Ayuthaya life. Larger residential structures at the front of the complex contain displays of Khmer, Hindu and Buddhist art, Ban Chiang ceramics and a collection of historic **Buddhas**, including a beautiful late U Thong–style image. In the noise and confusion of Bangkok, the gardens offer a tranquil retreat.

DON'T MISS...

- Lacquer Pavilion
- Buddha statue collection

PRACTICALITIES

- วังสวนผักกาด
- Map p263
- Th Si Ayuthaya
- admission 100B
- ⏲9am-4pm
- [S]Phaya Thai exit 4

6pm Sat & Sun; [S]Siam exit 2 & taxi) [FREE] This gallery, part of Chulalongkorn University's Faculty of Arts, emphasises modern spiritual themes and brilliantly coloured abstracts from emerging student artists.

LINGAM SHRINE MONUMENT

Map p260 (ศาลเจ้าแม่ทับทิม; Swissôtel Nai Lert Park, Th Witthayu (Wireless Rd); ⏲24hr; ⛴klorng boat to Tha Witthayu, [S]Phloen Chit exit 1) [FREE] Every village-neighbourhood has a local shrine, either a sacred banyan tree tied up with coloured scarves or a spirit house. But it isn't every day you see a phallus garden like this lingam shrine, tucked back behind the staff quarters of the Swissôtel Nai Lert Park.

Clusters of carved stone and wooden shafts surround a spirit house and shrine built by millionaire businessman Nai Loet to honour Jao Mae Thap Thim, a female deity thought to reside in the old banyan tree on the site. Someone who made an offering shortly after the shrine was built had a baby, and the shrine has received a steady stream of worshippers – mostly young women seeking fertility – ever since.

If facing the entrance of the hotel, follow the small concrete pathway to the right, which winds down into the building beside the car park. The shrine is at the end of the building next to the *klorng*.

100 TONSON GALLERY ART GALLERY

Map p260 (www.100tonsongallery.com; 100 Soi Tonson; ⏲11am-7pm Thu-Sun; [S]Chit Lom exit 4) [FREE] Housed in a spacious residential villa, and generally regarded as one of the city's top commercial galleries, 100 Tonson hosts a variety of contemporary exhibitions of all genres by local and international artists.

Ratchathewi

BANGKOK DOLL FACTORY & MUSEUM MUSEUM

Map p263 (พิพิธภัณฑ์ตุ๊กตาบางกอกดอลล์; ☎0 2245 3008; www.bangkokdolls.com; 85 Soi Ratchataphan (Soi Mo Leng); ⏲8am-5pm Mon-Sat; [S]Phaya Thai exit 3 & taxi) [FREE] This workshop was founded by Khunying Tongkorn Chandavimol in 1956 after she completed a doll-making course while living in Japan. Upon her return to Thailand, she began researching and making dolls, drawing from Thai mythology and historical periods.

MOTORCYCLE MADNESS

It's Friday rush hour in Bangkok and traffic is bumper-to-bumper as far as the eye can see. You need to be somewhere – fast. Assuming you don't have a police escort, the only way out is to hop on the back of a fearless motorcycle taxi, known as a *motorsai ráp jâhng*. Hang on tight as your orange-vested driver weaves past belching trucks, zips down tiny back-alleys and, when all else fails, treats the pavement as a bike lane. Even the niftiest túk-túk ('pronounced dúk dúk') struggles to keep up with a *motorsai*.

Motorsai are an essential lubricant for Bangkok's congested streets, with an estimated 200,000 on the road. They gather at street corners in ranks known as *win*. As well as transporting people and goods, they double as messengers for private companies. Since they can drive down narrow sois, *motorsai* are often the only form of public transport in parts of the city, providing the last leg of bus and train commutes. This is particularly true when there's no Skytrain or subway line.

Not all *motorsai* journeys are mad dashes across town. Plenty of people use them to putter up and down their soi, to run local errands or visit friends. But their finest hours come when traffic is so backed up that a regular taxi or bus just won't do – there's something exhilarating about passing a $50,000 BMW caught in a snarl-up. 'They make space where there is no space,' says Claudio Sopranzetti, an anthropology student at Harvard who spent a year researching *motorsai* drivers for his PhD.

Yet while nearly everyone relies on them, *motorsai* have a mixed reputation. Bangkokians swap hair-raising stories of drunken or reckless drivers who should be behind bars. Most parents shudder at the idea that their daughter might bring one home (nearly all are male). Then there's the underworld aspect: *motorsai* ranks are typically run by moonlighting cops or soldiers, a shady practice that former Prime Minister Thaksin Shinawatra tried to stamp out in 2003. He didn't quite succeed, but he won the loyalty of drivers who were fed up with paying their bosses for protection. Most drivers originally come from northeastern Thailand, where Thaksin's brand of economic populism made him a political rock star.

This loyalty to Thaksin, who lost power in 2006, is why *motorsai* drivers were so active in the red-shirt protests that convulsed Bangkok in 2009 and 2010. As well as joining mass demonstrations, drivers used their bikes to transport supplies into protest camps, bring red-shirt guards to the front lines and to keep tabs on troop movements. Journalists also relied on nimble *motorsai* to get them in and out of danger zones, particularly when the army moved in in May 2010.

Since then, some drivers have tried to steer a more neutral path through Thailand's colour-coded politics. They prefer to be seen as orange shirts, not red shirts (or yellow shirts). Their orange vests can be valuable property. Although each numbered vest is supposed to stay with its registered owner, drivers trade or sell them, fetching prices of up to 150,000B on busy corners or in posh neighbourhoods. Sopranzetti says that an average *motorsai* earns 400B to 500B a day. That isn't far off the salary of an office worker, but the hours are longer and the work more hazardous. Drivers must also pay for petrol and maintain their own motorcycle.

Motorsai first became popular in the 1980s as the city spread rapidly outwards and commuters found themselves stranded far from public transport. The peculiar layout of Bangkok – narrow sois, big roads, lots of dead ends – meant that motorcycles had the edge. Like so much of Bangkok's workings, it was an ad hoc response to a failure of central urban planning. Bangkok may be the world's least planned yet most livable city – and its *motorsai* drivers are the unsung heroes who help make it that way.

Simon Montlake, Asian-based journalist

Today her personal collection includes 400 dolls from around the world, plus important pieces from her own workshop, where you can watch the figures being crafted by hand.

The museum is rather tricky to find; take a taxi from BTS Phaya Thai and get the driver to call the museum for directions.

BAIYOKE II TOWER NOTABLE BUILDING

Map p263 (ตึกใบหยก ๒; 22 Th Ratchaprarop; admission 250B; ⏲9am-11pm; ⛴klorng boat to Tha Pratunam) Thailand's tallest tower soars to 88 storeys (85 of them above ground), the upper of which are often clad with some truly huge advertising. The main attraction here is the 84th-floor revolving observation deck. The views are as impressive as you'd expect (unless it's too smoggy) but only just enough to compensate for the tacky decor, uninspiring restaurant and inconvenient location.

VICTORY MONUMENT MONUMENT

Map p263 (อนุสาวรีย์ชัย; cnr Th Ratchawithi & Th Phayathai; ⏲24hr; [S]Victory Monument) [FREE] This obelisk monument was built by the then military government in 1941 to commemorate a 1940 campaign against the French in Laos. Today the monument is primarily a landmark for observing the social universe of local university students and countless commuters. It's worth exploring the neighbourhood around Victory Monument, which is reminiscent of provincial Thai towns, if not exactly hicksville. It's also something of a transport hub, with minivans to Ko Samet, Kanchanaburi and Ayuthaya stopping here, and there's a useful BTS stop.

🍴 EATING

🍴 Siam Square, Pratunam & Ploenchit

NUER KOO THAI $

Map p260 (4th fl, Siam Paragon, 991/1 Th Phra Ram I; mains 89-970B; ⏲11.30am-9.30pm; ❄; [S]Siam exits 3 & 5) Is this the future of the noodle stall? Mall-bound Nuer Koo does an upscale version of the formerly humble bowl of beef noodles. Choose your cut of beef – including Kobe beef from Japan – enjoy the rich broth and cool air-con, and quickly forget about the good old days.

SOM TAM NUA NORTHEASTERN THAI $

Map p260 (392/14 Soi 5, Siam Sq; mains 59-130B; ⏲10.45am-9.30pm; ❄; [S]Siam exit 4) It can't compete with the street stalls for flavour and authenticity, but if you need to be seen, particularly while in air-con and trendy surroundings, this is a good place to sample northeastern Thai specialities. Expect a line at dinner.

SANGUAN SRI THAI $

Map p260 (59/1 Th Witthayu (Wireless Rd); mains 40-150B; ⏲10am-3pm Mon-Sat; ❄; [S]Phloen Chit exit 5) This restaurant, essentially a concrete bunker filled with furniture circa 1973, can afford to remain decidedly *cher-i* (old-fashioned) simply because of its reputation. Mimic the area's hungry office staff and try the excellent *gaang pèt Ƀèt yâhng* (red curry with grilled duck breast) served over snowy white rice noodles.

NEW LIGHT COFFEE HOUSE INTERNATIONAL $

Map p260 (426/1-4 Soi Chulalongkorn 64; mains 60-200B; ⏲8am-midnight; ❄; [S]Siam exit 2) Travel back in time to 1960s-era Bangkok at this vintage diner popular with students from nearby Chulalongkorn University. Try old-school Western dishes (think 'grilled pork chop' and goulash), all of which come accompanied by a soft roll and green salad, or choose from the extensive Thai menu.

FOOD PLUS THAI $

Map p260 (btwn Soi 5 & Soi 6, Siam Sq; mains 30-70B; ⏲9am-3pm; [S]Siam exit 2) This claustrophobic alleyway is bursting with the wares of several *ráhn kôw gaang* (rice and curry stalls). Everything is made ahead of time, so simply point to what looks tasty. You'll be hard-pressed to spend more than 100B, and the flavours are unanimously authentic and delicious.

KOKO THAI $

Map p260 (262/2 Soi 3, Siam Sq; mains 70-220B; ⏲11am-9pm; ❄ 🖉; [S]Siam exit 2) This casual cafelike restaurant offers a lengthy vegie menu, not to mention a brief but solid repertoire of meat-based Thai dishes, such as a Penang curry served with tender pork, or fish deep-fried and served with Thai herbs. Perfect for a mixed crowd.

CRYSTAL JADE LA MIAN XIAO LONG BAO CHINESE $$

Map p260 (basement, Erawan Bangkok, 494 Th Ploenchit; mains 115-450B; ⏲11am-10pm; ❄ 🖉; [S]Chit Lom exit 8) The tongue-twistingly long name of this excellent Singaporean chain refers to the restaurant's signature *la mian* (wheat noodles) and the famous Shanghainese *xiao long pao* ('soup' dumplings). If you order the hand-pulled noodles (which you should do), allow the staff to cut them with kitchen shears, otherwise you'll end up with ample evidence of your meal on your shirt.

FOOD COURTS

The Siam Square area is home to many of Bangkok's malls, which means that it's also home to more than its share of mall-based food courts. They're a great way to dip your toe in the sea of Thai food as they're generally cheap, clean, air-conditioned and have English-language menus. At most, paying is done by exchanging cash for vouchers or a temporary credit card at one of several counters; your change is refunded at the same desk.

MBK Food Island (Map p260; 6th fl, MBK Center, cnr Th Phra Ram I & Th Phayathai; mains 35-150B; ⏲10am-10pm; ❄ ✎; [S]National Stadium exit 4) The granddaddy of the genre offers loads of vendors selling dishes from virtually every corner of Thailand and beyond. Standouts include a good vegetarian food stall (C8) and a decent Isan food vendor (C22).

Gourmet Paradise (Map p260; ground fl, Siam Paragon, 991/1 Th Phra Ram I; mains 35-500B; ⏲10am-10pm; ❄; [S]Siam exits 3 & 5) The perpetually busy Gourmet Paradise unites international fast-food chains, domestic restaurants and food-court-style stalls, with a particular emphasis on the sweet stuff.

Food Republic (Map p260; 4th fl, Siam Center, cnr Th Phra Ram I & Th Phayathai; mains 30-200B; ⏲10am-10pm; ❄ ✎; [S]Siam exit 1) The city's newest food court has a good mix of Thai and international (mostly Asian) outlets, all in an open, contemporary-feeling locale. We particularly enjoyed the Thai-Muslim dishes at the stall called 'Curry Rice'.

FoodPark (Map p260; 4th fl, Big C, 97/11 Th Ratchadamri; mains 30-90B; ⏲9am-9pm; ❄; [S]Chit Lom exit 9 to Sky Walk) The selections here are not going to inspire you to move east, but they are abundant and cheap, and representative of the kind of 'fast food' Thais enjoy eating.

Food Loft (Map p260; 6th fl, Central Chidlom, 1027 Th Ploenchit; mains 65-950B; ⏲10am-9pm; ❄ ✎; [S]Chit Lom exit 5) This department store pioneered the concept of the upscale food court, and mock-ups of the various Indian, Italian, Japanese and other international cuisines aid in the decision-making process.

LA MONITA — MEXICAN $$

Map p260 (☎0 2650 9581; www.lamonita.com; 888/26 Mahatun Plaza, Th Ploenchit; mains 75-550B; ⏲11.30am-10pm; ❄ ✎; [S]Phloen Chit exit 2) Admittedly, the menu is more Texas than Tijuana, but of all the places that have attempted Mexican in Bangkok over the years, we reckon La Monita has done the best job. Come for an inviting, pleasant atmosphere and a repertoire of hearty dishes such as *queso fundido* (a skillet of melted cheese) and burritos.

COCA SUKI — CHINESE, THAI $$

Map p260 (416/3-8 Th Henri Dunant; mains 78-488B; ⏲11am-11pm; ❄ ✎; [S]Siam exit 6) Immensely popular with Thai families, *sù·gêe* takes the form of a bubbling hotpot of broth and the raw ingredients to dip therein. Coca is one of the oldest purveyors of the dish, and this branch reflects the brand's efforts to appear more modern. Fans of spice be sure to request the tangy 'tom yam' broth.

ERAWAN TEA ROOM — THAI $$

Map p260 (2nd fl, Erawan Bangkok, 494 Th Ploenchit; mains 180-480B; ⏲10am-10pm; ❄ ✎; [S]Chit Lom exit 8) The oversized chairs, panoramic windows and variety of hot drinks make this one of Bangkok's best places to catch up with the paper. The lengthy menu of Thai standards will likely encourage you to linger longer, and the selection of jams and teas to take away allows you to re-create the experience at home.

FOUR SEASONS SUNDAY BRUNCH — INTERNATIONAL $$$

Map p260 (☎0 2250 1000; www.fourseasons.com/bangkok; ground fl, Four Seasons Hotel, 155 Th Ratchadamri; buffet 2950B; ⏲11.30am-3pm Sun; ❄ ✎; [S]Ratchadamri exit 4) All of the Four Seasons' highly regarded restaurants – Spice Market, Shintaro, Biscotti and Madison – set up steam tables for this decadent Sunday brunch buffet. Numerous cooking stations and champagne options take this light years beyond your normal Sunday brunch. It's popular, so be sure to reserve your table a couple of weeks in advance.

SRA BUA THAI $$$

Map p260 (☎0 2162 9000; www.kempinskibangkok.com; ground fl, Siam Kempinski Hotel, 991/9 off Th Phra Ram I; set meal 2700B; 🕒noon-3pm & 6-11pm; ❄; [S]Siam exits 3 & 5) Helmed by a Thai and a Dane whose Copenhagen restaurant, Kiin Kiin, snagged a Michelin star, Sra Bua takes an international approach to Thai food. Putting local ingredients through the wringer of molecular gastronomy, the couple have created unconventional Thai dishes such as 'frozen red curry with lobster salad'. Reservations recommended.

GAGGAN INDIAN $$$

Map p260 (☎0 2652 1700; www.eatatgaggan.com; 68/1 Soi Langsuan; set menu 1600B; 🕒6-11pm; ❄ ✍; [S]Ratchadamri exit 2) The white, refurbished villa that houses Gaggan seems more appropriate for an English-themed tea house than a restaurant serving self-proclaimed 'progressive Indian cuisine', but Gaggan is all about incongruity. The set menu here spans 10 courses, ranging from the daring (a ball of raita) to the traditional (some excellent tandoori), with bright flavours and unexpected but satisfying twists as a unifying thread.

🍴 Ratchathewi

TIDA ESARN NORTHEASTERN THAI $

Map p263 (1/2-5 Th Rang Nam; mains 60-250B; 🕒10.30am-10.30pm; [S]Victory Monument exit 2) Tida Esarn sells country-style Thai food in a decidedly urban setting. Appropriately, foreigners provide the bulk of the restaurant's customers, but the kitchen still insists on serving full-flavoured Isan-style dishes such as *súp nòr mái,* a tart salad of shredded bamboo.

MALLIKA RESTAURANT SOUTHERN THAI $$

Map p263 (21/36 Th Rang Nam; mains 90-500B; 🕒10am-10pm; ❄; [S]Victory Monument exit 2) Visit this corner of northern Bangkok for a taste of Thailand's southern provinces. The menu spans the region with spicy hits such as *kôo·a glîng* (minced meat fried with curry paste) or *gaang sôm* (a turmeric-laden seafood soup). Prices are slightly higher than elsewhere, but you're paying for quality.

PATHÉ THAI, INTERNATIONAL $$

Map p263 (www.patherestaurant.com; 507 Th Ratchawithi; mains 80-250B; 🕒2pm-1am; ❄; [S]Victory Monument exit 4) The modern Thai equivalent of a 1950s-era American diner, this popular place combines solid Thai food, a fun atmosphere and a jukebox playing scratched records. The menu is equally eclectic, and combines Thai and Western dishes and ingredients; be sure to save room for the deep-fried ice cream.

🍷 DRINKING & ENTERTAINMENT

🍷 Siam Square, Pratunam & Ploenchit

CO-CO WALK BAR

Map p260 (87/70 Th Phayathai; 🕒5pm-midnight; [S]Ratchathewi exit 2) This covered compound is a smorgasbord of pubs, bars and live

SIAM SQUARE'S SILVER SCREENS

Each Bangkok mall has its own cinema, but boasting 16 screens and more than 3000 seats, few can rival **Paragon Cineplex** (Map p260; ☎0 2129 4635; www.paragoncineplex.com; 5th fl, Siam Paragon, 991/1 Th Phra Ram I; [S]Siam exits 3 & 5). In addition to Thailand's largest IMAX screen, options include the Blue Ribbon Screen, a cinema with a maximum of 72 seats, where you're plied with pillows, blankets, complimentary snacks and drinks, and of course, a 15-minute massage; or Enigma, where in addition to a sofa-like love seat designed for couples, you'll be served cocktails and food (as well as blankets and a massage).

If you're looking for something with a bit more character, consider the old-school stand-alone theatres just across the street such as **Scala** (Map p260; ☎0 2251 2861; Soi 1, Siam Sq; [S]Siam exit 2) and **Lido** (Map p260; ☎0 2252 6498; www.apexsiam-square.com; btwn Soi 2 & Soi 3, Siam Sq; [S]Siam exit 2).

DON'T CALL ME LADYBOY

Prempreeda Pramoj Na Ayutthaya is a transwoman researcher and activist.

Why does Thailand appear to have so many transgender people? It's a cultural heritage based on a very old concept of gender that can even be found in ancient palm leaf manuscripts.

The Thai word ladyboy is sometimes used in English to refer to transgender people. How do you prefer to be called? I prefer (the Thai word) *gà·teu·i* (also spelt *kathoey*) because it goes back to an indigenous Thai belief that sex isn't binary. The words ladyboy and shemale are often used to sell sex and can stigmatise transgender people.

To outsiders, Thailand appears very open to homosexuals and transgender people – is this really the case? In everyday life, transgender people can live freely, but on a policy level we still face many difficulties.

What do you hope to achieve as an activist? I'm working to change the laws and policies so that homosexuals and transgender people can feel more comfortable in Thailand.

music popular with Thai university students. **Güts** has live acoustic music, **Chilling House Café** has the same and tacks on a few pool tables, **Muay Thai Restaurant** does Thai food, and for something confusingly international there's, well, **L'aventure Musical & Frenchy Bar**.

HYDE & SEEK — BAR

Map p260 (www.hydeandseek.com; ground fl, Athenee Residence, 65/1 Soi Ruam Rudi; ⏰11am-1am; [S]Phloen Chit exit 4) The tasty and comforting English-inspired bar snacks and meals have earned Hyde & Seek the right to call itself a 'gastro bar', but we reckon the real reasons to come are arguably Bangkok's most well-stocked liquor cabinet and some of the city's tastiest and most sophisticated cocktails.

RED SKY — BAR

Map p260 (55th fl, Centara Grand, CentralWorld, Th Ratchadamri; ⏰6-11.30pm; [S]Chit Lom exit 9 to Sky Walk, Siam exit 6 to Sky Walk) Perched on the 55th floor of a striking new skyscraper, Red Sky is Bangkok's newest and most formal rooftop dining venture.

DIPLOMAT BAR — LIVE MUSIC

Map p260 (ground fl, Conrad Hotel, 87 Th Witthayu (Wireless Rd); ⏰7pm-1am Sun-Thu, to 2am Fri & Sat; [S]Phloen Chit exit 5) Named for its location in the middle of the embassy district, this is one of the few hotel lounges that locals make a point of visiting. Choose from an expansive list of innovative Martinis and sip to live jazz, played gracefully at conversation level.

ROOF — BAR

Map p260 (25th fl, Siam@Siam, 865 Th Phra Ram I; ⏰6pm-12.30am; [S]National Stadium exit 1) In addition to views of central Bangkok from 25 floors up, the Roof offers a dedicated personal Martini sommelier and an extensive wine and champagne list. Party House One, on the ground floor of the same hotel, offers live music most nights.

TO-SIT — BAR

Map p260 (www.tosit.com; Soi 3, Siam Sq; [S]Siam exit 2) Live, loud and sappy music; cheap and spicy food; good friends and cold beer: To-Sit epitomises everything a Thai university student could wish for on a night out. There are branches all over town (check the website), but the Siam Square location has the advantage of being virtually the only option in an area that's buzzing during the day but dead at night.

FOREIGN CORRESPONDENTS' CLUB OF THAILAND — BAR, RESTAURANT

Map p260 (FCCT; www.fccthai.com; Penthouse, Maneeya Center, 518/5 Th Ploenchit; ⏰noon-2.30pm & 6pm-midnight; [S]Chit Lom exit 2) A bar-slash-restaurant, not to mention a bona fide gathering place for the city's hacks and photogs, the FCCT also hosts art exhibitions ranging in genre from photojournalism to contemporary painting. Check the website to see what's on.

🍷 Ratchathewi

SAXOPHONE PUB & RESTAURANT LIVE MUSIC

Map p263 (www.saxophonepub.com; 3/8 Th Phayathai; ⏲7.30pm-1.30am; [S]Victory Monument exit 2) Saxophone is still Bangkok's premier live-music venue – a dark, intimate space where you can pull up a chair just a few metres away from the band and see their every bead of sweat. If you like some mystique in your musicians, watch the blues, jazz, reggae or rock from the balcony.

SKY TRAIN JAZZ CLUB BAR

Map p263 (cnr Th Rang Nam & Th Phayathai; ⏲5pm-2am; [S]Victory Monument exit 2) An evening at this comically misnamed bar is more like chilling on the rooftop of your stoner buddy's flat than any jazz club we've ever been to. But there are indeed views of the BTS, jazz on occasion and a scrappy speakeasy atmosphere. To find it, look for the sign and proceed up the graffiti-strewn stairway until you reach the roof.

WINE PUB BAR

Map p263 (www.pullmanbangkokkingpower; 1st fl, Pullman Bangkok King Power, 8/2 Th Rang Nam; ⏲6pm-2am; [S]Victory Monument exit 2) If the upmarket but chilled setting and spinning DJ aren't compelling enough reasons to venture from your Sukhumvit comfort zone, consider that this is probably the least expensive place in town to drink wine. Check the website for revolving nibbles promotions that span everything from imported cheeses and cold cuts to tapas.

PLAYHOUSE THEATER CABARET CABARET

Map p260 (☎0 2215 0571; www.playhousethailand.com; basement, Asia Hotel, 296 Th Phayathai; admission 1200B; ⏲show times 8.15pm & 9.45pm; [S]Ratchathewi exit 1) Watching *gà·teu·i* (transgender people; also spelt kathoey) perform show tunes has, not surprisingly, become the latest 'must-do' fixture on the Bangkok tourist circuit. Playhouse caters to the trend with choreographed stage shows featuring Broadway high kicks and lip-synched pop performances.

RAINTREE LIVE MUSIC

Map p263 (116/63-64 Th Rang Nam; ⏲8pm-2am; [S]Victory Monument exit 2) This rustic pub is one of the few remaining places in town to hear 'songs for life' – Thai folk music with roots in the political movements of the 1960s and '70s. Tasty bar snacks also make it a clever place to have a bite to eat.

ROCK PUB LIVE MUSIC

Map p260 (www.therockpub-bangkok.com; 93/26-28 Th Phayathai; ⏲9.30pm-2am; [S]Ratchathewi exit 2) With posters of Iron Maiden as interior design, and black jeans and long hair as the dress code, this cavelike live-music bar is Thailand's unofficial Embassy of Heavy Metal.

🛍 SHOPPING

★MBK CENTER SHOPPING CENTRE

Map p260 (www.mbk-center.com; cnr Th Phra Ram I & Th Phayathai; ⏲10am-10pm; [S]National Stadium exit 4) This intimidatingly immense shopping mall is quickly becoming one of Bangkok's top attractions. Swedish and other languages can be heard as much as Thai, and on any given weekend half of Bangkok can be found here combing through an inexhaustible range of small stalls and shops. You can buy everything you need here: mobile phones, accessories, shoes, name brands, wallets, handbags and T-shirts.

The mall's 6th-floor **food court** is one of the city's most expansive. And although

WHAT'S YOUR NUMBER?

The 4th floor of MBK Center resembles something of a digital produce market. A confusing maze of stalls sell all the components to send you into the land of cellular: a new phone, a new number and a SIM card. Even if you'd rather keep yourself out of reach, do a walk-through to observe the chaos and the mania over phone numbers. Computer print-outs displaying all the available numbers for sale turn the phone numbers game into a commodities market. The luckier the phone number, the higher the price; upwards of thousands of dollars have been paid for numbers composed entirely of nines, considered lucky in honour of the current king, Rama IX (King Bhumibol Adulyadej; r 1946–present), and because the Thai word for 'nine' is similar to the word for 'progress'.

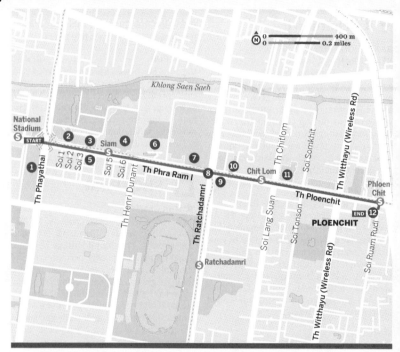

Neighbourhood Walk
Siam Square Shopping Spree

START MBK CENTER
END HYDE & SEEK
LENGTH APPROXIMATELY 3KM; TWO TO
FOUR HOURS

This walk cuts across the heart of Bangkok's most commercial district via elevated walkways, escalators and air-conditioned malls. Start no earlier than 10am, when most shopping centres open.

Begin at ❶ **MBK Center**, where you can pick up some new sneakers or fuel up for the rest of the walk at the mall's 6th-floor food court.

From MBK, it's possible to continue, more or less, without touching street level again. Following the elevated walkway to ❷ **Siam Discovery Center**, continue to ❸ **Siam Center** and ❹ **Siam Paragon** via linking walkways. Have a sweet snack at the latter's basement-level food court, or if you're missing the heat and exhaust, make a detour across Th Phra Ram 1 to the teen-themed shops and restaurants of ❺ **Siam Square**.

From Siam BTS station, continue east along the elevated walkway known as Sky Walk. After a couple of minutes, on your left you'll see ❻ **Wat Pathum Wanaram**, an incongruously located Buddhist temple. Turn left on the bridge that connects to ❼ **CentralWorld**, or continue forward until you reach busy ❽ **Ratchaprasong Intersection**, the area seized by red shirt protesters in 2010 and again in 2013-14. The intersection is also home to the busy ❾ **Erawan Shrine**. Just beyond the junction is ❿ **Narai Phand**, a government-sponsored handicraft emporium.

If there's anything you've forgotten, you can most likely pick it up at your last stop, ⓫ **Central Chidlom**, a seven-storey department store. Otherwise, end your walk, simultaneously balancing your chequebook and sipping one of Bangkok's best mixed drinks, at ⓬ **Hyde & Seek**.

you're not going to find many bargains, MBK is also one of the more convenient one-stop shopping destinations for photo equipment. **Foto File**, on the ground floor, has a good selection of used gear; the shop's sister venture, **Photo Thailand**, stocks all manner of new gear on the 3rd floor. There's well-stocked **Sunny Camera**, also on the 3rd floor, and **Big Camera**, on the 5th.

★SIAM SQUARE SHOPPING CENTRE

Map p260 (Th Phra Ram I; ⏰10am-10pm; [S]Siam exits 2, 4 & 6) Siam Square is ground zero for teenage culture in Bangkok. Pop music blares out of tinny speakers, and gangs of hipsters in various costumes ricochet between fast-food restaurants and closet-sized boutiques.

Digital Gateway (Map p260; cnr Th Phra Ram I & Soi 4; ⏰10am-9pm) stocks everything electronic, from computers to cameras. **DJ Siam** (Map p260; Soi 4) carries all the Thai indie and T-pop albums you'll need to speak 'teen'. Small shops peddle pop-hip styles along Soi 2 and Soi 3, but most outfits require a barely-there waist.

CENTRALWORLD SHOPPING CENTRE

Map p260 (www.centralworld.co.th; Th Ratchadamri; ⏰10am-10pm; [S]Chit Lom exit 9 to Sky Walk, Siam exit 6 to Sky Walk) Spanning eight storeys of more than 500 shops and 100 restaurants, CentralWorld is one of Southeast Asia's largest shopping centres. In addition to an **ice rink**, you'll find an extra-huge branch of bookstore **B2S**, and you could spend an hour sniffing around the fragrances at **Karmakamet** on the 2nd floor.

SIAM PARAGON SHOPPING CENTRE

Map p260 (www.siamparagon.co.th; 991/1 Th Phra Ram I; ⏰10am-10pm; [S]Siam exits 3 & 5) Paragon epitomises the city's fanaticism for the new, the excessive and absurd slogans. In addition to the usual high-end brands, there's a Lamborghini dealer on the 2nd floor should you need a ride home, and one floor up the **True Urban Park** 'lifestyle centre' featuring a cafe, internet access and a shop selling books, music and camera equipment.

Bookworms will fancy **Kinokuniya** (3rd floor), the largest English-language bookstore in Thailand, as well as an expansive branch of **Asia Books** (2nd floor). Even more audacious than the retail sections are the spectacular aquarium **Siam Ocean World**, an **IMAX theatre** and **Gourmet Paradise**, a seemingly never-ending basement level-food court. Whew.

> **LOCAL KNOWLEDGE**
>
> **LIVING LARGE**
>
> In your home town you may be considered average or even petite but, based on the Thai measuring stick, you're an extra large, clearly marked in the tag as 'LL' or, worse still, 'XL'. If that batters the body image, then skip the street markets, where you'll bust the seams from the waist up – if you can squirm that far into the openings. If you're larger than a US size 10 or an Australian size 14, you strike out altogether. Men will find that they exceed Thai clothes in length and shoulder width, as well as shoe sizes. For formal wear, many expats turn to custom orders through tailors. For ready-to-wear, many of the vendors at Pratunam Market and several stalls on the 6th floor of MBK Center stock the larger sizes.

PRATUNAM MARKET CLOTHING

Map p260 (cnr Th Phetchaburi & Th Ratchaprarop; ⏰10am-10pm; ⛴klorng boat to Tha Pratunam, [S]Ratchathewi exit 4) The emphasis here is on cheap clothes, and you could spend hours flipping through the T-shirts at the seemingly endless **Baiyoke Garment Center**.

The greater market area occupies the neighbourhood behind the shopfronts on the corner of Th Phetchaburi and Th Ratchaprarop, but it doesn't end here: across the street is the five-storey **Platinum Fashion Mall**, which sports the latest in no-brand couture.

SIAM CENTER SHOPPING CENTRE

Map p260 (Th Phra Ram I; ⏰10am-9pm; [S]Siam exit 1) Siam Center, Thailand's first shopping centre, was built in 1976 but, since a recent nip and tuck, hardly shows its age. Its 3rd floor is one of the best locations to check out established local labels such as **Flynow III**, **Senada Theory** and **Tango**.

SIAM DISCOVERY CENTER SHOPPING CENTRE

Map p260 (cnr Th Phra Ram I & Th Phayathai; ⏰10am-9pm; [S]Siam exit 1) This modern mall is, somewhat incongruously, one of the best

LOCAL BRANDS WORTH BUYING

Doi Tung (Map p260; www.doitung.org; 4th fl, Siam Discovery Center, cnr Th Phra Ram I & Th Phayathai; ⏰10am-9pm; [S]Siam exit 1) This royally funded enterprise sells beautiful hand-woven carpets, classy ceramics and domestic coffee beans.

Tango (Map p260; www.facebook.com/Tango.Leather; 3rd fl, Siam Center, Th Phra Ram 1; ⏰10am-9pm; [S]Siam exit 1) This homegrown brand specialises in funky leather goods, but you may not even recognise the medium under the layers of bright embroidery and chunky jewels.

Thann (Map p260; www.thann.info; 2nd fl, CentralWorld, Th Ratchadamri; ⏰10am-10pm; [S]Chit Lom exit 9 to Sky Walk, Siam exit 6 to Sky Walk) Smell good enough to eat with these botanical-based spa products. Products are all natural, rooted in Thai traditional medicine, and stylish enough to share space with brand-name beauty.

It's Happened To Be A Closet (Map p260; 1st fl, Siam Paragon, 991/1 Th Phra Ram I; ⏰10am-10pm; [S]Siam exits 3 & 5) Garbled grammar aside, this domestic label has gained a glowing reputation for its bright colours and bold patterns.

Flynow III (Map p260; www.flynowiii.com; 3rd fl, Siam Center, Th Phra Ram I; ⏰10am-9pm; [S]Siam exit 1) A long-standing leader in Bangkok's home-grown fashion scene, Flynow creates feminine couture that has appeared in several international shows.

Propaganda (Map p260; 4th fl, Siam Discovery Center, cnr Th Phra Ram I & Th Phayathai; ⏰10am-9pm; [S]Siam exit 1) Thai designer Chaiyut Plypetch dreamed up this brand's signature character, the devilish Mr P, who appears in anatomically correct cartoon lamps and other products.

places in town to stock up on camping gear, and within tent-pitching distance of each other on the 3rd floor are **Procam-Fis**, **Equinox Shop** and **North Face**. There's also a branch of **Madam Tussaud's** (Map p260; www.madametussauds.com/Bangkok/en/; 6th fl, Siam Discovery Center; adult/child 800/600B; ⏰10am-8pm; [S]Siam exit 1).

NARAI PHAND — SOUVENIRS

Map p260 (www.naraiphand.com; ground fl, President Tower, 973 Th Ploenchit; ⏰10am-8pm; [S]Chit Lom exit 7) Souvenir-quality handicrafts are given fixed prices and comfortable air-conditioning at this government-run facility. You won't find anything here that you haven't already seen at all of the tourist street markets, but it is a good stop if you're pressed for time or are spooked by haggling.

PINKY TAILORS — CLOTHING

Map p260 (www.pinkytailor.com; 888/40 Mahatun Plaza, Th Ploenchit; ⏰10am-7pm Mon-Sat; [S]Phloen Chit exits 2 & 4) Suit jackets have been Mr Pinky's speciality for 35 years. His custom-made dress shirts, for both men and women, also have dedicated fans. Located behind the Mahatun Building.

PANTIP PLAZA — SHOPPING CENTRE

Map p260 (604 Th Phetchaburi; ⏰10am-9pm; [S]Ratchathewi exit 4) If you can tolerate the crowds and annoying porn vendors ('DVD sex? DVD sex?'), Pantip, a multistorey computer and electronics warehouse, might just be your kinda paradise. Technorati will find pirated software and music, gear for hobbyists to enhance their machines, flea market–style peripherals, and other odds and ends. Up on the 5th floor is **IT City**, a reliable computer megastore that can provide VAT Refund forms for tourists.

MARCO TAILORS — CLOTHING

Map p260 (430/33 Soi 7, Siam Sq; ⏰9am-7pm Mon-Fri; [S]Siam exit 2) Dealing solely in men's suits, this long-standing and reliable tailor has a wide selection of banker-sensibility wools and cottons. If you're considering getting suited, be sure to set aside at least a week for the various fittings.

UTHAI'S GEMS — JEWELLERY

Map p260 (☎0 2253 8582; 28/7 Soi Ruam Rudi; ⏰10am-6pm Mon-Sat; [S]Phloen Chit exit 4) A showroom is in quiet Soi Ruam Rudi serving the discriminating embassy community. Nonhagglers appreciate his fixed prices and good service. Appointments recommended.

CENTRAL CHIDLOM SHOPPING CENTRE

Map p260 (www.central.co.th; 1027 Th Ploenchit; ⏰10am-10pm; [S]Chit Lom exit 5) Central is a modern Western-style department store with locations throughout the city. This flagship store, Thailand's largest, is the snazziest of all the branches.

CENTRAL EMBASSY SHOPPING CENTRE

Map p260 (www.centralembassy.com; cnr Th Ploenchit & Th Witthayu (Wireless Rd); ⏰10am-10pm; [S]Phloen Chit exit 1) At the time this guidebook was going to print, Thailand's first full-scale luxury mall had just opened. With a glitzy design said to be inspired by traditional Thai temples, the high-end retail haven houses top international brands such as Ralph Lauren and Saint Laurent. The shimmering 37-floor complex is also home to Bangkok's first Park Hyatt hotel, due to open in 2015.

SPORTS & ACTIVITIES

SPA 1930 SPA

Map p260 (☎0 2254 8606; www.spa1930.com; 42 Soi Tonson; Thai massage from 1200B, spa packages from 3800B; ⏰9.30am-9.30pm; [S]Chit Lom exit 4) Discreet and sophisticated, Spa 1930 rescues relaxers from the contrived spa ambience of New Age music and ingredients you'd rather see at a dinner party. The menu is simple (face, body care and body massage) and the scrubs and massage oils are logical players.

KIDZANIA PLAY CENTRE

Map p260 (☎0 2683 1888; bangkok.kidzania.com/en; 5th fl, Siam Paragon, 991/1 Th Phra Ram I; adult/child 650/400B; ⏰10am-5pm Mon-Fri, 10am-3pm & 4-9pm Sat & Sun; [S]Siam exits 3 & 5) Fly a plane, record an album, make your own sushi or, er, perform a root canal at this new and impressive learn-and-play centre.

THANN SANCTUARY SPA

Map p260 (☎0 2658 6557; www.thann.info/thann_sanctuary.php; 2nd fl, CentralWorld, Th Ratchadamri; Thai massage from 1500B, spa treatments from 2800B; ⏰10am-7.30pm; [S]Chit Lom exit 9 to Sky Walk, Siam exit 6 to Sky Walk) This local brand of herbal-based cosmetics has launched a series of mall-based spas – perfect for post-shopping therapy.

SF STRIKE BOWL BOWLING

Map p260 (☎0 2611 4555; 7th fl, MBK Center, cnr Th Phra Ram I & Th Phayathai; from 30B; ⏰10am-1am; [S]National Stadium exit 4) Thai teenagers crowd this psychedelically decorated bowling alley at all hours of the day and night. The cost varies, depending on what time you play.

YOGA ELEMENTS STUDIO YOGA

Map p260 (www.yogaelements.com; 23rd fl, Vanissa Bldg, 29 Th Chitlom; sessions from 520B; [S]Chit Lom exit 5) Run by American Adrian Cox, who trained at Om in New York and teaches primarily vinyasa and ashtanga, this is the most respected studio in town. The high-rise location helps you rise above it all, too.

PILATES STUDIO YOGA

Map p260 (☎0 2650 7797; www.pilatesbangkok.com; 888/58-9 Mahatun Plaza, Th Ploenchit; sessions from 550B; [S]Phloen Chit exit 2) The first choice for those in Bangkok looking for Pilates instruction and training.

ABSOLUTE YOGA YOGA

Map p260 (☎0 2252 4400; www.absoluteyogabangkok.com; 4th fl, Amarin Plaza, Th Ploenchit; membership per month from 2500B; [S]Chit Lom exit 6) This is the largest of Bangkok's yoga-studio businesses, teaching Bikram hot yoga plus a host of other styles.

UNION LANGUAGE SCHOOL LANGUAGE

Map p260 (☎0 2214 6033; www.unionlanguageschool.com; 7th fl, 328 CCT Office Bldg, Th Phayathai; tuition from 7000B; [S]Ratchathewi exit 1) Generally recognised as having the best and most rigorous Thai-language courses (many missionaries study here), Union employs a balance of structure- and communication-oriented methodologies in 80-hour, four-week modules.

AAA LANGUAGE

Map p260 (Advance Alliance Academy Thai Language School; ☎0 2655 5629; www.aaathai.com; 6th fl, 29 Vanissa Bldg, Th Chitlom; tuition from 7000B; [S]Chit Lom exit 3) Opened by a group of experienced Thai-language teachers from various schools, good-value AAA Thai has a loyal following.

Riverside, Silom & Lumphini

Neighbourhood Top Five

1 Dining at **nahm** (p127), quite possibly the best Thai restaurant in the city, and as of 2014, the best restaurant in Asia.

2 Soaking up the views at one of Bangkok's most famous tower-top bars, **Sky Bar** (p128).

3 Relaxing Bangkok-style among the exercisers and exercise-observers in **Lumphini Park** (p122), the 'lungs of the city'.

4 Confronting your fear of snakes at **Queen Saovabha Memorial Institute** (p121).

5 Ending the day (or starting the night) with a **dinner cruise** (p125) on Mae Nam Chao Phraya.

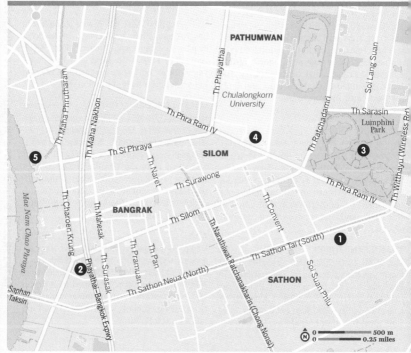

For more detail of this area see Map p264, p266 and p268 ➡

Explore: Riverside, Silom & Lumphini

Th Silom, with its towering hotels and office buildings, is Bangkok's de facto financial district, while Th Sathon is home to many of the city's embassies. Incongruously, lower Th Silom functions as Bangkok's lush gaybourhood. There's a dearth of sights in this part of town, so unless you're heading to Lumphini Park – at its best in the early morning – take advantage of the street stalls and upscale restaurants and combine your visit with lunch or dinner. The BTS stop at Sala Daeng and the MRT stop at Si Lom put you at lower Th Silom, perfect jumping-off points for either Lumphini Park or the area's restaurants and sights.

The Riverside area is significantly less flashy, and is a great area for an aimless wander among old buildings. This stretch of Mae Nam Chao Phraya (Chao Phraya River) was formerly Bangkok's international zone, but today boasts a particularly Chinese and Muslim feel. Most of the sights in this area can be seen in a morning; the BTS stop at Saphan Taksin is a good starting point.

Local Life

➡**Halal 'Hood** The intersection of Th Silom and Th Charoen Krung is home to several Muslim-Thai and Indian restaurants.

➡**Rainbow Flag** Lower Th Silom, particularly the strip from Soi 2 to Soi 4, is Bangkok's pinkest district, and is popular with both local and visiting gay men.

➡**Good Morning** Pretend you're Thai-Chinese by getting up at 5am and taking part in the early-morning stretching rituals at Lumphini Park. Or you can just show up at a slightly saner hour and watch.

➡**Art Attack** Those looking for a painting by a contemporary Burmese artist or an Ayuthaya-era Buddhist manuscript cabinet will undoubtedly find something interesting in one of the numerous art galleries and antique shops around Th Silom.

Getting There & Away

➡**BTS** To Riverside: Saphan Taksin. To Silom: Sala Daeng (interchange with MRT Si Lom). To Lumphini: Ratchadamri, Sala Daeng, Chong Nonsi, Surasak and Saphan Taksin.

➡**MRT** To Silom: Si Lom (interchange with BTS Sala Daeng). To Lumphini: Lumphini.

➡**River boat** To Riverside: Tha Si Phraya, Tha Oriental and Tha Sathon. To Lumphini: Tha Sathon.

➡**Bus** To Silom: air-con 76 and 77; ordinary 1, 15, 33 and 27.

Lonely Planet's Top Tip

Getting out on Mae Nam Chao Phraya is a great way to escape the Bangkok traffic and experience the city's maritime past. So it's fortunate that the city's riverside hotels also have some of the most attractive boats shuttling along the river (technically for hotel guests, but staff don't check). In most cases these free services run from Tha Sathon (also known as Central Pier) to their mother hotel, departing every 10 or 15 minutes. There's no squeeze, no charge and a uniformed crew to help you on and off.

RIVERSIDE, SILOM & LUMPHINI

✖ Best Places to Eat

➡ nahm (p127)
➡ Eat Me (p126)
➡ Muslim Restaurant (p122)
➡ Kai Thort Jay Kee (p126)
➡ Chennai Kitchen (p124)
➡ Never Ending Summer (p122)

For reviews, see p122.➡

🍷 Best Places to Drink

➡ Moon Bar (p128)
➡ Sky Bar (p128)
➡ Viva & Aviv (p128)

For reviews, see p128.➡

🔒 Best Places to Shop

➡ Asiatique (p130)
➡ River City (p130)
➡ Jim Thompson (p130)

For reviews, see p130.➡

👁 SIGHTS

👁 Riverside

OLD CUSTOMS HOUSE   HISTORICAL BUILDING

Map p266 (กรมศุลกากร: Soi 36. Th Charoen Krung; 🚣Tha Oriental) Old Customs House was once the gateway to Thailand, levying taxes on traders moving in and out of the kingdom. It was designed by an Italian architect and built in the 1890s; the front door opened onto its source of income (the river) and the grand facade was ceremonionsly decorated in columns and transom windows.

Today it's a crumbling yet hauntingly beautiful home to the fire brigade with sagging shutters, peeling yellow paint and laundry flapping on the balconies. For years the building has been used as a base for the waterborne fire brigade and the firefighters' families, meaning that the interior of the building can only be accessed by residents.

ASSUMPTION CATHEDRAL   CHURCH

Map p266 (อาสนวิหารอัสสัมชัญ; Soi 40 (Soi Oriental), Th Charoen Krung; ⏰7am-7pm; 🚣Tha Oriental) Marking the ascendancy of the French missionary influence in Bangkok during the reign of Rama II (King Phraphutthaloetla Naphalai; r 1809–24), this Romanesque church with its rich golden interior dates from 1910, and hosted a Mass by Pope John Paul II in 1984; his statue now stands

Hard-core movie buffs with a keen eye will recognise the Old Customs House from its cameo appearance in Wong Kar Wai's *In the Mood for Love* (2000).

outside the main door. The schools associated with the cathedral are considered some of the best in Thailand.

👁 Silom

SRI MARIAMMAN TEMPLE   TEMPLE

Map p264 (วัดพระศรีมหาอุมาเทวี (วัดแขก), Wat Phra Si Maha Umathewi; cnr Th Silom & Th Pan; ⏰6am-8pm; 🚇Surasak exit 3) **FREE** Arrestingly flamboyant, Sri Mariamman is a Hindu temple that is a wild collision of colours, shapes and deities. The official Thai name of the temple is Wat Phra Si Maha Umathewi, but sometimes it is shortened to its colloquial name Wat Khaek – *kàak* being a common expression for people of Indian descent. The literal translation is 'guest', an obvious euphemism for any group of people not particularly wanted as permanent residents; hence most Indian Thais don't appreciate the term.

The temple was built in the 1860s by Tamil immigrants and features a 6m facade of intertwined, full-colour Hindu

---

👁 TOP SIGHT
BANGKOKIAN MUSEUM

The Bangkokian Museum consists of a collection of three **antique structures** and illustrates an often-overlooked period of Bangkok's history. The main building was built in 1937 as a home for the Surawadee family and, as the signs inform us, was finished by Chinese carpenters on time and for less than the budgeted 2400B (which would barely buy a door handle today). It is filled with beautiful wooden furniture and the detritus of postwar family life, and offers a fascinating window into the period. An adjacent two-storey shophouse contains themed displays of similar items on the ground floor (don't miss the replicated traditional Thai kitchen), while the upper level **Bang Rak Museum** profiles Khet Bang Rak, the district in which the compound is located. The third building, at the back of the block, was built in 1929 as a surgery for an Indian doctor, though he died soon after arriving in Thailand. A visit takes the form of an informal guided tour in halting English, and photography is encouraged.

DON'T MISS...

➡ Antique wooden buildings

➡ Bang Rak Museum

PRACTICALITIES

➡ พิพิธภัณฑ์ชาวบางกอก

➡ Map p266

➡ 273 Soi 43, Th Charoen Krung

➡ ⏰10am-4pm Wed-Sun

➡ 🚣Tha Si Phraya

deities. While most of the people working in the temple hail from the Indian subcontinent, you will likely see plenty of Thai and Chinese devotees praying here as well. This is because the Hindu gods figure just as prominently in their individualistic approach to religion.

NEILSON HAYS LIBRARY   LIBRARY
Map p264 (www.neilsonhayslibrary.com; 195 Th Surawong; membership from 1900B; ☉9.30am-5pm Tue-Sun; ⓢSurasak exit 3) The oldest English-language library in Thailand dates back to 1922, and today remains the city's noblest place for a read – with the added benefit of air-con. It has a good selection of children's books and a decent selection of titles on Thailand. Nonmembers are expected to pay a 50B fee to use the facilities.

KATHMANDU PHOTO GALLERY   ART GALLERY
Map p264 (www.kathmandu-bkk.com; 87 Th Pan; ☉11am-7pm Tue-Sun; ⓢSurasak exit 3) FREE Bangkok's only gallery wholly dedicated to photography is housed in an attractively restored Sino-Portuguese shophouse. The owner, photographer Manit Sriwanichpoom, wanted Kathmandu to resemble photographers' shops of old, where customers could flip through photographs for sale. Manit's own work is on display on the ground floor, and the small but airy upstairs gallery plays host to changing exhibitions by local and international artists and photographers.

TANG GALLERY   ART GALLERY
Map p264 (5th fl, Silom Galleria, 919/1 Th Silom; ☉11am-7pm Mon-Sat; ⓢSurasak exit 3) FREE Bangkok's primary venue for modern artists from China has edged its way to become one of the city's top contemporary galleries. Check the posters in the lobby of its home, Silom Galleria, to see what's on.

NUMBER 1 GALLERY   ART GALLERY
Map p264 (www.number1gallery.com; 4th fl, Silom Galleria, 919/1 Th Silom; ☉10am-7pm Mon-Sat; ⓢSurasak exit 3) FREE This relatively new gallery has featured the attention-grabbing contemporary work of Thai artists such as Vasan Sitthiket, Sutee Kunavichayanont and Thaweesak Srithongdee.

THAVIBU GALLERY   ART GALLERY
Map p264 (www.thavibu.com; 4th fl, Silom Galleria, 919/1 Th Silom; ☉11am-7pm Tue-Sat; ⓢSurasak exit 3) FREE Thavibu is an amalgam of

Thailand, Vietnam and Myanmar (Burma). The gallery specialises in contemporary paintings by younger and emerging artists from the three countries.

H GALLERY   ART GALLERY
Map p264 (www.hgallerybkk.com; 201 Soi 12, Th Sathon Neua (North); ☉10am-6pm Wed-Sat, by appointment Tue; ⓢChong Nonsi exit 1) FREE Housed in a refurbished colonial-era wooden building, H is considered among the city's leading private galleries. It's also seen as a jumping-off point for Thai artists with international ambitions, such as Jakkai Siributr and Somboon Hormthienthong.

⊙ Lumphini & Around

QUEEN SAOVABHA MEMORIAL INSTITUTE   ZOO
Map p268 (สถานเสาวภา, Snake Farm; cnr Th Phra Ram IV & Th Henri Dunant; adult/child 200/50B; ☉9.30am-3.30pm Mon-Fri, to 1pm Sat & Sun; ⓜSi Lom exit 1, ⓢSala Daeng exit 3) Snake farms tend to gravitate towards carnivalesque rather than humanitarian, except at the Queen Saovabha Memorial Institute. Founded in 1923, the snake farm gathers antivenin from venomous snakes. This is done by milking the snakes' venom, injecting it into horses, and harvesting and purifying the antivenin they produce. The antivenins are then used to treat human victims of snake bites.

Regular **milkings** (☉11am Mon-Fri) and **snake-handling performances** (☉2.30pm Mon-Fri, 11am & 2.30pm Sat & Sun) are held at the outdoor amphitheatre.

The leafy grounds are home to a few caged snakes (and a constant soundtrack of rock music), but most attractions are found in the Simaseng Building, at the rear of the compound. The ground floor houses several varieties of snakes in glass cages.

MR KUKRIT PRAMOJ HOUSE   MUSEUM
Map p264 (บ้านหม่อมราชวงศ์คึกฤทธิ์ปราโมช; Soi 7 (Soi Phra Phinit), Th Narathiwat Ratchanakharin; adult/child 50/20B; ☉10am-4pm; ⓢChong Nonsi exit 2) Author and statesman Mom Ratchawong Kukrit Pramoj (1911–95) once resided in this charming complex now open to the public for tours. Surrounded by a manicured garden famed for its Thai bonsai trees, five teak buildings introduce visitors to traditional Thai architecture, arts and to the former resident, who wrote more than

TOP SIGHT
LUMPHINI PARK

Named after Buddha's birthplace in Nepal (Lumbini), Lumphini Park is central Bangkok's largest and most popular park. Its 58 hectares are home to an artificial lake surrounded by broad, well-tended lawns, wooded areas, walking paths and the odd scurrying monitor lizard to complement the shuffling Bangkokians – it's the best outdoor escape from Bangkok without leaving town.

The park was originally a royal reserve but in 1925 Rama VI (King Vajiravudh; r 1910–25) declared it a public space. In the years since it has matured and, as the concrete has risen all around, become the city's premier exercise space. One of the best times to visit is early morning, when the air is (relatively) fresh and legions of Chinese are practising t'ai chi, doing their best to mimic the aerobics instructor or doing the half-run half-walk version of jogging that makes a lot of sense in oppressive humidity. A weight-lifting area in one section becomes a miniature 'muscle beach' on weekends, when the park takes on a festive atmosphere as the day cools down into evening. Cold drinks are available at the entrances and street-food vendors set up tables outside the park's northwest corner from about 5pm.

DON'T MISS...

- Enormous monitor lizards
- Early-morning t'ai chi and evening aerobics

PRACTICALITIES

- สวนลุมพินี
- Map p268
- Bounded by Th Sarasin, Th Phra Ram IV, Th Witthayu (Wireless Rd) & Th Ratchadamri
- 🕑4.30am-9pm
- [M]Lumphini exit 3, Si Lom exit 1, [S]Sala Daeng exit 3, Ratchadamri exit 2

150 books (including the highly respected *Four Reigns*), served as prime minister of Thailand in 1974 and '75, and spent 20 years decorating this house.

🍴 EATING

🍴 Riverside

MUSLIM RESTAURANT MUSLIM-THAI **$**

Map p266 (1354-6 Th Charoen Krung; mains 40-140B; 🕑6.30am-5.30pm; ⛴Tha Oriental, [S]Saphan Taksin exit 1) Plant yourself in any wooden booth of this ancient eatery for a glimpse into what restaurants in Bangkok used to be like. The menu, much like the interior design, doesn't appear to have changed much in the restaurant's 70-year history, and the biryanis, curries and samosas are more Indian-influenced than Thai.

NAAZ MUSLIM-THAI **$**

Map p266 (24/9 Soi 45, Th Charoen Krung; mains 35-90B; 🕑8.30am-10pm Mon-Sat; ⛴Tha Oriental) Hidden in a nondescript alleyway is Naaz (pronounced 'Nát'), a tiny shophouse restaurant serving some of the city's richest *kôw mòk gài* (chicken biryani). Various daily specials include chicken masala and mutton korma, but we're most curious to visit on Thursday when the restaurant serves something called Karai Ghost.

INDIAN HUT INDIAN **$$**

Map p266 (www.indianhut-bangkok.com; 418 Th Surawong; mains 160-380B; 🕑11am-11pm; ❄✍; ⛴Tha Oriental) Despite the fast-food connotations in the name, this long-standing restaurant is classy and popular with visiting business people. The emphasis is on northern Indian cuisine, including excellent flatbreads, tandoor-baked meats and homemade paneer in a tomato and onion curry.

NEVER ENDING SUMMER THAI **$$$**

Map p266 (☎0 2861 0953; www.facebook.com/TheNeverEndingSummer; 41/5 Th Charoen Nakhon; mains 140-350B; 🕑11am-11pm; ❄; ⛴river-crossing ferry from Tha Si Phraya) Located in a former warehouse in a seemingly hidden compound by the river, the cheesy name doesn't do justice to this surprisingly sophisticated Thai restaurant. Join Bangkok's

Neighbourhood Walk
Riverside
Architecture Ramble

START BTS SAPHAN TAKSIN
END VIVA & AVIV
LENGTH APPROXIMATELY 3KM; TWO TO
FOUR HOURS

Bangkok isn't known for its secular architecture, but the area that runs along Mae Nam Chao Phraya is home to several noteworthy structures.

Board the BTS, heading towards the river, and get off at Saphan Taksin. Walk north along Th Charoen Krung, passing ancient **1** **shophouses** between Th Charoen Wiang and Th Si Wiang. Turn left on Soi 40 (Soi Oriental), home to the **2** **Mandarin Oriental**, Bangkok's oldest and most storied hotel. Directly across from the entrance is the classical Venetian-style facade of the **3** **East Asiatic Company**, built in 1901. Proceed beneath the overhead walkway linking two buildings to the red-brick **4** **Assumption Cathedral**.

Return to Soi 40 and take the first left. On your right is **5** **O.P. Plaza**, built as a department store in 1905. Pass the walls of the French embassy and turn left. Head towards the river and the **6** **Old Customs House**.

Backtrack and turn left beneath the green sign that says Haroon Mosque. You're now in **7** **Haroon village**, a Muslim enclave full of sleeping cats, playing kids and gingerbread wooden houses. Wind through Haroon and you'll eventually come to Soi 34, which will lead you back to Th Charoen Krung. Turn left and cross the street opposite the art deco **8** **General Post Office**. Turn right onto Soi 43 and proceed to the **9** **Bangkokian Museum**, home to three antique wooden homes.

Head back to Th Charoen Krung, cross the street and turn right. Turn left on Soi 30. Follow this road past the walls of the **10** **Portuguese Embassy**, Bangkok's oldest, to River City – not noteworthy in an architectural sense, but its riverside bar **11** **Viva & Aviv** is a good place to end the walk.

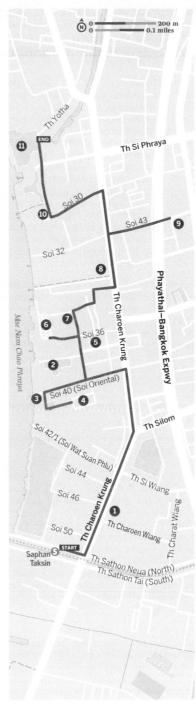

beautiful and edgy crowd for antiquated Thai dishes such as cubes of watermelon served with a dry 'dressing' of fish, sugar and deep-fried shallots, or fragrant green curry with pork and fresh bird's eye chili.

LE NORMANDIE FRENCH $$$

Map p266 (☑0 2236 0400; www.mandarin oriental.com; Mandarin Oriental Hotel, Soi 40 (Soi Oriental), Th Charoen Krung; mains 1400-3750B; ◎noon-2.30pm & 7-11pm Mon-Sat, 7-11pm Sun; ✳; 🛥Tha Oriental or hotel shuttle boat from Tha Sathon, Central Pier) Although today's Bangkok boasts a plethora of upmarket choices, Le Normandie has maintained its niche and is still the only place to go for a genuinely old-world 'continental' dining experience. A revolving cast of Michelin-starred guest chefs and some of the world's most decadent ingredients keep up the standard, and appropriately formal attire (including jacket) is required. Book ahead.

LORD JIM'S INTERNATIONAL $$$

Map p266 (☑0 2659 9000; Mandarin Oriental Hotel, Soi 40 (Soi Oriental), Th Charoen Krung; buffet 2050-2943B; ◎noon-2.30pm Mon-Fri, 11.30am-3pm Sat, 11am-3pm Sun; ✳ 🅿; 🛥Tha Oriental or hotel shuttle boat from Tha Sathon, Central Pier) Even if you can't afford to stay at the Oriental, you should save up for the hotel's decadent riverside buffet. Dishes such as foie gras are standard, and weekends, when reservations are recommended, see additional seafood stations.

✕ Silom

CHENNAI KITCHEN INDIAN $

Map p264 (10 Th Pan; mains 70-150B; ◎10am-3pm & 6-9pm; ✳ 🅿; 🅂Surasak exit 3) This thimble-sized mom-and-pop restaurant near the Hindu temple puts out some of the most solid southern Indian vegetarian food around. Yard-long dosai (a crispy southern Indian bread) is always a good choice, but if you're feeling indecisive (or exceptionally famished) go for the banana-leaf thali that seems to incorporate just about everything in the kitchen.

RAN NAM TAO HU YONG HER CHINESE $

Map p264 (68 Th Narathiwat Ratchanakharin; mains 40-205B; ◎11am-10pm; ✳; 🅂Chong Nonsi exit 3) Although the name of this blink-and-you'll-miss-it shophouse eatery translates as 'soy milk restaurant', the emphasis here

is on northern Chinese cuisine — a rarity in Bangkok. Try the Shanghainese speciality *xiao long bao,* described on the menu as 'small steamed bun', actually dumplings encasing a pork filling and rich hot broth that pours out when you bite into them.

KALAPAPRUEK THAI $

Map p264 (27 Th Pramuan; mains 80-120B; ◎8am-6pm Mon-Sat, to 3pm Sun; ✳; 🅂Surasak exit 3) This venerable Thai eatery has numerous branches and mall spin-offs around town, but we still fancy the original branch. The diverse menu spans Thai specialities from just about every region, daily specials and, occasionally, seasonal treats as well.

JAY SO NORTHEASTERN THAI $

Map p264 (146/1 Soi Phiphat 2; mains 20-80B; ◎11am-4pm Mon-Sat; Ⓜ Si Lom exit 2, 🅂Sala Daeng exit 2) Jay So has no menu, but a mortar and pestle and a huge grill are the telltale signs of ballistically spicy *sôm đam* (green papaya salad), sublime herb-stuffed grilled catfish and other northeastern Thai specialities. There's no English signage, so look for the white, Pepsi-decorated shack about halfway down Soi Phiphat 2.

KRUA 'AROY-AROY' THAI $

Map p264 (Th Pan; mains 40-100B; ◎8am-8.30pm; 🅂Surasak exit 3) Krua 'Aroy-Aroy' (Delicious Kitchen) is the kind of family-run Thai restaurant where nobody seems to mind a cat slumbering on the cash register. Stop by for some of the richest curries around, as well as the interesting daily specials including, on Thursdays, *kôw klúk gà-bì,* rice cooked in shrimp paste and served with sweet pork, shredded green mango and other toppings.

SOMTAM CONVENT NORTHEASTERN THAI $

Map p264 ('Hai; 2/4-5 Th Convent; mains 30-100B; ◎11am-9pm Mon-Fri, to 5pm Sat; ✳; Ⓜ Si Lom exit 2, 🅂Sala Daeng exit 2) Northeastern-style Thai food is usually relegated to less-than-hygienic stalls perched by the side of the road with no menu or English-speaking staff in sight. A less intimidating introduction to the wonders of *lâhp* (a minced meat 'salad'), *sôm đam* and other Isan delights can be had at this popular restaurant.

SOI 10 FOOD CENTRES THAI $

Map p264 (Soi 10, Th Silom; mains 20-60B; ◎8am-2pm Mon-Fri; Ⓜ Si Lom exit 2, 🅂Sala Daeng exit 1) These two adjacent hangarlike buildings tucked behind Soi 10 are the main lunchtime fueling stations for this area's office staff. Choices range from southern-style *kôw gaang* (point-and-choose curries ladled over rice) to virtually every form of Thai noodle.

MIZU'S KITCHEN JAPANESE, INTERNATIONAL **$**
Map p264 (32 Soi Patpong 1; mains 65-200B; ⊙noon-midnight; ❄; ⓂSi Lom exit 2, ⓢSala Daeng exit 1) This certifiable hole-in-the-wall place oozes character, not to mention the beefy essence of thousands of steaks served over the decades. Do order the house Sarika steak, and do take a hint from the regulars and use your chequered tablecloth to protect your clothes from the sizzle and spray of the hot plate when it arrives.

TALING PLING THAI **$$**
Map p264 (Baan Silom, Soi 19, Th Silom; mains 110-230B; ⊙11am-10pm; ❄; ⓢSurasak exit 3) Don't be fooled by the modern interior; despite the fancy new digs, longstanding Taling Pling continues to pull off a thick menu of full-flavoured Thai dishes. It's a good starting point for rich, central Thai-style dishes such as *gaang kôo·a*, 'crabmeat curry with wild betel leaves'. Tasty pies and cakes and refreshing drinks round out the choices.

DAIMASU JAPANESE **$$**
Map p264 (www.facebook.com/shichirinizakaya daimasu; 9/3 Soi Than Tawan; dishes 49-300B; ⊙11:30am-2pm & 6-11pm, to 10pm Sat & Sun; ❄⏀; ⓂSi Lom exit 2, ⓢSala Daeng exit 1) The

emphasis at this cosy, retro-themed Japanese restaurant is *yakiniku* (DIY grilled meat). But we also love the tasty, tiny sides ranging from crispy spears of cucumber in a savoury marinade, to a slightly bitter salad of paper-thin slices of eggplant.

SUSHI TSUKIJI JAPANESE **$$**
Map p264 (62/19-20 Th Thaniya; sushi per item 60-700B; ⊙11am-2pm, 5.30-10.30pm; ❄; ⓂSi Lom exit 2, ⓢSala Daeng exit 1) Th Thaniya is home to many hostess bars catering to visiting Japanese, so naturally, the quality of the street's Japanese restaurants is high. Our pick is Tsukiji, named after Tokyo's famous seafood market. Specialising in raw fish, dinner at this sleek sushi joint will leave a significant dent in the wallet, so come for lunch, when Tsukiji does sushi sets for as little as 198B.

FOODIE THAI **$$**
Map p264 (Soi Phiphat 2; mains 80-150B; ⊙11am-11pm; ❄; ⓢChong Nonsi exit 2) Has a lengthy menu of hard-to-find central and southern-style Thai dishes. Highlights include *yam sôm oh* (spicy-sour-sweet salad of pomelo) and spicy *prík kǐng 'blah dùk foo* (catfish fried in a curry paste until crispy).

BONITA CAFE & SOCIAL CLUB VEGETARIAN **$$**
Map p264 (56/3 Th Pan; mains 160-250B; ⊙11am-10pm Wed-Mon; ❄⏀✐; ⓢSurasak exit 3) Resembling grandma's living room, this homey restaurant serves predominantly Western-style vegan and raw dishes.

DINNER CRUISES

A dinner cruise along Mae Nam Chao Phraya is touted as an iconic Bangkok experience, and several companies cater to this. Yet it's worth mentioning that, in general, the vibe can be pretty cheesy, with loud live entertainment and mammoth boats so brightly lit inside you'd never know you were on the water. The food, typically served as a buffet, usually ranges from mediocre to forgettable. But the atmosphere of the river at night, bordered by illuminated temples and skyscrapers, and the cool breeze chasing the heat away, is usually enough to trump all of this.

A good one-stop centre for all your dinner cruise needs is the **River City Information Desk** (Map p266; ✆0 2639 4532, 0 2237 0077; www.rivercity.co.th; ground fl, River City, 23 Th Yotha; ⊙10am-10pm; ⚓Tha Si Phraya/River City, or shuttle boat from Tha Sathon), where tickets can be purchased for **Grand Pearl** (Map p266; ✆0 2861 0255; www.grandpearlcruise.com; 1700B; ⊙cruise 7.30-9.30pm), **Chaophraya Cruise** (Map p266; ✆0 2541 5599; www.chaophrayacruise.com; 1700B; ⊙cruise 7-9pm), **Wan Fah** (Map p266; ✆0 2622 7657; www.wanfah.in.th/eng/dinner; 1300B; ⊙cruise 7-9pm), **Chao Phraya Princess** (Map p266; ✆0 2860 3700; www.thaicruise.com; 1400B; ⊙cruise 7.45-9.45pm) and **White Orchid** (Map p266; ✆0 2476 5207; www.thairivercruise.com; 1400B; ⊙cruise 7.45-9.45pm). All cruises depart from River City Pier; take a look at the websites to see exactly what's on offer.

★ EAT ME
INTERNATIONAL **000**

Map p264 (☏0 2238 0931; www.eatmerest
aurant.com; Soi Phiphat 2; mains 340-1350B;
⊙3pm-1am; ❋ ☝; Ⓜ Si Lom exit 2, Ⓢ Sala Daeng
exit 2) The dishes at this longstanding restaurant, with descriptions like 'fig & blue
cheese ravioli w/walnuts, rosemary and
brown butter', or 'beef cheek tagine w/saf-
fron and dates', may sound all over the map
or perhaps even somewhat pretentious, but
they're actually just plain tasty. A buzzy,
casual-yet-sophisticated atmosphere, good
cocktails and a handsome wine list, and
some of the city's best desserts, are additional reasons why this is one of our favourite places in Bangkok to dine.

D'SENS
FRENCH **$$$**

Map p264 (☏0 2200 9000; www.dusit.com; 22nd
fl, Dusit Thani Hotel, 946 Th Phra Ram IV; set
lunch from 800B, set dinner from 3100B; mains
1300-1800B; ⊙11.30am-2pm & 6-10pm Mon-Fri,
6-10pm Sat; ❋; Ⓜ Si Lom exit 3, Ⓢ Sala Daeng exit
4) Perched like an air-traffic control tower
atop the Dusit Thani Hotel, D'Sens doesn't
only offer the best restaurant views in
Bangkok, it's also one of the city's best fine
dining experiences. The progressive menu
draws its influences from the traditions
of the south of France, emphasising high-
quality imported ingredients.

SOMBOON SEAFOOD
THAI **$$$**

Map p264 (☏0 2233 3104; www.somboonsea
food.com; cnr Th Surawong & Th Narathiwat Ratchanakharin (Chong Nonsi); mains 120-900B; ⊙4-
11.30pm; ❋; Ⓢ Chong Nonsi exit 3) Somboon, a
busy seafood hall with a reputation far and
wide, is known for doing the best curry-
powder crab in town. Soy-steamed sea bass
(*Ƀlah grà·pohng nêung see·éw*) is also a
speciality and, like all good Thai seafood,
should be enjoyed with an immense platter
of *kôw pàt Ƀoo* (fried rice with crab) and as
many friends as you can gather together.

LE DU
INTERNATIONAL **$$$**

Map p264 (☏09 2919 9969; www.ledubkk.
com; 399/3 Soi 7, Th Silom; mains 220-1200B;
⊙11.30am-2.30pm & 6-11pm Mon-Fri, 6-11pm
Sat; ❋ ☎ ☝; Ⓢ Chong Nonsi exit 2) A play on
the Thai word for season, Le Du, not sur-
prisingly, emphasises fresh, seasonal ingre-
dients that blend east and west. But don't
call it fusion: dishes such as 'spaghetti with
smoked duck, poached egg, tomato, bacon
and basil' are just plain tasty. For the full
experience, including the wonderful des-

serts, come for the four to seven course
tasting menus (from 990B to 1590B).

INDIGO
FRENCH **$$$**

Map p264 (6 Th Convent; mains 390-1850B;
⊙noon-11pm; ❋; Ⓜ Si Lom exit 2, Ⓢ Sala Daeng
exit 2) Set in a former schoolhouse, the
charming atmosphere appears to be the
main draw here. But the food actually delivers. Think your neighbourhood French
place, if your neighbourhood French place
had oysters flown in from Les Halles on
a weekly basis and an interesting cheese
selection.

✕ Lumphini & Around

KAI THORT JAY KEE
THAI **$$**

Map p268 (Soi Polo Fried Chicken; 137/1-3 Soi
Sanam Khlii (Soi Polo); mains 40-280B; ⊙11am-
9pm; ❋; Ⓜ Lumphini exit 3) This Cinderella of
a former street stall has become synony-
mous with fried chicken. Although the *sôm
đam* (green papaya salad), sticky rice and
lâhp (spicy 'salad' of minced meat) give the
impression of a northeastern Thai-style ea-
tery, the deep-fried bird is more southern
in origin. Regardless, smothered in a thick
layer of crispy deep-fried garlic, it is none
other than a truly Bangkok experience.

NGWANLEE LUNG SUAN
CHINESE, THAI **$$**

Map p268 (cnr Soi Lang Suan & Th Sarasin; mains
50-900B; ⊙7am-3am; Ⓢ Ratchadamri exit 2)
This open-air staple of copious consumption is going strong after decades. If you
can locate the entrance, squeeze in with the
postclubbing crowd and try some Chinese-
style street dishes you never dare to order
elsewhere, such as *jàp chài* (Chinese-style
stewed vegies) or *hŏy lai pàt nám prík pŏw*
(clams stir-fried with chilli sauce and Thai
basil).

ISSAYA SIAMESE CLUB
THAI **$$**

Map p268 (www.issaya.com; 4 Soi Sri Ak-
sorn; mains 150-580B; ⊙11.30am-2.30pm &
6-10.30pm; ❋ ☝; Ⓜ Khlong Toei exit 1 & taxi) In
a charming 1920s-era villa, Issaya is Thai
celebrity chef Ian Kittichai's first effort at
a domestic outpost serving the food of his
homeland. Dishes alternate between some-
what saucy, meaty dishes and lighter dishes
using produce from the restaurant's organic
garden. The restaurant can be a bit tricky to
find, and is best approached in a taxi via Soi
Ngam Duphli.

BANGKOK'S GAYBOURHOOD

The side streets off lower Th Silom are so gay that they make San Francisco look like rural Texas. Every night, a pink tractor beam draws gay locals and tourists to the in-your-face sex shows in nearby Duangthawee Plaza, the chilled open-air bars on Soi 4 and the booming clubs near Soi 2; below are our picks.

Bars

Soi 4 is a tiny alleyway packed with gay bars, most with strategically positioned seats to best observe the nightly parade.

Telephone Pub (Map p264; www.telephonepub.com; 114/11-13 Soi 4, Th Silom; ⊘6pm-1am; 🛜; Ⓜ Si Lom exit 2, ⓈSala Daeng exit 1) Telephone is famous for the phones that used to sit on every table, allowing you to ring up that hottie sitting across the room. Its popularity remains even if most of the phones are gone. The clientele is mostly 30-and-above white men with their Thai 'friends'.

Balcony (Map p264; www.balconypub.com; 86-88 Soi 4, Th Silom; ⊘5.30pm-1am; 🛜; Ⓜ Si Lom exit 2, ⓈSala Daeng exit 1) Located directly across from Telephone, this is yet another long-standing cafelike pub that features the occasional drag-queen performance.

Bearbie (Map p264; 2nd fl, 82 Soi 4, Th Silom; ⊘8pm-1am Tue-Thu, to 2am Fri-Sun; Ⓜ Si Lom exit 2, ⓈSala Daeng exit 1) A bear bar as perceived through the Thai lens, Bearbie replaces beards and bikers with local 'chubs' and teddy bear-themed karaoke rooms.

Duangthawee Plaza (Soi Twilight; Map p264; Soi Pratuchai; ⊘7pm-1am; Ⓜ Si Lom exit 2, ⓈSala Daeng exit 3) This strip of male-only go-go bars is the gay equivalent of nearby Th Patpong. Expect tacky sex shows by bored-looking young men.

Nightclubs

The area's clubs are located in dead-end Soi 2 and Soi 2/1; if the following are too packed, alternatives are just steps away.

DJ Station (Map p264; www.dj-station.com; 8/6-8 Soi 2, Th Silom; admission from 100B; ⊘10.30pm-3am; Ⓜ Si Lom exit 2, ⓈSala Daeng exit 1) One of Bangkok's and indeed Asia's most legendary gay dance clubs, here the crowd is a mix of Thai guppies (gay professionals), money boys and a few Westerners.

G Bangkok (Guys on Display; Map p264; Soi 2/1, Th Silom; admission 300B; ⊘8pm-late; Ⓜ Si Lom exit 2, ⓈSala Daeng exit 1) As the name suggests, Guys on Display is not averse to a little shirtless dancing. Open late, this is where to go after DJ Station has closed.

Saunas

In Bangkok, there's a fine line – often no line at all – between male massage and prostitution. Saunas, on the other hand, don't involve any transaction past the entrance fee.

Babylon (Map p268; www.babylonbangkok.com; 34 Soi Nandha; admission 260B; ⊘10.30am-10.30pm; Ⓜ Lumphini exit 2) Bangkok's first luxury sauna remains extremely popular with visitors, many from neighbouring Singapore and Hong Kong. B&B-style accommodation is also available.

 NAHM   THAI **$$$**
Map p268 (☎0 2625 3388; www.comohotels.com/metropolitanbangkok/dining/nahm; ground fl, Metropolitan Hotel, 27 Th Sathon Tai (South); set lunch 1100B, set dinner 2000B, mains 180-700B; ⊘noon-2pm Mon-Fri, 7-10.30pm daily; ❄; Ⓜ Lumphini exit 2) Australian chef-author David Thompson is behind what is almost certainly one of Bangkok's best Thai restaurants, and if you believe the critics, the best in all of Asia in 2014. Using ancient cookbooks as his inspiration, Thompson has given new life to previously extinct dishes such as 'smoked fish curry with prawns, chicken livers, cockles and black pepper'. Dinner takes the form of a multicourse set meal, while lunch features *kà·nŏm jeen* (thin rice noodles served with curries). If you're expecting bland, gentrified Thai food meant for foreigners, prepare to be disappointed. Reservations recommended.

RIVERSIDE, SILOM & LUMPHINI EATING

ZANOTTI
ITALIAN $$$

Map p268 (www.zanottigroup.com; 21/2 Th Sala Daeng; mains 190-1600B; ☺11.30am-2pm & 6-10.30pm; ✱; MSi Lom exit 3, SSala Daeng exit 4) Zanotti has a well-deserved reputation as one of Bangkok's best destinations for Italian. But we also fancy the dark woods and framed paintings of the gentlemen's club-like dining room, not to mention the professional and confident service – the latter a rarity in Bangkok. Come midday from Monday to Friday for the amazing-value set lunch that starts at only 350B.

CHOCOLATE BUFFET
INTERNATIONAL $$$

Map p268 (www.sukhothai.com; Sukhothai Hotel, 13/3 Th Sathon Tai (South); buffet 900B; ☺2-5pm Fri-Sun; ✱ ✈; MLumphini exit 2) If you love the sweet stuff, the Sukhothai Hotel offers a unique, almost entirely cocoa-based high tea.

🍷 DRINKING & NIGHTLIFE

🍸 Riverside

SKY BAR
BAR

Map p266 (www.lebua.com/sky-bar; 63rd fl, State Tower, 1055 Th Silom; ☺6pm-1am; SSaphan Taksin exit 3) Allegedly one of the highest alfresco bars in the world, Sky Bar, located on the 63rd floor of this upmarket restaurant compound, provides heart-stopping views over Chao Phraya River. Note that the dress code doesn't allow access to those wearing shorts and sandals.

VIVA & AVIV
BAR

Map p266 (www.vivaaviv.com; ground fl, River City, 23 Th Yotha; ☺11am-midnight; 🚢river ferry Tha Si Phraya/River City or shopping centre shuttle boat from Tha Sathon, Central Pier) An enviable riverside location, casual open-air seating and a funky atmosphere make this restaurant-ish bar a contender for Bangkok's best sunset cocktail destination. Expect a pun-heavy menu (sample item: I 'foc'cat cia' name!) of pizzas, meaty snacks and salads that really is no joke.

🍸 Silom

MAGGIE CHOO'S
BAR

Map p264 (www.facebook.com/maggiechoos; basement, Novotel Bangkok Fenix Silom, 320 Th Silom; ☺6.30pm-1.30am; SSuracak exit 1) A former bank vault with a Chinatown opium-den vibe, secret passageways and lounging women in silk dresses; with all this going on, it's easy to forget that the new Maggie Choo's is actually a bar. But creative yet expensive and somewhat sweet house cocktails, and a crowd that blends selfie-snapping locals and curious tourists, are reminders of this.

TAPAS ROOM
NIGHTCLUB

Map p264 (114/17-18 Soi 4, Th Silom; admission 100B; ☺9pm-2am; MSi Lom exit 2, SSala Daeng exit 1) Although it sits staunchly at the front of Bangkok's pinkest street, this long-standing two-level disco brings in just about everybody. Come from Thursday to Saturday, when the combination of DJs and live percussion brings the body count to critical level.

BARLEY
BAR

Map p264 (www.barleybistro.com; Food Channel, Th Silom; ☺8pm-late; MSi Lom exit 2, SSala Daeng exit 2) The seemingly incongruous combo of Belgian beer and Thai-influenced snacks somehow works at this new bar. Seating is on the breezy rooftop or inside, occasionally in the company of live bands. Barley is located in the Food Channel building, between Soi 5 and Soi 7.

🍸 Lumphini & Around

★ MOON BAR
BAR

Map p268 (www.banyantree.com; 61st fl, Banyan Tree Hotel, 21/100 Th Sathon (South) Tai; ☺5pm-1am; MLumphini exit 2) The Banyan Tree Hotel's Moon Bar kick-started the rooftop trend and, as Bangkok continues to grow at a mad pace, the view from 61 floors up only gets better. Arrive well before sunset and grab a coveted seat to the right of the bar for the most impressive views. Save your shorts and sandals for another locale.

WONG'S PLACE
BAR

Map p268 (27/3 Soi Si Bamphen; ☺9pm-late Tue-Sun; MLumphini exit 1) This dusty den is a time warp into the backpacker world of the early 1980s. The namesake owner died several years ago, but a relative removed the padlock and picked up where Wong left off. Wong's works equally well as a destination or a last resort, but don't bother knocking until midnight, keeping in mind that it stays open until the last person crawls out.

KU DÉ TA NIGHTCLUB

Map p264 (www.kudeta.com/bangkok; 38th & 39th fl, Sathorn Square Complex, 98 Th Sathon Neua (North); ⏰11am-1am, to 3am Fri & Sat; [S]Chong Nonsi exit 1) The biggest new thing on Bangkok's club scene – literally and figuratively – with seven bars, three restaurants and two clubs. Expect an entry fee of 500B after 10pm on Friday and Saturday.

PUSSY GALORE

Super Pussy! Pussy Collection! The neon signs leave little doubt about the dominant industry in Patpong, the world's most infamous strip of go-go bars and clubs running 'exotic' shows. There is enough skin on show in Patpong to make Hugh Hefner blush, and a trip to the upstairs clubs could mean you'll never look at a ping-pong ball or a dart the same way again.

For years opinion on Patpong has been polarised between those people who see it as an exploitative, immoral place that is the very definition of sleaze, and others for whom a trip to Bangkok is about little more than immersing themselves in planet Patpong. But Patpong has become such a caricature of itself that in recent times a third group has emerged: the curious tourist. Whatever your opinion, what you see in Patpong or in any of Bangkok's other high-profile 'adult entertainment' areas depends as much on your personal outlook on life as on the quality of your vision.

Prostitution is actually illegal in Thailand but there are as many as 2 million sex workers, the vast majority of whom – women and men – cater to Thai men. Many come from poorer regional areas, such as Isan in the northeast, while others might be students helping themselves through university. Sociologists suggest Thais often view sex through a less moralistic or romantic filter than Westerners. That doesn't mean Thai wives like their husbands using prostitutes, but it's only recently that the gradual empowerment of women through education and employment has led to a more vigorous questioning of this very widespread practice.

Patpong actually occupies two soi that run between Th Silom and Th Surawong in Bangkok's financial district. The two streets are privately owned by – and named for – the Thai-Chinese Patpongpanich family, who bought the land in the 1940s and initially built Patpong Soi 1 and its shophouses; Soi 2 was laid later. During the Vietnam War the first bars and clubs opened to cater to American soldiers on 'R&R'. The scene and its international reputation grew through the '70s and peaked in the '80s, when official Thai tourism campaigns made the sort of 'sights' available in Patpong a pillar of their marketing.

These days Patpong has mellowed considerably, if not matured. Thanks in part to the popular night market that fills the soi after 5pm, it draws so many tourists that it has become a sort of sex theme park. There are still plenty of the stereotypical middle-aged men ogling pole dancers, sitting in dark corners of the so-called 'blow-job bars' and paying 'bar fines' to take girls to hotels that charge by the hour. But you'll also be among other tourists and families who come to see what all the fuss is about.

Most tourists go no further than stolen glances into the ground-floor go-go bars, where women in bikinis drape themselves around stainless-steel poles. Others will be lured to the dimly lit upstairs clubs by men promising sex shows. But it should be said that the so-called 'erotic' shows usually feature bored-looking women performing acts that feel not so much erotic as demeaning to everyone involved. Several of these clubs are also infamous for their scams, usually involving the nonperforming (ie clothed, if just barely) staff descending on wide-eyed tourists like vultures on fresh meat. Before you know it you've bought a dozen drinks, racked up a bill for thousands of baht, and followed up with a loud, aggressive argument flanked by menacing-looking bouncers and threats of 'no money, no pussy!'.

Were we saying that Patpong had mellowed? Oh yes, there is a slightly softer side. Several bars have a little more, erm, class, and in restaurants such as Mizu's Kitchen in Patpong 1 you could forget where you are – almost.

⭐ ENTERTAINMENT

CALYPSO BANGKOK
CABARET

(⚐0 2688 1415; www.calypsocabaret.com; Asiatique, Soi 72-76, Th Charoen Krung; admission 1200B; ⊙show times 8.15pm & 9.45pm; ⛴shuttle ferry from Tha Sathon, Central Pier) Located in a corner of Asiatique market, Calypso is yet another destination for *gà·teu·i* (transgender, also spelt *kathoey*) cabaret.

BAMBOO BAR
LIVE MUSIC

Map p266 (⚐0 2236 0400; www.mandarinoriental.com/bangkok/fine-dining/the-bamboo-bar; ground fl, Mandarin Oriental, 48 Soi 40, Th Charoen Krung; ⊙9-11.45pm Sun-Thu, to 12.45am Fri & Sat; ⛴Tha Oriental or hotel shuttle boat from Tha Sathon, Central Pier) The Oriental's Bamboo Bar is famous for its live jazz lounge, which holds court inside a colonial-era cabin of lazy fans, broad-leafed palms and rattan decor.

THREE SIXTY
LIVE MUSIC

Map p266 (⚐0 2442 2000; 32nd fl, Millennium Hilton, 123 Th Charoen Nakhorn; ⊙5pm-1am; ⛴hotel shuttle boat from Tha Sathon, Central Pier) Frustrated with Bangkok? A set or two of live jazz in this elegant glass-encased perch 32 floors above the city will help you forget some of your troubles, or at the very least, give you a whole new perspective on the city.

SALA RIM NAAM
DINNER THEATRE

Map p266 (⚐0 2437 3080; www.mandarinoriental.com/bangkok/fine-dining/sala-rim-naam; ground fl, Mandarin Oriental Hotel, Soi 40, Th Charoen Krung; tickets 2400B; ⊙dinner & show 8.15-9.30pm; ⛴river ferry Tha Oriental or hotel shuttle boat from Tha Sathon, Central Pier) The historic Mandarin Oriental hosts dinner theatre in a sumptuous Thai pavilion located across the river in Thonburi. The price is well above average, reflecting the means of the hotel's client base, but the performance gets positive reviews.

PATPONG
RED-LIGHT DISTRICT

Map p264 (Soi Patpong 1 & 2, Th Silom; ⊙4pm-2am; MSi Lom exit 2, SSala Daeng exit 1) Possibly one of the most famous red-light districts in the world, today any 'charm' that the area used to possess has been eroded by modern tourism, and fake Rolexes and Diesel T-shirts are more ubiquitous than flesh. If you must, be sure to agree to the price of entry and drinks before taking a seat at one of Patpong's first-floor 'pussy shows', otherwise you're likely to receive an astronomical bill.

SHOPPING

ASIATIQUE
MARKET

(www.thaiasiatique.com; Soi 72-76, Th Charoen Krung; ⊙4-11pm; ⛴shuttle boat from Tha Sathon, Central Pier) At press time Bangkok's buzziest market, Asiatique takes the form of open-air warehouses of commerce next to Mae Nam Chao Phraya. Expect clothing, handicrafts, souvenirs and quite a few dining and drinking venues. Shuttle boats from Tha Sathon (Central Pier) run frequently.

RIVER CITY
ANTIQUES

Map p266 (www.rivercity.co.th; 23 Th Yotha; ⊙10am-10pm; ⛴Tha Si Phraya/River City or shopping centre shuttle boat from Tha Sathon, Central Pier) Several upscale art and antique shops occupy the 3rd and 4th floors of this riverside mall, yet as with many antique stores in Bangkok, the vast majority of pieces appear to come from Myanmar and, to a lesser extent, Cambodia.

A free shuttle boat to River City departs from Tha Sathon (Central Pier) pier every half hour, from 10am to 8pm.

JIM THOMPSON
TEXTILES

Map p264 (www.jimthompson.com; 9 Th Surawong; ⊙9am-9pm; MSi Lom exit 2, SSala Daeng exit 3) The surviving business of the international promoter of Thai silk, the largest Jim Thompson shop sells colourful silk handkerchiefs, place mats, wraps and cushions. The styles and motifs appeal to older, somewhat more conservative tastes. There's also a **factory outlet** (Map p264; 149/4-6 Th Surawong; ⊙9am-6pm; SSala Daeng exit 1) just up the road, which sells discontinued patterns at a significant discount.

CHIANG HENG
ACCESSORIES

Map p266 (1466 Th Charoen Krung, no no-script sign; ⊙10.30am-7pm; SSaphan Taksin exit 3) In need of a handmade stainless-steel wok, old-school enamel-coated crockery or a manually operated coconut-milk strainer? Then we suggest you stop by this third-generation family-run kitchen-supply store. Even if your cabinets are already stocked, a visit here is a glance into the type of spe-

LOCAL KNOWLEDGE

THE UNIQUITOUS 7-ELEVEN

Be extremely wary of any appointment that involves the words 'meet me at 7-Eleven'. In Bangkok alone, there are 2700 branches of 7-Eleven (known as *sair·wên* in Thai) – nearly half the number found in North America. In central Bangkok, 7-Elevens are so ubiquitous that it's not uncommon to see two branches staring at each other from across the street.

Although the company claims its stores carry more than 2000 items, the fresh flavours of Thai cuisine are not reflected in the wares of a typical Bangkok 7-Eleven, the food selections of which are even junkier than those of its counterpart in the West. Like all shops in Thailand, alcohol is only available from 11am to 2pm and 5pm to midnight, and branches of 7-Eleven located near hospitals, temples and schools do not sell alcohol or cigarettes at all (but do continue to sell unhealthy snack food).

All 7-Eleven stores carry a wide selection of drinks, a godsend in sweltering Bangkok. You can conveniently pay most of your bills at the service counter, and all manner of phonecards, prophylactics and 'literature' (although very few English-language newspapers) are also available. And sometimes the blast of air-conditioning alone is enough reason to stop by. But our single favourite item must be the dirt-cheap chilled scented towels for wiping away the accumulated grime and sweat before your next appointment.

cialised and cramped but atmospheric shops that have all but disappeared from Bangkok.

JULY CLOTHING
Map p264 (✆0 2233 0171; www.julytailor.com; 30/6 Th Sala Daeng; ⊙9am-7pm; Ⓜ Si Lom exit 2, Ⓢ Sala Daeng exit 4) Tailors to Thailand's royalty and elite, their suits don't come cheap and the cuts can be somewhat conservative, but the quality is unsurpassed.

HOUSE OF CHAO ANTIQUES
Map p264 (9/1 Th Decho; ⊙9.30am-7pm; Ⓢ Chong Nonsi exit 3) This three-storey antique shop, appropriately located in an antique house, has everything necessary to deck out your fantasy colonial-era mansion. Particularly interesting are the various weatherworn doors, doorways, gateways and trellises that can be found in the covered area behind the showroom.

TAMNAN MINGMUANG HANDICRAFTS
Map p264 (2nd fl, Thaniya Plaza, Th Thaniya; ⊙11am-8pm; Ⓜ Si Lom exit 2, Ⓢ Sala Daeng exit 1) As soon as you step through the doors of this museumlike shop, the earthy smell of dried grass and stained wood rushes to meet you. Rattan, *yahn lí·pow* (a fernlike vine) and water hyacinth woven into silklike patterns, and coconut shells carved into delicate bowls are among the exquisite pieces that will outlast flashier souvenirs available on the streets.

THAI HOME INDUSTRIES HANDICRAFTS
Map p266 (35 Soi 40, Th Charoen Krung; ⊙9am-6.30pm Mon-Sat; ☖ Tha Oriental) A visit to this templelike building and former monks' quarters is like discovering an abandoned attic of Asian booty. On our most recent visit, the display cases held an eclectic collection of cotton farmer shirts, handsome stainless-steel flatware and delicate mother-of-pearl spoons. Despite the odd assortment of items and lack of order (not to mention the dust), it's heaps more fun than the typically faceless Bangkok handicraft shop.

MAISON DES ARTS HANDICRAFTS
Map p266 (1334 Th Charoen Krung; ⊙11am-6pm Mon-Sat; ☖ Tha Oriental) Hand-hammered, stainless-steel tableware haphazardly occupies this warehouse retail shop. The bold style of the flatware dates back centuries and the staff applies no pressure to indecisive shoppers.

PATPONG NIGHT MARKET SOUVENIRS
Map p264 (Soi Patpong 1 & 2, Th Silom; ⊙6pm-midnight; Ⓜ Si Lom exit 2, Ⓢ Sala Daeng exit 1) You'll be faced with the competing distractions of strip-clubbing and shopping on this infamous street. And true to the area's illicit leanings, pirated goods (in particular watches) make a prominent appearance even amid a wholesome crowd of families and straight-laced couples. Bargain with

determination, as first quoted prices tend to be astronomically high.

SOI LALAI SAP   CLOTHING

Map p264 (Soi 5, Th Silom; ⊖9am-4pm Mon-Fri; MSi Lom exit 2, SSala Daeng exit 2) The ideal place to buy an authentic Thai secretary's uniform, this 'money-dissolving soi' has mobs of vendors selling insanely cheap but frumpy clothing, as well as heaps of snacks and housewares.

🏃 SPORTS & ACTIVITIES

ORIENTAL SPA   SPA

Map p266 (⌂0 2659 9000, ext 7440; www.mandarinoriental.com/bangkok/spa; Mandarin Oriental, 48 Soi 40, Th Charoen Krung; massage/spa packages from 2900B; ⊖6am-10pm; ⛴Tha Oriental or hotel shuttle boat from Tha Sathon, Central Pier) Regarded as among the premier spas in the world, the Oriental Spa also sets the standard for Asian-style spa treatment. Depending on where you flew in from, the jet lag massage might be a good option, but all treatments require advance booking.

SILOM THAI COOKING SCHOOL   COOKING

Map p264 (⌂08 4726 5669; www.bangkokthaicooking.com; 68 Soi 13, Th Silom; 1000B; ⊖lessons 9am-12.30pm, 1.40-5.30pm & 6-9pm; SChong Nonsi exit 3) The facilities are basic but Silom crams a visit to a local market and instruction of six dishes into four hours, making it the best bang for your baht. Hotel pick-up in central Bangkok is available.

BANYAN TREE SPA   SPA

Map p268 (⌂0 2679 1052; www.banyantreespa.com; 21st fl, Banyan Tree Hotel, 21/100 Th Sathon Tai (South); massage packages from 3200B; spa packages from 6000B; ⊖10am-10pm; MLumphini exit 2) A combination of highly trained staff and high-tech facilities has provided this hotel spa with a glowing reputation. Come for unique signature treatments based on Thai traditions, or the more futuristic-sounding 'Tranquility Hydro Mist'.

HEALTH LAND   MASSAGE

Map p264 (⌂0 2637 8883; www.healthlandspa.com; 120 Th Sathon Neua (North); massage 2hr

500B; ⊖9am midnight, SSurasak exit 3) This, the main branch of a long-standing Thai massage mini-empire, offers good-value, no-nonsense massage and spa treatments in a tidy environment.

RUEN NUAD MASSAGE STUDIO   MASSAGE

Map p264 (⌂0 2632 2662; 42 Th Convent; massage per hr 350B; ⊖10am-9pm; MSi Lom exit 2, SSala Daeng exit 2) Set in a refurbished wooden house, this charming place successfully avoids both the tackiness and New Agedness that characterise most Bangkok Thai-massage joints. Prices are approachable, too.

CO VAN KESSEL BANGKOK TOURS   CYCLING

Map p266 (⌂0 2639 7351; www.covankessel.com; ground fl, River City, 23 Th Yotha; tours from 950B; ⊖6am-7pm; ⛴Tha Si Phraya/River City) This Dutch-run outfit offers a variety of tours in Chinatown, Thonburi and Bangkok's green zones, many of which also involve boat rides. Tours depart from the company's office in the River City shopping centre.

BLUE ELEPHANT THAI COOKING SCHOOL   COOKING COURSE

Map p264 (⌂0 2673 9353; www.blueelephant.com; 233 Th Sathon Tai (South); course 2800B; ⊖lessons 8.45am-1.30pm & 1.30-4.30pm Mon-Sat; SSurasak exit 2) Bangkok's most chi-chi Thai cooking school offers two lessons daily. The morning class squeezes in a visit to a local market, while the afternoon session includes a detailed introduction to Thai ingredients.

ORIENTAL HOTEL THAI COOKING SCHOOL   COOKING COURSE

Map p266 (⌂0 2659 9000; www.mandarinoriental.com; Mandarin Oriental, 48 Soi 40, Th Charoen Krung; lessons 4000B; ⊖lessons 9am-1pm Mon-Sat; ⛴Tha Oriental or hotel shuttle boat from Tha Sathon, Central Pier) Located across the river in an antique wooden house, the Oriental's cooking class spans a daily revolving menu of four dishes. Cooking is significantly less 'hands on' than elsewhere, and is done in teams rather than individually.

Sukhumvit

Neighbourhood Top Five

❶ Spending a night out at **Badmotel** (p140) and other buzz-worthy bars and night-clubs the in-crowd would approve of.

❷ Rejuvenating at one of Th Sukhumvit's excellent-value spas, such as **Health Land** (p144).

❸ Sampling Th Sukhum-vit's generous spread of **international restaurants**, (p136).

❹ Witnessing a corner of northern Thailand in modern Bangkok at **Ban Kamthieng** (p135).

❺ Getting lost in **Khlong Toey Market** (p135), one of the city's largest.

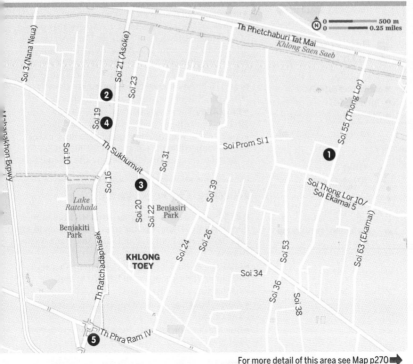

For more detail of this area see Map p270 ➡

Lonely Planet's Top Tip

All odd-numbered soi branching off Th Sukhumvit head north, while even numbers run south. Unfortunately, they don't line up sequentially (eg Soi 11 lies directly opposite Soi 8; Soi 39 is opposite Soi 26). Also, some larger soi are better known by alternative names, such as Soi Nana (Soi 3), Soi Asoke (Soi 21), Soi Thong Lor (Soi 55) and Soi Ekamai (Soi 63).

✗ Best Places to Eat

➡ Jidori-Ya Kenzou (p138)

➡ Little Beast (p138)

➡ Nasir Al-Masri (p138)

➡ Supanniga Eating Room (p137)

➡ Saras (p136)

For reviews, see p136. ➡

🍷 Best Places to Drink

➡ WTF (p139)

➡ Badmotel (p140)

➡ Tuba (p140)

➡ Cheap Charlie's (p140)

For reviews, see p139. ➡

☆ Best Nightclubs

➡ Grease (p140)

➡ Arena 10 (p140)

For reviews, see p139. ➡

Explore: Sukhumvit

You'll probably spend more time on Th Sukhumvit eating, drinking and perhaps sleeping (there's a high concentration of hotels here), rather than sightseeing. The BTS (Skytrain) runs along the length of Th Sukhumvit, making it a snap to reach just about anywhere in this chapter. BTS stops are also a convenient way to define the street's various vibes. Lower Sukhumvit, particularly the area around Nana BTS station, is a discombobulating mix of sexpats and Middle Eastern tourists; street markets and touts make this a frustrating zone to navigate nearly any time of day or night. Middle Sukhumvit, around BTS Asok/MRT Sukhumvit, is dominated by midrange hotels, upscale condos, international restaurants and businesses meant to appeal to tourists and resident foreigners. Starting at BTS Phrom Phong is where you'll find well-concealed compounds of wealthy Thai residents and tidy Japanese enclaves, while extending east from BTS Ekkamai, the feel becomes more provincial and more Thai.

Local Life

➡**Hi-So hangouts** This is Bangkok's ritziest zone, and is *the* area to observe hi-so (high society) Thais in their natural environment: chatting at a wine bar on Soi 55 (Thong Lor) or buying Fendi bags at Emporium (p143).

➡**International dining** Th Sukhumvit's various ethnic enclaves are a logical destination if you've grown tired of Thai food. Known colloquially as Little Arabia, Soi 3/1 is home to several Middle Eastern restaurants, while a handful of Korean restaurants can be found at Soi 12, and several Japanese restaurants are located near BTS Phrom Phong. Not surprisingly, there's relatively little interesting Thai food in the area.

➡**Club Alley** The streets that extend from Th Sukhumvit are home to many of Bangkok's most popular clubs. Ravers of uni age tend to head to Soi 63 (Ekamai), while the pampered elite play at Soi 55 (Thong Lor) and expats head to the clubs around Soi 11.

Getting There & Away

➡**BTS** Nana, Asok (interchange with MRT Sukhumvit), Phrom Phong, Thong Lo, Ekkamai, Phra Khanong, On Nut, Bang Chak, Punnawithi, Udom Suk, Bang Na and Bearing.

➡**MRT** Queen Sirikit National Convention Centre, Sukhumvit (interchange with BTS Asok) and Phetchaburi.

➡**Klorng boat** Tha Asoke, Tha Nana Neua and Tha Nana Chard.

➡**Bus** Air-con 501, 508, 511 and 513; ordinary 2, 25, 30, 48 and 72.

SIGHTS

THAILAND CREATIVE & DESIGN CENTER — GALLERY

Map p270 (ศูนย์สร้างสรรค์งานออกแบบ, TCDC; ☎0 2664 8448; www.tcdc.or.th; 6th fl, Emporium, cnr Th Sukhumvit & Soi 24; ⏲10.30am-9pm Tue-Sun; [S]Phrom Phong exit 3) The Thailand Creative & Design Center is a government-backed initiative that acts as both showroom and shop for Thai design. Rotating exhibitions feature profiles of international products and retrospectives of regional handicrafts and creativity. The centre includes a permanent library of design-related books and materials and is a good place to meet young Thai designers and students; the adjoining cafe has free wi-fi and good views.

KHLONG TOEY MARKET — MARKET

Map p270 (ตลาดคลองเตย; cnr Th Ratchadaphisek & Th Phra Ram IV; ⏲5-10am; [M]Khlong Toei exit 1) This wholesale market, one of the city's largest, is inevitably the origin of many of the meals you'll eat during your stay in Bangkok. Although some corners of the market can't exactly be described as photogenic, you'll still want to bring a camera to capture the cheery fishmongers and stacks of durians. Get there early, ideally before 10am, when most vendors have packed up and left.

CHUVIT GARDEN — PARK

Map p270 (Th Sukhumvit; ⏲6-10am & 4-8pm; [S]Nana exit 4) [FREE] The story behind this park is shadier than the plantings. Chuvit Kamolvisit, the benefactor of the park, was Bangkok's biggest massage-parlour owner. He was arrested in 2003 for illegally bulldozing, rather than legally evicting, tenants off the land where the park now stands. With all the media attention, he sang like a bird about the police bribes he handed out during his career and became an unlikely activist against police corruption.

Chuvit later ran unsuccessfully for Bangkok governor in 2004, and successfully for the Thai parliament in 2005 and 2011. This park was one of his early campaign promises. It's a pretty green patch in a neighbourhood lean on trees.

BENJAKITI PARK — PARK

Map p270 (สวนเบญจกิติ; Th Ratchadaphisek; ⏲5am-8pm; [M]Queen Sirikit National Convention Centre exit 3) This 130-*rai* (20.8-hectare) park is built on what was once a part of the Tobacco Monopoly, a vast, Crown-owned expanse

TOP SIGHT
SIAM SOCIETY & BAN KAMTHIENG

Stepping off cacophonous Soi 21 (Asoke) and into the Siam Society's Ban Kamthieng is as close to visiting a northern Thai village as you'll come in Bangkok. Ban Kamthieng is a traditional 19th-century home that was located on the banks of Mae Nam Ping (Ping River) in Chiang Mai. Now relocated to Bangkok, the house presents the daily customs and spiritual beliefs of the Lanna tradition. Communicating all the hard facts as well as any sterile museum (with detailed English signage and engaging video installations), Ban Kamthieng instils in the visitor a palpable sense of place, from the attached rice granary and handmade tools to the wooden loom and woven silks. You can't escape the noise of Bangkok completely, but the houses are refreshingly free of concrete and reflecting glass, and make a pleasant, interesting break.

Next door are the headquarters of the prestigious Siam Society (admission free), publisher of the renowned *Journal of the Siam Society* and a valiant preserver of traditional Thai culture. Those with a serious interest can use the **reference library**, which has the answers to almost any question you might have about Thailand (outside the political sphere, since the society is sponsored by the royal family).

DON'T MISS...

- Ban Kamthieng
- Siam Society's reference library

PRACTICALITIES

- สยามสมาคม & บ้านคำเที่ยง
- Map p270
- www.siam-society.com
- 131 Soi 21 (Asoke), Th Sukhumvit
- adult/child 100B/free
- ⏲9am-5pm Tue-Sat
- [M]Sukhumvit exit 1, [S]Asok exit 3 or 6

of low-rise factories and warehouses. There's an artificial lake that's good for jogging and cycling; **bikes** (Map p270; per hr 40B; ☉8am-7pm) can be hired around its 2km track.

EATING

SARAS
INDIAN $

Map p270 (www.saras.co.th; Soi 20, Th Sukhumvit; mains 90-200B; ☉8.30am-10.30pm; ❄✏; ⓂSukhumvit exit 2, ⓈAsok exit 4) Order at the counter to be rewarded with crispy dosai, regional set meals or rich curries (dishes are brought to your table). There are shelves of Punjabi sweets and *chaat* (sweet and savoury snacks), and perhaps most endearingly, chai is served in earthenware cups. We wish all fast food could be this satisfying.

BHARANI
THAI $

Map p270 (Sansab Boat Noodle; 96/14 Soi 23, Th Sukhumvit; mains 50-200B; ☉11am-10pm; ❄; ⓂSukhumvit exit 2, ⓈAsok exit 3) This cozy Thai restaurant dabbles in a bit of everything, from ox-tongue stew to rice fried with shrimp paste, but the real reason to come is for the rich, meaty 'boat noodles' – so called because they used to be sold from boats plying the *klorng* (canals; also spelt *khlong*) of Ayuthaya.

BOON TONG KIAT SINGAPORE
HAINANESE CHICKEN RICE
SINGAPOREAN $

Map p270 (440/5 Soi 55 (Thong Lor), Th Sukhumvit; mains 60-150B; ☉10am-10pm; ❄; ⓈThong Lo exit 3 & taxi) After taking in the exceedingly detailed and ambitious chicken rice manifesto written on the walls, order a plate of

the restaurant's namesake and witness how a dish can be so simple, yet so delicious. And while you're there you'd be daft not to order *rojak* (spicy/sour fruit 'salad') which is referred to here tongue-in-cheek as 'Singapore Som Tam'.

PIER 21
THAI $

Map p270 (5th fl, Terminal 21, cnr Th Sukhumvit & Soi 21 (Asoke); mains 39-200B; ☉10am-10pm; ❄✏; ⓂSukhumvit exit 3, ⓈAsok exit 3) Ascend a seemingly endless number of escalators to arrive at this noisy food court made up from vendors across the city. The selection is vast and the dishes are exceedingly cheap, even by Thai standards.

RUEA THONG
THAI $

Map p270 (331/2 Soi 55 (Thong Lor), Th Sukhumvit; mains 70-180B; ☉11.30am-2pm & 5-11pm Mon-Sat, 5-11pm Sun; ❄; ⓈThong Lo exit 3) A tiny, homey restaurant serving a wide menu of Thai dishes, including some spicy southern Thai specialities. Expect a crowd of local and expat regulars.

There's no English-language sign here, but Ruea Thong is located next door to Family Mart, near the corner of Soi Thong Lor 17.

SOI 38 NIGHT MARKET
THAI $

Map p270 (cnr Soi 38 & Th Sukhumvit; mains 30-60B; ☉8pm-3am; ⓈThong Lo exit 4) Not the best street food in town by a long shot, but after a hard night of clubbing on Sukhumvit, you can be forgiven for believing so. If you're sober, stick to the knot of 'famous' vendors tucked into an alley on the right-hand side as you enter the street; flame-fried *pàt tai* and herbal fish-ball noodles are standouts.

SUNDAY BRUNCH

Sunday brunch has become a modern Bangkok tradition, particularly among the members of the city's expat community, and the hotels along Th Sukhumvit offer some of the city's best spreads. Below are some of our favourites.

Rang Mahal (Map p270; ✆0 2261 7100; 26th fl, Rembrandt Hotel, 19 Soi 20, Th Sukhumvit; buffet 850B; ☉11am-2.30pm Sun; ❄✏; ⓂSukhumvit exit 2, ⓈAsok exit 6) Couple views from the 26th floor with an all-Indian buffet and a live band, and you have one of the most popular Sunday destinations for Bangkok's South Asian expat community.

Sunday Jazzy Brunch (Map p270; ✆0 2649 8888; 1st fl, Sheraton Grande Sukhumvit, 250 Th Sukhumvit; adult/child 2600/1200B; ☉noon-3pm Sun; ❄✏; ⓂSukhumvit exit 3, ⓈAsok exit 2) If you require more than just victuals, then consider the Sheraton's Sunday brunch, which unites all the hotel's restaurant outlets to a theme of live jazz.

Marriott Café (Map p270; ✆0 2656 7700; ground fl, JW Marriott, 4 Soi 2, Th Sukhumvit; buffet 1884B; ☉11.30am-3pm Sat & Sun; ❄✏; ⓈNana exit 3) The feastlike weekend brunch at this American hotel chain is likened to Thanksgiving year-round.

URBAN FARMERS

The last couple of years have seen a boom in so-called farmer's markets in Bangkok, most of which unfold around Th Sukhumvit.

Bangkok Farmers' Market (Map p270; www.facebook.com/bkkfm; K Village, Soi 26, Th Sukhumvit; 🕑last weekend of the month, 9am-5pm; 📝; [S]Phrom Phong exit 1 and taxi) The largest and most well-established market, it has purveyors of organic produce; restaurants, bakeries and vendors of artisinal ingredients and healthcare products also set up shop here.

Spring Epicurean Market (Map p270; www.facebook.com/springepicureanmarket; Spring restaurant, 199 Soi Phrom Si 1; 🕑last Sunday of the month, 8am-1pm; [S]Phrom Phong exit 3 & taxi) A small but fun mix of organic produce and artisinal foods; bring a blanket and have a picnic with your purchases on the restaurant's vast lawn.

Big Bite (www.eatingthaifood.com/big-bite-bangkok) Not exactly a farmers' market, this semi-annual event brings together heaps of vendors ranging from some of the city's best restaurants to some talented home cooks.

SUPANNIGA EATING ROOM — THAI $$

Map p270 (www.supannigaeatingroom.com; 160/11 Soi 55 (Thong Lor), Th Sukhumvit; mains 120-350B; 🕑11.30am-2.30pm & 5.30-11.30pm; ❄📝; [S]Thong Lo exit 3 & taxi) Thais are starting to take a serious interest in their own cuisine, and over the last few years Bangkok has seen an explosion of sophisticated-feeling places serving regional Thai dishes. The best of the lot is probably Supanniga, which focuses on the typically seafood-based, herb-forward dishes of Chanthaburi and Trat in eastern Thailand.

PIZZA ROMANA PALA — ITALIAN $$

Map p270 (Th Sukhumvit; pizza per slice 60-105B, mains 190-240B; 🕑11.30am-10pm; ❄📝; [M]Sukhumvit exit 3, [S]Asok exit 3) Strategically located at the intersection of BTS and MRT – ideal for that rush-hour snack – this place serves some of Bangkok's best pies. Pizzas are sold by the slice and are made using almost exclusively imported ingredients. Pala also boasts a deli, and in addition to antipasti and simple pasta dishes you can also pick up a chunk of *pecorino romano* or some salami.

SNAPPER — INTERNATIONAL $$

Map p270 (www.snapper-bangkok.com; 1/20-22 Soi 11, Th Sukhumvit; mains 200-1950B; 🕑5pm-midnight Mon-Fri, noon-midnight Sat & Sun; ❄; [S]Nana exit 3) Allegedly Bangkok's first restaurant serving New Zealand cuisine, Snapper specialises in Kiwi-style fish and chips. Choose from one of four sustainably harvested fish from New Zealand, your cut of fries, and the delicious homemade tartar sauce or a garlic aioli. A handful of other seafood dishes, salads and a brief wine list round out the selections.

NEW SRI FAH 33 — CHINESE, THAI $$

Map p270 (www.newsrifa33.com; 12/19-21 Soi 33, Th Sukhumvit; mains 80-450B; 🕑5pm-3am; ❄; [S]Phrom Phong exit 5) This former Chinatown shophouse restaurant, originally opened in 1955, has relocated to a tight but classy location in new Bangkok. Just about anything from the Thai-Chinese seafood-heavy menu is bound to satisfy, but we particularly love the stir-fried Chinese black olive with pork, and the stir-fried water mimosa.

FIREHOUSE — AMERICAN $$

Map p270 (www.firehousethailand.com; Soi 11, Th Sukhumvit; mains 160-909B; 🕑11.30am-3am Tue-Sat, to midnight Sun-Mon; ❄; [S]Nana exit 3) There's lots of debate about Bangkok's best burger, but Firehouse gets our vote. If burgers aren't your thing, try one of the hearty dishes influenced by US firefighter food. Open late, it's the perfect post-club meal.

TAPAS CAFÉ — SPANISH $$

Map p270 (www.tapasiarestaurants.com; 1/25 Soi 11, Th Sukhumvit; tapas 75-350B; 🕑11am-midnight; ❄📝; [S]Nana exit 3) Although it's the least expensive of Bangkok's Spanish joints, a visit to this friendly restaurant is in no way a compromise. Tasty tapas, refreshing sangria and a jazzy Latin vibe make Tapas Café well worth the visit. Tapas Café is located nearly next door to Suk 11 hostel.

CABBAGES & CONDOMS — THAI $$

Map p270 (www.pda.or.th/restaurant; Soi 12, Th Sukhumvit; mains 120-450B; 🕑11am-11pm; ❄📝;

M Sukhumvit exit 3, S Asok exit 2) 🍴 This long-standing garden restaurant is a safe place to gauge the Thai staples. It also stands for a safe cause: instead of after-meal mints, diners receive packaged condoms, and all proceeds go towards Population & Community Development Association (PDA), a sex education/AIDS prevention organisation.

LITTLE BEAST
INTERNATIONAL $$$

Map p270 (📞 0 2185 2670; www.facebook.com/littlebeastbar; 44/9-10 Soi Thong Lor 13; mains 300-750B; ⏰ 5.30pm-1am Tue-Sun; ✦ 🍃; S Phrom Phong exit 3 & taxi) With influences stemming from modern American cuisine, Little Beast isn't very Bangkok, but it is very good. Expect meaty mains, satisfying salads and some of the best desserts in town (the ice-cream sandwiches alone are worth a trip).

NASIR AL-MASRI
MIDDLE EASTERN $$$

Map p270 (4/6 Soi 3/1, Th Sukhumvit; mains 160-370B; ⏰ 24hr; ✦ 🍃; S Nana exit 1) One of several Middle Eastern restaurants on Soi 3/1, Nasir Al-Masri is easily recognisable by its thoroughly impressive floor-to-ceiling stainless steel 'theme'. Middle Eastern food generally means meat, meat and more meat, but there are also several delicious vegie-based *mezze* (small dishes).

QUINCE
INTERNATIONAL $$$

Map p270 (📞 0 2662 4178; www.quincebangkok.com; Soi 45, Th Sukhumvit; dishes 90-1800B; ⏰ 11.30am-10.30pm; ✦ 🍃; S Phrom Phong exit 3) Back in 2011, Quince made an audible splash in Bangkok's dining scene with its retro/industrial interior and eclectic, internationally influenced menu. The formula has since been copied ad nauseam, but Quince continues to put out the type of vibrant, full-flavoured dishes, many with palpable Middle Eastern or Spanish influences, that made it stand out in the first place. Reservations recommended.

APPIA
ITALIAN $$$

Map p270 (📞 0 2261 2057; www.appia-bangkok.com; 20/4 Soi 31, Th Sukhumvit; mains 350-900B; ⏰ 6.30-11pm Tue-Fri, 11.30am-2pm & 6.30-11pm Sat & Sun; ✦ 🍃; S Phrom Phong exit 5) Handmade pastas, slow-roasted meats and a

BEYOND SUSHI

Bangkok is home to a massive Japanese population, many of whom live around mid-Sukhumvit (indeed, on Google Maps this area is labelled as 'Japanese Village'). Along with these Japanese expats has come a sophisticated array of restaurants, some representing the only branches of certain chains outside of Japan. Not surprisingly, the dining options go way beyond maki rolls; some of our favourites:

Jidori-Ya Kenzou (Map p270; off Soi 26, Th Sukhumvit; dishes 60-350B; ⏰ 5pm-midnight Mon-Sat; ✦; S Phrom Phong exit 4) This cosy Japanese restaurant does excellent tofu dishes, delicious salads and great desserts – basically everything here is above average – but the highlight are the sublimely smokey, perfectly seasoned chicken skewers.

Ginzado (Map p270; 📞 0 2392 3247; Panjit Tower, 117 Soi 55 (Thong Lor), Th Sukhumvit; dishes 120-900B; ⏰ 5-11pm; ✦; S Thong Lo exit 3) Make a reservation or queue for some really excellent *yakitori* – DIY grilled beef – not to mention a mean *bibimbap* (rice and toppings served in a sizzling stone bowl). Ginzado is located between Soi Thong Lor 3 and Soi Thong Lor 5, through the large white archway.

Tenkaichi Yakiton Nagiya (Map p270; www.nagiya.com; Nihonmachi 105, 115 Soi 26, Th Sukhumvit; mains 90-160B; ⏰ 5pm-midnight; ✦; S Phrom Phong exit 1 & taxi) Originating in Tokyo, this hectic eatery is one of Bangkok's best – and most popular – *izakaya* (Japanese tavern-style restaurants). The highlights here are the warming *nabe* (do-it-yourself hotpots) and the smokey *yakitori* (grilled skewers of meat).

Imoya (Map p270; 3rd fl, Terminal Shop Cabin, 2/17-19 Soi 24, Th Sukhumvit; mains 40-400B; ⏰ 6pm-midnight; ✦; S Phrom Phong exit 4) A visit to this well-hidden restaurant, with its antique ads, wood panelling and wall of sake bottles, is like taking a trip back in time. Even the prices of the Japanese-style pub grub haven't caught up with modern times.

Fuji Super (Map p270; 593/29-39, Soi 33/1, Th Sukhumvit; S Phrom Phong exit 5) Central Bangkok or suburban Tokyo? It's hard to tell when inside this well-stocked supermarket that has additional branches around town.

SUPER MARKETS

Are you an American in need of a peanut-butter fix or an Aussie craving Vegemite? Th Sukhumvit is home to Bangkok's best-stocked international grocery stores.

Villa Market (Map p270; www.villamarket.com; Soi 33/1, Th Sukhumvit; ⏰24hr; [S]Phrom Phong exit 5) The main branch of this longstanding international grocery store is the place to pick up necessities from Cheerios to cheddar cheese. Additional Th Sukhumvit branches include **Soi 11** (Map p270; Soi 11, Th Sukhumvit; ⏰24hr; [S]Phrom Phong exit 5), **Soi 49** (Map p270; Soi 49, Th Sukhumvit; ⏰24hr; [S]Phrom Phong exit 3 & taxi) and **Soi 55** (Thong Lor; Map p270; Soi Thong Lor 15, Soi 55 (Thong Lor); ⏰24hr; [S]Thong Lo exit 3 & taxi); check the website for other locations.

Gourmet Market (Map p270; 5th fl, Emporium, cnr Soi 24 & Th Sukhumvit; ⏰10am-10pm; 🚆Phrom Phong exit 2) At Emporium; carries a wide range of Western-style staples.

carefully curated and relatively affordable wine list are the selling points of this new restaurant serving Roman-style cuisine. Reservations recommended.

BO.LAN — THAI $$$

Map p270 (☎0 2260 2962; www.bolan.co.th; 42 Soi Rongnarong Phichai Songkhram, Soi 26, Th Sukhumvit; set dinner 1980B; ⏰6pm-midnight Tue-Sun; ❄; [S]Phrom Phong exit 4) Upscale Thai is often more garnish than flavour, but Bo.lan, started up by two former chefs of London's Michelin-starred nahm, is the exception. Bo and Dylan (Bo.lan, a play on words that also means 'ancient') take a scholarly approach to Thai cuisine, and generous set meals featuring full-flavoured Thai dishes are the result. Reservations recommended.

MYEONG GA — KOREAN $$$

Map p270 (ground fl, Sukhumvit Plaza, cnr Soi 12 & Th Sukhumvit; mains 200-950B; ⏰11am-10pm Tue-Sun, 4-10pm Mon; ❄; [M]Sukhumvit exit 3, [S]Asok exit 2) Located on the ground floor of Sukhumvit Plaza (the multistorey complex also known as Korean Town), this restaurant is the city's best destination for authentic Seoul food. Go for the tasty prepared dishes or, if you've got a bit more time, the excellent, DIY Korean-style barbecue.

BEI OTTO — GERMAN $$$

Map p270 (www.beiotto.com; 1 Soi 20, Th Sukhumvit; mains 175-590B; ⏰11am-midnight; ❄✎; [M]Sukhumvit exit 2, [S]Asok exit 4) Claiming a Bangkok residence for nearly 30 years, Bei Otto's major culinary bragging point is its pork knuckles, reputedly the best in town. A good selection of German beers and an attached delicatessen with brilliant breads and super sausages makes it even more attractive to go Deutsch.

OPPOSITE MESS HALL — INTERNATIONAL $$$

Map p270 (www.oppositebangkok.com; 2nd fl, 27/2 Soi 51, Th Sukhumvit; mains 220-650B; ⏰6-11pm Tue-Sun; ❄✎; [S]Thong Lo exit 1) Much like the dishes it serves (example: 'savoury duck waffle, leg confit, pate, crispy skin and picalily relish'), Opposite can be hard to pin down. But how can you go wrong with a beautiful space, friendly service and really excellent cocktails? There's a menu, but the best strategy is to check the daily blackboard menu.

SOUL FOOD MAHANAKORN — THAI $$$

Map p270 (☎0 2714 7708; www.soulfoodmahanakorn.com; 56/10 Soi 55 (Thong Lor), Th Sukhumvit; mains 220-300B; ⏰5.30pm-midnight; ❄✎; [S]Thong Lo exit 3) Soul Food gets its buzz from its dual nature as both an inviting restaurant the menu spans tasty interpretations of rustic Thai dishes – and a bar serving deliciously boozy, Thai-influenced cocktails. Reservations recommended.

BACCO – OSTERIA DA SERGIO — ITALIAN $$$

Map p270 (www.bacco-bkk.com; 35/1 Soi 53, Th Sukhumvit; antipasti 200-800B, mains 350-1200B; ⏰11.30am-2.30pm & 5.30pm-midnight Mon-Fri, 11am-midnight Sat & Sun; ❄✎; [S]Thong Lo exit 1) The slightly cheesy interior of this *osteria* serves as a cover for one of Bangkok's better Italian menus. There's an abundance of delicious antipasti, but the emphasis here is on breads, from pizza to *piada* (flatbread), all of which are exceptional.

🍷 DRINKING & NIGHTLIFE

★WTF — BAR

Map p270 (www.wtfbangkok.com; 7 Soi 51, Th Sukhumvit; ⏰6pm-1am Tue-Sun; [S]Thong Lo exit 3)

No, not that WTF; Wonderful Thai Friendship is a funky, friendly neighbourhood bar that also packs in two floors of gallery space. Artsy locals and resident foreigners come for the old-school cocktails, live music and DJ events, poetry readings, art exhibitions and truly tasty bar snacks whose influences range from Macau to Spain. We, like them, give WTF our vote for Bangkok's best bar.

BADMOTEL BAR

Map p270 (www.facebook.com/badmotel; Soi 55 (Thong Lor), Th Sukhumvit; ⏰5pm-1.30am; [S]Thong Lo exit 3 & taxi) The new Badmotel blends modern and kitschy, cosmopolitan and Thai, in a way that has struck a nerve with Bangkok hipsters. This is manifest in drinks that combine Hale's Blue Boy, a Thai childhood drink staple, with rum, and bar snacks such as *nám prík ong* (a northern-style dip), here served with poppadum.

TUBA BAR

Map p270 (34 Room 11-12 A, Soi Ekamai 21, Soi 63 (Ekamai), Th Sukhumvit; ⏰11am-2am; [S]Ekkamai exit 1 & taxi) Part storage room for over-the-top vintage furniture, part restaurant, part friendly local boozer, this quirky bar doesn't lack in diversity, nor fun. Indulge in a whole bottle (they'll hold onto it if you don't finish it) and don't miss the moreish chicken wings or the delicious deep-fried *lâhp*.

CHEAP CHARLIE'S BAR

Map p270 (Soi 11, Th Sukhumvit; ⏰4.30-11.45pm Mon-Sat; [S]Nana exit 3) You're bound to have a hard time convincing your Thai friends to go to Th Sukhumvit only to sit at an outdoor wooden shack decorated with buffalo skulls and wagon wheels. Fittingly, Charlie's draws a staunchly foreign crowd who don't mind a bit of kitsch and sweat with their Singha.

GREASE NIGHTCLUB

Map p270 (www.greasebangkok.com; 46/12 Soi 49, Th Sukhumvit; ⏰6pm-4am Mon-Sat; [S]Phrom Phong exit 3 & taxi) Bangkok's newest, hottest nightclub is also one of its biggest – you could get lost in the four floors of dining venues, lounges and dance floors here.

ARENA 10 NIGHTCLUB

Map p270 (cnr Soi Ekamai 5 & Soi 63 (Ekamai), Th Sukhumvit; [S]Ekkamai exit 2 & taxi) This open-air entertainment zone is the destination of choice for Bangkok's young and beautiful – for the moment at least. **Demo** (Map p270; www.facebook.com/demobangkok; admission free; ⏰6pm-2am) combines blasting beats and a NYC warehouse vibe, while **Funky Villa** (Map p270; www.facebook.com/funkyvillabkk; ⏰7pm-2am), with its outdoor seating and Top 40 soundtrack, is more chilled. Fridays and Saturdays see a 400B entrance fee for foreigners.

BAR 23 BAR

Map p270 (Soi 16, Th Sukhumvit; ⏰7pm-1am Tue-Sat; [M]Sukhumvit exit 2, [S]Asok exit 6) The foreign NGO crowd and indie Thai types flock to this warehouse-like bar on weekends; cold Beerlao and a retro-rock soundtrack keep them until the late hours. It's about 500m down Soi 16, accessible from Th Ratchadaphisek.

NUNG-LEN NIGHTCLUB

Map p270 (www.nunglen.net; 217 Soi 63 (Ekamai), Th Sukhumvit; ⏰6pm-1am Mon-Sat; [S]Ekkamai exit 1 & taxi) Young, loud and Thai, Nung-Len (literally 'Sit and chill') is a popular den of live music and uni students on buzzy Th Ekamai. Get there before 10pm or you won't get in.

SHADES OF RETRO BAR

Map p270 (Soi Thararom 2, Soi 55 (Thong Lor), Th Sukhumvit; ⏰2pm-1am Mon-Sat; [S]Thong Lo exit 3 & taxi) As the name suggests, this eclectic place takes the current vintage fad to the max. You'll have to climb around Vespas and Naugahyde sofas to reach your seat, but you'll be rewarded with friendly service, a varied domestic soundtrack (the people behind Shades also run the domestic indie label Small Room) and free popcorn.

IRON FAIRIES BAR

Map p270 (www.theironfairies.com; 394 Soi 55 (Thong Lor), Th Sukhumvit; ⏰6pm-2am; [S]Thong Lo exit 3 & taxi) Imagine, if you can, an abandoned fairy factory in Paris c 1912, and you'll begin to get an idea of the vibe at this popular pub/wine bar. If you manage to wrangle one of a handful of seats, you can test their claim of serving Bangkok's best burgers. There's live music after 9.30pm.

BANGKOK BAR BAR

Map p270 (rooftop, The Opus, Soi Thong Lor 10; ⏰8pm-1am; [S]Thong Lo exit 3 & taxi) Bounce with Thai indie kids at this fun but astonishingly uncreatively named bar. There's live music, and the eats are strong enough to make Bangkok Bar a dinner destination in itself. We double-dog-dare you to walk a straight line after downing two Mad Dogs, Bangkok Bar's infamous house drink.

SOI 11

Although it's seen some significant changes in the last few years, Soi 11 has yet to relinquish its position as one of Bangkok's premier nightlife strips. Its selling point is its diversity, and options range from the streetside, VW van-based bars to sophisticated dens like Le Derrière, not to mention several dodgy late-night clubs. Some of our picks:

Q Bar (Map p270; www.qbarbangkok.com; 34 Soi 11, Th Sukhumvit; admission from 600B; ⏲8pm-2am; [S]Nana exit 3) In club years, Q Bar is fast approaching retirement age, but big-name guest DJs and a recent renovation have ensured that it still maintains a place in Bangkok's club scene. For something a bit more low-key, consider the attached Parisian-themed absinthe speakeasy, **Le Derrière** (Map p270; Q Bar, 34 Soi 11, Th Sukhumvit; ⏲9pm-3am; [S]Nana exit 3).

Apoteka (Map p270; www.facebook.com/ApotekaBangkok; Soi 11, Th Sukhumvit; ⏲5pm-1am Mon-Thu, 5pm-2am Fri-Sat, 3pm-1am Sun; [S]Nana exit 3) Antiques and a shophouse-like setting give Apoteka a fun, old-school feel. Solid drinks and blues-oriented bands every night from 9.30pm make it one of the better places in the area to sip to live music.

Above 11 (Map p270; ☎08 3542 1111; www.aboveeleven.com; 33rd fl, Fraser Suites Sukhumvit, Soi 11, Th Sukhumvit; ⏲6pm-2am; [S]Nana exit 3) Couple downward glances at Bangkok's most cosmopolitan neighbourhood with the Peruvian/Japanese bar snacks at this sophisticated rooftopper.

Levels (Map p270; www.levelsclub.com; 6th fl, Aloft, 35 Soi 11, Th Sukhumvit; ⏲9pm-late; [S]Nana exit 3) Come 1am, when most Soi 11 bars begin to close down, folks file into this popular hotel nightclub.

Alchemist (Map p270; www.thealchemistbkk.com; 1/19 Soi 11, Th Sukhumvit; ⏲5pm-midnight Tue-Sun; [S]Nana exit 3) A tiny bar with a big emphasis on cocktails, Alchemist claims to do Bangkok's best old fashioned, and we tend to agree.

Nest (Map p270; www.thenestbangkok.com; 8th fl, Le Fenix Hotel, 33/33 Soi 11, Th Sukhumvit; ⏲5pm-2am; [S]Nana exit 3) Perched eight floors up on the roof of Le Fenix Hotel, Nest is a chic maze of cleverly concealed sofas and inviting day-beds. A DJ soundtrack and one of the more thoughtful pub grub menus in town keep things down to earth.

Oskar (Map p270; www.oskar-bistro.com; 24 Soi 11, Th Sukhumvit; ⏲6pm-2am; [S]Nana exit 3) It touts itself as a bistro, but it's more like a cocktail bar dressed like a club with food.

NARZ — NIGHTCLUB

Map p270 (www.narzclubbangkok.net; 112 Soi Prasanmit, Th Sukhumvit; admission from 600B; ⏲9pm-late; [M]Sukhumvit exit 2, [S]Asok exit 3) Like a small clubbing neighbourhood, Narz consists of three vast zones boasting an equal variety of music. It's largely a domestic scene, but the odd guest DJ can pull a large crowd. Open later than most.

LONG TABLE — BAR

Map p270 (www.longtablebangkok.com; 25th fl, Column Bldg, 48 Soi 16, Th Sukhumvit; ⏲5pm-2am; [M]Sukhumvit exit 2, [S]Asok exit 6) Come to this slick, 25th-floor balcony to sip fruity cocktails and gloat at the poor sods stuck in traffic below. In addition to views, there's a menu of Thai-inspired dishes and generous happy-hour specials. It's about 200m down Soi 16, which is accessible via Th Ratchadaphisek.

HAPPY MONDAY — BAR

Map p270 (Ekkamai Shopping Mall, Soi Ekamai 10, Soi 63 (Ekamai), Th Sukhumvit; ⏲7pm-1am Mon-Sat; [S]Ekkamai exit 1 & taxi) This somewhat concealed pub follows the tried and true Ekamai/Thong Lor formula of retro furniture, a brief bar-snack menu and bizarrely named house drinks. The diverse soundtrack, spun by local and visiting DJs, sets it apart.

GLOW — NIGHTCLUB

Map p270 (www.glowbkk.com; 96/415 Soi Prasanmit, Th Sukhumvit; admission from 400B; ⏲7pm-2am; [M]Sukhumvit exit 2, [S]Asok exit 3) Glow is a small venue with a big reputation. Boasting a huge variety of vodkas and a recently upgraded sound system, the tunes range from hip-hop to electronica and just about everything in between.

SCRATCH DOG NIGHTCLUB

Map p270 (basement, Windsor Suites Hotel, 8-10 Soi 20, Th Sukhumvit; admission 400B; ⏲midnight-late; Ⓜ Sukhumvit exit 2, Ⓢ Asok exit 4) It's pretty much as corny as the name and the Goofy-as-DJ logo suggest, but Scratch Dog pulls in a mixed crowd and is probably the least dodgy of Bangkok's late-late-night clubs. Don't bother showing up before 2am.

☆ ENTERTAINMENT

LIVING ROOM LIVE MUSIC

Map p270 (☎0 2649 8888; www.thelivingroomatbangkok.com/en; Level 1, Sheraton Grande Sukhumvit, 250 Th Sukhumvit; ⏲6pm-midnight; Ⓜ Sukhumvit exit 3, Ⓢ Asok exit 2) Don't let looks deceive you: every night this bland hotel lounge transforms into the city's best venue for live jazz. True to the name, there's comfy, sofa-based seating, all of it within earshot of the music. Enquire ahead of time to see which sax master or hide-hitter is in town.

TITANIUM LIVE MUSIC

Map p270 (www.titaniumbangkok.com; 2/30 Soi 22, Th Sukhumvit; ⏲8pm-1am; Ⓢ Phrom Phong exit 6) Most come to this cheesy 'ice bar' for the chill, the skimpily dressed working girls and the flavoured vodka, but we come for Unicorn, an all-female house band.

SONIC LIVE MUSIC

Map p270 (www.facebook.com/SonicBangkok; 90 Soi 63 (Ekamai), Th Sukhumvit; ⏲6pm-2am; Ⓢ Ekkamai exit 4 & taxi) Drawing a mixture of Thai bands, touring indie acts, big-name DJs and a painfully hip crowd, the intermittently open Sonic has emerged as Bangkok's hottest venue for live music; check the website ahead of time to see what's on.

SOI COWBOY RED-LIGHT DISTRICT

Map p270 (Th Sukhumvit; ⏲4pm-2am; Ⓜ Sukhumvit exit 2, Ⓢ Asok exit 3) This single-lane strip of raunchy bars claims direct lineage to the post-Vietnam War R&R era. A real flesh trade functions amid the flashing neon.

NANA ENTERTAINMENT PLAZA RED-LIGHT DISTRICT

Map p270 (Soi 4 (Nana Tai), Th Sukhumvit; ⏲4pm-2am; Ⓢ Nana exit 2) Nana is a three-storey go-go bar complex where the sexpats are separated from the gawking tourists. It's also home to a few *gà·teu·i* (also spelled *kàthoey;* transgender person) bars.

SHOPPING

NANDAKWANG HANDICRAFTS

Map p270 (www.nandakwang.com; 108/2-3 Soi Prasanmit, Th Sukhumvit; ⏲9am-6.30pm Mon-Sat; Ⓜ Sukhumvit exit 2, Ⓢ Asok exit 3) The Bangkok satellite of a Chiang Mai store, Nandakwang sells a fun and colourful mix of cloth products. Cheery, chunky, hand-embroidered pillows are particularly attractive, and are also the best way to locate this shop, which doesn't have an English language sign.

BANGKOK'S SAVILE ROW

The strip of Th Sukhumvit between BTS stops Nana and Asok is home to tonnes of tailors – both reputable and otherwise. We list some of the former below.

Raja's Fashions (Map p270; ☎0 2253 8379; www.rajasfashions.com; 160/1 Th Sukhumvit; ⏲6.30am-10.30pm Mon-Sat; Ⓢ Nana exit 4) With his photographic memory for names, Bobby will make you feel as important as the long list of ambassadors, foreign politicians and officers he's fitted over his family's decades in the business.

Rajawongse (Map p270; www.dress-for-success.com; 130 Th Sukhumvit; ⏲10.30am-8pm Mon-Sat; Ⓢ Nana exit 2) Another legendary and longstanding Bangkok tailor; Jesse and Victor's creations are particularly renowned among American visitors and residents.

Ricky's Fashion House (Map p270; ☎0 2254 6887; www.rickysfashionhouse.com; 73/5 Th Sukhumvit; ⏲11am-10pm Mon-Sat & 1-5.30pm Sun; Ⓢ Nana exit 1) Ricky gets positive reviews from locals and resident foreigners alike for his more casual styles of custom-made trousers and shirts.

Nickermann's (Map p270; ☎0 2252 6682; www.nickermanns.net; basement, Landmark Hotel, 138 Th Sukhumvit; ⏲10am-8.30pm Mon-Sat, noon-6pm Sun; Ⓢ Nana exit 2) Corporate ladies rave about Nickermann's tailor-made power suits. Formal ball gowns are another area of expertise.

ZUDRANGMA RECORDS MUSIC

Map p270 (www.zudrangmarecords.com; 7/1 Soi 51, Th Sukhumvit; 🕒noon-10pm Tue-Sun; [S]Thong Lo exit 1) Located next door to the popular bar WTF, the headquarters of this retro/world label is a chance to finally combine the university-era pastimes of record-browsing and drinking. Come to snicker at corny old Thai vinyl covers or invest in some of the label's highly regarded compilations of classic *mŏr lam* and *lôok tûng* (both styles of Thai-country music).

TERMINAL 21 SHOPPING CENTRE

Map p270 (www.terminal21.co.th; cnr Th Sukhumvit & Soi 21 (Asoke); 🕒10am-10pm; [M]Sukhumvit exit 3, [S]Asok exit 3) Seemingly catering to a Thai need for wacky objects to be photographed in front of, this new mall is worth a visit for the spectacle as much as the shopping. Start at the basement-level 'airport' and proceed upwards through 'Paris', 'Tokyo' and other city-themed floors.

SOP MOEI ARTS HANDICRAFTS

Map p270 (www.sopmoeiarts.com; Soi 49/9, Th Sukhumvit; 🕒9.30am-5pm Tue-Sat; [S]Phrom Phong exit 3 & taxi) The Bangkok showroom of this nonprofit organisation features the vibrant cloth creations of Karen weavers in Mae Hong Son, in northern Thailand. Near the end of Soi 49/9, in the Racquet Club complex.

ALMETA HANDICRAFTS

Map p270 (www.almeta.com; 20/3 Soi 23, Th Sukhumvit; 🕒10am-6pm; [M]Sukhumvit exit 2, [S]Asoke exit 3) If the verdant colours of Thai silk remind you of frumpy society matrons, you're a candidate for Almeta's earth-tones similar in hue to raw sugar or lotus blossoms.

EMPORIUM SHOPPING CENTRE

Map p270 (www.emporiumthailand.com; cnr Soi 24 & Th Sukhumvit; 🕒10am-10pm; [S]Phrom Phong exit 2) You might not have access to the beautiful people's nightlife scene, but you can observe their spending rituals at this temple to red-hot and classic cool.

THANON SUKHUMVIT MARKET SOUVENIRS

Map p270 (btwn Soi 3 & Soi 15, Th Sukhumvit; 🕒11am-11pm Tue-Sun; [S]Nana exits 1 & 3) Leaving on the first flight out tomorrow morning? Never fear about gifts for those back home; here the street vendors will find you, with faux Fendi handbags, soccer kits, black-felt 'art', sunglasses and jewellery, to name a few. There are also ample stacks of nudie DVDs, Chinese throwing stars, penis-shaped lighters and other questionable gifts for your high school–aged brother.

LOCAL KNOWLEDGE

FAIR-TRADE FAIR

The twice-monthly **ThaiCraft Fair** (Map p270; www.thaicraft.org; 3rd fl, Jasmine City Bldg, cnr Soi 23 & Th Sukhumvit; 🕒10am-3pm; [M]Sukhumvit exit 2, [S]Asok exit 3) is a great chance to browse through the products of more than 60 community groups. For 20 years, ThaiCraft has marketed quality handicrafts made by artisans across all parts of Thailand, and recent fairs have seen products such as hand-made baskets and mulberry-bark notebooks. Check the website to see if the next one is being held during your visit.

DASA BOOK CAFÉ BOOKSTORE

Map p270 (www.dasabookcafe.com; 714/4 Th Sukhumvit; 🕒10am-8pm; [S]Phrom Phong exit 4) Boasting more than 16,000 books, Dasa is one of Bangkok's best-stocked used bookstores. A frequently updated list of stock (also available online) makes it easy to find that book you've been searching for; an attached cafe provides an excuse to linger.

SPORTS & ACTIVITIES

PUSSAPA THAI MASSAGE SCHOOL MASSAGE

Map p270 (☎0 2204 2922; www.thaimassage-bangkok.com/nuat1_egl.htm; 25/8 Soi 26, Th Sukhumvit; tuition from 8000B; 🕒lessons 9am-4pm; [S]Phrom Phong exit 4) Run by a longtime Japanese resident of Bangkok, the basic course in Thai massage here spans 30 hours over five days; there are shorter courses in foot massage and self massage. Thai massage is also available for 300B per hour.

HELPING HANDS COOKING

(☎08 4901 8717; www.cookingwithpoo.com; 1200B; 🕒lessons 8.30am-1pm) This popular cooking course was started by a native of Khlong Toey's slums and is held in her neighbourhood. Courses, which must be booked in advance, span four dishes and include a visit to Khlong Toey Market and transport to and from Emporium.

SPA CENTRAL

Th Sukhumvit is home to many of Bangkok's recommended and reputable massage studios, including the following:

Health Land (Map p270; ✆0 2261 1110; www.healthlandspa.com; 55/5 Soi 21 (Asoke); Thai massage 2hr 500B; ◷9am-midnight; Ⓜ Sukhumvit exit 1, Ⓢ Asok exit 5) A winning formula of affordable prices, expert treatments and pleasant facilities; branches on **Soi Ekamai 10** (Map p270; ✆0 2392 2233; 96/1 Soi Ekamai 10; Thai massage 2hr 500B; ◷9am-midnight; Ⓢ Ekkamai exit 2 & taxi) and Th Sathon Neua (p132).

Asia Herb Association (Map p270; ✆0 2261 7401; www.asiaherbassociation.com; 33/1 Soi 24; Thai massage per hr 400B, with herbal compress 1½hr 900B; ◷9am-midnight; Ⓢ Phrom Phong exit 4) With multiple branches along Th Sukhumvit, including at **Sawatdi** (Map p270; ✆0 2261 2201; 20/1 Soi 31 (Sawatdi); Thai massage per hr 400B, with herbal compress 1½hr 900B; ◷9am-midnight; Ⓢ Phrom Phong exit 5) and **Thong Lor** (Map p270; ✆0 2392 3631; 58/19-25 Soi 55 (Thong Lor); Thai massage per hr 400B, with herbal compress 1½hr 900B; ◷9am-midnight; Ⓢ Thong Lo exit 3), this Japanese-owned chain specialises in massage using *bràkòp* (traditional Thai herbal compresses).

Divana Massage & Spa (Map p270; ✆0 2261 6784; www.divanaspa.com; 7 Soi 25; massage from 1150B, spa packages from 2350B; ◷11am-9pm Mon-Fri, 10am-9pm Sat & Sun; Ⓜ Sukhumvit exit 2, Ⓢ Asok exit 6) Divana retains a unique Thai touch with a private and soothing setting in a garden house.

Coran (Map p270; ✆0 2726 9978; www.coranbangkok.com; 94-96/1 Soi Ekamai 10, Soi 63 (Ekamai); Thai massage per hr 600B; ◷11am-10pm; Ⓢ Ekkamai exit 4 & taxi) A classy, low-key spa in a Thai villa. Aroma and Thai-style massage are also available.

Lavana (Map p270; ✆0 2229 4510; www.lavanabangkok.com; 4 Soi 12; Thai massage per hr 450B; ◷9am-11pm; Ⓜ Sukhumvit, Ⓢ Asok) Another spa with an emphasis on traditional Thai healing using *bràkòp*. Oil massage is also available.

Eugenia Spa (Map p270; ✆08 8083 7300; www.theeugeniaspa.com; Eugenia hotel, 267 Soi 31 (Sawatdi); Thai massage from 800B, spa packages from 2000B; ◷10am-10pm) New spa with a charming vintage vibe, experienced staff and positive feedback from customers.

Rakuten (Map p270; ✆0 2258 9433; www.rakutenspa.com; 94 Soi 33; Thai massage per hr 250B; ◷noon-midnight; Ⓡ Phrom Phong exit 5) A Japanese-themed spa that gets good reports for its Thai-style massage.

So Thai Spa (Map p270; ✆0 2662 2691; www.sothaispa.com; 269 Soi 31; Thai massage from 750B, spa packages from 1300B; ◷10am-10pm; Ⓢ Phrom Phong exit 5) A foreign-run spa based out of a villa. Treatments won't break the bank and get good reports.

Baan Dalah (Map p270; ✆0 2653 3358; www.baandalahmindbodyspa.com; 2 Soi 8; Thai massage per hr 350B; ◷10am-midnight; Ⓢ Nana exit 4) A small, conveniently located spa with services ranging from foot massage to full-body Thai massage.

KRUDAM GYM
THAI BOXING

Map p270 (✆08 7111 7115, 08 4108 6652; www.krudamgym.com; Soi 24, Th Sukhumvit; per lesson 500B; ◷10am-9pm Mon-Fri, 10am-7.30pm Sat & Sun; Ⓢ Phrom Phong exit 2) Helmed by Dam Srichan, a former professional boxer, this small gym in downtown Bangkok offers 1½hr *moo·ay tai* (Thai boxing; also spelt muay thai) lessons for all skill levels, including for children. See website for times.

ABC AMAZING BANGKOK CYCLISTS
CYCLING

Map p270 (✆0 2665 6364; www.realasia.net; 10/5-7 Soi Aree, Soi 26, Th Sukhumvit; tours from 1300B; ◷daily tours at 8am, 10am, 1pm & 6pm; Ⓢ Phrom Phong exit 4) A long-running operation offering morning, afternoon and all-day bike tours of Bangkok and its suburbs.

FUN-ARIUM
PLAY CENTRE

Map p270 (✆0 2665 6555; www.funarium.co.th; 111/1 Soi 26, Th Sukhumvit; admission 110-320B; ◷9am-7pm; Ⓢ Phrom Phong exit 1 & taxi) Bangkok's largest indoor playground, with coffee and wi-fi to keep parents happy while the kids play.

Greater Bangkok

Neighbourhood Top Five

1 Getting lost in the **Chatuchak Weekend Market** (p147), one of the world's largest markets and a must-do Bangkok experience.

2 Partying at the bars and clubs on **Royal City Ave** (RCA; p153).

3 Travelling back in time at retro-themed market **Talat Rot Fai** (p150).

4 Ditching the smog and traffic and heading to **Ko Kret** (p151).

5 Experiencing the charms of provincial Thailand at **Nonthaburi Market** (p150).

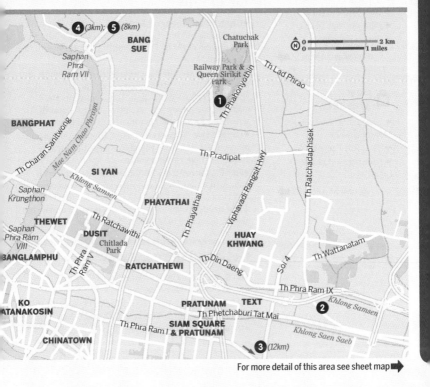

For more detail of this area see sheet map ➡

Lonely Planet's Top Tip

Make a point of arriving at Chatuchak Weekend Market as early as possible – around 10am is a good bet – as the crowds are much thinner and the temperatures are slightly lower.

Best Places to Eat

➡ Chatuchak Weekend Market (p147)

➡ Yusup (p152)

➡ Or Tor Kor Market (p151)

➡ Baan Suan Pai (p152)

➡ Salt (p152)

➡ Rosdee (p152)

For reviews, see p152.➡

Best Drinking & Entertainment

➡ Cosmic Café (p154)

➡ Parking Toys (p153)

➡ Slim/Flix (p153)

For reviews, see p152.➡

Best Markets

➡ Chatuchak Weekend Market (p147)

➡ Talat Rot Fai (p150)

➡ Nonthaburi Market (p150)

For reviews, see p155.➡

Explore: Greater Bangkok

Most people come to greater Bangkok with markets in mind – the northern suburbs are home to some of the city's best. Chatuchak Weekend Market, one of the world's largest, draws tens of thousands of shoppers every weekend and is a hectic but must-do Bangkok experience. The Nonthaburi Market is an expansive wet market that shows the city's provincial side, while the retro-themed Talat Rot Fai acts as a magnet for Bangkok's hipsters. Other reasons to visit Bangkok's suburbs include nightlife, with the RCA entertainment strip drawing thousands of partiers.

For the day markets you'll generally want to arrive as early as possible. Set aside at least half a day for Chatuchak. Getting to Nonthaburi Market by boat takes at least an hour; keep in mind that the market has pretty much packed up by 9am. Talat Rot Fai is usually open until around 11pm. Most clubs and live music venues don't get going until 11pm and close at 2am.

Most markets are within easy access of the northern extents of the BTS (Skytrain) and/or MRT (Metro). Reaching other destinations in Bangkok's 'burbs often involves a taxi ride from BTS or MRT terminal stations and a bit of luck. A smartphone with a mapping function will be an invaluable tool for helping you get to the right place and on time.

Local Life

➡**Chatuchak Weekend Market** It may be a huge draw for tourists, but it's still very much a local affair, with tens of thousands of Thais shuffling between stalls and eating snacks every Saturday and Sunday.

➡**RCA** For years, the dance clubs, live-music clubs and bars along Royal City Ave have been the first nightlife choice for most young Thais. In recent years the clientele has grown up – slightly, at least – and RCA now hosts locals and visitors of just about any age.

➡**Local Style** Greasers, cowboys, hippies, punks and mods: Talat Rot Fai is the place to see the various cliques of modern Thai youth.

➡**Full-Flavoured Eats** Although a bit of a schlep, an excursion to Bangkok's suburbs can be a profoundly tasty experience, with heaps of restaurants that don't tone down their flavours for foreigners. The city's outskirts are also a great place to sample regional Thai cuisine.

Getting There & Away

➡**BTS** Ari, Bang Chak, Chong Nonsi, Ekkamai, Mo Chit, Ratchathewi, Wongwian Yai.

➡**MRT** Chatuchak Park, Kamphaeng Phet, Phahon Yothin, Phra Ram 9, Thailand Cultural Centre.

➡**River ferry** Tha Nonthaburi, Tha Saphan Phra Pin Klao.

CHATUCHAK WEEKEND MARKET

Imagine all of Bangkok's markets fused together in a seemingly never-ending commerce-themed barrio. Now add a little artistic flair, a saunalike climate and bargaining crowds and you've got a rough sketch of Chatuchak (also spelled 'Jatujak' or nicknamed 'JJ'). Everything is sold here, from live snakes to *mŏr lam* CDs. Once you're deep in its bowels, it will seem like there is no order and no escape, but Chatuchak is actually arranged into relatively coherent sections.

Antiques, Handicrafts & Souvenirs

Section 1 is the place to go for Buddha statues, old LPs and random antiques.

More secular arts and crafts, like musical instruments and hill-tribe items, can be found in Sections 25 and 26. **Meng** (Section 26, Stall 195, Soi 8) features a mish-mash of quirky antiques from Thailand and Myanmar (Burma).

Baan Sin Thai (Section 24, Stall 130, Soi 1) sells *kŏhn* masks and old-school toys, while **Kitcharoen Dountri** (Section 8, Stall 464, Soi 15) specialises in Thai musical instruments, including flutes, whistles and drums, and CDs of classical Thai music.

Golden Shop (Section 17, Stall 19, Soi 1) is your bog-standard souvenir shop, and boasts an equal blend of tacky and worthwhile items, ranging from traditionally dressed dolls to commemorative plates. Other quirky gifts available at Chatuchak include the lifelike plastic Thai fruit and vegetables at **Marché** (Section 17, Stall 254, Soi 1) or their scaled-down miniature counterparts nearby at **Papachu** (Section 17, Stall 23, Soi 1).

Section 7 is a virtual open-air art gallery; we particularly like the Bangkok-themed murals at **Pariwat A-nantachina** (Section 7, Stall 118, Soi 2).

Several shops in Section 10, including **Tuptim Shop** (Section 10, Stall 261, Soi 19), sell Burmese lacquerware.

DON'T MISS...

➡ Cheap clothes
➡ One-of-a-kind souvenirs
➡ A market meal

PRACTICALITIES

➡ ตลาดนัดจตุจักร, Talat Nat Jatujak
➡ www.chatuchak.org
➡ Th Phahonyothin
➡ ◷9am-6pm Sat & Sun
➡ Ⓜ Chatuchak Park exit 1, Kamphaeng Phet exits 1 & 2, Ⓢ Mo Chit exit 1

IMPORTANT STUFF

There is an information centre and several banks with ATMs and foreign-exchange booths at the **Chatuchak Park offices**, near the northern end of the market's Soi 1, Soi 2 and Soi 3. Pay toilets are located sporadically throughout the market.

There are a few vendors out on weekday mornings, and open every day is nearby **Or Tor Kor Market (p151)**, a vegetable, plant and flower market, which also has a decent food court, opposite the market's southern side.

FINDING YOUR WAY AROUND

Schematic maps are located throughout Chatuchak; if you need more detail (not to mention insider tips), consider purchasing **Nancy Chandler's Map of Bangkok** (www.nancy chandler.net), available at most Bangkok bookstores.

Clothing & Accessories

Clothing dominates much of Chatuchak, starting in Section 8 and continuing through the even-numbered sections to 24. Sections 5 and 6 deal in used clothing for every Thai youth subculture, from punks to cowboys; Soi 7, where it transects Sections 12 and 14, is heavy on hip-hop and skate fashions. Tourist-sized clothes and textiles are found in sections 8 and 10.

Sections 2 and 3, particularly the tree-lined Soi 2 of the former, is the Siam Sq of Chatuchak, and is home to heaps of trendy independent labels. Moving north, Soi 4 in Section 4 boasts several shops selling locally designed T-shirts. In fact, Chatuchak as a whole is a particularly good place to pick up quirky T-shirts of all types.

For something more rustic, **Khaki-Nang** (Section 8, Stall 267-268, Soi 17) sells canvas clothing and tote bags, many featuring old-school Thai themes. And if you can't make it up to Chiang Mai, **Roi** (Section 25, Stall 268, Soi 4) and similar shops nearby are where you'll find hand-woven cotton scarves, clothes and other accessories from Thailand's north.

For accessories, several shops in Sections 24 and 26, such as **Orange Karen Silver** (Section 26, Stall 246, Soi 8), specialise in chunky silver jewellery and uncut semiprecious stones.

Eating & Drinking

Lots of Thai-style eating and snacking will stave off Chatuchak rage (cranky behaviour brought on by dehydration or hunger), and numerous food stalls are set up throughout the market, particularly between Sections 6 and 8. Long-established standouts include **Foon Talop** (Section 26, Stall 319, Soi 8; mains 40-100B; ⊙10am-6pm Sat & Sun), an incredibly popular Isan restaurant; **Café Ice** (Section 7, Stall 267, Soi 3; mains 100-300B; ⊙10am-6pm Sat & Sun), a Western-Thai fusion joint that does good *pàt tai* (fried noodles) and tasty fruit shakes; and **Saman Islam** (Section 16, Stall 34, Soi 24; mains 40-100B; ⊙10am-6pm Sat & Sun), a Thai-Muslim restaurant that serves a tasty chicken biryani. If you need air-con, pop into **Toh-Plue** (Section 27; mains 100-250B; ⊙9am-7pm; ﹡; ⓂMRT Kamphaeng Phet) for all the Thai standards. **Viva 8** (www.facebook.com/Viva8JJ; Section 8, Soi 16/1; mains 100-300B; ⊙9am-10pm Sat & Sun) features a bar, a DJ and, when we stopped by, a Spanish chef making huge platters of paella. As evening draws near, down a beer at **Viva's** (Section 26, Stall 149, Soi 6; ⊙10am-10pm Sat & Sun), a cafe-bar that features live music and stays open late, or cross Th Kamphaengphet 2 to the cosy whisky bars that keep nocturnal hours.

Housewares & Decor

The western edge of the market, particularly sections 8 to 26, features all manner of housewares, from cheap plastic buckets to expensive brass woks. This area is a particularly good place to stock up on inexpensive Thai ceramics, ranging from celadon to the traditional rooster-themed bowls from Lampang. **N & D Tablewares** (Section 25, Stall 185, Soi 4) has a huge variety of stainless-steel flatware, and **Ton-Tan** (Section 8, Stall 460, Soi 15/1) deals in coconut- and sugar-palm derived plates, bowls and other utensils.

Those looking to spice up the house should stop by **Spice Boom** (Section 26, Stall 246, Soi 8), where you can find dried herbs and spices for both consumption and decoration. Other notable olfactory indulgences include the handmade soaps, lotions, salts and scrubs at **D-narn** (Section 19, Stall 204, Soi 1) and the fragrant perfumes and essential oils at **AnyaDharu Scent Library** (Section 3, Stall 3, Soi 43/2).

Pets

Possibly the most fun you'll ever have window-shopping will be petting puppies and cuddling kittens in sections 13 and 15. Soi 9 of the former features several shops that deal solely in clothing for pets.

Plants & Gardening

The interior perimeter of sections 2 to 4 features a huge variety of potted plants, flowers, herbs and fruits, and the accessories needed to maintain them. Many of these shops are also open on weekday afternoons.

GREATER BANGKOK CHATUCHAK WEEKEND MARKET

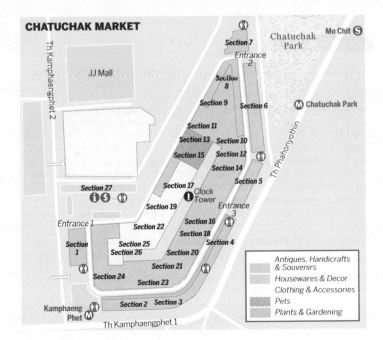

CHATUCHAK MARKET

SIGHTS

CHATUCHAK WEEKEND MARKET
MARKET

See p147.

ANCIENT CITY
MUSEUM

(เมืองโบราณ, Muang Boran; www.ancientcity.com; 296/1 Th Sukhumvit, Samut Prakan; adult/child 500/250B; ⏰8am-5pm) Don't have the time to see Thailand's most famous historic monuments? Then consider visiting scaled-down versions of them in what claims to be the largest open-air museum in the world.

Ancient City lies outside Samut Prakan, which is accessible via air-conditioned bus 511 from Bearing BTS station at the east end of Th Sukhumvit. Upon reaching the bus terminal at Pak Nam, board minibus 36, which passes the entrance to Ancient City.

Covering more than 80 hectares of peaceful countryside, Ancient City is littered with 109 facsimiles of famous Thai monuments. It's an excellent place to explore by bicycle (daily rental 50B) as it's usually quiet and rarely crowded.

TALAT ROT FAI
MARKET

(ตลาดรถไฟ; www.facebook.com/taradrodfi; Soi 51, Th Srinakharin; ⏰6pm-midnight Wed & Fri-Sun; [S]Udom Suk exit 2 & taxi) This market is all about the retro, with goods ranging from antique enamel platters to second-hand Vespas. With mobile snack vendors, VW van-based bars and even a few land-bound pubs, it's also much more than just a shopping destination.

NONTHABURI MARKET
MARKET

(ตลาดนนทบุรี; Tha Nam Nonthaburi, Nonthaburi; ⏰5-9am; ⛴Tha Nonthaburi) Located a short walk from Tha Nonthaburi, the northernmost extent of the Chao Phraya Express boats, this is one of the most expansive and atmospheric produce markets in the area.

To get to the market, take any north-bound Chao Phraya Express boat and get off at Tha Nonthaburi, the northernmost stop for most lines. The market is a two-minute walk east along the main road from the pier.

Exotic fruits, towers of dried chillies, smoky grills and the city's few remaining rickshaws form a very un-Bangkok backdrop here. Come early though, as most vendors are gone by 9am.

BANG NAM PHEUNG MARKET
MARKET

(ตลาดบางน้ำผึ้ง; Bang Nam Pheung; ⏰8am-3pm Sat & Sun; [S]Bang Na exit 2 & taxi) An easy es-

LOCAL KNOWLEDGE

BANGKOK'S GREEN LUNG

Joey Tulyanond is Chief Greening Officer at the Bangkok Tree House (p192), an ecofriendly resort on the Phra Pradaeng Peninsula.

How would you describe the Phra Pradaeng Peninsula? Serene and undisturbed. Geographically, the area is an island that is separated from Bangkok by the Chao Phraya River. Physically, it's as if the peninsula is lost in another time – in fact, if you wanted to see what Bangkok was like 200 years ago, this is the place to visit.

Why is it called Bangkok's 'green lung'? The people there are blessed with having a tropical jungle in their backyard, in addition to some very unique neighbours, from turquoise kingfishers to timid turtles.

What kind of people live there? Mostly local farmers and plantation owners, but more recently Bangkokians weary of city living and expats yearning for a slower and simpler life.

What kind of activities can visitors do there? A stroll through the lush green walkways along the fruit orchards always does it for me, but the weekend floating market Bang Nam Pheung Market (p150), the 200-*râi* (about 80 acres) botanical park Si Nakhon Kheun Khan Park (p151) and the dilapidated but stunning 250-year-old Bang Nam Pheung Nok temple (p151) are also worth a visit.

How does one get around? Bicycles, which can be rented at various locations, and which can be borrowed at the Bangkok Tree House.

Is it difficult to get to there? A skip on the BTS, a hop on the taxi and a jump on the green ferry and you are there.

WORTH A DETOUR

KO KRET

Bangkok's closest green getaway, **Ko Kret** (เกาะเกร็ด; adult/child 299/250B) is an artificial 'island', the result of a canal being dug nearly 300 years ago to shorten an oxbow bend in the Chao Phraya. Today Ko Kret is known for its hand-thrown terracotta pots (sold at markets throughout Bangkok) and its food. This island and the pottery tradition date back to one of Thailand's oldest settlements of Mon people, who were a dominant people of central Thailand between the 6th and 10th centuries AD. From **Wat Poramai Yikawat** (วัดปรมัยยิกาวาส; Ko Kret; ⊙9am-5pm) **FREE**, which has an interesting Mon-style marble Buddha, go in either direction to find working pottery centres on the east and north coasts.

Even more prevalent than pottery is food. At weekends, droves of Thais flock to Ko Kret to munch on deep-fried savouries, *kôw châa* (a Mon dish combining savoury/sweet titbits and chilled rice) and iced coffee. Arrive on a weekday and the eating options are much fewer, but you'll have the place to yourself.

Ko Kret is in Nonthaburi, about 12km north of central Bangkok. To get there, take bus 33 from Sanam Luang, bus 166 from the Victory Monument or a taxi to Pak Kret, before boarding the cross-river ferry (2B, 5am to 9pm) that leaves from Wat Sanam Neua. Alternatively, the Chao Phraya Express Boat's 'green flag' express goes as far north as Pak Kret on weekdays between 6.15am and 8.10am, and 3.30pm and 6.05pm (32B).

---

cape from the city, this buzzy, weekends-only market is located on the Phra Pradaeng Peninsula, a vast rural-feeling district often referred to as Bangkok's 'green lung'. Because it's a Thai market, the emphasis is on food, and it's a great place for unrestrained outdoor snacking.

To get there, take the BTS to Bang Na and jump in a taxi for the short ride to the pier at Wat Bang Nam Pheung Nork. From there, take the river-crossing ferry (4B) followed by a short motorcycle taxi (10B) ride.

The market is a stop on the many bike tours that criss-cross the peninsula, as are **Wat Bang Nam Pheung Nok** **FREE**, a 250-year-old temple near the pier, and **Si Nakhon Kheun Khan Park** (⊙6am-7pm) **FREE**, a vast botanical garden with a large lake and bird-watching tower.

OR TOR KOR MARKET   MARKET

(อค์การตลาดเพื่อเกษตรกร (ตลาด อ.ต.ก.); Th Kamphaengphet; ⊙8am-6pm; MKamphaeng Phet exit 3) Or Tor Kor is Bangkok's highest-quality fruit and agricultural market, and sights such as toddler-sized mangoes and dozens of pots full of curries amount to culinary trainspotting.

To get here, take the MRT to Kamphaeng Phet station and exit on the side opposite Chatuchak (the exit says 'Marketing Organization for Farmers').

The vast majority of vendors' goods are takeaway only, but a small food court and a few informal restaurants exist, including **Rot Det**, which does tasty stir-fries and curries, and **Sut Jai Kai Yaang**, just south of the market, which does spicy northeastern-style Thai.

ARTIST'S HOUSE   ART GALLERY

(บ้านศิลปิน, Khlong Bang Luang, Thonburi; ⊙10am-6pm; SWongwian Yai exit 2 & taxi) **FREE** Sort of a gallery, kind of a coffee shop, more a cultural centre... It's hard to pin down this old wooden house on Khlong Bang Luang. There's food available on weekends, as well as a free traditional Thai puppet show scheduled for 2pm, but the best excuse to come is simply to soak up the old-world canalside vibe.

Artist's House is most easily accessible via Soi 3, Th Charansanitwong; cross the canal at the bridge by the 7-Eleven, turn left and it's about 100m down.

BANGKOK UNIVERSITY
ART GALLERY   ART GALLERY

(BUG; bugallery.blogspot.com; 3rd fl, Bldg 9, City Campus, Th Phra Ram IV; ⊙10am-7pm Tue-Sat; SEkkamai exit 4 & taxi) **FREE** This spacious new compound is located at what is currently the country's most cutting-edge art school. Recent exhibitions have encompassed a variety of media by some of the country's top names, as well as the work of internationally recognised artists.

ERAWAN MUSEUM (CHANG SAM SIAN) MUSEUM

(พิพิธภัณฑ์ช้างเอราวัณ (ช้างสามเศียร); www.erawan-museum.com; Soi 119, Th Sukhumvit; adult/child 400/200B; ⏲8am-5pm) Located on the way to Ancient City and created by the same visionary, this museum is actually a five-storey sculpture of Erawan, Indra's three-headed elephant mount from Hindu mythology. The interior is filled with antique sculptures but is most impressive for the stained-glass ceiling.

The museum is 8km from Bangkok's Ekamai bus station. Any Samut Prakan–bound bus can drop you off; just tell the driver.

🍴 EATING

YUSUP MUSLIM-THAI $

(531/12 Kaset-Navamin Hwy; mains 50-120B; ⏲8.30am-3pm; [S]Mo Chit exit 3 & taxi) The Thai-language sign in front of this restaurant boldly says *rah·chah kôw mòk* (King of Biryani) and Yusup backs it up with flawless biryani, not to mention mouth-puckeringly sour oxtail soup and decadent *gaang mát·sà·màn* (Muslim curry).

To get here, take a taxi heading north from BTS Mo Chit and tell the driver to take you to the Kaset intersection and turn right on Th Kaset-Navamin. Yusup is on the left-hand side, about 1km past the first stoplight.

For dessert try *roh·dee wăhn*, a paratha-like crispy pancake topped with sweetened condensed milk and sugar – a dish that will send most carb-fearing Westerners running away screaming.

BAAN SUAN PAI VEGETARIAN, THAI $

(Banana Family Park, Th Phahonyothin; mains 15-30B; ⏲7am-3pm; 🥕; [S]Ari exit 1) This open-air vegie centre is worth the trip north of town. Expect a wide variety of vendors selling meat-free Thai-style dishes, drinks and desserts.

To find it, take exit 1 at Ari BTS and turn right down the narrow alleyway just after the petrol station.

PHAT THAI ARI THAI $

(Soi Phaholyothin Center, Th Phahonyothin; mains 80-120B; ⏲9am-8pm; [S]Ari exit 4) One of the city's better-known *pàt tai* shops is located a couple of blocks from the eponymous soi. Try the innovative 'noodle-less' version, where long strips of crispy green papaya are substituted for the traditional rice noodles from Chanthaburi.

Phat Thai Ari is located on the narrow soi that leads to Phaholyothin Center, just north of BTS Ari.

FATBIRD INTERNATIONAL $$

(☎0 2619 6609; www.facebook.com/fatbird; Soi 7 (Ari), Th Phahonyothin; mains 200-300B; ⏲5.30pm-midnight Tue-Sun; ❄; [S]Ari exit 3) The dishes at this buzzy new place, which span from tater tots to 'tom-yum-kung fried rice', don't quite cut it for dinner. But approach them as bar snacks, especially coupled with Fatbird's great drinks, eclectic shophouse atmosphere and decent soundtrack, and you have yourself a winner.

ROSDEE CHINESE-THAI $$

(2357 Th Sukhumvit; mains 70-2800B; ⏲8am-9pm; ❄; [S]Bang Chak exit 1) Rosdee is known for its consistently tasty, well-executed Chinese-Thai favourites such as the garlicky *or sòo·an* (oysters fried with egg and a sticky batter), or the house speciality, braised goose.

Rosdee is located on the corner with Soi 95/1, a short walk from the BTS stop at Bang Chak.

SALT INTERNATIONAL $$$

(www.saltbangkok.com; Soi 7 (Ari), Th Phahonyothin; mains 220-1350B; ⏲5pm-midnight Mon-Sat; ❄; [S]Ari exit 1) With a DJ booth flashing a strategically placed copy of *Larousse Gastronomique*, Salt is the kind of eclectic place that's currently shaping Bangkok's restaurant scene. Appropriately located in Ari, suburban Bangkok's trendiest 'hood, the menu ranges from sushi to wood-fired pizza, with a few forays into contemporary French.

🍷 DRINKING & NIGHTLIFE

AREE BAR

(cnr Soi Ari 4 (Nua) & Soi 7 (Ari), Th Phahonyothin; ⏲6pm-1am; [S]Ari exit 3) Exposed brick, chunky carpets and warm lighting give Aree a cosier feel than your average Bangkok bar. It also offers live music (from 8pm, Tuesday to Sunday), contemporary Thai

TAXI ALTARS: INSURANCE ON THE DASHBOARD

As your taxi races into Bangkok from the airport, your delight at being able to do the 30km trip for less than US$10 is soon replaced by uneasiness, anxiety and eventually outright fear – 150km/h is fast, you're tailgating the car in front and there's no seatbelt. You can rest assured (or not), however, that your driver will share none of these concerns.

All of which makes the humble taxi trip an instructive introduction to Thai culture. Buddhists believe in karma and thus that their fate is, to a large extent, predestined. Unlike Western ideas, which take a more scientific approach to road safety, many Thais believe factors such as speed, concentration, seatbelts and actual driving skills have no bearing whatsoever on your chances of being in a crash. Put simply, if you die a horrible death on the road, karma says you deserved it. The trouble is that when a passenger gets into a taxi they bring their karma and any bad spirits the passenger might have along for the ride. Which could upset the driver's own fate.

To counteract such bad influences most Bangkok taxi drivers turn the dashboard and ceiling into a sort of life-insurance shrine. The ceiling will have a *yantra* diagram drawn in white powder by a monk as a form of spiritual protection. This will often be accompanied by portraits of notable royals. Below this a red box dangling red tassels, beads and amulets hangs from the rear-vision mirror, while the dashboard is populated by Buddhist and royal statuettes, and quite possibly banknotes with the king's image prominent and more amulets. With luck (such as it exists in Thailand), the talismans will protect your driver from any bad karma you bring into the cab. Passengers, meanwhile, must simply hope that their driver's number is not up. If you feel like it might be, try saying *cháh cháh* soothingly – that is, ask your driver to slow down. For a look inside some of Bangkok's 100,000 or so taxis, check out **Still Life in Moving Vehicle** (www.lifeinmovingvehicle.blogspot.com).

drinking snacks, and a relatively sophisticated drinks list.

SLIM/FLIX
NIGHTCLUB

(29/22-32 Royal City Ave (RCA), off Th Phra Ram IX; ⊙9pm-2am; ⓂPhra Ram 9 exit 3 & taxi) Ideal for the indecisive raver, this immense three-in-one complex dominating one end of RCA features chilled house on one side (Flix), while the other (Slim) does the hip-hop/R&B soundtrack found across much of the city. Oh, and there's a restaurant thrown in there somewhere as well. Despite its size, this place is positively packed on Friday and Saturday nights, when foreigners must pay a 300B entry fee.

ROUTE 66
NIGHTCLUB

(www.route66club.com; 29/33-48 Royal City Ave (RCA), off Th Phra Ram IX; ⊙8pm-2am; ⓂPhra Ram 9 exit 3 & taxi) This place has been around just about as long as RCA, but a recent facelift has given it a new feel and a loyal following. Top 40 hip-hop rules the main space here, although there are several different themed 'levels', featuring anything from Thai pop to live music. Foreigners pay a 300B entry fee on Fridays and Saturdays.

CASTRO
NIGHTCLUB

(www.facebook.com/Castro.rca.bangkok; Block C, RCA, off Th Phra Ram IX; ⊙9.30pm-4.30am; ⓂPhra Ram 9 exit 3 & taxi) Coyote boys, late hours and a dark, anything-goes lounge: RCA's biggest gay bar has all the essentials for a night you might love to regret.

FAKE CLUB
NIGHTCLUB

(www.facebook.com/fakeclub.bangkok; Th Kamphaengphet; ⊙8pm-2am; ⓂKamphaeng Phet exit 1) The area directly west of Chatuchak Weekend Market remains a popular destination for Thai gay men. You'll still find a few students here, but the crowd is generally older and more sophisticated, as is the decor and music. Fake Club has live music from 11.30pm.

☆ ENTERTAINMENT

★ PARKING TOYS
LIVE MUSIC

(⌨0 2907 2228; 17/22 Soi Mayalap, off Kaset-Navamin Hwy; ⊙6pm-2am; ⓈMo Chit exit 3 & taxi) Parking Toys is one of Bangkok's best venues for live music, and hosts an eclectic revolving cast of fun bands ranging in genre from rockabilly to electro-funk jam acts.

To get here, take a taxi heading north from BTS Mo Chit and tell the driver to take you to the Kaset intersection and turn right on Th Kaset-Navamin; Parking Toys is just past the second stoplight on this road.

COSMIC CAFÉ
LIVE MUSIC

(www.facebook.com/cosmiccafe.bkk; Block C, Royal City Ave (RCA), off Th Phra Ram IX; ☺8pm-2am Mon-Sat; ⓜPhra Ram 9 exit 3 & taxi) Blessedly more low-key than most places on RCA, Cosmic calls itself a cafe but looks like a bar, and in recent years has become one of Bangkok's better live-music clubs. Despite the slight identity crisis, it's is a fun place to drink, rock to live music and meet, Thaistyle.

LUMPINEE BOXING STADIUM
THAI BOXING

(www.muaythailumpinee.net/en; Th Ramintra; tickets 3rd-class/2nd-class/ringside 1000/2000/3000B; ⓜChatuchak Park exit 2 & taxi, ⓢMo Chit exit 3 & taxi) The other of Bangkok's two premier Thai boxing rings recently moved to fancy new digs north of town. Matches occur on Tuesday and Friday from 6.30pm to 10.30pm, and Saturday at 4pm to 8pm and 8.30pm to midnight. At time of research there were plans underway for a Thai boxing museum and a school for foreign fighters.

TAWANDANG GERMAN BREWERY
LIVE MUSIC

(www.tawandang.co.th; cnr Th Phra Ram III & Th Narathiwat Ratchanakharin (Th Chong Nonsi); ☺5pm-1am; ⓢChong Nonsi exit 2 & taxi) It's Oktoberfest all year round at this hangar-sized music hall. The Thai-German food is tasty, the house-made brews are entirely potable, and the nightly stage shows make singing along a necessity. Music starts at 8.30pm.

MAMBO CABARET
CABARET

(☎0 2294 7381; www.mambocabaret.com; 59/28 Yannawa Tat Mai; tickets 800-1000B; ☺show times 7.15pm & 8.30pm; ⓢChong Nonsi exit 2 taxi) This transgender cabaret venue hosts choreographed stage shows featuring Broadway high-kicks and lip-synched pop tunes.

HOUSE
CINEMA

(www.houserama.com; 3rd fl, RCA Plaza, Royal City Avenue (RCA), off Th Phra Ram IX; ⓜPhra Ram 9 exit 3 & taxi) Bangkok's first art-house cinema, House shows lots of foreign flicks of the non-Hollywood type.

HOLLYWOOD
LIVE MUSIC

(Soi 8, Th Ratchadaphisek; ☺8pm-2am; ⓜPhra Ram 9 exit 3) Like taking a time machine back to the previous century, Hollywood is a holdover from the days when a night out in Bangkok meant corny live stage shows, wiggling around the whiskey-set table and neon, neon, neon. As is the case with many of its counterparts, you'll need to purchase a bottle of whiskey at the door to gain entry.

SIAM NIRAMIT
THEATRE

(☎0 2649 9222; www.siamniramit.com; 19 Th Thiam Ruammit; tickets 1500-2350B; ☺shows

---

A LITTLE BIG TIME

The suburbs north of Bangkok are home to handful of kid-orientated theme parks. All of the following lie north of Bangkok and are accessible via taxi from Mo Chit BTS station.

Safari World (☎0 2518 1000; www.safariworld.com; 99 Th Ramindra 1; adult/child 1200/900B; ☺9am-5pm; ⓢMo Chit exit 3 and taxi) Claiming to be the world's largest 'open zoo', Safari World is divided into two parts: a drive-through Safari Park and a Marine Park. In the Safari Park, visitors take a bus tour (windows remained closed) through an 'oasis for animals' separated into different habitats. The Marine Park focuses on stunts by dolphins and other trained animals; if that's not your thing you can go to the Safari Park only.

Siam Park City (☎0 2919 7200; www.siamparkcity.com; 203 Th Suansiam; adult/child 900/750B; ☺10am-6pm; ⓢMo Chit exit 1 & taxi) Siam Park City features more than 30 rides and a water park with the largest wave pool in the world.

Dream World (☎0 2577 8666; www.dreamworld.co.th/2011; 62 Moo 1, Th Rangsit-Nakornnayok, Pathum Thani; 800B; ☺10am-5pm Mon-Fri, to 7pm Sat & Sun; ⓢMo Chit exit 1 & taxi) Expansive amusement park that boasts a snow room.

8pm; MThailand Cultural Centre exit 1 & access by shuttle bus) A cultural theme park, this enchanted kingdom transports visitors to a Disneyfied version of ancient Siam with a technicoloured stage show of traditional performance depicting the Lanna Kingdom, the Buddhist heaven and Thai festivals.

A free shuttle-bus service is available at Thailand Cultural Centre MRT station, running every 15 minutes from 6pm to 7.45pm.

SHOPPING

FORTUNE TOWN   ELECTRONICS
(Th Ratchadaphisek; ◔10am-9pm; MPhra Ram 9 exit 1) If you need to supplement your digital life with cheap software, a camera or computer peripherals, this multistorey mall is a much saner alternative to Pantip Plaza (p116).

SPORTS & ACTIVITIES

BAIPAI THAI COOKING SCHOOL   COOKING
(☏0 2561 1404; www.baipai.com; 8/91 Soi 54, Th Ngam Wong Wan; 2200B; ◔lessons 9.30am-1.30pm & 1.30-5.30pm Mon-Sat) Housed in an attractive suburban villa, and taught by a small army of staff, Baipai offers two daily lessons of four dishes each. Transportation is available.

AMITA THAI COOKING CLASS   COOKING
(☏0 2466 8966; www.amitathaicooking.com; 162/17 Soi 14, Th Wutthakat, Thonburi; 3000B; ◔lessons 9.30am-1pm Thu-Tue) In a canalside house in Thonburi, a course here includes

a romp in a herb garden and instruction in four dishes. The fee covers transporation, including boat ride from Tha Maharaj.

MANOHRA CRUISES   DINNER CRUISE
(☏0 2476 0022; www.manohracruises.com; 1400-1990B; ◔cruise 7.30-9.30pm; ⛴hotel shuttle boat from Tha Sathon, Central Pier) This cruise takes place aboard a restored teak rice barge, and probably has the best food of Bangkok's various dinner cruises. It departs from Anantara Bangkok Riverside Resort & Spa, accessible via hotel shuttle boat from Tha Sathon (Central Pier).

HOUSE OF DHAMMA   MEDITATION
(☏0 2512 6083; www.houseofdhamma.com; 26/9 Soi 15, Th Lat Prao; fee by donation; ◔lessons 10am-5pm Wed-Sun; MPhahon Yothin exit 5) Helen Jandamit has opened her suburban Bangkok home to meditation retreats and classes in *vipassana* (insight meditation). Check the website to see what workshops are on offer and be sure to reserve a spot at least 10 days in advance.

MUAYTHAI INSTITUTE   THAI BOXING
(☏0 2992 0096; www.muaythai-institute. net; Rangsit Stadium, 336/932 Th Prachatipat, Pathum Thani; 10-day course from 8000B; MMo Chit exit 3 & taxi) Associated with the respected World Muay Thai Council, the institute offers a fundamental course in Thai boxing (consisting of three levels of expertise), as well as courses for instructors, referees and judges.

FAIRTEX MUAY THAI   THAI BOXING
(☏0 2386 6117; www.fairtexbangplee.com; 99/5 Mu 3, Soi Buthamanuson, Th Thaeparak, Samut Prakan; tuition & accommodation per day 1450-1850B; SChong Nonsi exit 2 & taxi) A popular, long-running Thai boxing camp south of Bangkok.

Day Trips from Bangkok

Ayuthaya Historical Park p157
Thailand's heroic former capital, Ayuthaya is a Unesco World Heritage site and a major pilgrimage site for anyone interested in ancient history.

Ko Samet p160
This island, only a few hours from Bangkok, has famously squeaky sand beaches and accommodation to fit any budget.

Amphawa p163
Amphawa's canal-side setting and ancient wooden houses look like they are straight out of a movie; its homestays provide a first-hand experience of this unique community.

Phetchaburi (Phetburi) p165
Phetchaburi's temples and peak-roofed wooden houses combine to form the epitome of central Thai life.

Kanchanaburi p169
Recent history is only a train ride away in Kanchanaburi, where vivid museums and touching monuments bring home the area's history as a WWII labour camp.

Khao Yai p173
Home to Khao Yai National Park, one of Thailand's biggest and best preserves, where mountainous monsoon forests boast hundreds of resident species.

Ancient ruins, a rural Thai vibe, tasty food, good-value accommodation – and all this only 70km from Bangkok: Ayuthaya is the easiest and most worthwhile escape from the Big Mango.

The riverside city served as the seat of one of ancient Thailand's most powerful kingdoms until 1767, when it was destroyed in warfare by the Burmese. Today, the ruins of the former capital, **Ayuthaya Historical Park**, are one of Thailand's biggest tourist sites. They're separated into two distinct districts: ruins 'on the island', in the central park of town west of Th Chee Kun, are most easily visited by bicycle (30B per day) or motorbike (200B per day); those 'off the island', opposite the river from the centre, are best visited by evening boat tour (150B per hour). For more detailed descriptions of the ruins, pick up the *Ayuthaya* booklet from the tourist information centre.

DON'T MISS...

➡ Wat Phra Si Sanphet

➡ Riverside setting at Wat Chai Wattanaram

➡ A crash course in local history at the Ayutthaya Tourist Center

➡ Ancient murals at Wat Ratburana

PRACTICALITIES

➡ individual sites 20-50B, day pass 220B

➡ ⊘8am-6pm

On the Island

Wat Phra Si Sanphet

This was once the largest **temple** (วัดพระศรีสรรเพชญ์; admission 50B; ⊘8am-6pm; P) in Ayuthaya and was used as the royal temple-palace by several kings. Built in the late 15th century, the compound contained a 16m standing Buddha coated with 250kg of gold, which was melted down and carted off by the Burmese conquerors. Its three Ayuthaya-style *chedi* (stupas) have come to be identified with Thai art more than any other style. The adjacent **Wat Phra Mongkhon Bophit** (วัดพระมงคลบพิตร; ⊘8.30am-4.30pm) FREE, built in the 1950s, houses one of the largest bronze, seated Buddhas in Thailand.

Ayutthaya Tourist Center

This **museum** (☎0 3524 6076; www.tourismthailand.org/ayutthaya; ⊘8.30am-4.30pm) FREE should be your first stop in Ayuthaya, as the excellent upstairs exhibition hall puts everything in context and describes the city's erstwhile glories, and the ground-floor TAT office has lots of maps and good advice.

Wat Ratburana

Wat Ratburana (วัดราชบูรณะ; admission 50B; ⊘8am-6pm) dates back to the early 15th century and contains *chedi* and faded murals that are among the oldest in the country.

Wat Lokayasutharam

This **temple** (วัดโลกยสุธาราม; off Th Khlong Thaw; ⊘8am-7pm) FREE features an impressive 28m-long reclining Buddha, ostensibly dating back to the early Ayuthaya period. A visit is worth the short bike trip it takes to reach it.

Wat Phra Mahathat

This **wát** (วัดพระมหาธาตุ; cnr Th Chee Kun & Th Naresuan; admission 50B; ⊘8am-6pm) has one of the first *brahng* (Khmer-style tower) built in the capital and an evocative Buddha head engulfed by finger-like tree roots – the most photographed site in Ayuthaya.

Wat Thammikarat

Wat Thammikarat (วัดธรรมิกราช; ⊘8am-7pm) FREE features overgrown *chedi* ruins and lion sculptures.

GETTING THERE & AWAY

Ayuthaya is 70km north of Bangkok. Minivans depart from a stall east of Bangkok's Victory Monument (60B, one hour, hourly 5.30am to 9pm). Buses depart Bangkok's Northern & Northeastern Bus Terminal (p225; 53B to 68B, 1½ hours, hourly 5am to 7pm). Northbound trains leave Hualamphong Station (p225; 15B to 185B, 1½ hours) every 30 minutes from 6.20am to 9pm (less frequently from 9.30am till 4pm). A taxi to Ayuthaya costs around 1000B.

Most visitors are on a big bus and a tight schedule. Instead explore by túk-túk, boat or bicycle.

INFORMATION

The **Tourist Information Centre** (TAT; ☑0 3524 6076; 108/22 Th Si Sanphet; ☉8.30am-4.30pm Mon-Fri) is in an art deco building west of the park.

Chao Sam Phraya National Museum

The city's largest **museum** (พิพิธภัณฑสถานแห่งชาติเจ้า สามพระยา; cnr Th Rotchana & Th Si Sanphet; adult/child 150B/free; ☉9am-4pm Wed-Sun; ℗) has 2400 items on show, ranging from a 2m-high bronze-cast Buddha head to glistening treasures found in the crypts of Wat Phra Mahathat and Wat Ratburana.

Wat Suwannaram

The two main structures of this **wát** (วัดสุวรรณาราม; off Th U Thong; ☉8am-7pm) FREE boast attractive murals, including a modern-era depiction of a famous Ayuthaya-era battle in the *wí-hăhn* (central sanctuary), and classic *jataka* (stories from the Buddha's past lives) in the adjacent *bòht* (ordination hall). Nearby **Pom Phet** (ป้อมเพชร) served as the island's initial line of defence for centuries. Only crumbling walls remain today, but the spot features breezy views and is also home to a ferry to the mainland.

Chantharakasem National Museum

Inside this national **museum** (พิพิธภัณฑสถานแห่งชาติ จันทรเกษม; Th U Thong; admission 100B; ☉9am-4pm Wed-Sun) is a collection of Buddhist art, sculptures, ancient weapons and lacquered cabinets. The museum is within the grounds of Wang Chan Kasem (Chan Kasem Palace), which was built for King Naresuan by his father in 1577.

Off the Island

Wat Chai Wattanaram

The ruined Ayuthaya-style tower and *chedi* of **Wat Chai Wattanaram** (วัดไชยวัฒนาราม; admission 50B; ☉8am-6pm), on the western bank of Mae Nam Chao Phraya (Chao Phraya River), boast the most attractive setting of any of the city's temples. The manicured Thai-style compound across the river belongs to the Thai royal family.

Wat Phanan Choeng

Southeast of town on Mae Nam Chao Phraya, this **wát** (วัดพนัญเชิง; admission 20B; ☉8am-7pm) was built before Ayuthaya became a Siamese capital. The temple's builders are unknown, but it appears to have been constructed in the early 14th century, so it's possibly Khmer. The main *wí-hăhn* contains a highly revered, 19m sitting Buddha image from which the wát derives its name.

Elephant Kraal

North of the city, the **Elephant Kraal** (เพนียดคล้องช้าง) FREE is a restoration of the wooden stockade once used for the annual round-up of wild elephants. A

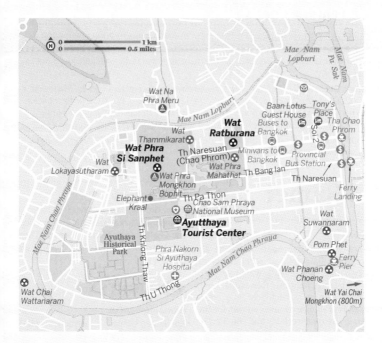

fence of huge teak logs enclosed the elephants. The king had a raised observation pavilion for the thrilling event.

Wat Yai Chai Mongkhon

Southeast of town, this **wát** (วัดใหญ่ชัยมงคล; admission 20B) is a quiet place built in 1357 by King U Thong and was once famous as a meditation centre. The compound contains a large *chedi,* and a community of *mâa chee* (Buddhist nuns) lives here.

Wat Na Phra Meru

This **temple** (วัดหน้าพระเมรุ; admission 20B; P) is notable because it escaped destruction when the Burmese army overran and sacked the city in 1767. The main *bòht* was built in 1546 and features fortress-like walls and pillars. The *bòht* interior contains an impressive carved wooden ceiling and a splendid 6m-high sitting Buddha in royal attire. Inside a smaller *wí·hǎhn* behind the *bòht* is a greenstone, European-pose (sitting in a chair) Buddha from Sri Lanka, said to be 1300 years old. The walls of the *wí·hǎhn* show traces of 18th- or 19th-century murals.

SLEEPING IN AYUTHAYA

Baan Lotus Guest House (☑ 0 3525 1988; 20 Th Pamaphrao; s 200B, d 450-600B; ⓟ ❋ ☎) Set in large, leafy grounds, this converted teak schoolhouse has a cool, clean feel and remains our favourite place to crash. Staff are as charmingly old-school as the building itself.

Tony's Place (☑ 0 3525 2578; www.tonyplace-ayutthaya.com; 12/18 Soi 2, Th Naresuan; r 300-1200B; ❋ ☎ ⍩) Budget rooms still offer just the basics, but the true flashpacker can hang out in renovated rooms that verge on the palatial, relatively speaking.

Iudia on the River (☑ 0 3532 3208; www.iudia.com; 11-12 Th U Thong; s 1550B, d 2750-5550B; ⓟ ❋ ☎ ⍩) Superbly designed rooms that fuse traditional Thai furnishings with modern finishes make this a fabulous spot.

Ko Samet เกาะเสม็ด

Explore

It takes at least five hours to reach Ko Samet from Bangkok, so schedule in at least two nights if you really want to experience the island's famously fine sands. Long weekends can be particularly busy, with thousands of Bangkokians beelining for the island; arrive on a weekday and you'll probably have Ko Samet to yourself.

The Best...

➡**Place to Eat** Red Ginger (p163)
➡**Place to Drink** Baywatch Bar (p163)
➡**Beach Ao Wong Deuan** (p162)

Top Tip

Ko Samet is a relatively dry island, making it an excellent place to visit during the rainy season (approximately June to October) when other tropical paradises might be underwater.

Getting There & Away

Minivan Minivans to Ban Phe (the pier for ferries to Ko Samet) depart from a stall just east of Bangkok's Victory Monument (200B, three hours, hourly from 6am to 8pm).
Bus Buses to Ban Phe leave from Bangkok's Eastern Bus Terminal (p225; 173B, four hours, hourly from 6am to 6pm).
Boat Boats to Ko Samet leave from Ban Phe's many piers. Most boats go to Tha Na Dan (return 100B, 30 to 45 minutes each way). You can also charter a speedboat (about 2500B depending on demand) for up to 10 people.

Need to Know

➡**Location** 200km southeast of Bangkok
➡**National Parks Main Office** (btwn Na Dan & Hat Sai Kaew; ⊙sunrise-sunset). There's another office at Ao Wong Deuan.

◉ SIGHTS

MERMAID STATUE   MONUMENT

Ko Samet earned a permanent place in Thai literature when classical Thai poet Sunthorn Phu set part of his epic 'Phra Aphaimani' on its shores. The story follows the travails of a prince exiled to an undersea kingdom governed by a lovesick female giant. A mermaid assists the prince in his escape to Ko Samet, where he defeats a giant by playing a magic flute. Today the poem is immortalised on the island by the

Ko Samet

Ko Samet

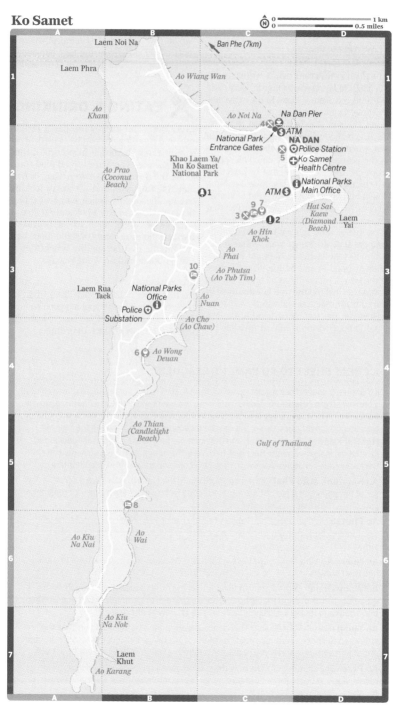

mermaid statue built on the rocky point separating Ao Hin Khok and Hat Sai Kaew.

KHAO LAEM YA/MU KO SAMET NATIONAL PARK   NATIONAL PARK

(อุทยานแห่งชาติเขาแหลมหญ้า-หมู่เกาะเสม็ด; ☎0 3865 3034; reserve@dnp.go.th; adult/child 200/100B; ⏰8.30am-4.30pm) In the early '80s, Ko Samet began receiving its first visitors: young Thais in search of a retreat from city life. It was made a national marine park in 1981, when there were only about 40 houses on the island. Rayong and Bangkok speculators saw the sudden interest in Ko Samet as a chance to cash in on an up-and-coming Phuket and began buying up land along the beaches. No one bothered about the fact that it was a national marine park. When *fa·ràng* (Westerners) soon followed, spurred on by rumours that Ko Samet was similar to Ko Samui '10 years ago', the National Parks Division stepped in and built a visitors' office on the island, ordered that all bungalows be moved back behind the tree line and started charging admission to the park.

However, the regulating hand of the National Parks Division is almost invisible beyond its role collecting fees at the admission gate. One successful measure, however, is a ban on new accommodation except where it replaces old sites, ensuring that bungalows remain thinly spread over most of the island.

✖️ EATING & DRINKING

Every hotel and guesthouse has a restaurant and choosing one can be as difficult as a walk along the beach inspecting menus along the way. There are several food stalls along the main drag between Tha Na Dan and Hat Sai Kaew, and it's worth looking out for the nightly beach barbecues, particularly along Ao Hin Khok and Ao Phai.

Likewise, every hotel has a beachside bar, and there are plenty of stand-alone bar-restaurants that occupy the beachfront at Hat Sai Kaew and Ao Wong Deuan.

RABEANG BAAN   THAI $

(Na Dan; dishes 70-120B; ⏰8am-10pm) Right by the ferry terminal, this spot has good enough food to make you forget you have to leave the island. It's busier at lunch than dinner.

A CHEAT SHEET TO KO SAMET'S BEACHES

Ko Samet is shaped like a golf tee, with the wide part in the north tapering away along a narrow strip to the south. Most boats from the mainland arrive at Tha Na Dan in the north, which is little more than a transit point for most visitors. Starting south of Tha Na Dan and moving clockwise, the most noteworthy beaches include the following:

Hat Sai Kaew (Diamond Beach) On the northeastern coast is the most developed stretch of beaches and the best nightlife. Wealthy Bangkokians file straight into Hat Sai Kaew's air-con bungalows with their designer sunglasses and designer dogs.

Ao Hin Khok & Ao Phai Scattered south along the eastern shore are a scruffier set of beaches that were once populated solely by backpackers but are increasingly catering to flashpackers and Bangkok expats.

Ao Phutsa (Ao Tub Tim) This wide and sandy beach is a favourite for solitude seekers, families and gay men who need access to 'civilisation' but not a lot of other stimulation.

Ao Nuan, Ao Cho (Ao Chaw) Less voluptuous beaches that appeal more to romantics than crowds.

Ao Wong Deuan Immediately to the south is the prom queen of the bunch, with a graceful stretch of sand that is home to an entourage of sardine-packed sun worshippers, package tourists, screaming jet skis and honky-tonk bars.

Ao Thian (Candlelight Beach) This beach is punctuated by big boulders that shelter small sandy spots, creating a castaway feel. Thai college kids claim these for all-night guitar jam sessions and if you're also on a tight budget, this beach is your best bet.

Ao Prao (Coconut Beach) The only developed beach on the steeper western side of the island, it hosts three upmarket resorts and moonlights as 'Paradise Beach' to those escaping winter climates.

SLEEPING IN KO SAMET

Due to the high demand, Ko Samet's prices can seem elevated compared with the amenities on offer, especially on weekends. A ramshackle hut starts at about 600B and with air-con this can climb to 1000B. Reservations aren't always honoured, so at peak times (most weekends and especially public-holiday weekends) it is advisable to arrive early, poised for the hunt.

Tok's (✆0 3864 4073; www.tok-littlehut.com; Ao Hin Khok; r 1500-2000B; ❄❂) Snazzy villas climb up a landscaped hillside with plenty of shade and flowering plants, making Tok's a respectable midranger.

Tubtim Resort (✆0 3864 4025; www.tubtimresort.com; Ao Phutsa; r 600-3600B; ❄@❂) Tubtim has dozens of bungalows climbing up a rugged hill from the beach. The pick are the modern, stylish bungalows with big windows and balconies that look straight down the beach; midpriced rooms are thoroughly comfortable, too. The resort's restaurant serves some of the best food on the island.

Samet Ville Resort (✆0 3865 1682; www.sametvilleresort.com; Ao Wai; r 1080-4500B; ❄❂) An unpretentious place with a range of rooms and cottages that suit most budgets. And the beach is great.

JEP'S RESTAURANT   INTERNATIONAL $
(Ao Hin Khok; mains 60-150B; ⏲7am-11pm) Canopied by the branches of an arching tree decorated with pendant lights, this pretty place does a little of everything right on the beach.

RED GINGER   INTERNATIONAL-THAI $$
(Na dan; dishes 125-285B; ⏲11am-10pm) Small but select menu of the French-Canadian chef's favourite dishes at this atmospheric eatery in between the pier and Hat Sai Kaew. Good salads, great oven-baked ribs. There's Thai food too.

BAYWATCH BAR   BAR
(Ao Wong Deuan; beers from 80B) A good spot for after-dark beach-gazing, with a fun crowd and strong cocktails.

NAGA BAR   BAR
(Ao Hin Khok; beers from 70B) This beachfront bar specialises in drinking games, with whisky buckets to give you courage.

Amphawa

Explore

Amphawa is located within day-trip distance from Bangkok, but is probably best approached as an overnighter. The trip is easy enough by bus or minivan or via a more circuitous route, and after you've seen the town, Amphawa is a good jumping-off point for other floating markets such as Damnoen Saduak (p174) and Tha Kha (p174).

The Best...
➡**Sight** Village Life (p164)
➡**Place to Eat** Amphawa Floating Market (p165)
➡**Place to Stay** Ploen Amphawa Resort (p165)

Top Tip
Amphawa is mobbed with tourists from Bangkok every weekend. For cheaper accommodation and a calmer environment, make a point of hitting the town during the week.

Getting There & Away
Minivan Frequent minivans run from a stall just north of Bangkok's Victory Monument to Samut Songkhram (73B, 1½ hours, frequent from 5.30am to 9pm). From there, you can hop in a sŏrng·tăa·ou (passenger pick-up truck; 8B) near the market for the 10-minute ride to Amphawa.
Bus From Bangkok's Southern Bus Terminal (p225), board any bus bound for Damnoen Saduak and ask to get off at Amphawa (80B, two hours, frequent from 6am to 9pm).

Need to Know
➡**Location** 80km southwest of Bangkok
➡**Tourist Office** (✆0 3475 2847; ⏲8.30am-4.30pm)

 **SIGHTS**

AMPHAWA VILLAGE VILLAGE

(อัมพวา) This canal-side village is a popular destination among city folk who seek out what many consider its quintessentially 'Thai' setting. This urban influx has sparked quite a few signs of gentrification, but the canals, old wooden buildings, atmospheric cafes and quaint waterborne traffic still retain heaps of charm. On the weekend, Amphawa puts on a fun floating market.

WAT AMPHAWAN CHETIYARAM BUDDHIST TEMPLE

(วัดอัมพวันเจติยาราม; ☉daylight) **FREE** Steps from Amphawa's central footbridge is this graceful temple thought to be located at the place of the family home of Rama II (King Phraphutthaloetla Naphalai; r 1809–24). The temple features accomplished murals.

THE LONG WAY TO AMPHAWA

Amphawa is only 80km from Bangkok, but if you play your cards right, you can reach the town via a long journey involving trains, boats, a motorcycle ride and a short jaunt in the back of a truck. Why? Because sometimes the journey is just as important as the destination.

The adventure begins at Thonburi's Wong Wian Yai (p225) train station. Just past the Wong Wian Yai traffic circle is a fairly ordinary food market that camouflages the unspectacular terminus of this commuter line. Hop on one of the hourly trains (10B to 25B, one hour, from 5.30am to 8.10pm) to Samut Sakhon.

After 15 minutes on the rattling train the city density yields to squat villages. From the window you can peek into homes, temples and shops built a carefully considered arm's length from the passing trains. Further on, palm trees, patchwork rice fields, and marshes filled with giant elephant ears and canna lilies line the route, punctuated by whistle-stop stations.

The backwater farms evaporate quickly as you enter Samut Sakhon, popularly known as Mahachai because it straddles the confluence of Mae Nam Tha Chin and Khlong Mahachai. This is a bustling port town, several kilometres upriver from the Gulf of Thailand, and the end of the first rail segment. Before the 17th century it was called Tha Jiin (Chinese Pier) because of the large number of Chinese junks that called here.

After working your way through one of the most hectic fresh markets in the country, you'll come to a vast harbour clogged with water hyacinths and wooden fishing boats. A few rusty cannons pointing towards the river testify to the existence of the town's crumbling fort, built to protect the kingdom from sea invaders.

Take the ferry across to Baan Laem (3B to 5B), jockeying for space with motorcycles that are driven by school teachers and people running errands. If the infrequent 5B ferry hasn't already deposited you there, take a motorcycle taxi (10B) for the 2km ride to Wat Chawng Lom, home to the Jao Mae Kuan Im Shrine, a 9m-high fountain in the shape of the Mahayana Buddhist Goddess of Mercy that is popular with regional tour groups. Beside the shrine is Tha Chalong, a train stop with three daily departures for Samut Songkhram at 10.10am, 1.30pm and 4.40pm (10B, one hour). The train rumbles out of the city on tracks that the surrounding forest threatens to engulf, and this little stretch of line genuinely feels a world away from the big smoke of Bangkok.

The jungle doesn't last long, and any illusion that you've entered a parallel universe free of concrete is shattered as you enter Samut Songkhram. And to complete the seismic shift you'll emerge directly into a hubbub of hectic market stalls. Between train arrivals and departures these stalls set up directly on the tracks, and must be hurriedly cleared away when the train arrives – it's quite an amazing scene.

Commonly known as Mae Klong, Samut Songkhram is a tidier version of Samut Sakhon and offers a great deal more as a destination. Owing to flat topography and abundant water sources, the area surrounding the provincial capital is well suited to the steady irrigation needed to grow guava, lychee and grapes. From Mae Klong Market pier *(tâh dà·làht mâa glorng)*, you can charter a boat (100B) or hop in a *sŏrng·tăa·ou* (8B) near the market for the 10-minute ride to Amphawa.

SLEEPING IN AMPHAWA

Amphawa is popular with Bangkok's weekend warriors and virtually every other house has opened its door to tourists in the form of homestays. These can range from little more than a mattress and a mosquito net to upscale guesthouse-style accommodation. Fan rooms start at about 200B while air-con rooms, many of which share bathrooms, begin at about 1000B. Prices are half this on weekdays. If you prefer something a bit more private, consider one of the following.

Ploen Amphawa Resort (☑08 1458 9411; www.ploenamphawa.com; Th Rim Khlong; r incl breakfast 1400-3000B; ❋ ☎) Not a resort at all, but rather a scant handful of rooms in a refurbished wooden home in the thick of the canal area.

ChababaanCham Resort (☑08 1984 1000; Th Rim Khlong; r incl breakfast 1500-2400B; ❋ ☎) A compound with modern but somewhat overpriced rooms and bungalows just off the canal.

Baan Ku Pu (☑0 3472 5920; Th Rim Khlong; d 1000B; ❋) A longstanding collection of wooden bungalows just a brief walk from the market area.

KING BUDDHALERTLA (PHUTTHA LOET LA) NAPHALAI MEMORIAL PARK   MUSEUM

(อุทยานพระบรมราชานุสรณ์ พระบาทสมเด็จ พระพุทธเลิศหล้านภาลัย (อุทยาน ร. ๒); admission 20B; ⊗8.30am-5pm) A short walk from Wat Amphwan Chetiyaram is an open-air museum consisting of a collection of traditional central-Thai houses set on four landscaped acres. Dedicated to Rama II, the houses contain rare Thai books and antiques from early-19th-century Siam.

FIREFLIES GUIDED TOURS   BOAT TOUR

(หิ่งห้อย) At night long-tail boats zip through Amphawa's sleeping waters to watch the Christmas-tree-like light dance of the *hìng hôy* (fireflies), most populous during the wet season. From Friday to Sunday, several operators at the piers near the main footbridge lead tours, charging 60B for a seat. On other days, it costs 500B for a two-hour charter.

DON HOI LOT   BEACH

(ดอนหอยหลอด) The area's second-most famous tourist attraction is a bank of fossilised shells at the mouth of Mae Nam Mae Klong (Mae Klong River), not far from Samut Songkhram. These shells come from *hǒy lòrt* (clams with a tubelike shell). While nearby seafood restaurants are popular with city folk year-round, the shell bank is best seen during April and May when the river surface has receded to its lowest level. To get there hop into a *sǒrng·tǎa·ou* (passenger pick-up truck, 10B, about 15 minutes) in front of Samut Songkhram's Somdet Phra Phuttalertla Hospital at the intersection of Th Prasitpattana and Th Tamnimit.

Or charter a boat from Mae Klong Market pier *(tâh dà·làht mâa glorng),* a scenic journey of around 45 minutes (about 1000B).

✗ EATING

There are several basic Thai restaurants in Amphawa; many more open on weekends.

AMPHAWA FLOATING MARKET   MARKET $

(ตลาดน้ำอัมพวา; Amphawa, Samut Songkhram; dishes 20-40B; ⊗4-9pm Fri-Sun) If you're in town on a weekend, plan your meals around this fun market where *pàt tai* and other noodle dishes are served directly from boats.

SEAFOOD RESTAURANTS   SEAFOOD $

(Samut Songkhram; mains 70-200B; ⊗10am-10pm) The road leading to Don Hoi Lot is lined with seafood restaurants, nearly all serving dishes made with *hǒy lòrt,* the area's eponymous shellfish.

Phetchaburi (Phetburi) เพชรบุรี

Explore

Phetchaburi (colloquially known as Phetburi) is only about two hours from Bangkok. It is probably best approached as an overnighter, although it's worth noting that the town's hotels are a dreary lot. Regardless,

Phctchaburi (Phctburi)

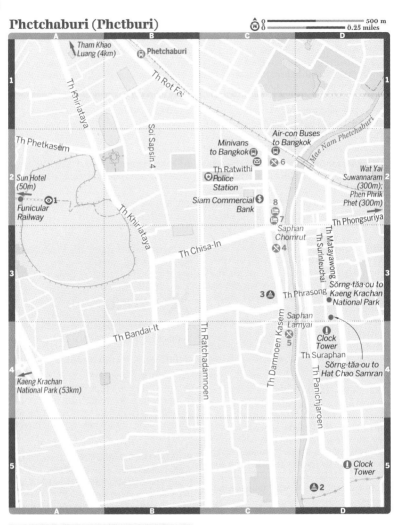

500 m
0.25 miles

DAY TRIPS FROM BANGKOK PHETCHABURI (PHETBURI)

Phetchaburi (Phetburi)

◎ Sights
1 Phra Nakhon Khiri Historical Park......A2
2 Wat Ko Kaew Sutharam......................D5
3 Wat Mahathat Worawihan..................C3

⊗ Eating
4 Khao Chae Nang Ram.........................C3
5 Mondee C4
6 Night Market......................................C2

⊜ Sleeping
7 J.J. Home C2
8 Sabaidee Resort................................C2

despite the number of worthwhile sights, very few foreign tourists make it to Phetchaburi, and you'll likely have the town to yourself.

If you have time, consider extending your stay to take in the jungle at Kaeng Krachan National Park or the beach at Hat Chao Samran.

....

The Best...
➡ **Sight** Phra Nakhon Khiri Historical Park (p167)

➡ **Place to Eat** Phen Phrik Phet (p169)

➡ **Place to Stay** Sun Hotel (p168)

Top Tip

The train is the slowest but arguably the most scenic way to reach Phetchaburi.

Getting There & Away

Minivan Frequent minivans ply from a stop just east of Bangkok's Victory Monument to Phetchaburi (100B, two hours, every 45 minutes from 6.15am to 8pm).

Bus Air-con buses run to/from Bangkok's Southern bus terminal (p225; 120B, two hours, 8.30am and 10.30am).

Train There are frequent services from Bangkok's Hualamphong Train Station (p99), and fares vary depending on the train and class (3rd class 84B to 388B, three hours, 12 daily from 1.53am to 4.47pm).

Need to Know

➜**Location** 166km south of Bangkok

 **SIGHTS**

PHRA NAKHON KHIRI HISTORICAL PARK
HISTORICAL SITE

(อุทยานประวัติศาสตร์พระนครคีรี; ☑0 3240 1006; 150B, tram return adult/child 40B/free; ☺park & tram 8.30am-4.30pm) Phetchaburi lives in the shadow of a looming hill (known locally as Khao Wang) studded with wát and topped by various components of Rama IV's (King Mongkut; r 1851–68) 1860 palace. The mountaintop is divided into three sections; the east peak bears a scaled-down version of **Wat Phra Kaew** (the Temple of the Emerald Buddha) and an unusual *chedi* made of granite blocks; the middle peak is dominated by **Phra That Chom Phet**, a 40m-high *chedi* that affords panoramic views from its upper level, while the western peak is home to Mongkut's palace, the eponymous **Phra Nakhon Khiri**, his observatory and other palace essentials built in Thai and Sino-European styles. To get here, make the strenuous upward climb or head to the west side of the hill and take the **funicular railway** straight up to the peak.

WAT MAHATHAT WORAWIHAN
BUDDHIST TEMPLE

(วัดมหาธาตุวรวิหาร; Th Damnoen Kasem; FREE) With its late-Ayuthaya/early-Ratanakosin adaptation of the *prahng* of Lopburi and

Phimai, this is Phetchaburi's most imposing temple. The beautiful murals inside the *wí-hăhn* illustrate the *jataka* and also show vivid snippets of everyday Thai life during the 19th century. The roof of the adjacent *bòht* holds some fine examples of stucco work, which is characteristic of the Phetchaburi school of art that can be seen on many of the city's temples.

WAT YAI SUWANNARAM
BUDDHIST TEMPLE

(วัดใหญ่สุวรรณาราม; Th Phongsuriya; ☺7am-6pm) FREE This expansive temple compound was originally built in Ayuthaya during the 17th century and was moved to Phetchaburi and renovated during the reign of Rama V (King Chulalongkorn; r 1868–1910). Legend has it that the gash in the ornately carved wooden doors of the lengthy wooden *săh-lah* (often spelt 'sala') dates to the Burmese attack. The faded murals inside the *bòht* date to the 1730s. Next to the *bòht*, set on a murky pond, is a beautifully designed old *hŏr drai* (Tripitaka library), though these days it's home only to pigeons.

WAT KO KAEW SUTHARAM
BUDDHIST TEMPLE

(วัดเกาะแก้วสุทธาราม, Wat Ko; off Th Matayawong; ☺7am-6pm) FREE Located at the edge of town, this temple compound dates back to the Ayuthaya era, and the *bòht* features early-18th-century murals that are among the oldest in Thailand. One panel depicts what appears to be a Jesuit priest wearing the robes of a Buddhist monk, while another shows foreigners undergoing Buddhist conversions. You'll probably have to ask the caretaker to open it for you.

SLEEPING IN PHETCHABURI (PHETBURI)

There is not much to choose from in the accommodation department, so don't get too excited.

Sun Hotel (☑0 3240 1000; www.sunhotelthailand.com; 43/33 Soi Phetkasem; r 900-1150B; ❈◎◎) Probably the best place to stay in town, the rooms here are huge, and come with TV, fridge, air-con and warm water, but not much character. The Sun is located opposite the back entrance to Phra Nakhon Khiri.

J.J. Home (☑08 1880 9286; a.sirapassorn@hotmail.com; 2 Th Chisa-In; r 200-500B; ❈◎) By the road, so a little noisy, but the rooms are spacious, clean and a decent deal. The more expensive options have private bathrooms and air-con.

Sabaidee Resort (☑0 3240 0194; sabai2505@gmail.com; 65-67 Th Klongkrachang; r 250-500B; ❈◎◎) Basic but well-kept bungalows and rooms, some fan only and all with shared bathrooms, set around a small garden. Pleasant staff and a popular spot for breakfast.

THAM KHAO LUANG   CAVE

(ถ้ำเขาหลวง; ⊙8am-6pm) **FREE** About 4km north of town is this cave sanctuary, which has three caverns filled with dozens of Buddha images in various poses – some of them originally placed by Rama IV. The best time to visit Khao Luang is around 5pm, when the school groups have gone and the evening light pierces the ceiling, surrounding artefacts with an ethereal glow. A round-trip *săhm·lór* from town should cost about 150B.

☉ Around Phetchaburi (Phetburi)

KAENG KRACHAN
NATIONAL PARK   NATIONAL PARK

(อุทยานแห่งชาติแก่งกระจาน; ☑0 3245 9293; www. dnp.go.th; 200B; ⊙visitors centre 8.30am-4.30pm) The largest national park in Thailand and home to the gorgeous Pala-U waterfalls, Kaeng Krachan National Park is easily reached from Phetchaburi. There are caves to explore, mountains, a huge lake and excellent birdwatching opportunities in the evergreen forest blanketing the park. Kaeng Krachan has fantastic trekking, and it is one of the few places to see Asian elephants roaming wild (if you're lucky).

Tourist infrastructure in the park is somewhat limited and roads can be rough. Park rangers can help arrange camping-gear rental, food and transport. The best months to visit are between November and April. Staffs at **Rabieng Rim Nam** (☑0 3242 5707; 1 Th Chisa-In; 950B per person for 4 people) can arrange trekking and birding tours that range from one day to multiple days if you don't want to figure out the logistics yourself.

There are various **bungalows** (☑0 2562 0760; www.dnp.go.th/parkreserve; from 1200B) within the park, mainly near the reservoir. There are also **camping grounds** (per person 60-90B), including a pleasant grassy one near the reservoir at the visitors centre (where there is also a modest restaurant). On the road leading to the park entrance are several simple resorts and bungalows.

The park is 50km from Phetchaburi. It can be reached by minivan (100B, hourly from 6.30am to 6pm) or *sŏrng tăa·ou* (passenger pick-up truck, 80B, 1½ hours, 6am to 2pm), both of which stop 4km from the park headquarters. To get to the higher camping grounds you'll have to charter a vehicle from the headquarters (1600B).

HAT CHAO SAMRAN   BEACH

(หาดเจ้าสำราญ) Lying 18km east of Phetchaburi, Hat Chao Samran is one of Thailand's oldest beach resorts, dating back to the reign of Rama VI (King Vajiravudh; r 1910–25). While the Thailand of today certainly has more appealing beaches, it's a pleasant enough place to laze your way through a day or two, punctuating your naps with cheap·seafood binges. A recent resurgence in popularity has brought with it 'boutique'-style bungalow accommodation. **Blue Sky** (☑0 3244 1399; www.bluesky -resort.com; 5 Mu 2, Hat Chao Samran; bungalows incl breakfast 1800-5000B; ◎❈) offers cute bungalows and rooms overlooking the garden or the sea. When you can relax no more, stumble next door to the ramshackle **Jaa Piak** (mains 50-280B; ⊙9am-9pm), which serves all manner of seafood including a mean horseshoe-crab egg salad (*yam kài maang dah tálair*).

To reach Hat Chao Samran, hop on a morning or afternoon *sŏrng tăa·ou* (30B, 35 minutes) across from Phetchaburi's clock tower (the one just east of Saphan Lamyai).

EATING

Phetchaburi is especially famous for its desserts, many of which can claim a royal pedigree. The desserts get their sweetness from the fruit of the sugar palms that dot the countryside around here. Two of the most famous sweets on offer include *môr gaang* (an egg and coconut-milk custard) and *kà·nŏm đahn* (bright yellow steamed buns sweetened with sugar-palm kernels).

PHEN PHRIK PHET NOODLES $
(173/1 Th Phongsuriya; mains from 35B; ⊙9am-3pm Wed-Mon) Located directly across from the entrance to Wat Yai Suwannaram, this local noodle legend makes delicious *gŏo·ay đĕe·o mŏo nám daang* (pork noodles in a fragrant dark broth). There's no English-language sign; look for the umbrellas, pots and potted plants.

KHAO CHAE NANG RAM CENTRAL THAI $
(Th Damnoen Kasem; dishes 20D; ⊙8am 5pm) *Kôw châa* (camphor-scented chilled rice served with sweet/savoury titbits) is a dish associated with Phetchaburi, and this roadside stall in front of a noodle restaurant is considered one of the best places to try it. There's no English-language sign; look for the cart under the old blue awning.

MONDEE CENTRAL THAI $
(dishes 25-100B; ⊙10am-midnight) During the day, this cosy wooden shack beside the river serves *kà·nŏm jeen* (fresh rice noodles served with a variety of curries). At night Mondee takes full advantage of the breezes and river view and serves decent central Thai fare with an emphasis on seafood. There's no English-language sign; it's located at the foot of the bridge.

NIGHT MARKET CENTRAL THAI $
(Th Ratwithi; dishes 25-60B; ⊙4-11pm) Located near the Bangkok-bound bus station, this busy night market does a variety of tasty Thai dishes, from noodles to curries.

Kanchanaburi

กาญจนบุรี

Explore

There are multiple ways to approach Kanchaburi's sights. Many choose to charter a boat, which for 800B will take up to six people on a 1½-hour tour of the area's big sights. With a bit more time, bike (50B per day) and motorcycle (200B per day) are cheaper, but still viable ways to get around. And if you have more time, there are tourist trains that (slowly) whisk visitors to Nam Tok, over the Death Railway Bridge and via Hellfire Pass. In fact, it's worth staying overnight in Kanchanaburi, as there's good-value accommodation. After the sun sets the river boom-booms its way through the night with disco and karaoke barges packed with Bangkokians letting their hair down, especially at weekends.

The Best...
➡**Sight** Death Railway Bridge (Bridge Over the River Kwai; p170)
➡**Place to Eat** Blue Rice (p173)
➡**Place to Drink** Sugar Member (p173)

Top Tip
Try as you might, you will find few Thais who have ever heard of the River Kwai. The river over which the Death Railway trundled is pronounced like 'quack' without the '-ck'.

Getting There & Away
Minivan Frequent minivans depart from a stall just west of Bangkok's Victory Monument to Kanchanaburi (120B, two hours, hourly from 5am to 8pm).
Bus Buses leave from the Southern Bus Terminal (p225) in Thonburi (95B to 110B, about two hours, frequent from 4am to 8pm) and the Northern & Northeastern bus Terminal (p225; 105B to 135B, two hours, every 90 minutes from 6am to 6pm).
Train Trains leave Bangkok Noi Train Station in Thonburi at 7.45am and 1.35pm (100B, two hours). To return to Bangkok, trains depart Kanchanaburi at 7.19am, 2.48pm and 5.41pm.

DAY TRIPS FROM BANGKOK KANCHANABURI

Kanchanaburi

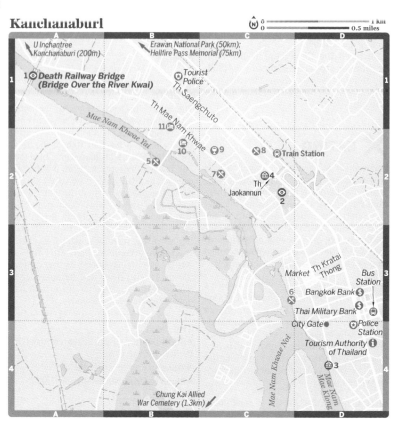

DAY TRIPS FROM BANGKOK KANCHANABURI

Need to Know

➡**Location** 130km west of Bangkok

➡**Tourism Authority of Thailand Office**
(TAT; ☏0 3451 1200; Th Saengchuto; ⊘8.30am-4.30pm)

◉ SIGHTS

⭐DEATH RAILWAY BRIDGE   HISTORICAL SITE
(สะพานข้ามแม่น้ำแคว, Bridge Over the River Kwai; Th Mae Nam Khwae) Despite its unspectacular appearance (it's an iron bridge), the bridge across Mae Nam Khwae is one of Kanchanaburi's most popular attractions. Indeed, Kanchanaburi can thank director David Lean and his Hollywood epic *The Bridge on the River Kwai* for a good proportion of the city's foreign visitors. The bridge, 2km north of town, was taken from Java by the Japanese and reassembled here with work beginning in 1942. It was bombed re-

peatedly during WWII and today only the curved spans are original; the two square sections were rebuilt with Japanese reparation money in 1946.

A rainbow-coloured minitrain runs regular trips (20B, 8am to 10am and noon to 2pm) across the bridge. Three trains daily (100B, 5.20am, 12.50pm and 3.15pm; about two hours) also cross the bridge en route to Nam Tok, via the infamous Hellfire Pass (p172). During the last week of November and first week of December a nightly sound-and-light show marks the Allied attack on the Death Railway in 1945.

⭐THAILAND-BURMA RAILWAY
CENTRE MUSEUM   MUSEUM
(ศูนย์รถไฟไทย-พม่า; www.tbrconline.com; 73 Th Jaokannun; adult/child 120/60B; ⊘9am-5pm) This is the pick of Kanchanaburi's war museums, with interactive exhibits, short films and clear descriptions providing the context of the Japanese aggression in

Kanchanaburi

Southeast Asia, detailing their plans for the railway and describing the horrors faced by those prisoners who worked and died constructing it. Give yourself a full hour to read through the museum, and stop for a coffee upstairs for sweeping views across the cemetery. Half-/full-day tours (2400/4900B) can be arranged from here.

★ **ALLIED WAR CEMETERY** HISTORICAL SITE
(สุสานทหารพันธมิตรดอนรัก; Th Saengchuto; ◎24hr) FREE This cemetery is the final resting place of about 7000 prisoners who died while working on the railway. The cemetery is meticulously maintained by the **Commonwealth War Graves Commission** (www.cwgc.org), and the rows of headstones are identical except for the names and the short, moving epitaphs. It's just around the corner from the riverside guesthouses.

JEATH WAR MUSEUM MUSEUM
(พิพิธภัณฑ์สงคราม; Th Wisuttharangsi; admission 30B; ◎8am-5pm) The simple Jeath War Museum operates in the grounds of a local temple and is housed in a re-creation of the long bamboo huts used by the POWs as shelter. Inside are various photographs, drawings, maps, weapons, paintings by POWs and other war memorabilia. The acronym Jeath represents the ill-fated meeting of Japan, England, Australia/America, Thailand and Holland at Kanchanaburi during WWII.

**CHUNG KAI ALLIED
WAR CEMETERY** HISTORICAL SITE
(สุสานทหารพันธมิตรช่องไก่; ◎7am-6pm) FREE This less-visited cemetery, where about

THE DEATH RAILWAY

Kanchanaburi's history includes a brutal cameo (later promoted to starring) role in WWII. The town was home to a Japanese-run prisoner of war camp, from which Allied soldiers and many others were used to build the notorious Death Railway, linking Bangkok with Burma (now Myanmar). Carving a rail bed out of the 415km stretch of rugged terrain was a brutally ambitious plan by the Japanese, intended to meet an equally remarkable goal of providing an alternative supply route for the Japanese conquest of Burma and other countries to the west. Japanese engineers estimated that the task would take five years to complete. But the railway was completed in a mere 14 months, entirely by forced labour that had little access to either machines or nutrition. A Japanese brothel train inaugurated the line.

Close to 100,000 labourers died as a result of the hard labour, torture or starvation; 13,000 of them were POWs, mainly from Britain, Australia, the Netherlands, New Zealand and the US, while the rest were Asians recruited largely from Burma, Thailand and Malaysia. The POWs' story was chronicled in Pierre Boulle's novel *The Bridge on the River Kwai* and later popularised by the movie of the same name. Many visitors come here specifically to pay their respects to the fallen POWs at the Allied cemeteries.

The original bridge was used by the Japanese for 20 months before it was bombed by Allied planes in 1945. As for the railway itself, only the 130km stretch from Bangkok to Nam Tok remains. The rest was either carted off by Karen and Mon tribespeople for use in the construction of local buildings and bridges, recycled by Thai Railways or reclaimed by the jungle.

1700 graves are kept, is a short and scenic bike ride from central Kanchanaburi. Take the bridge across the river through picturesque corn and sugarcane fields until you reach the cemetery on your left.

◉ Around Kanchanaburi

HELLFIRE PASS MEMORIAL · MUSEUM

(ช่องเขาขาด; Rte 323; museum admission by donation; ◷grounds 9am-4.30pm, museum to 4pm) Viewing the bridge and war museums doesn't quite communicate the immense task of bending the landscape with human muscle that was involved in building the Death Railway. A better understanding comes from a visit to the excellent Hellfire Pass Memorial, an Australian-Thai Chamber of Commerce memorial and museum dedicated to the POW labourers, 75km north of Kanchanaburi. A crew of 1000 prisoners worked for 12 weeks to cut a pass through the mountainous area dubbed Hellfire Pass. Nearly 70% of them died in the process. An interactive museum is enhanced by several short films. Below the museum is a walking trail along the track itself and through Hellfire Pass.

Hellfire Pass and the so-called Tiger Temple are accessed via the road running west from Kanchanaburi to Sangkhlaburi and the Myanmar border. It's easy to arrange tours from Kanchanaburi, or take a bus towards Sangkhlaburi (80B, 1½ hours,

frequent) and ask the driver to drop you near your destination. The last bus back to Kanchanaburi passes here at 4.45pm.

ERAWAN NATIONAL PARK · NATIONAL PARK

(อุทยานแห่งชาติเอราวัณ; admission 200B; ◷8am-4pm) Northwest of Kanchanaburi town is the area's natural playground. Erawan National Park sports a watery mane of waterfalls and is visited by locals and tourists out for a day trip of photographs, picnics and swimming.

SAI YOK NATIONAL PARK · NATIONAL PARK

(อุทยานแห่งชาติไทรโยก; ☎0 3468 6024; www.dnp.go.th; 200B) Sai Yok National Park has waterfalls, limestone caves, hot springs and accommodation. Tour organisers in Kanchanaburi can arrange day outings to these parks on various expeditions: river kayaking, elephant trekking, waterfall spotting and bamboo rafting.

WAT THAM KHAO PUN · CAVE

(วัดถ้ำเขาปูน; admission by donation; ◷7am-4pm) The limestone hills surrounding Kanchanaburi are famous for their temple caves, an underground communion of animistic spirit worship and traditional Buddhism. Winding arteries burrow into the guts of the caves past bulbous calcium deposits and altars for reclining or meditating Buddhas, surrounded by offerings from pilgrims. Wat Tham Khao Pun is one of the closest cave temples, and is best reached by bicycle. The temple is about 4km from the

SLEEPING IN KANCHANABURI

Travellers tend to navigate towards a 1km stretch of Th Mae Nam Khwae, where budget guesthouses offer riverfront views on raft houses. In contrast, there are several new boutique midrange spots on this strip and just out of town.

Blue Star Guest House (☎0 3451 2161; bluestar_guesthouse@yahoo.com; 241 Th Mae Nam Khwae; r 200-850B; P✳☎) Arguably the best of the raft-house options, nature wraps itself around Blue Star, creating a feeling of remoteness and tranquillity. Cheaper rooms have cold showers.

Sabai@Kan (☎0 3462 5544; www.sabaiatkan.com; 317/4 Th Mae Nam Khwae; r 1400-1700B; P✳☎☒) With the kind of king-size beds you just want to jump on, this pretty boutique resort does everything well. Rooms overlook a swimming pool and have heaps of natural light. Service is excellent.

U Inchantree Kanchanaburi (☎0 3452 1584; www.ukanchanaburi.com; 443 Th Mae Nam Khwae; r/ste incl breakfast 3600/4237B; P✳@☎☒) Granted, the rooms here are pretty small for the price tag, but they're packed with clever amenities (an iPod and widescreen TV) and the hotel's location, on an attractive bend in Mae Nam Khwae within eyeshot of the famous bridge, is probably the best in town. Located 300m north of the Death Railway Bridge.

TIGER SANCTUARY OR TOURIST TRAP?

Perhaps the most controversial tourist attraction in Thailand, the Tiger Temple continues to divide opinion. True, it's one of the few places in the world where you can get so close to these magnificent creatures. On the other hand, numerous allegations about animal welfare continue to dog the temple. In return for the 600B entrance fee (it's the same for adults and children), visitors get to walk the big cats to a canyon, where tourists are then briskly herded around a group of chained-up tigers to have their photos taken. A morning program of events costs a hefty 5000B.

This former sanctuary for abandoned cubs denies allegations that the tigers are ill-treated, drugged or traded and has been planning major developments for years, but progress seems slow. Some tour operators now decline to take visitors to the Tiger Temple, and Lonely Planet no longer recommends visiting.

Reports emerged in August 2013 of a UK student being badly mauled at the Tiger Temple; www.careforthewild.org has a detailed report about alleged abuses.

TAT office and 1km southwest of the Chung Kai cemetery across the railroad tracks and midway up the hill.

EATING & DRINKING

Kanchanaburi is not a culinary destination, and guesthouse-style and tourist-oriented restaurants serving bland Thai standards seem to dominate. It is, however, something of a nightlife town, and bars extend nearly the entire length of Th Mae Nam Khwae. Of these, tacky hostess bars dominate the southern end, backpacker-friendly pubs define the middle, and open-air bar-restaurants for the Thai crowd can be found at the street's northern end.

★BLUE RICE
THAI $
(153/4 Mu 4 Ban Tamakahm; dishes 95-150B; P🛇🅿️📶) A perfect riverside setting, brilliant menu and fantastic flavours make this a winner. Chef Apple puts a fresh spin on Thai classics, such as the eponymous rice, *yam sôm oh* (pomelo salad) and chicken soup with banana plant.

★MANGOSTEEN CAFE
CAFE $
(☎08 1793 5814; www.mangosteencafe.net; 13 Th Mae Nam Khwae; dishes 70-150B; ⊘9.30am-10pm; ❄🛇📶🅿️) Browse the 1000 or so books on offer while munching through the divine pizza toasties and sipping real coffee.

NIGHT MARKET
MARKET $
(Th Saengchuto; dishes 30-60B; ⊘6-11pm) An expansive market featuring everything

from Thai-Muslim nosh to *pàt tai* unfolds every night in front of the bus station.

FLOATING RESTAURANTS
THAI $$
(Th Song Khwae; dishes 80-200B; ⊘6-11pm) Down on the river are several large floating restaurants where the quality of the food varies, but it's hard not to enjoy the atmosphere.

SUGAR MEMBER
BAR
(Th Mae Nam Khwae) Has hip, friendly staff who will sip whisky buckets with you all night.

Khao Yai เขาใหญ่

Explore

Khao Yai is only about 200km from Bangkok, but the area is best approached as an overnight trip. There are two strategies to doing this, depending on your interests. If you've come for the nature, the logical option is to sleep at the park (or at a guesthouse that provides tours to the park), which can be reached via public transport. If you're looking for a more leisurely weekend getaway to take in the restaurants, resorts, wineries and other attractions that surround the actual park, you'll need to hire a car.

The Best...

Top Tip

The best time to visit Khao Yai National Park is in the dry season (December to June), but during the rainy season river rafting and waterfall-spotting will be more dramatic.

FLOATING MARKETS

Pictures of floating markets (dà·làht nám) jammed full of wooden canoes pregnant with colourful exotic fruits have defined the official tourist profile of Thailand for decades. The idyllic scenes are as iconic as the Grand Palace or the Reclining Buddha, but they are also almost completely contrived for, and dependent upon, foreign and domestic tourists – roads and motorcycles have long moved Thais' daily errands onto dry ground. That said, if you can see them for what they are, a few of Thailand's floating markets are worth a visit.

Tha Kha Floating Market (ตลาดน้ำท่าคา; Tha Kha, Samut Songkhram; ⊘7am-noon, 2nd, 7th & 12th day of waxing & waning moons plus Sat & Sun) This, the most 'real' feeling floating market, is also the most difficult to reach. A handful of vendors convene along an open rural klorng (canal, also spelt khlong) lined with coconut palms and old wooden houses. Boat rides (20B per person, 45 minutes) can be arranged along the canal, and there are lots of tasty snacks and fruits for sale. To get here, take one of the morning sŏrng·tăa·ou (passenger pick-up trucks, 20B, 45 minutes) from Samut Songkhram's market area.

Amphawa Floating Market (p165) The Amphawa Floating Market, located in Samut Songkhram Province, convenes near Wat Amphawa. The emphasis is on edibles and tourist knick-knacks, and because the market is only there on weekends and is popular with tourists from Bangkok, things can get pretty hectic.

Taling Chan Floating Market (ตลาดน้ำตลิ่งชัน; Khlong Bangkok Noi, Thonburi; ⊘7am-4pm Sat & Sun) Located just outside Bangkok on the access road to Khlong Bangkok Noi, Taling Chan looks like any other fresh-food market busy with produce vendors from nearby farms. But the twist emerges at the canal where several floating docks serve as informal dining rooms, and the kitchens are canoes tethered to the docks. Taling Chan is in Thonburi and can be reached via taxi from Wongwian Yai BTS station or via air-con bus 79 (16B, 25 minutes), which makes stops on Th Ratchadamnoen Klang. Long-tail boats from any large Bangkok pier can also be hired for a trip to Taling Chan and the nearby Khlong Chak Phra.

Damnoen Saduak Floating Market (ตลาดน้ำดำเนินสะดวก; Damnoen Saduak, Ratchaburi Province; ⊘7am-noon) This 100-year-old floating market – the country's most famous – is now essentially a floating souvenir stand filled with package tourists. This in itself can be a fascinating insight into Thai culture, as the vast majority of tourists here are Thais, and watching the approach to this cultural 'theme park' is instructive. But beyond the market, the residential canals are quite peaceful and can be explored by hiring a boat (per person 100B) for a longer duration. Trips stop at small family businesses, including a Thai candy maker, a pomelo farm and a knife crafter. Air-con bus 79, with stops on Th Ratchadamnoen Klang, and minivans (Map p263) from the Victory Monument both connect to the Southern Bus Terminal in Thonburi, from where you can find buses to Damnoen Saduak (80B, two hours, frequent from 6am to 9pm).

Don Wai Market (ตลาดดอนหวาย; Don Wai, Nakhon Pathom; ⊘6am-6pm) Not technically a swimmer, this market claims a riverbank location in Nakhon Pathom Province, having originally started in the early 20th century as a floating market for pomelo and jackfruit growers and traders. As with many tourist attractions geared towards Thais, the main attraction is food, including fruit, traditional sweets and bèt pah·lóh (five-spice stewed duck), which can be consumed aboard large boats that cruise Mae Nam Nakhorn Chaisi (Nakhon Chaisi River; 60B, one hour). The easiest way to reach Don Wai Market is to take a minibus (45B, 35 minutes) from beside Central Pinklao in Thonburi.

THAILAND'S NAPA VALLEY

The cool highlands surrounding Khao Yai are home to a nascent wine industry. These have been dubbed the 'New Latitude' wines because, at between 14 and 18 degrees north, they fall far outside the traditional wine-grape growing latitudes of between 30 and 50 degrees north or south of the equator. **PB Valley Khao Yai Winery** (☑0 3622 6415; www.khaoyaiwinery.com; tour 200B; ☺tours 10.30am, 1.30pm & 3.30pm) and **GranMonte Estate** (☑0 4400 9544; www.granmonte.com; ☺tours 11am, 1pm & 3pm Sat, Sun & holidays) are among the winemakers managing to coax shiraz and chenin blanc grapes from the relatively tropical climate. The wines do seem to improve year by year, though they still have a way to go. Both offer free tastings and GranMonte also has some appealing rooms overlooking the vineyards from 4200B.

Getting There & Away

Minivan Frequent minivans ply from a stall just north of Bangkok's Victory Monument to Pak Chong (180B, 2½ hours, hourly 6am to 8pm) and, upon request, to Khao Yai National Park (300B).

Bus From Bangkok's Northern & Northeastern Bus Terminal (p225), buses to Khorat (Nakhon Ratchasima) stop in Pak Chong (60B to 150B, three hours). From Pak Chong, take a *sŏrng·tăa·ou* (40B, 40 minutes, every 30 minutes from 6am to 5pm) to the park entrance. From there, it's another 14km to the visitor centre, which can be reached by chartering a vehicle (500B).

Hire Car For more freedom, hire a car and drive.

Need to Know

➡**Location** 196km northeast of Bangkok

➡**Tourist Office** (☑0 3731 2282; tatnayok@tat.or.th; 182/88 Mu 1, Th Suwannason)

⊙ SIGHTS

★**KHAO YAI NATIONAL PARK**   NATIONAL PARK
(อุทยานแห่งชาติเขาใหญ่; ☑08 6092 6529; adult/child 400/200B, car 50B) Cool and lush, Khao Yai National Park is an easy escape into the primordial jungle. The 2168-sq-km park, part of a Unesco World Heritage site, spans five forest types, from rainforest to monsoon, and is the primary residence of, among many others, shy tigers and elephants, noisy gibbons, colourful tropical birds and countless audible, yet invisible, insects. Khao Yai is a major birding destination with large flocks of hornbills and several migrators, including the flycatcher from Europe. Caves in the park are the

preferred resting place for wrinkle-lipped bats. In the grasslands, batik-printed butterflies dissect flowers with their surgical tongues.

The park has several accessible trails for self-tours, but birders or animal trackers should consider hiring a jungle guide to increase their appreciation of the environment and to spot more than the tree-swinging gibbons and blood-sucking leeches (the rainy season is the worst time for the latter). In total, there are 12 maintained trails criss-crossing the entire park; not ideal if you want to walk end to end. Access to transport is another reason why a tour might be more convenient, although Thai visitors with cars are usually happy to pick up pedestrians.

A two-hour walk from the **visitor centre** (☑08 6092 6529; ☺8am-9pm) leads to the **Nong Pak Chee Observation Tower** (หอส่องสัตว์หนองผักชี), which is a good early-morning spot for seeing insect-feeding birds, occasional thirsty elephants and sambar deer; make reservations at the visitor centre. It's important to understand that spotting the park's reclusive tigers and elephants is considered a bonus, with most people happy just to admire the frothy waterfalls that drain the peaks of Big Mountain. The park's centrepiece is **Nam Tok Haew Suwat** (น้ำตกเหวสุวัต), a 25m-high cascade that puts on a thundering show in the rainy season. **Nam Tok Haew Narok** (น้ำตกเหวนรก) is its larger cousin with three pooling tiers and a towering 150m drop.

PALIO   SHOPPING CENTRE
(www.palio-khaoyai.com; Km 17 Th Thanarat; ☺10am-7pm Mon-Fri, 9am-9pm Sat & Sun) We can't imagine a more jarring contrast to one of Asia's premier protected natural areas than this wacky open-air shopping

SLEEPING IN KHAO YAI

Th Thanarat is home to several midrange to upscale resorts targeted at Thai tourists.

Greenleaf Guesthouse (☑0 4436 5073; www.greenleaftour.com; Th Thanarat, Km 7.5; r 200-300B; 🅿 🛜) The extremely basic but clean rooms here are virtually the area's only budget option. Greenleaf isn't located near anything of interest, but the folks who run it do half- and full-day tours of Khao Yai National Park.

Park Lodging (☑0 2562 0760; www.dnp.go.th/parkreserve; tents 150-400B; r & bungalow 800-3500B, 30% discount Mon-Thu) The Department of National Parks provides a range of clean, simple lodgings scattered through the park. It's best to book online, where you can get more detail on locations and facilities, though bookings are also possible at the information centre.

Hotel des Artists (☑0 4429 7444; www.hotelartists.com; Km 22, Th Thanarat; r/bungalow incl breakfast 5000/6000B; 🅿 ❄ ✳ @ 🛜 ⛱) Breaking from the Khao Yai norm, this tasteful hotel goes for French-colonial chic rather than a nature theme; though with its gorgeous mountain views out back you won't forget where you are.

centre. Modelled after a Tuscan village, Palio is indicative of what the Khao Yai area has increasingly become over the last decade: a weekend playground for upper-middle-class Thais. Inside, you'll find shops, cafes, bars and hordes of Thais taking photos of each other with digital SLRs. There's plenty to eat, and on weekends, live music until 9pm.

EATING

In recent years, the area surrounding Khao Yai National Park has become a minor culinary destination, with restaurants featuring cuisines ranging from upmarket Italian to Muslim-Thai. The towns that surround the park have lively night markets but if you don't have a car, you'll find restaurants within the park.

KHRUA KHAO YAI INTERNATIONAL-THAI $
(Km 13.5, Th Thanarat; mains 60-150B; ☺9am-8pm Sun-Thu, to 10pm Fri & Sat) This open-air hut is hugely popular with visiting Bangkokians because it serves a hefty menu of satisfying Thai and *fa·ràng* dishes. The English-language menu is limited, so we

recommend pointing to whatever the table next to you is eating, which is likely to be the delicious home-smoked ham or a mushroom dish. There's no signage in English; Khrua Khao Yai is located roughly halfway between Pak Chong and the entrance to Khao Yai, near the well-posted turn off to Belle Villa and several other resorts.

DAIRY HOME INTERNATIONAL-THAI $
(Km 144, Th Mitraphab/Rte 2; mains 50-300B; ☺9am-8pm) If a weekend of intense jungle exploring or wine tasting has left you with a need for meat, stop by this organic dairy for steak or homemade sausages, or of course, a milk shake or ice cream. Arrive earlier in the day and it also does basic breakfasts and real coffee drinks.

NARKNAVA MUSLIM-THAI $
(Khao Mok Hi So; www.narknavafarm.com; Km 8, Th Phansuk-Kud Khala; mains 50-150B; ☺8am-7pm Tue-Sun) Muslim and even Middle Eastern fare are unexpected cuisines in this neck of the woods, but Narknava is an established favourite for its infamous chicken biryani – infamous, because at 100B it's super expensive by Thai standards. Unusually, the food is much better than the website images suggest.

🛏 Sleeping

If your idea of the typical Bangkok hotel was influenced by The Hangover Part II, you'll be pleased to learn that the city is home to a diverse spread of modern hostels, guesthouses and hotels. To make matters better, much of Bangkok's accommodation offers excellent value, and competition is so intense that fat discounts are almost always available.

Hostels

Those counting every baht can get a dorm bed (or a closet-like room) with a shared bathroom for between 250B and about 500B. The latest trend in Bangkok is slick 'flashpacker' hostels that blur the line between budget and midrange. A bed at these starts at about 500B.

Guesthouses

In Bangkok, this designation usually refers to any sort of budget accommodation rather than a room in a family home, although we use it to describe the latter. Guesthouses and similar budget hotels are generally found in somewhat inconveniently located corners of old Bangkok (Banglamphu, Chinatown and Thewet), which means that the money you're saving in rent will probably go for taxi fares. Rates begin at about 600B.

Hotels

Bangkok's midrange hotels often have all the appearance of a Western-style hotel, but without the predictability. If you're on a lower-midrange budget, and don't care much about aesthetics, some very acceptable rooms can be had for between 1500B and 2000B. If your budget is higher, it really pays to book ahead, as online discounts here can be substantial. You'll find several midrange hotels along lower Th Sukhumvit and in Banglamphu.

Luxury, Business & Boutique Hotels

Bangkok is home to a huge number of top-end hotels ranging from boutique (small but cosy) to luxury (big and brash). Most hotels of this type are located on Th Sukhumvit and

Th Silom, or along Mae Nam Chao Phraya (Chao Phraya River). Rooms generally start between 6000B and 9000B before hefty online discounts.

Amenities

Wi-fi is nearly universal across the spectrum, but air-conditioning and lifts are not.

BUDGET

The cheapest hostels and guesthouses often share bathrooms and may not even supply a towel. Some remain fan-cooled or, in the case of dorms, will only run the air-con between certain hours. Wi-fi, if available, is often free at the cheaper places. If on offer, breakfast at most Bangkok hostels and budget hotels is little more than instant coffee and toast.

MIDRANGE

Increasingly, midrange has come to mean a room with air-con, a fridge, hot water, free or inexpensive wi-fi and TV. It's not uncommon for a room to boast all of these but lack a view, or even windows. Breakfast can range from 'buffets' based around toast and oily fried eggs to more thoughtful meals involving yoghurt or tropical fruit.

TOP END

Top-end hotels supply all the amenities you'd expect at this range. The more thoughtful places have amenities such as en suite computers and free wi-fi; otherwise, expect to pay a premium for wi-fi. In sweaty Bangkok, pools are almost standard, not to mention fitness and business centres, restaurants and bars. Breakfast is often buffet-style.

SLEEPING

NEED TO KNOW

Price Ranges
Accommodation in this book is broken down into three categories. We've listed high-season walk-in rates for a double room, excluding the 'plus-plus' that most top-end places charge, which in Thailand is made up of 10% service and 7% government tax.

$	less than 1000B a night
$$	1000B to 3000B a night
$$$	more than 3000B a night

Accommodation Websites
The best time for discounts is outside of Bangkok's peak seasons, which are November to March and July and August.

Lonely Planet's Hotels & Hostels (www.hotels.lonelyplanet.com) Find reviews and make bookings.

Travelfish (www.travelfish.org) Independent reviews with lots of reader feedback.

Lonely Planet's Top Choices

Siam Heritage (p187) Homey touches and warm service make this the closest you may come to sleeping in a Thai home.

AriyasomVilla (p190) Sumptuous refurbished villa with a classy B&B vibe.

Loy La Long (p187) Boutique with an appealingly rustic, retro, riverside feel.

Phra-Nakorn Norn-Len (p182) An artsy, fun hotel compound in a refreshingly untouristed 'hood.

Lamphu Treehouse (p181) Cheerful budget vibe meets top-end quality at a midrange price.

Best by Budget

$
Lub*d (p183)
Chern (p180)
Khaosan Baan Thai (p183)
Suk 11 (p189)
NapPark Hostel (p183)

$$
Feung Nakorn Balcony (p181)
Littlest Guesthouse (p187)
Smile Society (p186)
Napa Place (p189)
Glow Trinity Silom (p186)

$$$
Metropolitan by COMO (p188)
Mandarin Oriental (p188)
Peninsula Hotel (p188)
Bhuthorn (p187)
Bangkok Tree House (p192)

Best for Romantics

Old Bangkok Inn (p182)
Mandarin Oriental (p188)

Siam (p184)
Sala Rattanakosin (p180)

Best Contemporary Cool

Ma Du Zi (p191)
LUXX XL (p185)
W Bangkok (p189)
Fusion Suites (p190)
Aloft (p191)
Refill Now! (p192)

Best Affordable Luxury

Hansar (p185)
S31 (p191)
Shangri-La Hotel (p189)
Vie (p185)

Best Artsy Stays

Mystic Place (p192)
Silom Art Hostel (p183)
Seven (p191)
Shanghai Mansion (p184)
Sofitel So (p189)

Best Rooms with Views

Inn A Day (p180)
Millennium Hilton (p188)
Siam@Siam (p184)
Arun Residence (p187)

Best for Time Travel

Baan Dinso (p187)
Praya Palazzo (p182)
Hotel Muse (p185)
Eugenia (p190)
Chakrabongse Villas (p180)

Where to Stay

Neighbourhood	For	Against
Ko Ratanakosin & Thonburi	Bangkok's most famous sights at your door; occasional river views; (relatively) fresh air; old-school Bangkok feel.	Difficult to reach; few budget options; lack of dining and drinking venues; touts.
Banglamphu	Close to main sights; proximity to classic Bangkok 'hood; lots of good-value budget beds; fun, intergalactic melting-pot feel; virtually interminable dining options; one of the city's best nightlife areas.	Getting to and from the area can be troublesome; Th Khao San can be noisy and rowdy; budget places can have low standards; relentless touts.
Thewet & Dusit	Good budget options; riverside village feel; fresh air; close to a handful of visit-worthy sights.	Few midrange and upscale options; not very convenient access to rest of Bangkok; relatively few dining and drinking options; comatose at night.
Chinatown	Some interesting budget and midrange options; off the beaten track; easy access to worthwhile sights and some of the city's best food; close to Bangkok's main train station.	Noisy; polluted; touts; hectic; few non-eating-related nightlife options; access to rest of Bangkok not very convenient.
Siam Square, Pratunam, Ploenchit & Ratchathewi	Wide spread of accommodation alternatives; mega-convenient access to shopping (and air-conditioning); steps away from BTS.	Touts; unpristine environment; relative lack of dining and entertainment options in immediate area; lacks character.
Riverside, Silom & Lumphini	Some of the city's best upscale accommodation; river boats and river views; super-convenient access to BTS and MRT; lots of dining and nightlife options; gay-friendly.	Can be noisy and polluted; budget options can be pretty dire; hyper-urban feel away from the river.
Sukhumvit	Some of the city's most sophisticated hotels; lots of midrange options; easy access to BTS and MRT; international dining; easy access to some of the city's best bars; home to several reputable spas and massage parlours.	Annoying street vendors and sexpat vibe; noisy; hyper-touristy.
Greater Bangkok	Less hectic setting; good value; depending on location, convenient airport access.	Transport can be inconvenient; lack of drinking and entertainment options.

SLEEPING

🛏 Ko Ratanakosin & Thonburi

AROM D HOSTEL
HOSTEL $

Map p252 (☎0 2622 1055; www.aromdhostel.com; 336 Th Maha Rat; incl breakfast dm 800B, r 2250-2500B; ❄ @ 🛜; 🚤Tha Tien) The dorm beds and rooms here are united by a cutesy design theme and a host of inviting communal areas including a rooftop deck, computers, a ground-floor cafe and TV room.

ROYAL THA TIEN VILLAGE
HOTEL $$

Map p252 (☎08 9555 1683; www.facebook.com/theroyalthatienvillage; 392/29 Soi Phen Phat; r 1000-1200B; ❄ @ 🛜; 🚤Tha Tien) The five rooms in this converted shophouse are relatively unassuming, but TV, fridge, air-con, lots of space and shiny wood floors, not to mention a cosy homestay atmosphere, edge this place into the recommendable category.

CHETUPHON GATE
HOTEL $$

Map p252 (☎0 2622 2060; www.chetuphon-gate.com; 370-372 Soi Pratu Nok Yung; r 1800-2200B; ❄ @ 🛜; 🚤Tha Tien) Nine new and attractive rooms located above a coffee shop; some can feel rather tight, so opt for the 'deluxe' rooms, which feature beds on an elevated platform and a bit more space.

CHAKRABONGSE VILLAS
HOTEL $$$

Map p252 (☎0 2622 1900; www.chakrabongsevillas.com; 396/1 Th Maha Rat; incl breakfast r 5000B, ste 10,000-25,000B; ❄ @ 🛜🚤; 🚤Tha Tien) This compound incorporates three sumptuous but cramped rooms and four larger suites and villas, some with great river views, all surrounding a still-functioning royal palace dating back to 1908. There's a pool, jungle-like gardens and an elevated deck for romantic riverside dining. No walk-ins.

INN A DAY
HOTEL $$$

Map p252 (☎0 2221 0577; www.innaday.com; 57-61 Th Maha Rat; incl breakfast r 3200-4200B, ste 7500-9000B; ❄ @ 🛜; 🚤Tha Tien) The brand new Inn A Day wows with its hyper-cool retro/industrial theme (the hotel is located in a former sugar factory) and its location (it towers over the river and Wat Arun). Rooms aren't huge, but include unique touches such as clear neon shower stalls, while the top-floor suites have two levels and huge clawfoot tubs.

SALA RATTANAKOSIN
HOTEL $$$

Map p252 (☎0 2622 1388; www.salaresorts.com/rattanakosin; Soi Tha Tian; incl breakfast r 3100-4900B, ste 9000B; ❄ @ 🛜; 🚤Tha Tien) This new place boasts a sleek, modernist feel – an intriguing contrast with the former warehouse it's located in. The 17 rooms, decked out in black and white, and boasting open-plan bathrooms and big windows looking out on the river and Wat Arun, can't be described as vast, but will satisfy the fashion-conscious.

AURUM: THE RIVER PLACE
HOTEL $$$

Map p252 (☎0 2622 2248; www.aurum-bangkok.com; 394/27-29 Soi Pansuk; r incl breakfast 3700-4600B; ❄ @ 🛜; 🚤Tha Tien) The 12 modern rooms here don't necessarily reflect the grand European exterior of this refurbished shophouse. Nonetheless they're comfortable and well appointed, and most offer fleeting views of Mae Nam Chao Phraya.

🛏 Banglamphu

CHERN
HOSTEL $

Map p254 (☎0 2621 1133; www.chernbangkok.com; 17 Soi Ratchasak; dm 400B, r 1200-1500B; ❄ @ 🛜; 🚤klorng boat to Tha Phan Fah) A modern hostel has been coaxed out of this former factory. A convenient, untouristed location makes it stand apart from its brethren, while open spaces and white tones create an almost afterlife-like feel. The four- and eight-bed dorms are above average, but we particularly liked the private rooms; equipped with attractive minimalist furnishings, vast desk, TV, safe, fridge and lots of space, they're a steal at this price.

FORTVILLE GUESTHOUSE
HOTEL $

Map p254 (☎0 2282 3932; www.fortvilleguesthouse.com; 9 Th Phra Sumen; r 790-1120B; ❄ @ 🛜; 🚤Tha Phra Athit, Banglamphu) With an exterior that combines elements of a modern church or castle, and an interior that relies on mirrors and industrial themes, the design concept of this unique hotel is tough to pin down. Rooms are small, but the more expensive ones include perks such as a fridge, balcony and free wi-fi. A quirky, stylish good-value hotel.

RAJATA HOTEL
HOTEL $

Map p254 (☎0 2628 8084; www.rajatahotel.com; 46 Soi 6, Th Samsen; r 1000B; ❄ @ 🛜; 🚤Tha Phra Athit, Banglamphu) A defiantly old-school hotel, an unassuming but comfortable choice for those who don't want to stay on Th Khao San but don't want to be too far away.

KHAOSAN IMMJAI
HOSTEL $

Map p254 (📞0 2629 3088; www.khaosan immjai.com; Soi 1, Th Samsen; dm incl breakfast 350-420B; ❄ @ 🛜; 🚊Tha Phra Athit, Banglamphu) There's nothing flashy or particularly exceptional about this new hostel, but a homey feel and positive feedback edge it into the recommendable column. Dorms, which range from four to 14 beds, are clean, done out in pastel tones and have ample natural light, and include lots of convenient amenities (washing machines, computers, etc), although none of the latter are free.

WILD ORCHID VILLA
HOTEL $

Map p254 (📞0 2629 4378; www.wildorchidvilla. com; 8 Soi Chana Songkhram; r 600-1500B; ❄ 🛜; 🚊Tha Phra Athit, Banglamphu) The cheapies here are some of the tiniest we've seen anywhere, but all rooms are clean and neat, and come in a bright, friendly package. Exceedingly popular, so it's best to book ahead.

★LAMPHU TREEHOUSE
HOTEL $$

Map p254 (📞0 2282 0991; www.lamphutree hotel.com; 155 Wanchat Bridge, off Th Prachathipatai; incl breakfast r 1450-2500B, ste 3600-4900B; ❄ @ 🛜 🏊; 🚊Tha Phan Fah) Despite the name, this attractive midranger has its feet firmly on land, and as such represents brilliant value. The wood-panelled rooms are attractive and inviting, and the rooftop bar, pool, internet cafe, restaurant and quiet canal-side location ensure that you may never feel the need to leave. A new annexe a couple of blocks away increases your odds of snagging an elusive reservation. Highly recommended, but be sure to book at least a month in advance.

FEUNG NAKORN BALCONY
HOTEL $$

Map p258 (📞0 2622 1100; www.feungnakorn. com; 125 Th Fuang Nakhon; dm incl breakfast 600B, incl breakfast r 1650B, ste 2000-3000B; ❄ @ 🛜; 🚊klorng boat to Tha Phan Fah) Located in a former school, the 42 rooms here surround an inviting garden courtyard and are generally large, bright and cheery. Amenities such as a free minibar, safe and flatscreen TV are standard, and the hotel has a quiet and secluded location away from the strip, with capable staff. A charming and inviting, if not extremely great-value, place to stay.

HOTEL DÉ MOC
HOTEL $$

Map p254 (📞0 2282 2831; www.hoteldemoc.com; 78 Th Prachathipatai; r incl breakfast 2549-2804B; ❄ @ 🛜 🏊; 🚊Tha Phan Fah) The rooms at this 1960s-era hotel feel spacious, with high ceilings and generous windows, although the furnishings, like the exterior, are still stuck in the previous century. The grounds include an inviting and retro-feeling pool and cafe, and complimentary transport to Th Khao San and free bike rental are thoughtful perks. Hefty online discounts are available.

SAM SEN SAM PLACE
GUESTHOUSE $$

Map p257 (📞0 2628 7067; www.samsensam. com; 48 Soi 3, Th Samsen; r incl breakfast 590-2500B; ❄ @ 🛜; 🚊Tha Phra Athit, Banglamphu) One of the homiest places around, this colourful, refurbished antique villa gets glowing reports about its friendly service and quiet location. Note that the cheapest rooms are fan-cooled and share a bathroom.

RAMBUTTRI VILLAGE INN
HOSTEL $$

Map p254 (📞0 2282 9162; www.rambuttrivillage. com; 95 Soi Ram Buttri; r incl breakfast 1030-1600B; ❄ 🛜 🏊; 🚊Tha Phra Athit, Banglamphu) If you're willing to subject yourself to the relentless barrage of tailors ('Excuse me, suit?'), this newish hotel has an abundance of good-value rooms. A ground-floor courtyard with restaurants and shops also makes it a convenient place to stay.

PANNEE RESIDENCE
HOTEL $$

Map p254 (📞0 2629 4560; www.panneeresi dence.com; 117 Th Din So; r incl breakfast 1100-1700B; ❄ @ 🛜; 🚊klorng boat to Tha Phan Fah) Pannee is a multistorey hotel offering tidy, if somewhat characterless, rooms. The cheapest rooms are pretty tiny, but like all the others include a safe, TV and fridge. An upper-floor patio with outdoor rain showers and daybeds for sunbathing provides a bit more room to stretch, and convenient proximity to Bangkok's big sights makes the decision easy.

SOURIRE
HOTEL $$

Map p254 (📞0 2280 2180; www.sourirebangkok. com; Soi Chao Phraya Si Phiphat; r incl breakfast 1500-3500B; ❄ @ 🛜; 🚊Tha Phan Fah) More home than hotel, with 38 rooms that exude a calming feel. Soft lighting, comfortable, sturdy furniture and the friendly owners complete the package. To reach the hotel,

SLEEPING BANGLAMPHU

follow Soi Chao Phraya Si Phiphat to the end and knock on the tall brown wooden door immediately on your left.

DIAMOND HOUSE — HOTEL $$

Map p254 (☏0 2629 4008; www.thaidiamondhouse.com; 4 Th Samsen, r 1100-1700B, ste 3600B; ✻@🛜; 🚇Tha Phra Athit, Banglamphu) Despite sharing real estate with a Chinese temple, there's a no conflict of design at this eccentric hotel. Most rooms have beds on raised platforms, and are outfitted with stained glass, dark, lush colours and chic furnishings. There's a lack of windows, and some of the suites aren't much larger than the cheaper rooms, but a rooftop deck and an outdoor Jacuzzi (!) attempt to make up for this.

VILLA CHA-CHA — HOTEL $$

Map p254 (☏0 2280 1025; www.villachacha.com; 36 Th Tani; r 1000-3200B; ✻🛜☳; 🚇Tha Phra Athit, Banglamphu) Wind your way between Balinese statues, lounging residents, a rambling restaurant and a tiny pool to emerge at this seemingly hidden but popular hotel. Rooms are capable – bar the clumsy stabs made at interior design (think topless art school portraits) – but the real draw is the hyper-social, resortlike atmosphere.

BAAN DINSO @ RATCHADAMNOEN — HOTEL $$

Map p254 (☏08 6815 3300; www.baandinso.com; 78/3 Th Ratchadamnoen Klang; r incl breakfast 800-3100B; ✻🛜; 🚇klorng boat to Tha Phan Fah) Overlooking arguably the most famous intersection in Bangkok, the rooms here run the spectrum from modern but tiny singles to spacious 'Grand' rooms, all with fleeting views of the Democracy Monument.

RIKKA INN — HOTEL $$

Map p254 (☏0 2282 7511; www.rikkainn.com; 259 Th Khao San; r 1150-1450B; ✻@🛜☳; 🚇Tha Phra Athit, Banglamphu) With tight but attractive rooms, a rooftop pool and a location in the middle of all the action on Th Khao San, the Rikka is one of the area's most conveniently located and better-value midrangers.

NEW SIAM RIVERSIDE — HOTEL $$

Map p254 (☏0 2629 3535; www.newsiam.net; 21 Th Phra Athit; r incl breakfast 1490-3990B; ✻@☳; 🚇Tha Phra Athit, Banglamphu) One of a couple of newish places along Th Phra Athit taking advantage of the riverside setting, this hotel has comfortable rooms with tiny bathrooms. But the real value comes

from the amenities (internet, travel agent, restaurant) and the location on one of the city's more pleasant streets. Book ahead.

OLD BANGKOK INN — HOTEL $$$

Map p254 (☏0 2629 1787; www.oldbangkokinn.com; 609 Th Phra Sumen; incl breakfast r 4000-9000B; ✻@🛜; 🚇klorng boat to Tha Phan Fah) The dictionary definition of a honeymoon hotel, this refurbished antique shophouse has 10 rooms that are decadent and sumptuous, blending rich colours and heavy wood furnishings. All have computers for personal use, and some have two levels and semi-outdoor bathrooms.

PRAYA PALAZZO — HOTEL $$$

Map p254 (☏0 2883 2998; www.prayapalazzo.com; 757/1 Somdej Prapinklao Soi 2, Thonburi; incl breakfast r 7000-9000B, ste 12,000-19,000B; ✻🛜☳; 🚇Tha Phra Athit, Banglamphu) After lying dormant for nearly 30 years, this elegant 19th-century mansion has been reborn as an attractive riverside boutique hotel. The 17 rooms can feel rather tight, and river views can be elusive, but the meticulous renovation, handsome antique furnishings and a bucolic atmosphere convene in a boutique with authentic old-world charm. Significant online discounts available.

🛏 Thewet & Dusit

TAEWEZ GUESTHOUSE — HOTEL $

Map p257 (☏0 2280 8856; www.taewez.com; 23/12 Th Si Ayuthaya; r 390-820B; ✻@🛜; 🚇Tha Thewet) Popular with French travellers; the cheapest rooms here are bare and share bathrooms.

★PHRA-NAKORN NORN-LEN — HOTEL $$

Map p257 (☏0 2628 8188; www.phranakorn-nornlen.com; 46 Soi Thewet 1; r incl breakfast 1800-3600B; ✻@🛜; 🚇Tha Thewet) Set in an expansive garden compound decorated like the Bangkok of yesteryear, this bright and cheery hotel is a fun and atmospheric, if not necessarily stupendous-value place to stay. The 31 rooms are attractively furnished with old-timey antiques and wall paintings, and there's massage and endless opportunities for peaceful relaxing.

BAAN MANUSARN — GUESTHOUSE $$

Map p257 (☏08 1855 6062; www.baanmanusarn-guesthome.com; Th Krung Kasem; r incl breakfast 1400B; ✻@🛜; 🚇Tha Thewet) Steps from Tha

BATHROOMLESS IN BANGKOK
....

If you're on a budget and don't mind sharing a bathroom, Bangkok has heaps of options for you, ranging from high-tech dorm beds in a brand-new hostel to private bedrooms in a riverside house. And best of all, at the places below, we found the bathrooms to be clean and convenient, and sharing will hardly feel like a compromise. Some of our picks:

Lub*d (Map p260; ☎ 0 2634 7999; www.siamsquare.lubd.com; Th Phra Ram I; dm 750B, r 1800-2400B; ❄ @ �) ([S] National Stadium exit 1) The title is a play on the Thai *làp dee*, meaning 'sleep well', but the fun atmosphere here might make you want to stay up all night. There's an inviting communal area stocked with games and a bar, and thoughtful facilities ranging from washing machines to a theatre room. Only double rooms have en suite bathroom. If this one's full, there's another branch just off **Th Silom** (Map p264; ☎ 0 2634 7999; 4 Th Decho; dm 550-650B, r 1400-1800B; ❄ @ ☞; [S] Chong Nonsi exit 2).

Khaosan Baan Thai (Map p257; ☎ 0 2628 5559; www.khaosanbaanthai.com; 11/1 Soi 3, Th Samsen; r incl breakfast 390-730B; ❄ @ ☞; ⛴ Tha Phra Athit, Banglamphu) This tiny wooden house holds 10 rooms decked out in cheery pastels and hand-painted bunny pictures. Half the rooms are fan-cooled, most are little more than a mattress on the floor, and all share bathrooms, but warm service and an authentic homestay vibe compensate.

Silom Art Hostel (Map p264; ☎ 0 2635 8070; www.silomarthostel.com; 198/19-22 Soi 14, Th Silom; dm 400-550B, r 1200-1500B; ❄ @ ☞; [S] Chong Nonsi exit 3) Quirky, artsy, bright and fun, combining recycled materials, bizarre furnishings and colourful wall paintings to arrive at a hostel that's quite unlike anywhere else in town. Rooms (with en suite bathrooms) and dorm beds are functional and comfy, with appealing communal areas.

NapPark Hostel (Map p254; ☎ 0 2282 2324; www.nappark.com; 5 Th Tani; dm 570-750B; ❄ @ ☞; ⛴ Tha Phra Athit, Banglamphu) A well-run hostel with dorm rooms of various sizes; all have podlike beds with power points, mini-TV, reading lamp and wi-fi. Free bikes and supersocial communal areas mean you may not actually get the chance to plug in.

HQ Hostel (Map p264; ☎ 0 2233 1598; www.hqhostel.com; 5/3-4 Soi 3, Th Silom; dm 380-730B, r 1300-1700B; ❄ @ ☞; [M] Si Lom exit 2, [S] Sala Daeng exit 2) HQ is a flashpacker hostel in the polished-concrete-and-industrial-style mould. It includes four- to 10-bed dorms, a few doubles (S Type rooms have en suite) and inviting communal areas in a narrow multistorey building in the middle of Bangkok's financial district.

Saphaipae (Map p264; ☎ 0 2238 2322; www.saphaipae.com; 35 Th Surasak; dm 400-550B, r 1800-2500B; ❄ @ ☞; [S] Surasak exit 1) The bright colours, chunky furnishings and bold murals in the lobby of this new hostel give it the vibe of a day-care centre for travellers – a feel that continues through to the playful communal areas and rooms (the more expensive of which have en suite). Dorms and rooms are thoughtful and well-equipped, and there's heaps of useful travel resources and facilities.

Suneta Hostel Khaosan (Map p254; ☎ 0 2629 0150; www.sunetahostel.com; 209-211 Th Kraisi; dm incl breakfast 440-590B; r incl breakfast 900-1090B; ❄ @ ☞; ⛴ Tha Phra Athit, Banglamphu) This young hostel is getting rave reviews for its retro-themed design, comfy dorms and friendly service.

S1 Hostel (Map p268; ☎ 0 2679 7777; www.facebook.com/S1hostelBangkok; 35/1-4 Soi Ngam Duphli; dm 330-380B, r 700-1300B; ❄ @ ☞; [M] Lumphini exit 1) A huge new hostel with dorm beds and private rooms (the latter with en suite) decked out in a simple yet attractive primary-colour scheme. A host of facilities (laundry, kitchen, rooftop garden) and a convenient location near the MRT make it great value.

HI-Sukhumvit (Map p270; ☎ 0 2391 9338; www.hisukhumvit.com; 23 Soi 38, Th Sukhumvit; dm incl breakfast 350B; r incl breakfast 690-1590B; ❄ @ ☞; [S] Thong Lo exit 4) The dorms here are admittedly rather plain, but clean bathrooms and a location in a quiet residential area with easy access to street food make it comfortable and convenient.

New Road Guesthouse (Map p266; ☎ 0 2630 9371; www.newroadguesthouse.com; 1216/1 Th Charoen Krung; dm 250B, r 550-1600B; ❄ @ ☞; ⛴ Tha Oriental) The dorms here, among the cheapest accommodation in all of Bangkok, are surprisingly clean and welcoming.

Thewet is this rambling shophouse with four homey-feeling rooms. All are spacious with beautiful wood floors, but the two 'family' rooms are the most generous, and all but the smallest have balconies.

SAMSEN 5 LODGE GUESTHOUSE $$

Map p257 (✆0 2628 9799; www.samsen5lodge bangkok.com; 58/1 Soi 5, Th Samsen; r incl breakfast 1500-2000B; ❉🛜; 🚢Tha Thewet) It doesn't get much cosier than the three rooms in this rambling home. Rooms aren't huge, but are given colour by artsy/retro design touches. The comfy homestay feel is heightened by a lauded Thai-style breakfast and a location just outside the tourist zone.

SIAM HOTEL $$$

Map p257 (✆0 2206 6999; www.thesiamhotel. com; 3/2 Th Khao; incl breakfast r 16,300-22,500B, villa 31,000-37,200B; ❉@🛜⛱; 🚢Tha Thewet, hotel shuttle boat from Tha Sathon, Central Pier) Zoom back to the 1930s in this incongruously new riverside hotel, where art deco influences, copious marble and beautiful antiques define the look. Rooms are spacious and well-appointed, while villas up the ante with rooftop balcony and plunge pool. Yet it's not just about navel-gazing, with activities ranging from Thai boxing lessons to a private theatre available to keep you busy.

SSIP BOUTIQUE HOTEL $$$

Map p257 (✆0 2282 6489; www.ssiphotelthailand. com; 42 Th Phitsanulok; r incl breakfast 5800-7800B; ❉@🛜; 🚢Tha Thewet) Handsome tiles, heavy wood furniture, antique furnishings: the 20 rooms here have meticulously recreated an old-school Bangkok feel. Modern amenities (TV, fridge, safe) and thoughtful staff ensure a thoroughly contemporary stay.

🛏 Chinatown

SIAM CLASSIC GUESTHOUSE $

Map p258 (✆0 2639 6363; 336/10 Trok Chalong Krung; r incl breakfast 500-1200B; ❉@🛜; Ⓜ Hua Lamphong exit 1) Rooms don't have much furniture, but effort has been made at making them comfortable, tidy and even a bit stylish. An inviting communal area encourages meeting and chatting, and the whole place has a welcoming homestay vibe.

@HUA LAMPHONG HOSTEL $

Map p258 (✆0 2639 1925; www.at-hualamphong. com; 326/1 Th Phra Ram IV; dm 400-450B, r

690-950B; ❉@🛜; 🚢Tha Ratchawong, Ⓜ Hua Lamphong) Plain-yet-clean dorm beds and rooms can be found in this new-feeling hostel across the street from the train station.

SHANGHAI MANSION HOTEL $$$

Map p258 (✆0 2221 2121; www.shanghaimansion.com; 479-481 Th Yaowarat; incl breakfast r 3200B, ste 4500B; ❉@🛜; 🚢Tha Ratchawong, Ⓜ Hua Lamphong exit 1 & taxi) Easily the most consciously stylish place to stay in Chinatown, if not in all of Bangkok. This award-winning boutique hotel screams Shanghai circa 1935 with stained glass, an abundance of lamps, bold colours and cheeky Chinatown kitsch. If you're willing to splurge, ask for one of the bigger streetside rooms with tall windows that allow more natural light.

🛏 Siam Square, Pratunam, Ploenchit & Ratchathewi

HI MID BANGKOK HOSTEL $

Map p263 (✆0 2644 5744; www.midbangkok.com; 481/3 Th Ratchawithi; incl breakfast dm 490B, r 1550-2400B; ❉@🛜; Ⓢ Victory Monument exit 4) Contemporary elements (industrial influences, smooth concrete) and old-school Bangkok touches (faux-antique tiles, wood furniture) mix at this inviting hostel. Dorm rooms are cosy and share clean bathrooms, while private rooms are spacious and have lots of natural light, if somewhat bare (only the larger deluxe rooms have TV).

RENO HOTEL HOTEL $$

Map p260 (✆0 2215 0026; www.renohotel.co.th; 40 Soi Kasem San 1; r incl breakfast 1590-2390B; ❉@🛜⛱; Ⓢ National Stadium exit 1) Rooms are relatively large, if somewhat dark, and reflect the renovations evident in the lobby and exterior. But the cafe and pool of this Vietnam War–era hotel still cling to the past.

WENDY HOUSE HOSTEL $$

Map p260 (✆0 2214 1149; www.wendyguesthouse.com; 36/2 Soi Kasem San 1; r incl breakfast 1100-1490B; ❉@🛜; Ⓢ National Stadium exit 1) The rooms here are small and basic, but exceedingly clean and relatively well stocked (TV, fridge) for this price range.

SIAM@SIAM HOTEL $$$

Map p260 (✆0 2217 3000; www.siamatsiam. com; 865 Th Phra Ram I; r incl breakfast 7000-11,200B; ❉@🛜⛱; Ⓢ National Stadium exit 1)

A seemingly random mishmash of colours and industrial/recycled materials in the lobby here result in a style one could only describe as 'junkyard chic' – but in a good way, of course. The rooms, which largely continue the theme, are between the 14th and 24th floors, and offer terrific city views. There's a spa, a rooftop restaurant and a pool on the 11th floor.

HANSAR — BOUTIQUE HOTEL **$$$**

Map p260 (☎0 2209 1234; www.hansarbangkok.com; 3 Soi Mahadlekluang 2; incl breakfast r 5225B, ste 5700-24,000B; ❄@📶🏊; [S]Ratchadamri exit 4) The Hansar can claim that elusive intersection of style and value. All 94 rooms here are handsome and feature huge bathrooms and giant desks, but the smallest (and cheapest) studios are probably the best deal, as they have a kitchenette, washing machine, stand-alone tub, free wi-fi and balcony.

OKURA PRESTIGE — HOTEL **$$$**

Map p260 (☎0 2687 9000; www.okurabangkok.com; 57 Th Witthayu (Wireless Rd); incl breakfast r 14,000-25,000B, ste 29,000-150,000B; [P]❄@📶🏊; [S]Phloen Chit exit 5) The Bangkok venture of a Japanese chain – to date the first branch outside its homeland – is, unlike other recent, big-name openings in Bangkok, distinctly unflashy. But we like the minimalist, almost contemplative feel of the lobby and 240 rooms, and the subtle but thoughtful, often distinctly Japanese, touches. Significant online discounts available.

FOUR SEASONS HOTEL — HOTEL **$$$**

Map p260 (☎0 2126 8866; www.fourseasons.com/bangkok; 155 Th Ratchadamri; r 12,490-20,490B, ste 19,490-85,490B; ❄@📶🏊; 🚉Ratchadamri exit 4) A spectacular mural descending a grand staircase, ceilings with neck-craning artwork… the initial classy impression continues into rooms here, which combine Thai elements with heavy hardwood furniture and modern yet subtle amenities. If you've got deep pockets, consider the two-room Explorers Suite, decked out with beautiful swathes of Jim Thompson Thai silk. This being a Four Seasons hotel, you can rest assured that service is first-rate.

VIE — HOTEL **$$$**

Map p260 (☎0 2309 3939; www.viehotelbangkok.com; 117/39-40 Th Phayathai; incl breakfast r 4943B, ste 6591-23,304B; ❄@📶🏊; [S]Ratchathewi exit 2) Vie combines convenient location and casual atmosphere in one attractive package. The service gets good reports, there's an emphasis on wining and dining, and if you're considering upgrading, the spacious duplex suites offer great city views.

LIT — HOTEL **$$$**

Map p260 (☎0 2612 3456; www.litbangkok.com; 36/1 Soi Kasem San 1; r 7000-8000B, ste 9000-10,000B; ❄@📶🏊; [S]National Stadium exit 1) This modern, architecturally striking hotel has a variety of room styles united by a light theme. Check out a few, as they vary significantly, and some features, including a shower that can be seen from the living room, aren't necessarily for everybody.

LUXX XL — HOTEL **$$$**

Map p268 (☎0 2684 1111; www.staywithluxx.com; 82/8 Soi Lang Suan; incl breakfast r 2038-2379B, ste 2888-24,544B; ❄@📶🏊; [S]Ratchadamri exit 2) LUXX oozes with a minimalist hipness that wouldn't be out of place in London or New York. Floor-to-ceiling windows allow heaps of natural light, suites have an added kitchenette and all rooms are decked out with appropriately stylish furnishings. There's another slightly cheaper (and smaller) **branch** (Map p264; ☎0 2635 8800; 6/11 Th Decho; incl breakfast r 1784-2124B, ste 2633; ❄@📶; [S]Chong Nongsi exit 3).

PULLMAN BANGKOK KING POWER — HOTEL **$$$**

Map p263 (☎0 2680 9999; www.pullmanbangkokkingpower.com; 8/2 Th Rang Nam; incl breakfast r 3381-3981B, ste 5282-6282B; ❄@📶🏊; [S]Victory Monument exit 2) The Pullman is a great choice for those who want to stay in a business-class hotel but would rather not stay downtown. Rooms are smart and modern, and the Pullman's restaurants are among the best-value Western dining options in town. Located a brief walk from the BTS stop at Victory Monument.

HOTEL MUSE — BOUTIQUE HOTEL **$$$**

Map p260 (☎0 2630 4000; www.hotelmusebangkok.com; 55/555 Soi Lang Suan; incl breakfast r 5696-7638B, ste 11,500-35,500B; ❄@📶🏊; [S]Ratchadamri exit 2) Gaining inspiration from the golden era of travel of the late 19th-century, this hotel straddles the past and the present. Rooms feel dark and decadent – the vibe set by the faux-antique furniture, textured wallpaper and clawfoot tubs – but also feature modern amenities and great city views. It's run by Accor, so the service is on par with the surroundings.

🛏 Riverside, Silom & Lumphini

MILE MAP HOSTEL
HOSTEL $

Map p264 (📞0 2635 1212; 36/4 Th Pan; dm 295-330B, r 690-1300B, 🌀❄, ⓢSurasak exit 3) Despite the quasi-industrial theme, this new hostel feels inviting, warm and fun. The 10-bed dorms are one of the best deals in town, and the private rooms have a funky, minimalist feel, although not much natural light.

ETZZZ HOSTEL
HOSTEL $

Map p268 (📞0 2286 9424; www.etzhostel.com; 5/3 Soi Ngam Duphli; dm 250-450B, r 900B; 🌀@❄; ⓜLumphini exit 1) The private rooms at this brand-new shophouse-based hostel are overpriced, but the tidy dorm, shiny facilities and convenient location are draws.

SMILE SOCIETY
HOTEL $$

Map p264 (📞08 1343 1754, 08 1442 5800; www.smilesocietyhostel.com; 30/3-4 Soi 6, Th Silom; incl breakfast dm 420B, r 900-1880B; 🌀@❄; ⓜSi Lom exit 2, ⓢSala Daeng exit 1) Part boutique, part hostel, this four-storey shophouse combines small but comfortable and well-equipped rooms and dorms with spotless shared bathrooms. A central location, overwhelmingly positive feedback, and helpful, English-speaking staff are other perks.

GLOW TRINITY SILOM
HOTEL $$

Map p264 (📞0 2231 5050; www.zinchospitality.com/glowbyzinc/silom; 150 Soi Phiphat 2; incl breakfast r 1900-2600B, ste 3600B; 🌀@❄❄; ⓢChong Nonsi exit 2) A sophisticated-feeling hotel at a midrange price, Glow has modern, tech-equipped rooms, professional service, and pool and fitness facilities just next door. The suites aren't really worth the extra baht unless you really need a bit more space and a bigger TV.

W HOME
GUESTHOUSE $$

(📞0 2291 5622; www.whomebangkok.com; Yaek 8, Soi 79, Th Charoen Krung; r incl breakfast 1590-1700B; 🌀@❄; ⓢSaphan Taksin exit 2 & taxi) Located a bit off the grid, but that's part of the charm at this 60-year-old renovated house. Welcoming hosts, four small but attractive and thoughfully furnished rooms (only one with en suite bathroom), inviting communal areas and an authentic homestay atmosphere round out the package.

SWAN HOTEL
HOTEL $$

Map p266 (📞0 2235 9271; www.swanhotelbkk.com; 31 Soi 36, Th Charoen Krung; r incl breakfast 1200-2000B; 🌀@❄❄; ⓢTha Oriental) The 1960s-era furnishings date this classic Bangkok hotel despite recent renovations. But rooms are airy and virtually spotless, and the antiquated vibe provides the Swan, in particular its pool, with a groovy, retro feel.

BAAN SALADAENG
HOTEL $$

Map p268 (📞0 2636 3038; www.baansaladaeng.com; 69/2 Soi Sala Daeng 3; incl breakfast r 1100-1600B, ste 2300B; 🌀❄; ⓜSi Lom exit 2, ⓢSala Daeng exit 4) Of the handful of pint-sized boutique hotels on Th Sala Daeng, this is the most welcoming. The lobby's cheery primary-colour theme carries on into the 11 rooms, with those on the upper floors being the largest and airiest. Gay friendly.

HANSAAH GUESTHOUSE
GUESTHOUSE $$

Map p268 (📞08 5159 2811; www.hansaah.com; 44/7 Soi Si Bamphen; r incl breakfast 1650-2150B; 🌀❄; ⓜLumphini exit 1) The seven rooms, above a restaurant in a converted shophouse, feel homey and come equipped with the usual amenities. A good choice for those wishing for an anonymous, unhotel-like stay.

ROSE HOTEL
HOTEL $$

Map p264 (📞0 2266 8268; www.rosehotelbkk.com; 118 Th Surawong; incl breakfast r 1950-2250B, ste 3300-3800B; 🌀@❄❄; ⓜSi Lom exit 2, ⓢSala Daeng exit 1) Don't let the unremarkable exterior fool you: the convenient location, modern rooms, pool, gym and sauna make this Vietnam War–era vet a pretty solid deal. The only downside is the over-priced wi-fi (per day 300B).

ESCAPE AT SATHORN TERRACE
HOTEL $$

Map p266 (📞0 2630 9810; www.sathornterrace.com; 210 Th Sathon Neua (North); r incl breakfast 1500-2650B; 🌀❄; ⓢSaphan Taksin exit 3) If you can ignore the characterless and somewhat noisy location, rooms here a good deal. Many have lots of space, basic kitchenettes and large fridges – great for those who want to make themselves at home.

BANGKOK CHRISTIAN GUEST HOUSE
HOTEL $$

Map p264 (📞0 2233 2206; www.bcgh.org; 123 Soi Sala Daeng 2; r incl breakfast 1100-2860B; 🌀❄; ⓜSi Lom exit 2, ⓢSala Daeng exit 2) This rather institutional-feeling guesthouse is a wise choice for families on a budget, as some rooms have as many as five beds and there's a 2nd-floor children's play area.

CHAYDON SATHORN HOTEL $$
Map p268 (☎0 2343 6333; www.chaydonsathorn.com; 31 Th Sathon Tai (South); r incl breakfast 2000-2600B; ❄@📶🏊; [M]Lumphini exit 2)
The former King's Hotel has been reborn as a no-frills midranger, right in the middle of the embassy district. The primary colours and bold lines of the design scheme make up for the lack of natural light in some rooms. Online discounts available through the website.

★**SIAM HERITAGE** HOTEL $$$
Map p264 (☎0 2353 6101; www.thesiamheritage.com; 115/1 Th Surawong; incl breakfast r 2900B,

SMALLER IS BETTER

The research for this edition revealed several attractive hotels and guesthouses with fewer than 10 rooms. Some of our faves:

Arun Residence (Map p252; ☎0 2221 9158; www.arunresidence.com; 36-38 Soi Pratu Nokyung; incl breakfast r 4000-4200B, ste 5800B; ❄@📶; ⛴Tha Tien) Although strategically located on the river directly across from Wat Arun, this multilevel wooden house boasts much more than just brilliant views. The six rooms here manage to feel both homey and stylish, some being tall and loftlike, while others cojoin two rooms (the best is the top-floor suite with its own balcony).

Loy La Long (Map p258; ☎0 2639 1390; www.loylalong.com; 1620/2 Th Songwat; incl breakfast dm 1300B, r 2100-4000B; ❄@📶; ⛴Tha Ratchawong, [M]Hua Lamphong exit 1 & taxi) Rustic, retro, charming – the six rooms in this 100-year-old wooden house can lay claim to more than their fair share of personality. And united by breezy, inviting nooks and crannies, and a unique location elevated over Mae Nam Chao Phraya, the whole place is also privy to a hidden, almost secret, feel.

Bhuthorn (Map p254; ☎0 2622 2270; www.thebhuthorn.com; 96-98 Th Phraeng Phuthon; r incl breakfast 4500-6300B; ❄@📶; ⛴klorng boat to Tha Phan Fah) Travel a century back in time by booking one of the three rooms in this beautiful antique shophouse located in a classic Bangkok neighbourhood. They're not particularly huge, but are big on atmosphere and come equipped with both antique furnishings and modern amenities. The sister hotel, **Asadang** (Map p258; ☎08 5180 7100; 94-94/1 Th Atsadang; r incl breakfast 4500-5600B; ❄@📶; ⛴Tha Tien), a couple of blocks away, offers a similar package.

Littlest Guesthouse (Map p264; ☎0 2675 6763; www.littlestguesthouse.com; 77 Th Sathon Tai (South); r incl breakfast 2500B; ❄📶; [S]Surasak exit 2) In a secluded alleyway steps from the BTS is this tiny, home-bound boutique. Rooms are spacious and spotless, attractively decked out in contemporary/artsy furnishings, and boasting lots of natural light.

Café Ice Residence (Map p264; ☎0 2636 7831; cafeiceresidences@gmail.com; 44/4 Soi Phiphat 2; r incl breakfast 1900-3300B; ❄@📶; [S]Chong Nonsi exit 2) More home than hotel, the nine rooms in this spotless, classy villa are inviting, spacious and comfy. Filled with subtle yet attractive furnishings, they share a location with a Thai restaurant.

Loog Choob Homestay (Map p257; ☎08 5328 2475; www.loogchoob.com; 463/5-8 Th Luk Luang; incl breakfast r 1900B, ste 3300-3800B; ❄@📶; [S]Phaya Thai exit 3 & taxi) Five rooms in a former gem factory outside the tourist zone might sound iffy, but the rooms are stylish and inviting, with a huge array of thoughtful amenities and friendly, heartfelt service.

Baan Dinso (Map p254; ☎0 2621 2808; www.baandinso.com; 113 Trok Sin; r incl breakfast 1400-3500B; ❄@📶; ⛴klorng boat to Tha Phan Fah) This antique wooden villa may not represent the best value in Bangkok, but for a nostalgic feel and palpable sense of place, it's almost impossible to beat. Of the nine small-yet-spotless rooms, five have en suite bathrooms, while all have access to functional and inviting communal areas.

Baan Tepa Boutique House (Map p257; ☎0 2281 4332; www.baantepa.com; 245/1 Soi 9, Th Si Ayuthaya; r incl breakfast 1100-1800B; ❄@📶; ⛴Tha Thewet) The eight rooms in this 80-year-old wooden house are small, and the decor edges towards the chintzy, but the charm and hospitality are abundant and authentic.

ste 4000-9300B; ✱@🛜🏊; MSi Lom exit 2, SSala Daeng exit 1) Off busy Th Surawong, this classy boutique hotel oozes homey Thai charm – probably because the owners live in the same building. The 73 rooms are decked out in silk and dark woods with classy design touches and thoughtful amenities. There's an inviting rooftop garden/pool/spa, and it's all cared for by charming and professional staff. Highly recommended.

★**METROPOLITAN BY COMO** HOTEL $$$

Map p268 (📞0 2625 3333; www.comohotels. com/metropolitanbangkok; 27 Th Sathon Tai (South); r incl breakfast 9220-11,220B, ste incl breakfast 12,200-78,720B; ✱@🛜🏊; MLumphini exit 2) The exterior of Bangkok's former YMCA has changed relatively little, but a peek inside reveals one of the city's sleekest, sexiest hotels. A recent renovation has all 171 rooms looking better than ever in striking tones of black, white and yellow. It's worth noting that the 'City' rooms tend to feel a bit tight, while the two-storey penthouse suites feel like small homes.

MANDARIN ORIENTAL HOTEL $$$

Map p266 (📞0 2659 9000; www.mandarinoriental.com; 48 Soi 40, Th Charoen Krung; r incl breakfast 15,150-30,000B; ste incl breakfast 27,500-160,000B; ✱@🛜🏊; 🚤Tha Oriental, or hotel shuttle boat from Tha Sathon, Central Pier) For the true Bangkok experience, a stay at this grand old riverside hotel is a must. The majority of rooms are in the modern and recently refurbished New Wing, but we prefer the old-world ambience of the Garden and Authors' Wings. The hotel is also home to one of the region's most acclaimed spas, a legendary fine dining restaurant and a cooking school.

PENINSULA HOTEL HOTEL $$$

Map p266 (📞0 2861 2888; www.peninsula.com; 333 Th Charoen Nakhon, Thonburi; incl breakfast r 14,000-25,000B, ste 70,000-130,000B; ✱@🛜🏊; 🚤hotel shuttle boat from Tha Sathon, Central Pier) After 16 years in Bangkok, the Pen still seems to have it all: the location (towering over the river in Thonburi), the rep (consistently one of the highest-ranking luxury hotels in the world) and one of the highest levels of service in town. If money is no obstacle, stay on one of the upper floors where you literally have all of Bangkok at your feet.

SUKHOTHAI HOTEL HOTEL $$$

Map p268 (📞0 2344 8888; www.sukhothai.com; 13/3 Th Sathon Tai (South); incl breakfast r 11,000-12,000B, ste 14,000-79,500B; ✱@🛜🏊; MLumphini exit 2) If you can afford the outlay, this is one of Bangkok's classiest luxury options. As the name suggests, the Sukhothai employs brick stupas, courtyards and antique sculptures to create a peaceful, almost templelike atmosphere. The recently remodelled rooms contrast this with high-tech TVs, phones and yes, toilets.

MILLENNIUM HILTON HOTEL $$$

Map p266 (📞0 2442 2000; www.bangkok.hilton. com; 123 Th Charoen Nakorn, Thonburi; incl

FROM LITERATI TO GLITTERATI

Now a famous grand dame, the Mandarin Oriental (p188) started as the seafarers' version of a Th Khao San guesthouse. The original owners, two Danish sea captains, traded the nest to Hans Niels Andersen, the founder of the formidable East Asiatic Company. Andersen transformed the hotel into a civilised palace of grand architecture and luxury standards. He hired an Italian architect, S Cardu, to design what is now the Authors' Wing, which was the city's most fantastic building not constructed by the king.

The rest of the hotel's history relies on its famous guests. A Polish-born sailor named Joseph Conrad stayed here in 1888. The hotel brought him good luck: he got his first command on the ship *Otago*, from Bangkok to Port Adelaide, Australia, which in turn gave him ideas for several early stories. W Somerset Maugham stumbled into the hotel with an advanced case of malaria. In his feverish state, he heard the German manager arguing with the doctor about how a death in the hotel would hurt business. Maugham's overland Southeast Asian journey is recorded in *Gentleman in the Parlour: A Record of a Journey from Rangoon to Haiphong*, which gave literary appeal to the hotel. Other notable guests have included Noel Coward, Graham Greene, John le Carré, James Michener, Gore Vidal and, er, Barbara Cartland. Some modern-day writers claim that an Oriental stay will overcome writer's block – though we suspect any writer staying these days would need a very generous advance indeed.

breakfast r 10,000-12,000B, ste 13,000-13,800B; ✹@🛜🛏; 🚤hotel shuttle boat from Tha Sathon, Central Pier) As soon as you enter the dramatic lobby, it's obvious that this is Bangkok's youngest, most modern riverside hotel. Rooms, all of which boast widescreen river views, carry on the theme and are decked out with funky furniture and Thai-themed photos. A glass elevator and an artificial beach are just some of the fun touches.

W BANGKOK HOTEL $$$
Map p264 (☎0 2344 4314; www.whotels.com/ bangkok; 106 Th Sathon Neua (North); incl breakfast r 9000-10,350B, ste 11,250-154,350B; ✹@🛜🛏; 🚇Chong Nonsi exit 1) A huge, stylish, big-chain newbie, the W has young-feeling rooms with cheeky touches (think Thai boxing-themed furnishings) and high-tech amenities. Glitter and glass, a lobby bar and a pool that glows are some of the other touches that make this Bangkok's clubbiest hotel.

SHANGRI-LA HOTEL HOTEL $$$
Map p266 (☎0 2236 7777; www.shangri-la.com; 89 Soi 42/1 (Soi Wat Suan Phlu); r incl breakfast 7600-11,300B, ste incl breakfast 12,800-120,000B; ✹@🛏; 🚇Saphan Taksin exit 1) A recent facelift has the longstanding Shangri-La looking better than ever. A convenient location near the BTS, generous rates, a resortlike riverside atmosphere, plus ample activities and amenities, make it a clever choice for families.

SOFITEL SO HOTEL $$$
Map p268 (☎0 2624 0000; www.sofitel.com; 2 Th Sathon Neua (North); incl breakfast r 15,654-31,450B; ✹@🛜🛏; 🚇Lumphini exit 2) Taking inspiration from (and featuring amazing views of) Lumphini Park, this is one of a handful of large-yet-hip name-brand hotels to open in the last couple of years. A four-elements-inspired design theme sees no two rooms looking quite the same, but all feeling spacious, stylish, modern and young.

LE MÉRIDIEN BANGKOK HOTEL $$$
Map p264 (☎0 2232 8888; www.lemeridien.com/ bangkoksurawong; 40/5 Th Surawong; r 6000-8000B, ste 15,000-29,000B; ✹@🛏; 🚇Si Lom exit 2, 🚇Sala Daeng exit 1) The look at this new, design-oriented hotel is modern Asian, with bamboo, dark timber and earthy colours delivered in clean lines throughout the 282 rooms and edgy restaurants. The location is convenient, if somewhat hectic, and floor-to-ceiling windows ensure uninterrupted views of the Patpong action and make the rooms seem bigger than they are.

🛏 Sukhumvit

SUK 11 HOSTEL $
Map p270 (☎0 2253 5927; www.suk11.com; 1/33 Soi 11, Th Sukhumvit; r incl breakfast 500-1600B; ✹@🛜; 🚇Nana exit 3) Very well run and popular, this rustic guesthouse is an oasis of woods and greenery in the urban jungle that is Th Sukhumvit. The basic rooms are clean and comfy, if a bit dark, and the cheapest ones share bathrooms. Although the building holds nearly 70 rooms, you'll still need to book at least two weeks ahead.

BED BANGKOK HOSTEL $
Map p270 (☎0 2655 7604; www.bedbangkok. com; 11/20 Soi 1, Th Sukhumvit; dm 390B, r 800-1200B; ✹@🛜; 🚇Phloen Chit exit 3) This new hostel manages to maintain a homey feel despite the industrial design theme. The convenient location and friendly service make up for the rather hard dorm beds.

PREME HOSTEL $
Map p270 (☎0 2259 6908; www.premehostel. com; 2 Soi 25, Th Sukhumvit; incl breakfast dm 500-600B, r 1200-1800B; ✹@🛜; 🚇Sukhumvit exit 2, 🚇Asok exit 6) This tidy hostel packs 68 plain, but more-than-adequate, budget rooms, as well as some of the better dorms around with semi-private bathrooms.

ATLANTA HOTEL $
Map p270 (☎0 2252 1650; www.theatlantahotel bangkok.com; 78 Soi 2, Th Sukhumvit; r incl breakfast 690-800B, ste incl breakfast 950-1950B; ✹@🛜🛏; 🚇Nana exit 2) Defiantly antiquated and equal parts frumpy and grumpy, this crumbling gem has changed very little since its construction in 1952. The opulent lobby stands in stark contrast to the simple rooms, and the frantic anti-sex tourist tone can be rather disturbing, but the inviting pool (allegedly the country's first hotel pool) and delightful restaurant (for guests only) are just enough incentive to get past these.

NAPA PLACE HOTEL $$
Map p270 (☎0 2661 5525; www.napaplace.com; 11/3 Soi Napha Sap 2; r incl breakfast 2200-2400B, ste incl breakfast 3400-4100B; ✹@🛜; 🚇Thong Lo exit 2) Hidden in the confines of a typical Bangkok urban compound is what must be the city's homiest accommodation. The 12

SLEEPING SUKHUMVIT

expansive rooms have been decorated with dark woods from the family's former business, light brown cloths from the hands of Thai weavers, while the cosy communal areas couldn't be much different from the suburban living room you grew up in.

SACHA'S HOTEL UNO
HOTEL $$

Map p270 (📞0 2651 2180; www.sachas.hotel-uno.com; 28/19 Soi 19, Th Sukhumvit; r incl breakfast 1800-2300B; ❄@🛜; MSukhumvit exit 1, SAsok exit 1) These 56 rooms in adjacent buildings are pretty compact, and are neither the 'five-star' promised in the marketing nor quite as impressive as the lobbies suggest. Still, they are very well wired for business, and the 'deluxe' rooms in the main building, in particular, won't disappoint at these prices.

FUSION SUITES
HOTEL $$

Map p270 (📞0 2665 2644; www.fusionbangkok.com; 143/61-62 Soi 21 (Asoke), Th Sukhumvit; r incl breakfast 2600-5200B; ❄@🛜; MSukhumvit exit 1, SAsok exit 1) A disproportionately funky hotel for this price range; unconventional furnishings provide rooms with heaps of style, although the cheapest can feel a bit dark.

BAAN SUKHUMVIT
HOTEL $$

Map p270 (📞0 2258 5630; www.baansukhumvit.com; 392/38-39 Soi 20, Th Sukhumvit; r incl breakfast 1440-1540B; ❄@🛜; MSukhumvit exit 1, SAsok exit 1) With only 12 rooms, this hotel exudes a cosy feel. Rooms lack bells and whistles, but are subtly attractive; the more expensive include a bit more space, a bathtub and a safe.

FEDERAL HOTEL
HOTEL $$

Map p270 (📞0 2253 0175; www.federalbangkok.com; 27 Soi 11, Th Sukhumvit; r incl breakfast 1400-1600B; ❄@🛜; SNana exit 4) You wouldn't know it from the exterior, but after more than 50 years 'Club Fed' finally decided to get a makeover. The upstairs rooms are comfortable and almost contemporary, but elements of the ground-floor rooms still scream 1967. The real draws are the convenient location, the frangipani-lined pool and the time-warped US-style coffeeshop.

ON8
HOTEL $$

Map p270 (📞0 2254 8866; www.on8bangkok.com; 162 Th Sukhumvit; r incl breakfast 2000-2800B; ❄@🛜; SNana exit 4) Wind through expat bars to this highly designed 40-room hotel where space is at a premium. The three cat-egories of room differ only in size and outlook (ie none or an opaque window, which is appropriate given what you'd be looking at). They all have big flat-screen TVs, safes, small desks and appealing decor.

STABLE LODGE
HOTEL $$

Map p270 (📞0 2653 0017; www.stablelodge.com; 39 Soi 8, Th Sukhumvit; r 1550-1750B; ❄@🛜; SNana exit 4) To be honest, we were slightly disappointed that the faux-Tudor theme of the downstairs restaurant didn't carry on into the rooms, but could find no other faults. A recent renovation has given a bit of life to the simple rooms here, and the spacious balconies still offer great city views.

⭐ ARIYASOMVILLA
HOTEL $$$

Map p270 (📞0 2254 8880; www.ariyasom.com; 65 Soi 1, Th Sukhumvit; r incl breakfast 5353-11,682B; ❄@🛜; SPhloen Chit exit 3) Located at the end of Soi 1 behind a virtual wall of frangipani, this beautifully renovated 1940s-era villa is one of the worst-kept accommodation secrets in Bangkok. If you can score a reservation, you'll be privy to one of 24 spacious rooms, meticulously outfitted with thoughtful Thai design touches and beautiful antique furniture. There's a spa and an inviting tropical pool, and breakfast is vegetarian and served in the villa's stunning glass-encased dining room.

EUGENIA
HOTEL $$$

Map p270 (📞0 2259 9011; www.theeugenia.com; 267 Soi 31 (Sawadti), Th Sukhumvit; r incl breakfast 5157-6516B; ❄@🛜; SPhrom Phong exit 6 & taxi) A stay in this hotel, decked out in antique furniture and animal skins, is like travelling to Burmah circa 1936. Don't fear though; you won't have to ask the 'boy' to draw you a bath – modern amenities such as flat-screen TVs and free domestic and international calls are also provided. Ask about the vintage-car airport transfers.

SHERATON GRANDE SUKHUMVIT
HOTEL $$$

Map p270 (📞0 2649 8888; www.luxurycollection.com/bangkok; 250 Th Sukhumvit; incl breakfast r 10,000-12,500B, ste 18,000-55,500B; ❄@🛜; MSukhumvit exit 3, SAsok exit 2) This conveniently located, business-oriented hotel offers some of the most spacious rooms in town and fills them with a generous array of amenities. By the time you read this, an impending renovation may have already made what was already a very good hotel an excellent hotel.

MA DU ZI
HOTEL **$$$**

Map p270 (☑0 2615 6400; www.maduzihotel.com; cnr Th Ratchadaphisek & Soi 16, Th Sukhumvit; incl breakfast r 6500-7500B; ste 9000-12,500B; ✳@☞; ⓜSukhumvit exit 3, ⓢAsok exit 6) The name is Thai for 'come take a look', somewhat of a misnomer for this reservations-only, no walk-ins hotel. If you've gained access, behind the gate you'll find a modern, attractive mid-sized boutique steeped in dark, chic tones and designs. We particularly liked the immense bathrooms, equipped with a walk-in tub and minimalist shower.

ALOFT
HOTEL **$$$**

Map p270 (☑0 2207 7000; www.alofthotels.com/bangkoksukhumvit11; 35 Soi 11, Th Sukhumvit; incl breakfast r 4700-5750B; ste 7700-15,700B; ✳@☞✳; ⓢNana exit 5) Fun seems to be the operative term for this young-feeling hotel – even down to its seemingly strategic location on Soi 11, steps from heaps of clubs and bars. The lobby sets the theme with bold colours, a fusball table and lots of TVs, while free wi-fi, an attached nightclub and generous online specials prove that the sentiment runs more than just skin deep.

SEVEN
HOTEL **$$$**

Map p270 (☑0 2662 0951; www.sleepatseven.com; 3/15 Soi 31, Th Sukhumvit; r incl breakfast 4708-7062B; ✳☞; ⓢPhrom Phong exit 5) This tiny hotel manages to be chic and homey, stylish and comfortable, Thai and international all at the same time. Each of the five rooms is decked out in a different colour that corresponds to Thai astrology, and thoughtful amenities and friendly service abound.

S31
HOTEL **$$$**

Map p270 (☑0 2260 1111; www.s31hotel.com; 545 Soi 31, Th Sukhumvit; incl breakfast r 4000B; ste 7000-60,000B; ✳☞✳; ⓢPhrom Phong exit 5) The bold patterns and graphics of its interior and exterior make this a fun, young-feeling choice. Touches like kitchenettes with large fridge, super-huge beds and free courses (cooking, Thai boxing and yoga) prove that the style also has substance. Significant discounts can be found online, and additional branches can be found on Soi 15 and Soi 33.

RAMADA HOTEL & SUITES
HOTEL **$$$**

Map p270 (☑0 2664 7000; www.ramadasuites bangkok.com; 22 Soi 12, Th Sukhumvit; incl break-

---

LUXURY FOR LESS IN EXECUTIVE APARTMENTS

Bangkok is loaded with serviced apartment buildings aimed at the executive market, from midrange comfort to no-sacrifice-is-too-great luxury. Most apartments will take short-term guests as well as longer stayers – and by booking ahead you can get a luxury apartment with much more space than a hotel room for the same or less money. It's a great way to stay, especially for a family that needs more space than two hotel rooms.

Several luxury buildings are on centrally located Soi Lang Suan, between Chit Lom BTS station and Lumphini Park, while others gather on the other side of Lumphini Park in the Silom business district, and along Th Sukhumvit. The **Centrepoint** (☑0 2630 6345; www.centrepoint.com) group is the biggest manager of serviced apartments, with eight buildings across Bangkok. Others we like:

Siri Sathorn (Map p268; ☑0 2266 2345; www.sirisathorn.com; 27 Soi Sala Daeng 1, Th Silom; ste daily 6000-20,000B, per month 80,000-240,000B; ✳@☞✳; ⓜSi Lom exit 2, ⓢSala Daeng exit 2) Chic modern apartments starting at 60 sq metres; also includes shuttle bus, spa and satisfying service.

Urbana Langsuan (Map p260; ☑0 2250 6666; www.bangkok.frasershospitality.com; 55 Th Lang Suan; r daily 2300-3200B; ✳@☞✳; ⓢChit Lom exit 4) Architecturally stunning, with decor, facilities, service and location to match.

House by the Pond (Map p270; ☑0 2259 3543; www.housebythepond.com; 230/3 Soi Sainumthip 2, Soi 20, Th Sukhumvit; r daily 1400-2500B, per month 17,500-34,000B; ✳@☞✳; ⓢPhrom Phong exit 6) More affordable, older-style apartments.

For more options try these websites:

➡ **www.sabaai.com** Most professional site for apartments.

➡ **www.mrroomfinder.com** Wide range, detailed search options.

➡ **www.bangkokapartments.info** Cheap places.

➡ **www.airbnb.com** Apartment rentals.

AIRPORT ACCOMMODATION

If you have a super-early departure or late arrival it's worth considering a hotel near one of Bangkok's two airports. That said, it's worth keeping in mind that Bangkok taxis are cheap and early-morning traffic means the trip doesn't take that long.

Novotel Suvarnabhumi Airport Hotel (☎0 2131 1111; www.novotelairportbkk.com; r incl breakfast 7301-9216B, ste incl breakfast 10,174B; ❄@📶; [S]Phra Khanong exit 3 and taxi, 🚆Suvarnabhumi Airport & hotel shuttle bus) Has 600-plus luxurious rooms, and located within the Suvarnabhumi International Airport compound.

Grand Inn Come Hotel (☎0 2738 8189; www.grandinncome-hotel.com; 99 Mu 6, Th Kingkaew; r 1400-2300B, ste 4500-5000B; ❄@📶) Solid midranger 10km from Suvarnabhumi, with airport shuttle and 'lively' karaoke bar.

Amari Airport Hotel (☎0 2566 1020; www.amari.com/donmuang; 333 Th Choet Wutthakat; r 1750-2150B, ste 3150B; ❄@📶🏊; [M]Chatuchak Park exit 2 & taxi, [S]Mo Chit exit 3 & taxi) Directly opposite Don Muang International Airport.

fast r 3000-3800B, ste 3800-4200B; ❄@📶🏊; [M]Sukhumvit exit 3, [S]Asok exit 5) Tucked into a quiet residential area, there are no surprises here, just an attractive and low-key hotel with long-stay options and professional service. Go for the suites, which for only a bit more have a kitchenette and sitting room.

Greater Bangkok

REFILL NOW! HOSTEL $

(☎0 2713 2044; www.refillnow.co.th; 191 Soi Pridi Bhanom Yong 42, Soi 71, Th Sukhumvit; dm 325B, r 899-2077B; ❄@📶🏊; [S]Phra Khanong exit 3 & taxi, 🚆Ramkhamhaeng & taxi) This is the kind of place that might make you think twice about sleeping in a dorm. Rooms and dorms are stylishly minimalist and the latter have flirtatious pull screens between each double-bunk; women-only dorms are also available. There's an achingly hip chill-out area and, upstairs, a massage centre.

Refill Now! is near trendy Th Thong Lo and only 20 minutes from the airport by taxi, or 15 minutes by City Link to Ramkhamhaeng Station, then a 50B taxi. On the BTS, get off at Phra Khanong and take a taxi or moto taxi down Soi 71, turn right on Soi 42 and left; or best of all come by *klorng* (canal, also spelt *khlong*) taxi to Tha Khlong Tong and walk.

MYSTIC PLACE HOTEL $$

(☎0 2270 3344; www.mysticplacebkk.com; 224/5-9 Th Pradiphat; r incl breakfast 1530-1870B; ❄@📶; [S]Saphan Khwai exit 2 & taxi) This hotel unites 36 rooms, each of which is individually and playfully designed. One of the rooms we checked out combined a chair upholstered with stuffed animals and walls covered with graffiti, while another was swathed in eye-contorting op art. Heaps of fun and perpetually popular, so be sure to book ahead.

BE MY GUEST BED & BREAKFAST GUESTHOUSE $$

(☎0 2692 4037; www.bemyguestbnb.com; 212/4 Soi 1, Soi 7 (Na Thong), Th Ratchadaphisek; s/d incl breakfast 900/1400B; ❄@📶; [M]Thailand Cultural Centre exit 4 & taxi) With only four rooms and the owner living upstairs, you really are the eponymous guest at this friendly, tidy guesthouse. Rooms are neat but simple, and are supplemented by user-friendly communal areas, personal service and a genuinely homey feel. Be sure to contact in advance, both to ensure vacancy and to ask for detailed instructions on locating the place.

★**BANGKOK TREE HOUSE** HOTEL $$$

(☎08 1453 1100; www.bangkoktreehouse.com; near Wat Bang Nam Pheung Nork; bungalow incl breakfast 6000-10,000B; ❄@📶🏊; [S]Bang Na exit 2 & taxi) The 12 multilevel bungalows are stylishly sculpted from sustainable and recycled materials, resulting in a vibe that calls to mind a sophisticated, eco-friendly summer camp. Amenities include private computers equipped with movies, free mobile phone and bicycle use, and free ice cream. To get here, take the BTS to Bang Na and jump in a taxi for the short ride to the pier at Wat Bang Nam Pheung Nork. From there, take the river-crossing ferry (4B, from 5am to 9.30pm), and continue by motorcycle taxi (10B) or on foot (call in advance for directions).

Understand Bangkok

Bangkok Today

As Thailand's seat of power and hotbed of political activism, Bangkok entered 2014 on shaky ground. Crippling antigovernment protests resumed after two years of relative stability under Prime Minister Yingluck Shinawatra. Protesters forced Yingluck to call a snap election, only later to collaborate with the opposition Democrat Party to boycott and obstruct the polls, which were ultimately nullified. Inconclusive election results led to the Yingluck government's expulsion from office and a military takeover.

Best on Film

Mon Rak Transistor (directed by Pen-Ek Ratanaruang; 2001) An aspiring *loôk tûng* (Thai country music) singer trades his bucolic life for one of struggle in the big city.

Nang Nak (directed by Nonzee Nimibutr; 1999) This classic Thai tale is a fascinating peek at Thai beliefs, not to mention at the provincial village that existed before Bangkok was taken over by concrete.

Best in Print

Sightseeing (Rattawut Lapcharoensap; 2004) Written by an American-born Thai who later moved to Bangkok, the short stories in this book provide a look at the lives of normal Thais who live in the type of suburbs and towns most visitors will never see.

Four Reigns (Kukrit Pramoj; Thai 1953, English 1981) *Four Reigns* follows the fictional life of Phloi, a minor courtier during the Bangkok palace's last days of absolute monarchy.

Democratic Stalemate

Yingluck's political adversity is part and parcel of Thailand's decade-long crisis, one largely linked to her brother, former prime minister, Thaksin Shinawatra. Before a military coup deposed him in 2006, Thaksin's performance over five years in power was mixed, characterised by conflicts of interest, abuses of power and human rights violations on the one hand, and policy innovations, popular rural income redistribution and electoral successes on the other. While hounded by corruption allegations, Thaksin provided a sense of upward mobility to the neglected masses and addressed the longstanding grievances of Thailand's rural heartland, profoundly changing the face of Thai politics. Facing a corruption conviction and jail time, Thaksin and his ruling Pheu Thai Party pressed for a blanket amnesty in November 2013. This amnesty gambit was the catalyst for the reconstitution of the anti-Thaksin coalition, this time led by the Democrat Party's Suthep Thaugsuban under the aegis of the People's Democratic Reform Committee (PDRC).

Yingluck tried to backtrack on the amnesty bill, but the PDRC gained traction, with protesters taking over sections of Bangkok. Yingluck was forced to call an election for 2 February, but the polls were ultimately nullified by Thailand's Constitutional Court. As Yingluck was denied a new electoral mandate, charges against her, including alleged corruption in her involvement with a failed rice scheme (p214), and a failed constitutional amendment to make the senate fully elected, were seen as efforts of both the judiciary and watchdog agencies, such as the National Anti-Corruption Commission, to bring down her administration. These efforts were ultimately successful when in May 2014, Thailand's Constitutional Court found Yingluck and nine members of her cabinet guilty of abuse of power. Yet only weeks after

Yingluck was forced to step down, the Thai military seized power. At press time, a plan for a return to civilian rule had yet to be announced, and the coup d'etat is likely to elicit a backlash from pro-Thaksin red shirts, leading to increased political instability and tension in the long term.

Royal Twilight

Those who have followed Thai politics in recent years have witnessed a gruelling transformation from kingdom to democracy where loyal subjects are increasingly becoming informed citizens. The standoff between those in favour of electoral democracy, with its reliance on elected politicians, and those who favour the moral authority of a monarchy, will underpin Thai politics indefinitely. Electoral democracy can be accompanied by corruption, whereas moral authority from unelected sources is undemocratic.

This confrontation takes place during the twilight of the remarkable 67-year reign of a respected monarch, 86-year-old King Bhumibol Adulyadej (Rama IX), who has presided over Thailand's transformation from a village backwater to a modernised nation. His passing will spell the end of Thailand as we know it, raising the spectre of a volatile succession. The next monarch is unlikely to command as much moral authority, and the institution will need to be recalibrated to fit democratic times. The transformation of economy and society has given rise to new expectations of accountability and a greater share of the pie for the downtrodden masses. Thailand's dilemma is to ensure that democratic institutions are the ultimate winner in the ongoing struggle.

Thai Resilience

Thailand has weathered many storms in recent years: military coups, an economic crisis, ongoing political turmoil as the establishment yellow shirts battle the populist red shirts, devastating and politically challenging natural disasters, and the uncertainty of a new order as the reign of beloved King Bhumibol Adulyadej comes to an end.

There is no definitive answer to what is next, except that all will transpire against the backdrop of a revered king's passing and the political transformation in its wake. Still, visitors flock to Bangkok. Thailand's beaches in the south and mountainous resorts in the north are crowded. And the economy manages to grow, thanks to Thailand's geography, natural endowments, and a resourceful and hospitable people who take life in their stride. Thailand's existential sociopolitical crisis is likely to be offset by its mass of tourist attractions and future economic development.

– Thitinan Pongsudhirak, Professor of International al Political Economy and Director of the Institute of Security and International Studies at Chulalongkorn University, Bangkok.

population per sq km

BANGKOK THAILAND

≈ 130 people

belief systems
(% of population)

94 Buddhist

3 Muslim

2 Christian

1 other

if Bangkok were 100 people

75 would be Thai
14 would be Chinese
11 would be other

History

Since the late 18th century, the history of Bangkok has essentially been the history of Thailand. Many of the country's defining events have unfolded here, and today the language, culture and food of the city have come to represent those of the entire country. This situation may once have seemed impossible, given the city's origins as little more than an obscure Chinese trading port, but, today boasting a population of more than 10 million, Bangkok will most likely continue to shape Thailand's history for some time to come.

From the Beginning

Ayuthaya & Thonburi

King Taksin's execution was in the custom reserved for royalty – sealing him inside a velvet sack to ensure no royal blood touched the ground before beating him to death with a scented sandalwood club.

Before it became the capital of Siam – as Thailand was then known – in 1782, the tiny settlement known as Bang Makok was merely a backwater village opposite the larger Thonburi Si Mahasamut on the banks of Mae Nam Chao Phraya, not far from the Gulf of Siam.

Thonburi had been founded by a group of wealthy Siamese during the reign of King Chakkraphat (r 1548–68) as an important relay point for sea- and river-borne trade between the Gulf of Siam and Ayuthaya, 86km upriver. Ayuthaya served as the royal capital of Siam from 1350 to 1767, and throughout this time European powers tried without success to colonise the kingdom.

Eventually, an Asian power subdued the capital when the Burmese sacked Ayuthaya in 1767. Many Siamese were marched off to Pegu (Bago, Myanmar today), where they were forced to serve the Burmese court. However, the remaining Siamese regrouped under Phraya Taksin, a half-Chinese, half-Thai general who decided to move the capital further south along Mae Nam Chao Phraya, closer to the Gulf of Siam. Thonburi was a logical choice for the new capital.

The Chakri Dynasty & the Birth of Bangkok

Taksin eventually succumbed to mental illness and was executed, and one of his key generals, Phraya Chakri, came to power and was crowned

TIMELINE	1548–68	1768	1779
	Thonburi Si Mahasamut, at the time little more than a Chinese trading post on the right bank of Mae Nam Chao Phraya, is founded.	King Taksin the Great moves the Thai capital from Ayuthaya to Thonburi Si Mahasamut, a location he regarded as beneficial for both trade and defence.	After a brutal war of territorial expansion, the Emerald Buddha, Thailand's most sacred Buddha image, is brought to Bangkok from Laos, along with hundreds of Laotian slaves.

in 1782 as Phraphutthayotfa. Fearing Thonburi to be vulnerable to Burmese attack from the west, Chakri moved the Siamese capital across the river to Bang Makok (Olive Plum riverbank), named for the trees that grew there in abundance. As the first monarch of the new Chakri royal dynasty – which continues to this day – Phraya Chakri was posthumously dubbed Rama I.

The first task set before the planners of the new city was to create hallowed ground for royal palaces and Buddhist monasteries. Astrologers divined that construction of the new royal palace should begin on 6 May 1782, and ceremonies consecrated Rama I's transfer to a temporary new residence a month later.

In time, Ayuthaya's control of tribute states in Laos and western Cambodia was transferred to Bangkok, and thousands of prisoners of war were brought to the capital to work. Bangkok also had ample access to free Thai labour via the *prâi lõoang* (commoner/noble) system, under which all commoners were required to provide labour to the state in lieu of taxes.

Using this immense pool of labour, Rama I augmented Bangkok's natural canal and river system with hundreds of artificial waterways feeding into Thailand's hydraulic lifeline, the broad Mae Nam Chao Phraya. Rama I also ordered the construction of 10km of city walls and *klorng rôrp grung* (canals around the city) to create a royal 'island' – Ko Ratanakosin – between Mae Nam Chao Phraya and the canal loop.

Temple and canal construction remained the highlight of early development in Bangkok until the reign of Rama III (King Phranangklao; r 1824–51), when attention turned to upgrading the port for international sea trade. The city soon became a regional centre for Chinese trading ships, slowly surpassing in importance even the British port at Singapore.

The Age of Politics

European Influence & the 1932 Revolution

Facing increasing pressure from British colonies in neighbouring Burma and Malaya, in 1855 Rama IV (King Mongkut; r 1851–68) signed the Bowring Treaty with Britain. This agreement marked Siam's break from exclusive economic involvement with China, a relationship that had dominated the previous century.

The signing of this document, and the subsequent ascension of Rama V (King Chulalongkorn; r 1868–1910) led to the largest period of European influence on Siam. Wishing to head off any potential invasion plans, Rama V ceded Laos and Cambodia to the French, and northern Malaya to the British between 1893 and 1910. The two European

Water-borne traffic, supplemented by a meagre network of footpaths, dominated Bangkok well into the middle of the 19th century.

Rama IV was the first monarch to show his face to the Thai public.

1782	1785	1821	1851
Rama I re-establishes the Siamese court across the river from Thonburi, resulting in the creation of both the current Thai capital and the Chakri dynasty.	The majority of the construction of Ko Ratanakosin, Bangkok's royal district, including famous landmarks such as the Grand Palace and Wat Phra Kaew, is finished.	A boatload of opium marks the visit of the first Western trader to Bangkok; the trade of this substance is eventually banned nearly 20 years later.	Rama IV, the fourth king of the Chakri dynasty, comes to power, courts relations with the West and encourages the study of modern science in Siam.

powers, for their part, were happy to use Siam as a buffer state between their respective colonial domains.

Rama V gave Bangkok 120 new roads during his reign, inspired by street plans from Batavia (the Dutch colonial centre now known as Jakarta), Calcutta, Penang and Singapore. Germans were hired to design and build railways emanating from the capital, while the Dutch contributed the design of Bangkok's Hualamphong train station, today considered a minor masterpiece of civic art deco.

In 1893 Bangkok opened its first railway line, extending 22km from Bangkok to Pak Nam, where Mae Nam Chao Phraya enters the Gulf of Siam. A 20km electric tramway opened the following year, paralleling the left bank of Mae Nam Chao Phraya.

Americans established Siam's first printing press along with the kingdom's first newspaper in 1864. The first Siamese-language newspaper, *Darunovadha,* came along in 1874, and by 1900 Bangkok boasted three daily English-language newspapers: the *Bangkok Times, Siam Observer* and *Siam Free Press.*

As Bangkok prospered, many wealthy merchant families sent their children to study in Europe. Students of humbler socio-economic status who excelled at school had access to government scholarships for overseas study as well. In 1924 a handful of Siamese students in Paris formed the Promoters of Political Change, a group that met to discuss ideas for a future Siamese government modelled on Western democracy.

A bloodless revolution in 1932, initiated by the Promoters of Political Change and a willing Rama VII (King Prajadhipok; r 1925–35), transformed Siam from an absolute monarchy into a constitutional one. Bangkok thus found itself the nerve centre of a vast new civil service, which, coupled with its growing success as a world port, transformed the city into a mecca for Siamese seeking economic opportunities.

In 1861 Bangkok's European diplomats and merchants delivered a petition to Rama IV requesting roadways so they could enjoy horse riding for physical fitness and pleasure. The royal government acquiesced, and established a handful of roads suitable for horse-drawn carriages and rickshaws.

WWII & the Struggle for Democracy

Phibul Songkhram, appointed prime minister by the People's Party in December 1938, changed the country's name from Siam to Thailand and introduced the Western solar calendar. Phibul, who in 1941 allowed Japanese regiments access to the Gulf of Thailand, resigned in 1944 under pressure from the Thai underground resistance, and was eventually exiled to Japan. Bangkok resumed its pace towards modernisation, even after Phibul returned to Thailand in 1948 and took over the leadership again via a military coup. Over the next 15 years, bridges were built over Mae Nam Chao Phraya, canals were filled in to provide space for new roads, and multistorey buildings began crowding out traditional teak structures.

1855	1868	1893	1910
Bangkok, now Siam's major trading centre, begins to feel pressure from colonial influences; Rama IV signs the Bowring Treaty, which liberalises foreign trade in Siam.	At the age of 15, Chulalongkorn, the oldest son of Rama IV, becomes the fifth king of the Chakri dynasty upon the death of his father.	After a territorial dispute, France sends gunboats to threaten Bangkok, forcing Siam to give up most of its territory east of Mekong River; Siam gains its modern boundaries.	Vajiravudh becomes the sixth king of the Chakri dynasty after the death of his older brother; he fails to produce a male heir during his reign.

EXTENDED FAMILIES IN THAILAND'S ROYAL COURT

Until polygamy was outlawed by Rama VI (King Vajiravudh; r 1910–25), it was expected of Thai monarchs to maintain a harem consisting of numerous 'major' and 'minor' wives and the children of these relationships. This led to some truly vast families: Rama I (King Phraphutthayotfa; r 1782–1809) had 42 children by 28 mothers; Rama II (King Phraphutthaloetla Naphalai; r 1809–24), 73 children by 40 mothers; Rama III (King Phranangklao; r 1824–51), 51 children by 37 mothers (he would eventually accumulate a total of 242 wives and consorts); Rama IV (King Mongkut; r 1851–68), 82 children by 35 mothers; and Rama V (King Chulalongkorn; r 1868–1910), 77 children by 40 mothers. In the case of Rama V, his seven 'major' wives were all half-sisters or first cousins, a conscious effort to maintain the purity of the bloodline of the Chakri dynasty. Other consorts or 'minor' wives were often the daughters of families wishing to gain greater ties with the royal family.

In contrast to the precedent set by his predecessors, Rama VI had one wife and one child, a girl born only a few hours before his death. As a result, his brother, Prajadhipok, was appointed as his successor. Rama VII also had only one wife and failed to produce any heirs. After abdicating in 1935 he did not exercise his right to appoint a successor, so lines were drawn back to Rama V, and the grandson of one of his remaining 'major' wives, nine-year-old Ananda Mahidol, was chosen to be the next king.

From 1964 to 1973 – the peak years of the second Indochina War – Thai army officers Thanom Kittikachorn and Praphat Charusathien ruled Thailand and allowed the US to establish several army bases within Thai borders to support the US campaign in Indochina. During this time Bangkok gained notoriety as a 'rest and recreation' (R&R) spot for foreign troops stationed in Southeast Asia.

In October 1973 the Thai military brutally suppressed a large prodemocracy student demonstration at Bangkok's Thammasat University, but Rama IX (King Bhumibol Adulyadej; r 1946–present) and General Krit Sivara, who sympathised with the students, refused to support further bloodshed, forcing Thanom and Praphat to leave Thailand. Oxford-educated Kukrit Pramoj took charge of a 14-party coalition government and steered a leftist agenda past the conservative parliament.

The military regained control in 1976 after right-wing, paramilitary civilian groups assaulted a group of 2000 students holding a sit-in at Thammasat. Officially, 46 people died in the incident, although the number may be much higher, and more than a thousand were arrested. Many students fled Bangkok and joined the People's Liberation Army of Thailand (PLAT), an armed communist insurgency based in the hills, which had been active in Thailand since the 1930s.

1917	1932	1935–46	1939
Bangkok's first Western-style institute of higher education, Chulalongkorn University, is founded; it's still regarded as the country's most prestigious.	A bloodless coup transforms Siam from an absolute to a constitutional monarchy; deposed king, Rama VII, remains on the throne until he resigns three years later.	Ananda Mahidol, grandson of one of Rama V's 'major' wives, is appointed king; his reign ends abruptly when he is shot dead in his room in mysterious circumstances.	The country's name is changed from Siam to Thailand.

RAMA IX

A common backdrop in Bangkok are images of King Bhumibol Adulyadej, Thailand's longest-reigning monarch and the longest-reigning living monarch in the world. Also known in English as Rama IX (the ninth king of the Chakri dynasty), Bhumibol Adulyadej was born in 1927 in the USA, where his father Prince Mahidol was studying medicine at Harvard University.

Fluent in English, French, German and Thai, Bhumibol ascended the throne in 1946 following the death of his brother Rama VIII (King Ananda Mahidol; r 1935–46), who reigned for just over 11 years before dying under mysterious circumstances.

An ardent jazz composer and saxophonist when he was younger, Rama IX has hosted jam sessions with the likes of jazz greats Woody Herman and Benny Goodman. His compositions are often played on Thai radio. The king is also recognised for his extensive development projects, particularly in rural areas of Thailand. For a relatively objective English-language biography of the king's accomplishments, *King Bhumibol Adulyadej: A Life's Work* (Editions Didier Millet, 2010) is available in most Bangkok bookstores.

Rama IX and Queen Sirikit have four children: Princess Ubol Ratana (b 1951), Crown Prince Maha Vajiralongkorn (b 1952), Princess Maha Chakri Sirindhorn (b 1955) and Princess Chulabhorn (b 1957).

After more than 60 years in power, and having spent most of the last few years in hospital with very few public appearances, Rama IX is preparing for his succession. For the last few years the Crown Prince has performed most of the royal ceremonies the king would normally perform, such as presiding over the Royal Ploughing Ceremony, changing the attire on the Emerald Buddha and handing out academic degrees at university commencements.

Along with nation and religion, the monarchy is very highly regarded in Thai society. Negative comment about the king or any member of the royal family is a social as well as legal taboo.

Bangkok continued to seesaw between civilian and military rule for the next 15 years. Although a general amnesty in 1982 brought an end to the PLAT, and students, workers and farmers returned to their homes, a new era of political tolerance exposed the military once again to civilian fire.

In May 1992 several huge demonstrations demanding the resignation of the next in a long line of military dictators, General Suchinda Kraprayoon, rocked Bangkok and the large provincial capitals. Charismatic Bangkok governor Chamlong Srimuang, winner of the 1992 Magsaysay Award (a humanitarian service award issued in the Philippines) for his role in galvanising the public to reject Suchinda, led the protests. After confrontations between the protesters and the military near the

1946	1951–63	1962	1973
Pridi Phanomyong becomes Thailand's first democratically elected prime minister; after a military coup, Pridi is forced to flee Thailand, returning only briefly one more time.	Field marshal Sarit Thanarat wrests power from Phibun Songkhram, abolishes the constitution and embarks on one of the most authoritarian regimes in modern Thai history.	US involvement in the Indochina War leads to economic and infrastructural expansion of Bangkok; dissatisfaction with the Thai government leads to communist insurgency.	Student protests lead to violent military suppression; 1971 coup leader Thanom Kittikachorn is exiled by Rama IX; Kukrit Pramoj's civilian government takes charge.

Democracy Monument resulted in nearly 50 deaths and hundreds of injuries, Rama IX summoned both Suchinda and Chamlong for a rare public scolding. Suchinda resigned, having been in power for less than six weeks.

A mere 13 sq km in 1900, Bangkok grew to an astounding metropolitan area of more than 330 sq km by the end of the 20th century. Today the greater city encompasses not only Bangkok proper, but also the former capital of Thonburi across Mae Nam Chao Phraya to the west, along with the densely populated 'suburb' provinces, Samut Prakan to the east and Nonthaburi to the north. More than half of Thailand's urban population lives in Bangkok.

The Recent Past

The Crisis & the People's Constitution

Bangkok approached the new millennium riding a tide of events that set new ways of governing and living in the capital. The most defining moment occurred in July 1997 when – after several months of warning signs that nearly everyone in Thailand and the international community ignored – the Thai currency fell into a deflationary tailspin and the national economy screeched to a virtual halt. Bangkok, which rode at the forefront of the 1980s double-digit economic boom, suffered more than elsewhere in the country in terms of job losses and massive income erosion.

Two months after the crash, the Thai parliament voted in a new constitution that guaranteed – at least on paper – more human and civil rights than had ever been granted in Thailand previously. The so-called 'people's constitution' fostered great hope in a population left emotionally battered by the 1997 economic crisis.

Thaksin Shinawatra: CEO Prime Minister

In January 2001, billionaire former police colonel Thaksin Shinawatra became prime minister after winning a landslide victory in nationwide elections – the first in Thailand under the strict guidelines established in the 1997 constitution. Thaksin's new party, called Thai Rak Thai (TRT; Thais Love Thailand), swept into power on a populist agenda that seemed at odds with the man's enormous wealth and influence.

The sixth-richest ruler in the world as of late 2003, Thaksin owned the country's only private TV station through his family-owned Shin Corporation, the country's largest telecommunications company. Shin Corporation also owned Asia's first privately owned satellite company, Shin Satellite, and a large stake in Thai AirAsia, a subsidiary of the Malaysia-based airline AirAsia.

In 2001, days before he became prime minister, Thaksin Shinawatra transferred his shares in Shin Corporation to his siblings, chauffeur and even household servants in an apparent attempt to conceal his true assets. Eventually the country's constitutional court would clear him of all fraud charges.

1981	1985	1992	1997
General Prem Tinsulanonda is appointed prime minister after a military coup and is largely able to stabilise Thai politics over the next eight years.	Chamlong Srimuang is elected mayor of Bangkok; three years later, after forming his own largely Buddhist-based political group, the Palang Dharma Party, he is elected mayor again.	Protests led by Chamlong Srimuang against 1991 coup leader Suchinda Kraprayoon lead to violent confrontations; Suchinda resigns following a public scolding by Rama IX.	Thailand devalues the baht, triggering the Asian economic crisis; massive unemployment and personal debt, and a crash of the Thai stock market, follow.

Despite numerous controversies, during the February 2005 general elections Thaksin became the first Thai leader in history to be re-elected to a consecutive second term.

However, time was running short for Thaksin and his party. The final straw came in January 2006, when Thaksin announced that his family had sold off its controlling interest in Shin Corporation to a Singaporean investment firm. Since deals made through the Stock Exchange of Thailand (SET) were exempt from capital-gains tax, Thaksin's family paid no tax on the US$1.9 billion sale, which enraged Bangkok's middle class.

Many of the PM's most highly placed supporters also turned against him. Most prominently, media mogul and former friend, Sondhi Limthongkul organised a series of anti-Thaksin rallies in Bangkok, culminating in a rally at Bangkok's Royal Plaza on 4 and 5 February 2006 that drew tens of thousands of protesters.

Thaksin's ministers responded by dissolving the national assembly and scheduling snap elections for 2 April 2006, three years ahead of schedule. Thaksin initially claimed victory, but after a conference with the king, announced that he would take a break from politics.

The Coup & the Red/Yellow Divide

On the evening of 19 September 2006, while Thaksin was attending a UN conference in New York City, the Thai military took power in a bloodless coup. Calling themselves the Council for Democratic Reform under the Constitutional Monarch, the junta cited the TRT government's alleged lèse-majesté (treason), corruption, interference in state agencies and creation of social divisions as justification for the coup. Thaksin quickly flew to London, where he remained in exile until his UK visa was revoked in 2008.

In a nationwide referendum held on 19 August 2007, Thais approved a military-drafted constitution. Under the new constitution, elections were finally held in late 2007. After forming a loose coalition with several other parties, parliament chose veteran politician and close Thaksin ally Samak Sundaravej as prime minister.

Not surprisingly, Samak was regarded as little more than a proxy of Thaksin by his opponents, and shortly after taking office he became the target of a series of large-scale protests held by the Peoples' Alliance for Democracy (PAD), the same group of mostly Bangkok-based middle-class royalists who had called for Thaksin's resignation in the lead up to the 2006 coup. By this point, the PAD had already begun wearing their trademark yellow to show their allegiance to the king.

In August 2008, several thousand yellow-shirted PAD protesters took over Government House in Bangkok. The takeover was followed by spo-

Historical Reads

....

Thailand: A Short History (David K Wyatt)

....

A History of Thailand (Chris Baker & Pasuk Phongpaichit)

....

Chronicle of Thailand (Editions Didier Millet)

....

Reading Thai Murals (David K Wyatt)

1999	2001	2004	9 June 2006
The BTS (Skytrain), Bangkok's first expansive metro system, opens in commemoration of Rama IX's 6th cycle (72nd) birthday.	Thaksin Shinawatra, Thailand's richest man, is elected prime minister on a populist platform in what some have called the most open, corruption-free election in Thai history.	The MRT, Bangkok's first underground public transport system, is opened; an accident the next year injures 140 and causes the system to shut down for two weeks.	Thailand celebrates the 60th anniversary of Rama IX's ascension to the throne; the Thai king continues to be the longest-serving monarch in the world.

THAILAND'S COLOURS OF PROTEST

Most Thais are aware of the day of the week they were born, and in Thai astrology each day is associated with a particular colour. However, in the aftermath of the 2006 coup, these previously benign hues started to take on a much more political meaning.

To show their alleged support for the royal family, the anti-Thaksin Peoples' Alliance for Democracy (PAD) adopted yellow as their uniform. This goes back to 2006, when in an effort to celebrate the 60th anniversary of Rama IX's ascension to the throne, Thais were encouraged to wear yellow, the colour associated with Monday, the king's birthday. A couple of years later, pink was added to the repertoire when protesters wore the colour as a nod to a previous occasion when the king safely emerged from a lengthy hospital visit wearing a bright pink blazer.

To differentiate themselves, the pro-Thaksin United Front for Democracy against Dictatorship (UDD) began to wear red, and soon thereafter became known colloquially as the 'red shirts'. To add to the political rainbow, during the riots of April 2009 that disrupted an Asean summit in Pattaya, a blue-shirted faction emerged, apparently aligned with a former Thaksin ally and allegedly sponsored by the Ministry of the Interior. And during the political crisis of 2010, a 'no colour' group of peace activists and a 'black shirt' faction, believed to consist of rogue elements of the Thai military, also emerged. During the protests in 2013 and 2014, antigovernment protesters ditched yellow shirts in favour of the Thai flag, the red, white and blue stripes of which were co-opted on ribbons, buttons, shirts and iPhone cases.

radic violent clashes between the PAD and the United Front for Democracy against Dictatorship (UDD), a loose association of red-shirted Thaksin supporters who had set up camp nearby at Sanam Luang.

On 25 November, hundreds of armed PAD protesters stormed Bangkok's Suvarnabhumi and Don Muang Airports, entering the passenger terminals and seizing control of the control towers. Thousands of additional PAD sympathisers eventually flooded Suvarnabhumi, leading to the cancellation of all flights and leaving as many as 230,000 domestic and international passengers stranded. The stand-off lasted until 2 December, when the Supreme Court wielded its power yet again in order to ban Samak's successor, Prime Minister Somchai Wongsawat, from politics and ordered his political party and two coalition parties dissolved.

In addition to financial loss, the events of 2008 also had a significant social cost in that Thailand, a country that had mostly experienced a relatively high level of domestic stability and harmony throughout its modern history, was now effectively polarised between the predominately middle- and upper-class, urban-based PAD and the largely working-class, rural UDD.

19 September 2006	August 2007	November 2008	April 2010
A bloodless coup sees the Thai military take power from Thaksin while he is at a UN meeting in New York; he remains in exile.	In a nationwide referendum, voters agree to approve a military-drafted constitution, Thailand's 17th since becoming a constitutional monarchy in 1932.	Thousands of yellow-shirted anti-Thaksin protesters – the Peoples' Alliance for Democracy (PAD) – take over Bangkok's airports; tourist numbers drop.	Pro-Thaksin supporters clash with troops in central Bangkok, leading to 25 deaths, several hundred injuries and the torching of several buildings.

In December 2008 a tenuous new coalition was formed, led by Abhisit Vejjajiva, the Oxford-educated leader of the Democrat Party. Despite Abhisit being young, photogenic, articulate and allegedly untainted by corruption, his perceived association with the PAD did little to placate the UDD, and in February 2010 the 'red shirts' and self-proclaimed prodemocracy activists united to demand that Prime Minister Abhisit Vejjajiva stand down

In April 2010, violent clashes between police and protesters (numbering up to tens of thousands) resulted in 25 deaths. Red-shirted protesters barricaded themselves into an area stretching from Lumphini Park to the shopping district near Siam Square, effectively shutting down parts of central Bangkok. In May the protesters were eventually dispersed by force, but not before at least 36 buildings were set alight and at least 15 people killed. The death toll from the 2010 conflicts amounted to nearly 100 people, making it Thailand's most violent political unrest in 20 years.

Yingluck Shinawatra: Thaksin's 'Clone'

Parliamentary elections in 2011 saw the election of Yingluck Shinawatra, the younger sister of the still-exiled Thaksin. A former businesswoman, Yingluck had no prior political experience and has been described by her older brother as his 'clone'. Yingluck's leadership was tested almost immediately, when in mid-2011 the outskirts of Bangkok were hit by the most devastating floods in decades. Although nearly all of central Bangkok was spared from flooding, it was largely perceived that this was done at the expense of upcountry regions.

In 2011, Yingluck Shinawatra became the first female prime minister in Thai history.

Yingluck's tenure progressed relatively uneventfully until 2013, when she had to deal with the fallout from both a botched rice scheme (p214) and a proposed bill that would have granted amnesty to her brother, potentially allowing Thaksin to return to Thailand without facing trial for previous corruption convictions. The bill was rejected, but Yingluck's intentions were made clear. Within weeks, antigovernment protesters, led by former Democrat MP Suthep Thaugsuban, were staging frequent rallies, eventually taking over sections of central Bangkok in early 2014. After occasionally violent clashes that led to the deaths of 28 people and a nullified election, in May 2014 Thailand's Constitutional Court found Yingluck and nine members of her cabinet guilty of abuse of power, forcing them to stand down. A caretaker government was appointed, only for the Thai military to declare martial law on May 20, and two days later, officially announce that they had seized power of the country. At press time, the military had yet to reveal a timeframe for a return to civilian rule.

July 2011	5 August 2011	October 2013–May 2014	22 May 2014
Heavy monsoon rains lead to floods covering much of central Thailand, including parts of Bangkok, although protective measures spare nearly all the city's central districts.	Parliament approves the election of Thailand's first female prime minister, Yingluck Shinawatra, younger sister of deposed former prime minister Thaksin Shinawatra.	Antigovernment protesters seize key sections of Bangkok; violent incidents lead to 825 injuries and 28 deaths.	The Thai military seizes control of the country in what is Thailand's 12th coup d'etat since having abolished absolute monarchy in 1932.

People & Culture

Bangkok is both utterly Thai and totally foreign. Old and new ways clash and mingle, constantly redrawing the lines of what it means to be 'Thai'. But despite the international veneer, a Thai value system – built primarily on religious and monarchical devotion – is ticking away, guiding every aspect of life. Almost all Thais, even the most conspicuously consuming, are dedicated Buddhists who aim to be reborn into a better life by making merit (giving donations to temples or feeding monks), regarding merit-making as the key to their earthly success.

People of Bangkok

Bangkok accommodates every rung of the economic ladder, from the aristocrat to the slum dweller. It is the new start for the economic hopefuls and the last chance for the economic refugees. The lucky ones from the bottom rung form the working-class backbone of the city – taxi drivers, food vendors, maids, nannies and even prostitutes. Many hail from the northeastern provinces and send hard-earned baht back to their families in small rural villages. At the very bottom are the dispossessed, who live in squatter communities on marginal, often polluted land. While the Thai economy has surged, a truly comprehensive social net has yet to be constructed. Meanwhile, Bangkok is also the great incubator for Thailand's new generation of young creatives, from designers to architects, and has long nurtured the archetype of the country's middle class.

The city has also represented economic opportunity for foreign immigrants. Approximately half of its population claims some Chinese ancestry, be it Cantonese, Hainanese, Hokkien or Teochew. Although the first Chinese labourers faced discrimination from the Thais, their descendants' success in business, finance and public affairs helped to elevate the status of Chinese and Thai-Chinese families.

Immigrants from South Asia also migrated to Bangkok and comprise the second-largest Asian minority. Sikhs from northern India typically make their living in tailoring, while Sinhalese, Bangladeshis, Nepalis and Pakistanis can be found in the import-export or retail trade.

Thailand Demographics

Population: 66.7 million

Fertility rate: 1.6

Percentage of people over 65: 8.5%

Urbanisation rate: 34%

Life expectancy: 74 years

The Thai Character

Much of Thailand's cultural value system is hinged upon respect for the family, religion and monarchy. Within that system each person knows his or her place and Thai children are strictly instructed in the importance of group conformity, respecting elders and suppressing confrontational views. In most social situations, establishing harmony often takes a leading role and Thais take personal pride in making others feel at ease.

Other notable cultural characteristics include a strong belief in the concept of saving face and an equally strong regard for *sà·nùk,* Thai-style fun.

Religion

Theravada Buddhism

Around 90% of Bangkokians are Buddhists, who believe that individuals work out their own paths to *nibbana* (nirvana) through a combination of good works, meditation and study of the *dhamma* (Buddhist philosophy).

The social and administrative centre for Thai Buddhism is the wát (temple or monastery), a walled compound containing several buildings constructed in the traditional Thai style with steep, swooping roof lines and colourful interior murals; the most important structures contain solemn Buddha statues cast in bronze.

Walk the streets of Bangkok early in the morning and you'll catch the flash of shaved heads bobbing above bright ochre robes, as monks all over the city engage in *bin·tá·bàht,* the daily house-to-house alms-food gathering. Thai men are expected to shave their heads and don monastic robes temporarily at least once in their lives.

Cultural Readings

....

Being Dharma: The Essence of the Buddha's Teachings (2001; Ajahn Chah)

....

Very Thai (2013; Philip Cornwell-Smith)

....

Thailand at Random: Facts, Figures, Quotes and Anecdotes on Thailand (2012; Editions Didier Millet)

....

Sacred Tattoos of Thailand (2011; Joe Cummings)

Guardian Spirits

Animism predates the arrival of all other religions in Bangkok, and it still plays an important role in the everyday life of most city residents. Believing that *prá poom* (guardian spirits) inhabit rivers, canals, trees and other natural features, and that these spirits must be placated whenever humans trespass upon or make use of these features, the Thais build spirit shrines to house the displaced spirits. These dollhouse-like structures perch on wood or cement pillars next to their homes and receive daily offerings of rice, fruit, flowers and water.

Other Religions

Thai royal ceremony remains almost exclusively the domain of one of the most ancient religious traditions still functioning in the kingdom, Brahmanism. White-robed, topknotted priests of Indian descent keep alive an arcane collection of rituals that, it is generally believed, must be performed at regular intervals to sustain the three pillars of Thai nationhood: sovereignty, religion and the monarchy.

Green-hued onion domes looming over rooftops belong to mosques and mark the immediate neighbourhood as Muslim, while brightly painted and ornately carved cement spires indicate a Hindu temple. Wander down congested Th Chakraphet in the Phahurat district to find Gurdwara Siri Guru Singh Sabha, a Sikh temple where visitors are very welcome. A handful of steepled Christian churches, including a few historic ones, have been built over the centuries and can be found near the banks of Mae Nam Chao Phraya. In Chinatown, large round doorways topped with heavily inscribed Chinese characters and flanked by red paper lanterns mark the location of *săhn jôw,* Chinese temples dedicated to the worship of Buddhist, Taoist and Confucian deities.

Monarchy

All Thai kings are referred to as 'Rama', one of the incarnations of the Hindu god Vishnu. The Thais' relationship with their king is deeply spiritual and intensely personal. Most view their king as a father figure (the king's birthday is the national celebration of Father's Day). The reigning monarch, King Bhumibol Adulyadej, also known as Rama IX, inherited automatic reverence when he assumed the throne in 1946, but he captured the Thai people's hearts with his actions.

In June 2006, the king celebrated his 60th year on the throne, an event regarded by many Thais as bittersweet because the ageing king

WHAT'S A WÁT?

Bangkok is home to hundreds of wáts, temple compounds that have traditionally been at the centre of community life.

Buildings & Structures

Even the smallest wát will usually have a *bóht, wí·hǎhn* and monks' living quarters.

➡ **Bóht** The ordination hall, most sacred prayer room at a wát. Aside from the fact it does not house the main Buddha image, you'll know the *bóht* because it is usually more ornately decorated and has eight cornerstones to mark its boundary.

➡ **Chedi (stupa)** A large bell-shaped tower usually containing five structural elements symbolising (from bottom to top) earth, water, fire, wind and void; depending on the wát, relics of the Buddha, a Thai king or some other notable are housed inside.

➡ **Drum Tower** Elevates the ceremonial drum beaten by novices.

➡ **Mon·dòp** An open-sided, square building with four arches and a pyramidal roof, used to worship religious objects or texts.

➡ **ʋrahng** A towering phallic spire of Khmer origin serving the same religious purpose as a *chedi*.

➡ **Sǎh·lah (sala)** A pavilion, often open-sided, for relaxation, lessons or miscellaneous activities.

➡ **Wí·hǎhn (vihara)** The sanctuary for the temple's main Buddha image and where laypeople come to make their offerings. Classic architecture typically has a three-tiered roof representing the triple gems: the Buddha (the teacher), Dharma (the teaching) and Sangha (the followers).

Buddha Images

Elongated earlobes, no evidence of bone or muscle, arms that reach to the knees, a third eye: these are some of the 32 characteristics, originating from 3rd-century India, that govern the depiction of the Buddha in sculpture and denote his divine nature. Other symbols to be aware of are the various hand positions and 'postures', which depict periods in the life of the Buddha.

➡ **Sitting** Teaching or meditating. If the right hand is pointed towards the earth, the Buddha is subduing the demons of desire. If the hands are folded in the lap, the Buddha is meditating.

➡ **Reclining** The exact moment of the Buddha's passing into *parinibbana* (post death nirvana).

➡ **Standing** Bestowing blessings or taming evil forces.

➡ **Walking** The Buddha after his return to earth from heaven.

may soon leave the helm of the Thai nation. His son, Crown Prince Maha Vajiralongkorn, has been chosen to succeed him, but it is the king's daughter, Princess Mahachakri Sirindhorn, that many Thais feel a deeper connection with because she has followed in her father's philanthropic footsteps.

It's worth mentioning that, in Thai society, not only is criticising the monarchy an extreme social faux pas, it's also illegal.

Visual Arts

Divine Inspiration

The wát served as a locus for the highest expressions of Thai art for roughly 800 years, from the Lanna to Ratanakosin eras. Accordingly, Bangkok's 400-plus Buddhist temples are brimming with the figuratively imaginative, if thematically formulaic, art of Thailand's foremost muralists. Always instructional in intent, such painted images range

THE CHINESE INFLUENCE

In many ways Bangkok is a Chinese, as much as a Thai, city. The presence of the Chinese in Bangkok dates back to before the founding of the city, when Thonburi Si Mahasamut was little more than a Chinese trading outpost on Mae Nam Chao Phraya (Chao Phraya River). In the 1780s, during the construction of the new capital under Rama I (King Phraphutthayotfa; r 1782–1809), Hokkien, Teochew and Hakka Chinese were hired as labourers. The Chinese already living in the area were relocated to the districts of Yaowarat and Sampeng, today known as Bangkok's Chinatown.

During the reign of Rama I, many Chinese began to move up in status and wealth. They controlled many of Bangkok's shops and businesses, and because of increased trading ties with China, were responsible for an immense expansion in Thailand's market economy. Visiting Europeans during the 1820s were astonished by the number of Chinese trading ships on Mae Nam Chao Phraya, and some assumed that the Chinese formed the majority of Bangkok's population.

The newfound wealth of certain Chinese trading families created one of Thailand's first elite classes that was not directly related to royalty. Known as *jôw sŏo·a*, these 'merchant lords' eventually obtained additional status by accepting official posts and royal titles, as well as offering their daughters to the royal family. At one point, Rama V (King Chulalongkorn; r 1868–1910) took a Chinese consort. By the time of the 2001 census, more than half the people in Bangkok were able to lay claim to some Chinese ancestry.

During the reign of Rama III (King Phranangklao; r 1824–51), the Thai capital began to absorb many elements of Chinese food, design, fashion and literature. This growing ubiquity of Chinese culture, coupled with the tendency of the Chinese men to marry Thai women and assimilate into Thai culture, had, by the beginning of the 20th century, resulted in relatively little difference between the Chinese and their Siamese counterparts.

Arts Reading

Flavours: Thai Contemporary Art (2005; Steven Pettifor)

Bangkok Design: Thai Ideas in Textiles & Furniture (2006; Brian Mertens)

Buddhist Temples of Thailand: A Visual Journey Through Thailand's 40 Most Historic Wats (2010; Joe Cummings)

The Thai House: History and Evolution (2002; Ruethai Chaichongrak)

The Arts of Thailand (1998; Steve Van Beek)

from the depiction of the *jataka* (stories of the Buddha's past lives) and scenes from the Indian Hindu epic *Ramayana,* to elaborate scenes detailing daily life in Thailand.

The Modern Era

Although the origins of Thai art can be traced back to religion, today's cultural currents are as likely to be swayed by Korean soap operas, Japanese manga comics, Chinese mass merchandising, European fashion and American street culture as traditional Thai life. These influences are fuelling introspection among artists, with more art being created that pertains to the condition of the self and the societal constraints imposed upon it. Whereas a decade ago artists seemed to be the defenders of a precious national identity, now themes have become more personal and reflective. Though such approaches seem more aligned to the modern Western artist's mindset, there still remains an inextricable leaning towards a more spiritual, and ostensibly Buddhist, path.

Music

Classical Thai

Classical central-Thai music *(pleng tai deum)* features a dazzling array of textures and subtleties, hair-raising tempos and pastoral melodies. The classical orchestra *(bèe-pâht)* can include as few as five players or might have more than 20. Leading the band is *bèe,* a straight-lined woodwind instrument with a reed mouthpiece and an oboe-like tone; you'll hear it most at *moo·ay tai* (Thai boxing; also spelt *muay thai*) matches. The four-stringed *phin,* plucked like a guitar, lends subtle counterpoint, while *rá·nâht èhk,* a bamboo-keyed percussion instrument resembling the xylophone, carries the main melodies. The slender *sor,* a bowed instrument with a coconut-shell soundbox, provides soaring embellishments, as does the *klòo·i,* a wooden Thai flute.

Lôok Tûng & Mŏr Lam

Popular Thai music has borrowed much from Western music, particularly in instrumentation, but retains a distinct flavour of its own. The bestselling of all modern musical genres in Thailand remains *lôok tûng.* Literally 'children of the fields', *lôok tûng* dates back to the 1940s, is comparable to country and western in the USA, and is a genre that tends to appeal most to working-class Thais. Subject matter almost always concerns tales of lost love, tragic early death and the dire circumstances of farmers who work day in and day out and, at the end of the year, still owe money to the bank.

Another genre more firmly rooted in northeastern Thailand, and nearly as popular in Bangkok, is *mŏr lam.* Based on the songs played on the Lao-Isan *kaan,* a wind instrument devised of a double row of bamboo-like reeds fitted into a hardwood soundbox, *mŏr lam* features a simple but insistent bass beat and plaintive vocal melodies.

Songs for Life

The 1970s ushered in a new music style inspired by the politically conscious folk rock of the US and Europe, which the Thais dubbed *pleng pêu·a chee·wít* (literally 'music for life') after Marxist Jit Phumisak's earlier Art for Life movement. Closely identified with the Thai band Caravan – which still performs regularly – the introduction of this style was the most significant musical shift in Thailand since *lôok tûng* arose in the 1940s.

Pleng pêua chee·wít has political and environmental topics rather than the usual love themes. During the authoritarian dictatorships of the '70s many of Caravan's songs were banned. Following the massacre of student demonstrators in 1976, some members of the band fled to the hills to take up with armed communist groups.

T-Pop & Indie

In recent years, Thailand has also developed a thriving teen-pop industry – sometimes referred to as T-Pop – centred on artists who have been chosen for their good looks, and then matched with syrupy song arrangements. Labels GMM Grammy and RS Productions are the heavyweights of this genre, and their rivalry has resulted in a flood of copycat acts.

In the 1990s an alternative pop scene – known as *glorng sĕh·ree* ('free drum') or *pleng đâi din* ('underground music') – grew in Bangkok. Moderndog, a Britpop-inspired band of four Chulalongkorn University graduates, is generally credited with bringing independent Thai music into the mainstream, and their success prompted an explosion of similar bands and indie recording labels.

Cinema

Thailand has a lively homespun movie industry and produces nearly 50 comedies, dramas and horror films every year. Cinema is possibly the country's most significant contemporary cultural export, and several Thai films of the last two decades have emerged as international film festival darlings.

Bangkok Film launched Thailand's film industry with the first Thai-directed silent movie, *Chok Sorng Chan,* in 1927. Silent films proved to be more popular than talkies right into the 1960s, and as late as

PEOPLE & CULTURE CINEMA

Recommended Thai Playlist

The Sound of Siam: Leftfield Luk Thung, Jazz & Molam in Thailand 1964–1975 (Soundway Records compilation)

Bird Hits for Fan: Love Hits (Bird Thongchai)

Moderndog-Soem Sukhaphap (Moderndog)

Mint (Silly Fools)

Palmy (Palmy)

Romantic Comedy (Apartmentkhunpa)

Begins (Big Ass)

Lum Num Sading Love You (The Richman Toy)

Noo Aow Yoo (Ja Kunhoo)

1969 Thai studios were still producing them from 16mm stock. Perhaps partially influenced by India's famed masala movies – which enjoyed a strong following in post-WWII Bangkok – film companies blended romance, comedy, melodrama and adventure to give Thai audiences a little bit of everything.

The Thai movie industry almost died during the '80s and '90s, swamped by Hollywood extravaganzas and the boom era's taste for anything imported. From a 1970s peak of about 200 releases per year, the Thai output shrank to an average of only 10 films a year by 1997. The Southeast Asian economic crisis that year threatened to further bludgeon the ailing industry, but the lack of funding coupled with foreign competition brought about a new emphasis on quality rather than quantity. The current era boasts a new generation of seriously good Thai directors, several of whom studied film abroad during Thailand's '80s and early '90s boom period. Thai and foreign critics alike speak of a current Thai 'new wave', who, avoiding the soap operatics of the past, favour gritty realism, artistic innovation and a strengthened Thai identity.

Recommended Thai Movies

Mon Rak Transistor (2001; directed by Pen-Ek Ratanaruang)

Uncle Boonmee Who Can Recall His Past Lives (2010; directed by Apichatpong Weerasethakul)

Ong Bak (2003; directed by Prachya Pinkaew)

Satree Lex (Iron Ladies; 2000; directed by Yongyoot Thongkongtoon)

Fah Talai Jone (Tears of the Black Tiger; 2000; directed by Wisit Sasantieng)

Suriyothai (2001; directed by Chatrichalerm Yukol)

Nang Nak (1999; directed by Nonzee Nimibutr)

Traditional Theatre & Dance

Kŏhn

Scenes performed in traditional *kŏhn* (and *lá·kon* performances) – a dance drama formerly reserved for court performances – come from the 'epic journey' tale of the *Ramakian* (the Thai version of the Hindu epic, the *Ramayana*), with parallels in the Greek Odyssey and the myth of Jason and the Argonauts. In all *kŏhn* performances, four types of characters are represented – male humans, female humans, monkeys and demons. Monkey and demon figures are always masked with the elaborate head coverings often seen in tourist promo material. Behind the masks and make-up, all actors are male. Traditional *kŏhn* is very expensive to produce – Ravana's retinue alone (Ravana is the principal villain of the *Ramakian*) consists of more than 100 demons, each with a distinctive mask.

Lá·kon

The more formal *lá·kon nai* (inner *lá·kon,* which means that it is performed inside the palace) was originally performed for lower nobility by all-female ensembles. Today it's a dying art, even more so than royal *kŏhn*. In addition to scenes from the *Ramakian*, *lá·kon nai* performances may include traditional Thai folk tales; whatever the story, text is always sung. *Lá·kon nôrk* (outer *lá·kon,* performed outside the palace) deals exclusively with folk tales and features a mix of sung and spoken text, sometimes with improvisation. Male and female performers are permitted. Like *kŏhn* and *lá·kon nai,* performances of *lá·kon nôrk* are increasingly rare.

A variation on *lá·kon* that has evolved specifically for shrine worship, *lá·kon gâa bon* involves an ensemble of about 20, including musicians. At an important shrine such as Bangkok's Lak Meuang, four troupes may alternate, each for a week at a time, as each performance lasts from 9am to 3pm and there is usually a long list of worshippers waiting to hire them.

Translations of Thai short stories and novels can be downloaded as e-books at www.thaifiction.com.

Lí·gair

In outlying working-class neighbourhoods of Bangkok you may be lucky enough to come across the gaudy, raucous *lí·gair*. This theatrical art form is thought to have descended from drama-rituals brought to

BANGKOK FICTION

First-time visitors to virtually any of Bangkok's English-language bookstores will notice an abundance of novels with titles such as *The Butterfly Trap, Confessions of a Bangkok Private Eye, Even Thai Girls Cry, Fast Eddie's Lucky 7 A Go Go, Lady of Pattaya, The Go Go Dancer Who Stole My Viagra, My Name Lon You Like Me?, The Pole Dancer,* and *Thai Touch*. Welcome to the Bangkok school of fiction, a genre, as the titles suggest, defined by its obsession with crime, exoticism and Thai women.

The birth of this genre can be traced back to Jack Reynolds' 1956 novel, *A Woman of Bangkok*. Recently reprinted, the book continues to be an acknowledged influence for many Bangkok-based writers, and Reynolds' formula of Western-man-meets-beautiful-but-dangerous-Thai-woman – occasionally spiced up with a dose of crime – is a staple of the modern genre.

Standouts include John Burdett's *Bangkok 8* (2003), a page-turner in which a half-Thai, half-*fa·ràng* (Westerner) police detective investigates the python-and-cobras murder of a US marine in Bangkok. Along the way we're treated to vivid portraits of Bangkok's gritty nightlife scene and insights into Thai Buddhism. The book's four sequels have sold well in the US.

Christopher G Moore, a Canadian who has lived in Bangkok for the last two decades, has authored more than 20 mostly Bangkok-based crime novels to positive praise both in Thailand and abroad. His description of Bangkok's sleazy Thermae Coffee House (called 'Zeno' in *A Killing Smile*) is the closest literature comes to evoking the perpetual male adolescence to which such places cater.

Private Dancer, by popular English thriller author Stephen Leather, is another classic example of Bangkok fiction, despite having only been available via download until recently.

Jake Needham's 1999 thriller *The Big Mango* provides tongue-in-cheek references to the Bangkok bargirl scene and later became the first expat novel to be translated into Thai.

PEOPLE & CULTURE TRADITIONAL THEATRE & DANCE

southern Thailand by Arab and Malay traders. The first native public performance in central Thailand came about when a group of Thai Muslims staged *lí·gair* for Rama V in Bangkok during the funeral commemoration of Queen Sunantha. *Lí·gair* grew very popular under Rama VI, peaked in the early 20th century and has been fading slowly since the 1960s.

Lá·kon Lék

Lá·kon lék (little theatre; also known as *hùn lŏo·ang,* or royal puppets), like *kŏhn,* was once reserved for court performances. Metre-high marionettes made of *kòi* paper and wire, wearing elaborate costumes modelled on those of the *kŏhn,* were used to convey similar themes, music and dance movements.

Two to three puppet masters were required to manipulate each *hùn lŏo·ang* – including arms, legs, hands, even fingers and eyes – by means of wires attached to long poles. Stories were drawn from Thai folk tales, particularly *Phra Aphaimani* (a classical Thai literary work), and occasionally from the *Ramakian*. Surviving examples of a smaller, 30cm court version called *hùn lék* (little puppets) are occasionally used in live performances; only one puppeteer is required for each marionette in *hùn lék*.

Another form of Thai puppet theatre, *hùn grà·bòrk* (cylinder puppets) is based on popular Hainanese puppet shows. It uses 30cm hand puppets carved from wood and viewed only from the waist up.

Recommended Fiction

The Lioness in Bloom: Modern Thai Fiction about Women (translated by Susan Fulop Kepner)

Bangkok 8 (John Burdett)

Four Reigns (Si Phaendin; Kukrit Pramoj)

Sightseeing (Rattawut Lapcharoensap)

Jasmine Nights (SP Somtow)

Eating in Thailand

There's an entire universe of amazing dishes once you get beyond *pàd tai* and green curry, and for many visitors food is one of the main reasons for choosing Thailand as a destination. Even more remarkable, however, is the love for Thai food among the locals: Thais become just as excited as tourists when faced with a bowl of well-prepared noodles or when seated at a renowned hawker stall. This unabashed enthusiasm for eating, not to mention an abundance of fascinating ingredients and influences, has generated one of the most fun and diverse food scenes anywhere in the world.

How Thais Eat

The people behind Eating Thai Food (www. eatingthaifood. com) have put together an 88-page illustrated PDF guide to identifying and ordering Thai dishes for foreign visitors.

Aside from the occasional indulgence in deep-fried savouries, most Thais sustain themselves on a varied and healthy diet of many fruits, rice and vegetables mixed with smaller amounts of animal protein and fat. Satisfaction seems to come not from eating large amounts of food at any one meal, but rather from nibbling at a variety of dishes with as many different flavours as possible throughout the day.

Nor are certain kinds of food restricted to certain times of day. Practically anything can be eaten first thing in the morning, whether it's sweet, salty or chilli-ridden. *Kôw gaang* (curry over rice) is a very popular morning meal, as are *kôw něe·o mŏo tôrt* (deep-fried pork with sticky rice) and *kôw man gài* (sliced chicken cooked in chicken broth and served over rice).

Lighter morning choices, especially for Thais of Chinese descent, include *Ъah·tôrng·gŏh* (deep-fried bits of dough) dipped in warm *nám đow·hôo* (soy milk). Thais also eat noodles, whether fried or in soup, with great gusto in the morning, or as a substantial snack at any time of the day or night.

As the staple with which almost all Thai dishes are eaten (noodles are still seen as a Chinese import), *kôw* (rice) is considered an indispensable part of the daily diet. Most Bangkok families will put on a pot of rice, or start the rice cooker, just after rising in the morning to prepare a base for the day's menu.

Finding its way into almost every meal is *Ъlah* (fish), even if it's only in the form of *nám Ъlah* (a thin amber sauce made from fermented anchovies), which is used to salt Thai dishes, much as soy sauce is used in eastern Asia. Pork is undoubtedly the preferred protein, with chicken in second place. Beef is seldom eaten in Bangkok, particularly by Thais of Chinese descent who subscribe to a Buddhist teaching that forbids eating 'large' animals.

Thais are prodigious consumers of fruit. Vendors push glass-and-wood carts filled with a rainbow of fresh sliced papaya, pineapple, watermelon and mango, and a more muted palette of salt-pickled or candied seasonal fruits. These are usually served in a small plastic bag with a thin bamboo stick to use as an eating utensil.

Because many restaurants in Thailand are able to serve dishes at an only slightly higher price than they would cost to make at home, Thais dine out far more often than their Western counterparts. Dining with others is always preferred because it means everyone has a chance to sample several dishes. When forced to fly solo by circumstances – such as during lunch breaks at work – a single diner usually sticks to one-plate dishes such as fried rice or curry over rice.

The Four Flavours

Simply put, sweet, sour, salty and spicy are the parameters that define Thai food, and although many associate the cuisine with spiciness, virtually every dish is an exercise in balancing these four tastes. This balance might be obtained by a squeeze of lime juice, a spoonful of sugar and a glug of fish sauce, or a tablespoon of fermented soybeans and a strategic splash of vinegar. Bitter also factors into many Thai dishes, and often comes from the addition of a vegetable or herb. Regardless of the source, the goal is the same: a favourable balance of four clear, vibrant flavours.

Staples & Specialities

Rice & Noodles

In Thailand, to eat is to eat rice, and for most of the country, a meal is not acceptable without this staple. Rice is customarily served alongside main dishes such as curries, stir-fries or soups, which are lumped together as *gàp kôw* (with rice). When you order plain rice in a restaurant you use the term *kôw ่blòw* ('plain rice') or *kôw sŏo·ay* ('beautiful rice').

You'll find four basic kinds of noodle in Thailand. Hardly surprising, given the Thai fixation on rice, is the overwhelming popularity of *sên gŏo·ay ฺdĕe·o*, noodles made from rice flour mixed with water to form a paste, which is then steamed to form wide, flat sheets. The sheets are folded and sliced into various widths.

Also made from rice, *kà·nŏm jeen* is produced by pushing rice-flour paste through a sieve into boiling water, much the way Italian-style pasta is made. *Kà·nŏm jeen* is a popular morning market meal that is eaten doused with various spicy curries and topped with a self-selection of fresh and pickled vegetables and herbs.

The third kind of noodle, *bà·mèe*, is made from wheat flour and egg. It's yellowish in colour and sold only in fresh bundles.

Finally there's *wún·sên*, an almost clear noodle made from mung-bean starch and water. Often sold in dried bunches, *wún·sên* (literally

> *Thai Food* by David Thompson is widely considered the most authoritative English-language book on Thai cooking. Thompson's latest book, *Thai Street Food*, focuses on less-formal street cuisine.

(CON)FUSION CUISINE

A popular dish at restaurants across Thailand is *kôw pàt à·me·rí·gan,* 'American fried rice'. Taking the form of rice fried with ketchup, raisins and peas, sides of ham and deep-fried hot dogs, and topped with a fried egg, the dish is, well, every bit as revolting as it sounds. But at least there's an interesting history behind it: American fried rice apparently dates back to the Vietnam War era, when thousands of US troops were based in northeastern Thailand. A local cook apparently decided to take the ubiquitous 'American Breakfast' (also known as ABF: fried eggs with ham and/or hot dogs, and white bread, typically eaten with ketchup) and make it 'Thai' by frying the various elements with rice.

This culinary cross-pollination is only a recent example of the tendency of Thai cooks to pick and choose from the variety of cuisines at their disposal. Other (significantly more palatable) examples include *gaang mát·sà·màn,* 'Muslim curry', a now classic blend of Thai and Middle Eastern cooking styles, and the famous *pàt tai,* essentially a blend of Chinese cooking methods and ingredients (frying, rice noodles) with Thai flavours (fish sauce, chilli, tamarind).

RICE POLITICS

Despite its relatively small size, Thailand maintains the world's fifth largest amount of land dedicated to growing rice, an industry that employs more than half the country's arable land and a significant portion of its population. Rice is so central to Thai food culture that the most common term for 'eat' is *gin kôw* (literally, 'consume rice') and one of the most common greetings is *Gin kôw rěu yang?* (Have you consumed rice yet?). Given these factors, perhaps it's not surprising that the tiny grain harbours the potential to bring down the country's most powerful leaders.

Bar the occasional rally by Vietnam, Thailand has been the world's predominate rice exporter for more than 30 years. Perhaps given confidence by this long standing status quo, in 2011 the government led by Prime Minister Yingluck Shinawatra thought to further ensconce Thailand's reign of rice. They would do this by buying the country's rice for as much as 76% above market rates and stockpiling it. The rationale was that the world market would be starved for the grain, driving prices artificially high, at which point Thailand would sell its reserves at a handsome profit.

A risky economic gamble at best, but Yingluck and her political advisors neglected one significant factor: India. The country had traditionally not exported much of its rice, having long maintained a policy of self-sufficiency. Yet in a symphony of bad timing for Thailand, in 2011 India abandoned this policy, subsequently dumping 10 million tonnes of rice on the world market. Vietnam, seeing the writing on the wall, correspondingly put its rice on deep discount. Fast-forward a year and Thailand had fallen to the world's third-largest exporter of rice. This loss of pride and profit, coupled with the government's inability to swiftly recompense the growers the promised inflated rates for their rice, led to no small level of discontent.

For opponents of the Yingluck-led government, the rice debacle was the misstep they had been waiting for. Protesters pounced, taking over parts of central Bangkok and screaming corruption, describing the botched policy as 'indirect vote buying'. The unpaid bills may also have been the element that made Thailand's rice farmers, traditionally diehard supporters of Yingluck's Pheu Thai party, reconsider their loyalty.

'jelly thread') is prepared by soaking in hot water for a few minutes. The most common use of the noodle is in *yam wún sên,* a hot and tangy salad made with lime juice, fresh sliced *prík kêe nŏo* (tiny chillies), shrimp, ground pork and various seasonings.

Curries & Soups

In Thai, *gaang* (it sounds somewhat similar to the English 'gang') is often translated as 'curry', but it actually describes any dish with a lot of liquid and can thus refer to soups (such as *gaang jèut*) as well as the classic chilli-paste-based curries for which Thai cuisine is famous. The preparation of the latter begins with a *krêu·ang gaang,* created by mashing, pounding and grinding an array of fresh ingredients with a stone mortar and pestle to form an aromatic, extremely pungent-tasting and rather thick paste. Typical ingredients in a *krêu·ang gaang* include dried chilli, galangal, lemongrass, Kaffir lime zest, shallots, garlic, shrimp paste and salt.

Another food celebrity that falls into the soupy category is *dôm yam,* the famous Thai spicy-and-sour soup. Fuelling the fire beneath *dôm yam*'s often velvety surface are fresh *prík kêe nŏo* (tiny chillies) or, alternatively, half a teaspoonful of *nám prík pŏw* (a roasted chilli paste). Lemongrass, Kaffir lime leaf and lime juice give *dôm yam* its characteristic tang.

Stir-Fries & Deep-Fries

The simplest dishes in the Thai culinary repertoire are the various *pàt* (stir-fries), introduced to Thailand by the Chinese, who are world famous for being able to stir-fry a whole banquet in a single wok.

The list of *pàt* dishes seems endless. Many cling to their Chinese roots, such as the ubiquitous *pàt pàk bûng fai daang* (morning glory flash-fried with garlic and chilli), while some are Thai-Chinese hybrids, such as *pàt pèt* (literally 'hot stir-fry'), in which the main ingredients, typically meat or fish, are quickly stir-fried with red curry paste.

Tôrt (deep-frying in oil) is mainly reserved for snacks such as *glôo·ay tôrt* (deep-fried bananas) or *bò·bée·a* (egg rolls). An exception is *blah tôrt* (deep-fried fish), which is a common way to prepare fish.

Hot & Tangy Salads

Standing right alongside curries in terms of Thai-ness is the ubiquitous *yam,* a hot and tangy 'salad' typically based around seafood, meat or vegetables.

Lime juice provides the tang, while the abundant use of fresh chilli generates the heat. Most *yam* are served at room temperature or just slightly warmed by any cooked ingredients. The dish functions equally well as part of a meal, or on its own as *gàp glâam,* snack food to accompany a night of boozing.

Nám Prík

Although they're more home than restaurant food, *nám prík,* spicy chilli-based 'dips' are, for the locals at least, among the most emblematic of all Thai dishes. Typically eaten with rice and steamed or fresh vegetables and herbs, they're also among the most regional of Thai dishes, and you could probably pinpoint the province you're in by simply looking at the *nám prík* on offer.

Fruits

Being a tropical country, Thailand excels in the fruit department. *Má·môo·ang* (mangoes) alone come in a dozen varieties that are eaten at different stages of ripeness. Other common fruit include *sàp·bà·rót* (pineapple), *má·lá·gor* (papaya) and *daang moh* (watermelon), all of which are sold from ubiquitous vendor carts and are accompanied by a dipping mix of salt, sugar and ground chilli.

Some of the more unusual types of fruit you're likely to come across in Bangkok's fresh markets and supermarkets:

Kà·nǔn Jackfruit hails from India. The giant green pod conceals dozens of waxy yellow sections that taste like a blend of pineapple and bananas (it reminds us of Juicy Fruit chewing gum). At its peak from January to May.

Tú·ree·an Due to its intense odour and weapon-like appearance, the durian is possibly Southeast Asia's most infamous fruit, the flesh of which can suggest everything from custard to onions. Available from May to August.

Lín·jèe The pink skin of the lychee conceals an addictive translucent flesh similar in flavour to a grape. Available from April to June.

Ngó Known in English as rambutan, *ngó* has a tough hairy skin (*rambut* is the Malay word for hair) that holds a clear, sweet-tasting flesh and a large pit. Available from May to September.

Lam yai This indigenous fruit, known in English as longan, hides a sweet and fragrant flesh under its brittle shell. Often dried and used in juices or as a snack. Available from June to August.

Thailand is the world's third-largest exporter of rice, and in 2013 exported approximately 6.6 million tonnes of the grain.

Maintained by a Thai woman living in the US, She Simmers (www.shesimmers.com) is a good source of recipes for those making Thai food outside Thailand.

MUITO OBRIGADO

Try to imagine a Thai curry without the chillies, *pàt tai* without the peanuts, or papaya salad without the papaya. Many of the ingredients used on a daily basis by Thais are recent introductions courtesy of European traders and missionaries. During the early 16th century, while Spanish and Portuguese explorers were first reaching the shores of Southeast Asia, there was also subsequent expansion and discovery in the Americas. The Portuguese in particular were quick to seize the exciting products coming from the New World and market them in the East, thus most likely having introduced such modern-day Asian staples as tomatoes, potatoes, corn, lettuce, cabbage, chillies, papayas, guavas, pineapples, pumpkins, sweet potatoes, peanuts and tobacco.

Chillies in particular seem to have struck a chord with Thais, and are thought to have first arrived in Ayuthaya via the Portuguese around 1550. Before their arrival, the natives got their heat from bitter-hot herbs and roots such as ginger and pepper.

And not only did the Portuguese introduce some crucial ingredients to the Thai kitchen, but also some enduring cooking techniques, particularly in the area of sweets. The bright-yellow duck egg and syrup-based treats you see at many Thai markets are direct descendants of Portuguese desserts known as *fios de ovos* ('egg threads') and *ovos moles*. And in the area surrounding the Church of Santa Cruz (p99), a former Portuguese enclave, you can still find *kà·nŏm fa·ràng,* a bun-like snack baked over coals.

Má·feuang An import from the Americas, the starfruit or carambola is refreshingly crispy and slightly tart. Available from October to December.

Chom·pôo Resembling a small pear, the indigenous rose apple is a delicate and crispy fruit with a slightly bitter flavour and a mild rose scent. Available from February to June.

Nóy nàh Known in English as custard apple, this native of the Americas has a soft and slightly gritty texture and predominantly sweet flavour. Available from June to September.

Mang·kút Known as mangosteen in English, the thick purple skin of this Queen of Fruit conceals a creamy white flesh that is equal parts rich and tangy. Available from May to October.

Sôm oh The flesh of this indigenous fruit, known in English as pomelo, comes in large sections and is generally sweeter than the grapefruit it resembles. Available August to November.

Bangkok's Top 50 Street Food Stalls by Chawadee Nualkhair also functions well as a general introduction and guide to Thai-style informal dining.

Sweets

English-language Thai menus often have a section called 'Desserts', but the concept takes two slightly different forms in Thailand. *Kŏrng wăhn,* which translates as 'sweet things', are small, rich sweets that often boast a slightly salty flavour. Prime ingredients for *kŏrng wăhn* include grated coconut, coconut milk, rice flour (from white rice or sticky rice), cooked sticky rice, tapioca, mung-bean starch, boiled taro and various fruits.

Thai sweets similar to the European concept of pastries are called *kà·nŏm*. Probably the most popular type of *kà·nŏm* in Thailand are the bite-sized items wrapped in banana leaves, especially *kôw dôm gà·tí* and *kôw dôm mát*. Both consist of sticky rice grains steamed with *gà·tí* (coconut milk) inside a banana-leaf wrapper to form a solid, almost taffy-like, mass.

Although foreigners don't seem to immediately take to most Thai sweets, two dishes few visitors have trouble with are *roh·đee,* the back-packer staple 'banana pancakes' slathered with sugar and condensed milk, and *ai·đim gà·tí,* Thai-style coconut ice cream. At more traditional shops, the ice cream is garnished with toppings such as kidney beans or sticky rice, and is a brilliant snack on a sweltering Thai afternoon.

Drinks
Coffee, Tea & Fruit Drinks

Thais are big coffee drinkers, and good-quality arabica and robusta are cultivated in the hilly areas of northern and southern Thailand. The traditional filtering system is nothing more than a narrow cloth bag attached to a steel handle. This type of coffee is served in a glass, mixed with sugar and sweetened with condensed milk – if you don't want either, be sure to specify *gah·faa dam* (black coffee) followed with *mâi sài nám·đahn* (without sugar).

Black tea, both local and imported, is available at the same places that serve real coffee. *Chah tai,* Thai-style tea, derives its characteristic orange-red colour from tamarind seed added after curing.

Fruit drinks appear all over Thailand and are an excellent way to rehydrate after water becomes unpalatable. Most *nám pŏn·lá·mái* (fruit juices) are served with a touch of sugar and salt and a whole lot of ice. Many foreigners object to the salt, but it serves a metabolic role in helping the body to cope with tropical temperatures.

Vegetarians & Vegans

Vegetarianism isn't a widespread trend in Thailand, but many of the tourist-oriented restaurants cater to vegetarians, and there are also a handful of *ráhn ah·hăhn mang·sà·wí·rát* (vegetarian restaurants) in Bangkok where the food is served buffet-style and is very inexpensive. Dishes are almost always 100% vegan (ie no meat, poultry, fish or fish sauce, dairy or egg products).

During the Vegetarian Festival, celebrated by Chinese Buddhists in September/October, many restaurants and street stalls in Bangkok go meatless for one month. During the remainder of the year, the down-loadable *Vegetarian Thai Food Guide* (www.eatingthaifood.com/vege tarian-thai-food-guide) is a handy resource.

The phrase 'I'm vegetarian' in Thai is *pŏm gin jair* (for men) or *đì·chăn gin jair* (for women). Loosely translated this means 'I eat only vegetarian food', which includes no eggs and no dairy products – in other words, total vegan.

Habits & Customs

Like most of Thai culture, eating conventions appear relaxed and informal but are orchestrated by many implied rules.

Whether at home or in a restaurant, Thai meals are always served 'family-style', that is, from common serving platters, and the plates appear in whatever order the kitchen can prepare them. When serving yourself from a common platter, put no more than one spoonful onto your plate at a time. Heaping your plate with all 'your' portions at once will look greedy to Thais unfamiliar with Western conventions. Another important factor in a Thai meal is achieving a balance of flavours and textures. Traditionally, the party orders a curry, a steamed or fried

Pok Pok, by Andy Ricker and JJ Goode, features recipes of the rustic regional Thai dishes served at Ricker's eponymous Portland, Oregon, and New York City restaurants.

fish, a stir-fried vegetable dish and a soup, taking great care to balance cool and hot, sour and sweet, salty and plain.

Originally Thai food was eaten with the fingers, and it still is in certain regions of the kingdom. In the early 1900s, Thais began setting their tables with fork and spoon to affect a 'royal' setting, and it wasn't long before fork-and-spoon dining became the norm in Bangkok and later spread throughout the kingdom. To use these tools the Thai way, use a serving spoon, or alternatively your own, to take a single mouthful of food from a central dish, and ladle it over a portion of your rice. The fork is then used to push the now food-soaked portion of rice back onto the spoon before entering the mouth.

If you're not offered chopsticks, don't ask for them. Chopsticks are reserved for eating Chinese-style food from bowls, or for eating in all-Chinese restaurants. In either case you will be supplied with chopsticks without having to ask. Unlike their counterparts in many Western countries, restaurateurs in Thailand won't assume you don't know how to use them.

Keep up with the ever-changing food scene in Bangkok by following BK's restaurant section (www.bk.asia-city.com/restaurants).

The Sex Industry in Thailand

Thailand has had a long and complex relationship with prostitution that persists today. It is also an international sex tourism destination, a designation that began around the time of the Vietnam War. The industry targeted to foreigners is very visible with multiple red-light districts in Bangkok alone, but there is also a more clandestine domestic sex industry and myriad informal channels of sex-for-hire.

An Illegal – and Vast – Industry

Prostitution is technically illegal in Thailand. However, anti-prostitution laws are often ambiguous and unenforced. Some analysts have argued that the high demand for sexual services in Thailand limits the likelihood of the industry being curtailed; however, limiting abusive practices within the industry is the goal of many activists and government agencies.

It is difficult to determine the number of sex workers in Thailand, the demographics of the industry or its economic strength. This is because there are many indirect forms of prostitution, the illegality of the industry makes research difficult, and different organisations use different approaches to collect data. In 2003, measures to legalise prostitution cited the Thai sex industry as being worth US$4.3 billion (about 3% of GDP), employing roughly 200,000 sex workers. A study conducted in 2003 by Thailand's Chulalongkorn University estimated 2.8 million sex workers, of which 1.98 million were adult women, 20,000 were adult men and 800,000 were children, defined as any person under the age of 18.

Help stop child-sex tourism by reporting suspicious behaviour on a dedicated hotline (☏1300) or by reporting the individual directly to the embassy of their home country.

History & Cultural Attitudes

Prostitution has been widespread in Thailand since long before the country gained a reputation among international sex tourists. Throughout Thai history the practice was accepted and common among many sectors of society, though it has not always been respected by society as a whole.

Due to international pressure from the UN, prostitution was declared illegal in 1960, though entertainment places (go-go bars, beer bars, massage parlours, karaoke bars and bathhouses) are governed by a separate law passed in 1966. These establishments are licensed and can legally provide nonsexual services (such as dancing, massage, a drinking buddy); sexual services occur through these venues but they are not technically the businesses' primary purpose.

With the arrival of the US military forces in Southeast Asia during the Vietnam War era, enterprising forces adapted the existing framework to suit foreigners, in turn creating an international sex-tourism industry that persists today. Indeed, this foreigner-oriented sex industry is still a prominent part of Thailand's tourist economy.

In 1998 the International Labour Organization, a UN agency, advised Southeast Asian countries, including Thailand, to recognise prostitution as an economic sector and income generator. It is estimated that one-third of the entertainment establishments are registered with the government and the majority pay an informal tax in the form of police bribes.

Economic Motivations

Regardless of their background, most women in the sex industry are there for financial reasons: many find that sex work is one of the highest-paying jobs for their level of education, and they have financial obligations (be it dependants or debts). The most comprehensive data on the economics of sex workers comes from a 1993 survey by Kritaya Archavanitkul. The report found that sex workers made a mean income of 17,000B per month (US$18 per day), the equivalent of a mid-level civil servant job, a position acquired through advanced education and family connections. At the time of the study, most sex workers did not have a high-school degree.

The International Labour Organization estimates a Thai sex workers' salary at 270B (US$9) a day, the average wage of a Thai service-industry worker.

These economic factors provide a strong incentive for rural, unskilled women (and to a lesser extent, men) to engage in sex work.

As with many in Thai society, a large percentage of sex workers' wages are remitted back to their home villages to support their families (parents, siblings and children). Kritaya's 1993 report found that between 1800B and 6100B per month was sent back home to rural communities. The remittance-receiving households typically bought durable goods (TVs and washing machines), bigger houses and motorcycles or automobiles. Their wealth displayed their daughters' success in the industry and acted as a free advertisement for the next generation of sex workers.

The Coalition Against Trafficking in Women (CATW; www.catwinternational.org) is an NGO that works internationally to combat prostitution and trafficking in women and children.

Working Conditions

The unintended consequence of prostitution prohibitions is the lawless working environment it creates for women who enter the industry. Sex work becomes the domain of criminal networks that are often involved in other illicit activities and circumvent the laws through bribes and violence.

Sex workers are not afforded the rights of other workers: there is no minimum wage; no required vacation pay, sick leave or break time; no deductions for social security or employee-sponsored health insurance; and no legal redress.

Bars can set their own punitive rules that fine a worker if she doesn't smile enough, arrives late or doesn't meet the drink quota. Empower,

HIV/AIDS

Thailand was lauded for its rapid and effective response to the AIDS epidemic through an aggressive condom-use campaign in the 1990s. Infection rates of female sex workers declined to 5% by 2007 but rates have recently doubled among informal sex workers (street prostitutes). Analysts warn that the country is on the verge of a resurgence as public education efforts have declined and cultural attitudes towards sex have changed. Of the country's 610,000 people living with HIV/AIDS, intravenous drug users make up the largest portion (30% to 50% in 2007).

THE EXPERTS' VIEWS: THAILAND'S SEX INDUSTRY

In an effort to provide an alternate view on one of Thailand's most contentious issues, we approached members of Empower (www.empowerfoundation.org), a Thailand-based NGO that fights for safe and fair standards in the sex industry and equal rights in society, and Associate Professor Virada Somswasdi, Head of the Women's Studies Center, Chiang Mai University. We asked a few of the most common questions we've heard from visitors to Bangkok about Thailand's sex industry.

Why does the sex industry appear to be so open and tolerated in Thailand? Are Thai attitudes regarding the sex trade different than those of the West?

Professor Virada In any society – West, East and beyond, Thailand is no exception – where a deep-rooted and dominant patriarchal social structure controls sexuality and abuses women's bodies, combined with the huge vested interests of 'the industry' and a highly corruptible level of law enforcement, any 'illegal' deeds will go untouched or with a low response.

Empower Because it is so open and many people are in the business and they seem to make no harm to the public. And because the work is an economic opportunity for many women who need a job that pays enough to support herself and her family.

What are the biggest problems with the sex industry as it exists now in Thailand?

Professor Virada Degradation of women and their wellbeing, sexual exploitation, violence against women, gender inequality and sex tourism. The thin and very blurred line between trafficking in women and prostitution.

Empower Applying criminal laws to try and enforce moral judgement turns workers and the business into criminals to be punished, not humans to be supported.

Why do Thai women (and to a lesser extent, men) become sex workers?

Professor Virada It's about dominance of male sexuality that 'the industry' continues and expands to serve its clients, taking advantage of lower economic, social and political capabilities of women and girls to traffic and lure them into prostitution under the name of 'choice' or 'consent'.

Empower It's the job they chose over other jobs because it offers the most freedom, variety and opportunities.

Many people in the West tend to associate Thailand with child prostitution – is this still a significant problem in the country?

Professor Virada Yes, the establishments involved in commercial sexual exploitation and prostitution still target girls more and more, focusing on those from neighbouring countries of Thailand.

Empower As far as Empower's 25 years of experience, we have been working with adult women and have only seen child prostitution if we watch a documentary.

Should prostitution in Thailand be legalised? What are the potential positives and negatives of this?

Professor Virada Legalising prostitution will merely benefit pimps, traffickers and the sex industry; it will increase child prostitution, clandestine, hidden, illegal and street prostitution; it does not promote women's health, nor enhance women's choices; women in systems of prostitution do not want the sex industry legalised.

Empower We don't think that there should be law to either legalise or criminalise sex work, but rather that [sex workers] should be considered workers or employers under the labour protection law.

As told to Austin Bush.

an NGO that fights for safe and fair standards in the sex industry, reported that most sex workers will owe money to the bar at the end of the month through these deductions. In effect, the women have to pay to be prostitutes and the fines disguise a pimp relationship.

Through lobbying efforts, groups such as Empower hope that lawmakers will recognise all workers at entertainment places (including dishwashers and cooks as well as 'working girls') as employees subject to labour and safety protections.

Other commentators, such as the Coalition Against Trafficking in Women (CATW), argue that legalising prostitution is not the answer, because such a move would legitimise a practice that is always going to be dangerous and exploitative for the women involved. Instead, these groups focus on how to enable the women to leave prostitution and make their way into different types of work.

Organisations working across borders to stop child prostitution include Ecpat (End Child Prostitution & Trafficking; www.ecpat.net) and its Australian affiliate Child Wise (www.childwise.net).

Child Prostitution & Human Trafficking

According to Ecpat (End Child Prostitution & Trafficking), there are currently 30,000 to 40,000 children involved in prostitution in Thailand, though estimates are unreliable. According to Chulalongkorn University, the number of children is as high as 800,000.

In 1996, Thailand passed a reform law to address the issue of child prostitution (defined into two tiers: 15 to 18 years old and under 15). Fines and jail time are assigned to customers, establishment owners and even parents involved in child prostitution (under the old law only prostitutes were culpable). Many countries also have extraterritorial legislation that allows nationals to be prosecuted in their own country for such crimes committed in Thailand.

Urban job centres such as Bangkok have large populations of displaced and marginalised people (immigrants from Myanmar, ethnic hill-tribe members and impoverished rural Thais). Children of these fractured families often turn to street begging, which is an entryway into prostitution usually through low-level criminal gangs.

Thailand is also a conduit and destination for people trafficking (including children) from Myanmar, Laos, Cambodia and China. According to the UN, human trafficking is a crime against humanity and involves recruiting, transporting, transferring, harbouring and receiving a person through force, fraud or coercion for purposes of exploitation. In 2007, the US State Department labelled Thailand as not meeting the minimum standards for prevention of human trafficking.

It is difficult to obtain reliable data about trafficked people, including minors, but a 1997 report on foreign child labour, by Kritaya Archavanitkul, found that there were 16,423 non-Thai prostitutes working in the country and that 30% were children under the age of 18 (a total of 4900). Other studies estimated that there were 100,000 to 200,000 foreign-born children in the Thai workforce but these figures do not determine the type of work being done.

This chapter was written by China Williams, Lonely Planet author

Survival Guide

Transport

GETTING TO BANGKOK

Most travellers will arrive in Bangkok via air, but for those entering the city on ground transport, or who have plans to move onward, below is a summary of the city's major transport hubs.

Flights, tours and rail tickets can be booked online at lonelyplanet.com/bookings.

Air

Located 30km east of central Bangkok, **Suvarnabhumi International Airport** (✆0 2132 1888; www.suvarnabhumiairport. com) began commercial international and domestic service in 2006. The airport's name is pronounced sù·wan·ná·poom, and it inherited the airport code (BKK) previously held by the old airport at Don Muang. The airport website has real-time details of arrivals and departures.

Bangkok's other airport, **Don Muang International Airport** (DMK; ✆0 2535 1111; www.donmuangairportonline. com), 25km north of central Bangkok, was retired from service in 2006 only to reopen later as Bangkok's de-facto budget hub.

Travel to/from Suvarnabhumi International Airport

TRAIN
The **Airport Rail Link** (www. bangkokairporttrain.com) connecting central Bangkok and Suvarnabhumi International Airport is comprised of a local service, which makes six stops before terminating at Phaya Thai station (30 minutes, 45B), connected by a walkway to the BTS (Skytrain) of the same name, as well as an express service that runs without stopping between the airport and Makkasan or Phaya Thai stations (15 to 17 minutes, 90B). Makkasan, also known as Bangkok City Air Terminal, is a short walk from Phetchaburi MRT (metro) station, and if you show up at least three hours before your departure, also has check-in facilities for passengers flying on Thai Airways. Both lines run from 6am to midnight.

TAXI
➡ Metered taxis are available kerbside at floor 1 – ignore the 'official airport taxi' touts who approach you inside the terminal.

➡ Typical metered fares from the airport are as follows: 200B to 250B to Th Sukhumvit; 250B to 300B to Th Khao San; 400B to Mo Chit. Toll charges (paid by the passengers) vary between 25B and 60B. Note that there's an additional 50B surcharge added to all fares departing from the airport, payable directly to the driver.

CLIMATE CHANGE & TRAVEL

Every form of transport that relies on carbon-based fuel generates CO_2, the main cause of human-induced climate change. Modern travel is dependent on aeroplanes, which might use less fuel per kilometre per person than most cars but travel much greater distances. The altitude at which aircraft emit gases (including CO_2) and particles also contributes to their climate change impact. Many websites offer 'carbon calculators' that allow people to estimate the carbon emissions generated by their journey and, for those who wish to do so, to offset the impact of the greenhouse gases emitted with contributions to portfolios of climate-friendly initiatives throughout the world. Lonely Planet offsets the carbon footprint of all staff and author travel.

➡ You can hail a taxi directly from the street for airport trips or you can arrange one through the hotels or by calling ☎1681 (which charges a 20B dispatch surcharge).

BUS & MINIVAN

➡ A public transport centre is 3km from the airport and includes a bus terminal with buses to a handful of provinces and inner-city-bound buses and minivans. A free airport shuttle connects the transport centre with the passenger terminals.

➡ Bus lines city-bound tourists are likely to use include line 551 to BTS Victory Monument station (40B, frequent from 5am to 10pm) and 552 to BTS On Nut in the Sukhumvit area (25B, frequent from 5am to 10pm). From these points, you can continue by public transport or taxi to your hotel.

➡ From town, you can take the BTS to On Nut, then from near the market entrance opposite Tesco Lotus, take minivan 552 (25B, frequent from 5am to 10pm), or BTS to Victory Monument, then the minivan to Suvarnabhumi International Airport (40B, every 30 minutes from 5am to 9pm).

Travel to/from Don Muang International Airport

BUS

➡ From outside the arrivals hall, there are two airport bus lines from Don Muang: A1 makes a stop at BTS Mo Chit (30B, hourly, from 9am to midnight); A2 makes stops at BTS Mo Chit and BTS Victory Monument (30B, hourly, from 9am to midnight).

➡ Public buses stop on the highway in front of the airport. Useful lines include 29, with a stop at Victory Monument BTS station before terminating at Hualamphong Train Station (24 hours); line 59, with a stop near Th Khao San (24 hours); and line 538, stopping at Victory Monument BTS station (4am to 10pm); fares are approximately 30B.

TAXI

As at Suvarnabhumi, public taxis leave from outside the arrivals hall and there is a 50B airport charge added to the meter fare.

TRAIN

The walkway that crosses from the airport to the Amari Airport Hotel also provides access to Don Muang Train Station, which has trains to Hualamphong Train Station every one to 1½ hours from 4am to 11.30am and then roughly every hour from 2pm to 9.30pm (from 5B to 10B).

Bus

Buses using government bus stations are far more reliable and less prone to incidents of theft than those departing from Th Khao San or other tourist centres.

Eastern Bus Terminal (Ekamai; Map p270; ☎0 2391 2504; Soi 40, Th Sukhumvit; [S]Ekkamai exit 2) Go to this station for buses to cities on or near the eastern gulf coast including Ban Phe (for Ko Samet), Pattaya, Rayong, Chanthaburi and Trat (for Ko Chang).

Northern & Northeastern Bus Terminal (Mo Chit; ☎northeastern routes 0 2936 2852, ext 602/605, northern routes 0 2936 2841, ext 325/614; Th Kamphaeng Phet; [M]Kamphaeng Phet exit 1 & taxi, [S]Mo Chit exit 3 & taxi) Commonly called Mor Chit, this station serves destinations in northern and northeastern Thailand.

Southern Bus Terminal (Sai Tai Mai; ☎0 2894 6122; Th Boromaratchachonanee) Located across Saphan Phra Pinklao in the far western suburbs, Sai Tai Mai serves all points south – hello Phuket, Surat Thani, Krabi, Hat Yai – as well as Kanchanaburi and western Thailand. The easiest way to reach the station is by taxi, or you can take bus 79, 159, 201 or 516 from Th Ratchadamnoen Klang, or the **minivan** (Map p263) or bus 40 from the Victory Monument (p109).

Minivan

Privately run minivans, called *rót đôo*, are a fast and relatively comfortable way to get between Bangkok and neighbouring provinces. Several minivans depart from various points surrounding the Victory Monument (p109).

Train

Hualamphong (Map p258; ☎0 2220 4334, call centre 1690; www.railway.co.th; off Th Phra Ram IV; [M]Hua Lamphong exit 2) The city's main train terminus. It's advisable to ignore all touts here and avoid the travel agencies. To check timetables and prices for other destinations call the **State Railway of Thailand** (SRT; ☎1690; www.railway.co.th) or look at its website.

Wong Wian Yai (off Th Phra Jao Taksin; [S]Wongwian Yai exit 4 & taxi) This tiny hidden station is the jumping-off point for the commuter line to Samut Sakhon (also known as Mahachai).

Bangkok Noi (Map p252; off Th Itsaraphap; [S]Wongwian Yai exit 4 & taxi) A miniscule train station with (overpriced) departures for Kanchanaburi.

GETTING AROUND

Bangkok may seem chaotic and impenetrable at first, but its transport system is gradually improving, and although you'll almost certainly find yourself stuck in traffic at some point, the jams aren't as legendary as they used to be. For most of the day and night, Bangkok's 70,000 clean and dirt-cheap taxis are the most expedient choice – although it's important to note that Bangkok traffic is nothing if not unpredictable. During rush hour, the BTS, MRT, river ferries and *klorng* (canal, also spelt *khlong*) ferries are much wiser options. Locals and many local expats swear by the ubiquitous motorcycle taxis, but the accidents we've seen suggest that they're not really worth the risk.

BTS & MRT

The elevated **BTS** (☏0 2617 7300, tourist information 0 2617 7340; www.bts.co.th), also known as the Skytrain (*rót fai fáa*), whisks you through 'new' Bangkok (Silom, Sukhumvit and Siam Sq). The interchange between the two lines is at Siam station, and trains run frequently from 6am to midnight. Fares range from 15B to 52B, or 120B for a one-day pass. Most ticket machines only accept coins, but change is available at the information booths.

Bangkok's underground **MRT** (www.bangkokmetro.co.th) or Metro is most helpful for people staying in the Sukhumvit or Silom area to reach the train station at Hualamphong. Fares cost 16B to 40B, or 120B for a one-day pass. It runs frequently 6am to midnight.

Taxi

Although many first-time visitors are hesitant to use them, in general, Bangkok's taxis are new and spacious and the drivers are courteous and helpful, making them an excellent way to get around.

All taxis are required to use their meters, which start at 35B, and fares to most places within central Bangkok cost 60B to 90B. Freeway tolls – 25B to 60B depending on where you start – must be paid by the passenger.

Taxi Radio (☏1681; www.taxiradio.co.th) and other 24-hour 'phone-a-cab' services are available for 20B above the metered fare.

If you leave something in a taxi your best chance of getting it back (still pretty slim) is to call ☏1644.

BANGKOK ADDRESSES

➡ Any city as large and unplanned as Bangkok can be tough to get around. Street names often seem unpronounceable, compounded by the inconsistency of romanised Thai spellings. For example, the street sometimes spelt as 'Rajdamri' is actually pronounced 'Ratchadamri' (with the appropriate tones, of course), or in abbreviated form as Rat damri. The 'v' in Sukhumvit should be pronounced like a 'w'... One of the most popular locations for foreign embassies is known both as Wireless Rd and Th Witthayu (*wí·tá·yú* is Thai for 'radio').

➡ Many street addresses show a string of numbers divided by slashes and hyphens, for example, 48/3-5 Soi 1, Th Sukhumvit. The reason is that undeveloped property in Bangkok was originally bought and sold in lots. The number before the slash refers to the original lot number. The numbers following the slash indicate buildings (or entrances to buildings) constructed within that lot. The pre-slash numbers appear in the order in which they were added to city plans, while the post-slash numbers are arbitrarily assigned by developers. As a result numbers along a given street don't always run consecutively.

➡ The Thai word *tà·nǒn* (usually spelt 'thanon') means road, street or avenue. Hence Ratchadamnoen Rd (sometimes referred to as Ratchadamnoen Ave) is always called Thanon (Th) Ratchadamnoen in Thai.

➡ A soi is a small street or lane that runs off a larger street. In our example, the address referred to as 48/3-5 Soi 1, Th Sukhumvit will be located off Th Sukhumvit on Soi 1. Alternative ways of writing the same address include 48/3-5 Th Sukhumvit Soi 1, or even just 48/3-5 Sukhumvit 1. Some Bangkok soi have become so large that they can be referred to both as thanon and soi, eg Soi Sarasin/Th Sarasin and Soi Asoke/Th Asoke. Smaller than a soi is a *tròrk* (usually spelt 'trok') or alley. Well-known alleys in Bangkok include Chinatown's Trok Itsaranuphap and Banglamphu's Trok Rong Mai.

Boat

River Ferries

The **Chao Phraya Express Boat** (☑0 2623 6001; www.chaophrayaexpressboat.com) operates the main ferry service along Mae Nam Chao Phraya. The central pier is known as Tha Sathon, Saphan Taksin or sometimes Central Pier, and connects to the BTS at Saphan Taksin station.

The service runs from 6am to 10pm. You can buy tickets (10B to 40B) at the pier or on board; hold on to your ticket as proof of purchase (an occasional formality).

The most common boats are the orange-flagged express boats. These run between Wat Rajsingkorn, south of Bangkok, to Nonthaburi, north, stopping at most major piers (15B, frequent from 6am to 7pm). A yellow-flagged tourist boat (40B, every 30 minutes from 9am to 10pm) runs from Tha Sathon (Central Pier) (Map p266) to Tha Phra Athit (Banglamphu) (Map p254) with stops at six major sightseeing piers and barely comprehensible English-language commentary. Vendors at Tha Sathon (Central Pier) tout a 150B all-day pass, but unless you're doing a lot of boat travel, it's not great value.

There are also dozens of cross-river ferries, which charge from 3B to 3.50B and run every few minutes until late at night.

Private long-tail boats can be hired for sightseeing trips at Tha Phra Athit (Banglamphu), Tha Chang (Map p252), Tha Tien (Map p252) and Tha Oriental (Map p266).

Klorng Boats

Canal taxi boats run along Khlong Saen Saep (Banglamphu to Ramkhamhaeng) and are an easy way to get between Banglamphu

and Jim Thompson's House, the Siam Sq shopping centres –get off at Tha Saphan Hua Chang (Map p260) for both – and other points further east along Th Sukhumvit after a mandatory change of boat at Tha Pratunam (Map p260). These boats are mostly used by daily commuters and pull into the piers for just a few seconds – jump straight on or you'll be left behind. Fares range from 10B to 20B and boats run from 5.30am to 8.30pm.

Motorcycle Taxis

Motorcycle taxis (known as *motorsai*) serve two purposes in Bangkok. Most commonly and popularly they form an integral part of the public-transport network, running from the corner of a main thoroughfare, such as Th Sukhumvit, to the far ends of sois that run off that thoroughfare. Riders wear coloured, numbered vests and gather at either end of their soi, usually charging 10B to 20B for the trip (without a helmet unless you ask).

Their other purpose is as a means of beating the traffic. You tell your rider where you want to go, negotiate a price (from 20B for a short trip up to about 150B going across town), strap on the helmet (they will insist for longer trips) and say a prayer to whichever god you're into.

For more information see the boxed text on Bangkok's *motorsai* (p108).

Túk-Túk

Bangkok's iconic túk-túk (pronounced *đúk đúk;* a type of motorised rickshaw) are used by Thais for short hops not worth paying the taxi flag fall for. For foreigners, however, these emphysema-inducing machines are part of the Bangkok experience, so despite the fact they overcharge outrageously and you can't see anything due to the low roof, pretty much everyone takes a túk-túk at least once. It's worth knowing, however, that túk-túk are notorious for taking little 'detours' to commission-paying gem and silk shops and massage parlours. En route to 'special' temples, you'll meet 'helpful' locals who will steer you to even more rip-off opportunities. Ignore anyone offering too-good-to-be-true 10B trips.

The vast majority of túk-túk drivers ask too much from tourists (expat *fa·ràng* never use them). Expect to be quoted a 100B fare, if not more, for even the shortest trip. Try bargaining them down to about 60B for a short trip, preferably at night when the pollution (hopefully) won't be quite so bad. Once you've done it, you'll find taxis are cheaper, cleaner, cooler and quieter.

Car

For short-term visitors, you will find parking and driving a car in Bangkok more trouble than it is worth. If you need private transport, consider hiring a car and driver through your hotel or hire a taxi driver that you find trustworthy. One reputable operator is **Julie Taxi** (☏08 1846 2014, 08 5115 5455; www. facebook.com/TourWithJulie Taxi), which offers a variety of vehicles and excellent service.

But if you still want to give it a go, all the big car-hire companies have offices in Bangkok and at Suvarnab-humi airport. Rates start at around 1000B per day for a small car. A passport plus a valid licence from your home country (with English translation if necessary) or an International Driving Permit are required for all rentals.

Reliable car-hire companies include the following, all of which also have counters at Suvarnabhumi International Airport:

Avis (Map p268; ☏0 2251 1131; www.avisthailand.com; 40 Th Sathon Neua (North); ⏰7.30am-7.30pm; Ⓜ Lumphini exit 2) Cars and motorcycles can be hired through this international chain. Rates start at around 1000B per day, excluding insurance. An International Driving Permit and passport are required for all rentals.

Budget (☏0 2203 9222; www.budget.co.th; 19/23 Bldg A, Royal City Ave (RCA); ⏰8am-7pm; Ⓜ Phra Ram 9 exit 3 & taxi) A reliable car-hire place.

Thai Rent A Car (Map p270; ☏0 2737 8888; www.thairentacar.com; 2371 Th Petchaburi Tat Mai; ⏰8.30am-5.30am Mon-Sat; Ⓢ Thong Lo exit 3 & taxi) If you're not dissuaded, cars and motorcycles can be rented through this local chain, which has a branch at Suvarnabhumi International Airport. Rates start at around 1000B per day, excluding insurance. An International Driving Permit and passport are required for all rentals.

Bus

Bangkok's public buses are run by the **Bangkok Mass Transit Authority** (☏0 2246 0973; www.bmta. co.th). As the routes are not always clear, and with Bangkok taxis being such a good deal, you'd really have to be pinching pennies to rely on buses as a way to get around Bangkok. However, if you're determined, air-con bus fares range from 11B to 30B, and fares for fan-cooled buses start at 5B or 7B. Most of the bus lines run between 5am and 10pm or 11pm, except for the 'all-night' buses, which run from 3am or 4am to midmorning. You'll most likely require the help of thinknet's *Bangkok Bus Guide*.

TOURS

Bangkok has a variety of walking, bicycle and guided tours (p49).

Directory A–Z

Customs Regulations

➡ White-uniformed customs officers prohibit the import or export of the usual goods (porn, weapons, drugs). If you're caught with drugs in particular, expect life never to be the same again. The usual 200 cigarettes or 250g of tobacco are allowed in without duty, along with up to 1L of wine or spirits.

➡ For details about regulations, see www.customs.go.th.

➡ Licences are required for exporting religious images and other antiquities (p43).

Electricity

220V/50Hz

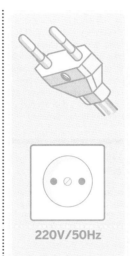

220V/50Hz

Embassies & Consulates

Australian Embassy (Map p268; ☎0 2344 6300; www. thailand.embassy.gov.au; 37 Th Sathon Tai (South), Bangkok; ⊙8.30am-4.30pm Mon-Fri; MLumphini exit 2)

Cambodian Embassy (☎0 2957 5851; 518/4 Th Pracha Uthit/Soi Ramkhamhaeng 39, Bangkok; ⊙9am-noon Mon-Fri; MPhra Ram 9 exit 3 & taxi)

Canadian Embassy (Map p268; ☎0 2646 4300; www. canadainternational.gc.ca; 15th fl, Abdulrahim Pl, 990 Th Phra Ram IV, Bangkok; ⊙7.30am-

12.15pm & 1-4.15pm Mon-Thu, to 1pm Fri; MSi Lom exit 2, SSala Daeng exit 4)

French Embassy (Map p266; ☎0 2657 5100; www. ambafrance-th.org; 35 Soi 36, Th Charoen Krung, Bangkok; ⊙8.30am-noon Mon-Fri; ⛴Tha Oriental) Consulates in Phuket and Surat Thani.

German Embassy (Map p268; ☎0 2287 9000; www. bangkok.diplo.de; 9 Th Sathon Tai (South), Bangkok; ⊙8.30-11am Mon-Fri; MLumphini exit 2)

Irish Consulate (Map p264; ☎0 2632 6720; www.ireland inthailand.com; 4th fl, Thaniya Bldg, 62 Th Silom, Bangkok; ⊙8.30am-12.30pm Mon-Fri; MSi Lom exit 2, ☒Sala Daeng exit 1)

Laotian Embassy (☎0 2539 6667; 502/1-3 Soi Sahakarn-pramoon, Th Pracha Uthit (Soi Ramkhamhaeng 39); ⊙8am-noon & 1-4pm Mon-Fri; MPhra Ram 9 exit 3 & taxi)

Malaysian Embassy (Map p268; ☎0 2629 6800; www. kln.gov.my/web/tha_bangkok/home; 35 Th Sathon Tai (South); ⊙8am-4pm; MLumphini exit 2) Consulate in Songkhla.

Myanmar Embassy (Map p264; ☎0 2233 7250; www. myanmarembassybkk.com; 132 Th Sathon Neua (North), Bangkok; ⊙9am-4.30pm (embassy),

9am-noon & 1-3pm Mon-Fri (visas); **S** Surasak exit 3)

Netherlands Embassy
(Map p260; ☏ 0 2309 5200; http://thailand.nlembassy. org; 15 Soi Tonson, Bangkok; ◷ 8.30-11.30am Mon-Wed, 8.30-11.30am & 1.30-3pm Thu (consular office); **S** Chit Lom exit 4)

New Zealand Embassy
(Map p260; ☏ 0 2254 2530; www.nzembassy.com/thailand; 14th fl, M Thai Tower, All Seasons Pl, 87 Th Witthayu (Wireless Rd), Bangkok; ◷ 8am-noon & 1-2.30pm Mon-Fri; **S** Phloen Chit exit 5)

UK Embassy (Map p260; ☏ 0 2305 8333; www.gov.uk/government/world/organisations/british-embassy-bangkok; 14 Th Witthayu (Wireless Rd), Bangkok; ◷ 8am-4.30pm Mon-Thu, to 1pm Fri; **S** Phloen Chit exit 5) Consulates in Chiang Mai and Pattaya.

US Embassy (Map p260; ☏ 0 2205 4000; http://bangkok.usembassy.gov; 120/22 Th Witthayu (Wireless Rd); ◷ 7am-4pm Mon-Fri; **S** Phloen Chit exit 5)

Emergency

Ambulance (☏ via police 191) In a medical emergency, it's probably best to call a hospital direct, and it will dispatch an ambulance. See Medical Services for recommended hospitals.

Fire (☏ 199) You're unlikely to find an English-speaker at this number, so it's best to use the default 191 emergency number.

Police (☏ 191)

Tourist Police (☏ 24hr hotline 1155) The best way to deal with most problems requiring police (usually a rip-off or theft) is to contact the tourist police, who are used to dealing with foreigners and can be very helpful in cases of arrest. The English-speaking unit investigates criminal activity involving tourists and can act as a bilingual liaison with the regular police. Although they typically have no jurisdiction over the kinds of cases handled by regular cops, they should be able to help with translation, contacting your embassy and/or arranging a police report you can take to your insurer.

Health

While urban horror stories can make a trip to Bangkok seem frighteningly dangerous, few travellers experience anything more than an upset stomach and the resulting clenched-cheek waddles to the bathroom. If you do have a problem, Bangkok has some very good hospitals.

Air Pollution

Bangkok has a bad reputation for air pollution, and on bad days the combination of heat, dust and motor fumes can be a powerful brew of potentially toxic air. The good news is that more-efficient vehicles (and fewer of them thanks to the BTS Skytrain and MRT Metro), and less industrial pollution mean Bangkok's skies are much cleaner than they used to be.

Flu

Thailand has seen a number of nasty influenza strains in recent years, most notably the bird (H5N1) and swine (H1N1) varieties. That said, it's no worse than any other country in the region and is probably better prepared than most of the world for any major outbreak because the government has stockpiled tens of millions of Tamiflu doses.

Food

If a place looks clean and well run and the vendor also looks clean and healthy, then the food is probably safe. In general, the food in busy restaurants is cooked and eaten quite quickly with little standing around, and is probably not reheated. The same applies to street stalls.

Heat

By the standards of most visitors Bangkok is somewhere between hot and seriously (expletive) hot all year round. Usually that will mean nothing more than sweat-soaked clothing, discomfort and excessive tiredness. However, heat exhaustion

---

PRACTICALITIES

➡ Bangkok's predominant English-language newspapers are the **Bangkok Post** (www.bangkokpost.com) and the business-heavy **Nation** (www.nationmultimedia.com).

➡ The *International New York Times* and weeklies such as the *Economist* and *Time* are sold at numerous news stands.

➡ **Bangkok 101** (www.bangkok101.com) is a tourist-friendly listings magazine.

➡ The metric system is used for weights and measures.

➡ Smoking in restaurants and bars has been banned since 2008.

is not uncommon, and dehydration is the main contributor. Symptoms include feeling weak, headache, irritability, nausea or vomiting, sweaty skin, a fast, weak pulse and a normal or slightly elevated body temperature. Treatment involves getting out of the heat and/or sun and cooling the victim down by fanning and applying cool, wet cloths to the skin, laying the victim flat with their legs raised and rehydrating with electrolyte drinks or water containing a quarter teaspoon of salt per litre. Heatstroke is more serious and requires more urgent action. Symptoms come on suddenly and include weakness, nausea, a hot, dry body with a temperature of more than 41°C, dizziness, confusion, loss of coordination, seizures and, eventually, collapse and loss of consciousness. Seek medical help and begin cooling by getting the victim out of the heat, removing their clothes, fanning them and applying cool, wet cloths or ice to their body, especially to the groin and armpits.

HIV & AIDS

In Thailand around 95% of HIV transmission occurs through sexual activity, and the remainder through natal transmission or illicit intravenous drug use. HIV/AIDS can also be spread through infected blood transfusions, although this risk is virtually nil in Thailand due to rigorous blood-screening procedures. If you want to be pierced or tattooed, be sure to check that the needles are new.

Water & Ice

Don't drink tap water, but do remember that all water served in restaurants or to guests in offices or homes in Bangkok comes from purified sources. It's not necessary to ask for bottled water in these places unless you prefer it. Ice is generally produced from purified water under

hygienic conditions and is therefore theoretically safe.

Internet Access

➡ There's no shortage of internet cafes in Bangkok competing to offer the cheapest and fastest connection. Rates vary depending on the concentration and affluence of net-heads – Banglamphu is cheaper than Sukhumvit or Silom, with rates as low as 15B per hour.

➡ Most internet shops have Skype and headsets so international calls can be made for the price of surfing the web.

➡ A convenient place to take care of your communication needs in the centre of Bangkok is the **TrueMove Shop** (Map p260; www.truemove.com; Soi 2, Siam Sq; ☉7am-10pm; ⒮Siam exit 4). It has high-speed internet computers equipped with Skype, sells phones and mobile subscriptions, and can also provide information on citywide wi-fi access for computers and phones.

➡ Wi-fi, mostly free of charge, is becoming more ubiquitous around Bangkok. For relatively authoritative lists of wi-fi hot spots in Bangkok, go to www.bkkpages.com (under 'Directory') or www.stickmanweekly.com/WiFi/BangkokFreeWirelessInternetWiFi.htm.

Legal Matters

➡ Thailand's police don't enjoy a squeaky clean reputation, but as a foreigner, and especially a tourist, you probably won't have much to do with them. While some expats will talk of being targeted for fines while driving, most anecdotal evidence suggests Thai police will usually go out of their way not to arrest a foreigner breaking minor laws.

➡ Most Thai police view drug-takers as a social scourge and

consequently see it as their duty to enforce the letter of the law; for others it's an opportunity to make untaxed income via bribes. Which direction they'll go often depends on drug quantities; small-time offenders are sometimes offered the chance to pay their way out of an arrest, while traffickers usually go to jail.

➡ Smoking is banned in all indoor spaces, including bars and pubs. The ban extends to open-air public spaces, which means lighting up outside a shopping centre, in particular, might earn you a polite request to butt out. If you throw your cigarette butt on the ground, however, you could then be hit with a hefty littering fine.

➡ If you are arrested for any offence, police will allow you to make a phone call to your embassy or consulate if you have one, or to a friend or relative. There's a whole set of legal codes governing the length of time and manner in which you can be detained before being charged or put on trial. Police have a lot of discretion and are more likely to bend these codes in your favour than the reverse. However, as with police worldwide, if you don't show respect you will only make matters worse, so keep a cool head.

Medical Services

More than Thailand's main health-care hub, Bangkok has become a major destination for medical tourism, with patients flying in for treatment from all over the world.

Hospitals

The following hospitals have English-speaking doctors.
BNH (Map p264;☏0 2686 2700; www.bnhhospital.com; 9 Th Convent; Ⓜ Si Lom exit 2, ⒮Sala Daeng exit 2)

Bangkok Christian Hospital (Map p264;☎0 2235 1000; www.bangkokchristian hospital.org; 124 Th Silom; Ⓜ️Si Lom exit 2, Ⓢ️Sala Daeng exit 1)

Bumrungrad International Hospital (Map p270; ☎0 2667 1000; www.bumrun-grad.com; 33 Soi 3, Th Sukhumvit; Ⓢ️Phloen Chit exit 3)

Samitivej Hospital (Map p270;☎0 2711 8000; www. samitivejhospitals.com; 133 Soi 49, Th Sukhumvit; Ⓢ️Phrom Phong exit 3 & taxi)

Dentists

Business is good in the teeth game, partly because so many fa·ràng are combining their holiday with a spot of cheap root canal or some 'personal outlook' care – a teeth-whitening treatment by any other name. Prices are a bargain compared with Western countries, and the quality of dentistry is generally good.

Bangkok Dental Spa (Map p270;☎0 2651 0807; www. bangkokdentalspa.com; 2nd fl, Methawattana Bldg, 27 Soi 19, Th Sukhumvit; ☺by appointment only; Ⓜ️Sukhumvit exit 3, ⓐAsok exit 1) This is not a typo. Combines oral hygiene with spa services (foot and body massage).

DC-One the Dental Clinic (Map p268;☎0 2240 2800; www.dc-one.com; 31 Th Yen Akat; ☺by appointment only; Ⓜ️Lumphini exit 2 & taxi) Reputation for excellent work and relatively high prices; popular with UN staff and diplomats.

Dental Hospital (Map p270; ☎0 2260 5000; www.dental-hospitalbangkok.com; 88/88 Soi 49, Th Sukhumvit; ☺9am-8pm Mon-Sat, to 4.30pm Sun; Ⓢ️Phrom Phong exit 3 & taxi) A private dental clinic with fluent English-speaking dentists.

Siam Family Dental

Clinic (Map p260;☎08 1987 7700; www.siamfamilydental. com; 209 Th Phayathai; ☺11am-8pm Mon-Fri, 10am-7pm Sat & Sun; Ⓢ️Siam exit 2) Teeth-whitening is big here.

Pharmacies

Pharmacies are plentiful, and in central areas most pharmacists will speak English. If you don't find what you need in a Boots, Watsons or local pharmacy, try one of the hospitals.

Money

The basic unit of Thai currency is the baht. There are 100 satang in one baht – though the only place you'll be able to spend them is in the ubiquitous 7-Elevens. Coins come in denominations of 25 satang, 50 satang, 1B, 2B, 5B and 10B. Paper currency comes in denominations of 20B (green), 50B (blue), 100B (red), 500B (purple) and 1000B (beige).

ATMs

You won't need a map to find an ATM in Bangkok – they're everywhere. Bank ATMs accept major international credit cards and many will also cough up cash (Thai baht only) if your card is affiliated with the Cirrus or Plus networks (typically for a fee of 150B). You can withdraw up to 20,000B per day from most ATMs.

Changing Money

Banks or legal money-changers offer the optimum foreign-exchange rates. When buying baht, US dollars and euros are the most readily accepted currencies, and travellers cheques receive better rates than cash. British pounds, Australian dollars, Singapore dollars and Hong Kong dollars are also widely accepted. As banks often charge commission and duty for

each travellers cheque cashed, you'll save on commissions if you use larger cheque denominations.

Credit Cards

Credit cards as well as debit cards can be used for purchases at many shops and pretty much any hotel or restaurant, though you'll probably have to pay cash for your pàt tai. The most commonly accepted cards are Visa and MasterCard, followed by Amex and JCB. To report a lost or stolen card, call the following numbers:

Amex (☎0 2273 5544)

MasterCard (☎001 800 11887 0663)

Visa (☎001 800 11 535 0660)

Tipping

Tipping is not a traditional part of Thai life and, except in big hotels and posh restaurants, tips are appreciated but not expected.

Opening Hours

Opening hours for businesses in this book are listed if they differ from the following.

Banks 9.30am to 3.30pm Monday to Friday; banks in shopping centres and tourist areas are often open longer hours (generally until 8pm), including weekends.

Bars & Nightclubs Bars 6pm to midnight (officially); bars close during elections and certain religious public holidays. Nightclubs 8pm to 2am. Closing times vary due to local enforcement of curfew laws.

Government Offices 8.30am to 4.30pm Monday to Friday. Often closed between noon and 1pm.

Restaurants Local Thai places all day from 10am to 8pm or 9pm; formal restaurants around 11am to 2pm and 6pm to 10pm.

Shops Local stores 10am to 6pm daily; department stores 10am to 10pm daily.

Post

Thailand has an efficient postal service, and both domestic and international rates are very reasonable.

Main Post Office (Map p266;☑0 2233 1050; Th Charoen Krung; ☉8am-8pm Mon-Fri, to 1pm Sat & Sun; ☻Tha Oriental) Near Soi 35.

Public Holidays

Government offices and banks close their doors on the following public holidays. For the precise dates of lunar holidays, see the Tourism Authority of Thailand (TAT) website www.tourismthai land.org/travel-information.

1 January New Year's Day

February (date varies) Makha Bucha Day, Buddhist holy day

6 April Chakri Day, commemorating the founder of the Chakri dynasty, Rama I

13–14 April Songkran Festival, traditional Thai new Year and water festival

1 May Labour Day

5 May Coronation Day, commemorating the 1946 coronation of HM the King and HM the Queen

May/June (date varies) Visakha Bucha, Buddhist holy day

July (date varies) Asanha Bucha, Buddhist holy day

12 August Queen's Birthday

23 October Chulalongkorn Day

October/November (date varies) Ork Phansaa, the end of Buddhist 'lent'

5 December King's Birthday

10 December Constitution Day

31 December New Year's Eve

Safe Travel

Bangkok is a safe city and incidents of violence against tourists are rare. That said, there is a repertoire of well-polished scams. But don't be spooked; commit the following to memory and you'll most likely enjoy a scam-free visit:

Gem scam We're begging you, if you aren't a gem trader, then don't buy unset stones in Thailand – period.

Closed today Ignore any 'friendly' local who tells you that an attraction is closed for a Buddhist holiday or for cleaning. These are set-ups for trips to a bogus gem sale.

Túk-túk rides for 10B Say goodbye to your day's itinerary if you climb aboard this ubiquitous scam. These alleged 'tours' bypass all the sights and instead cruise to all the fly-by-night gem and tailor shops that pay commissions.

Flat-fare taxi ride Flatly refuse any driver who quotes a flat fare (usually between 100B and 150B for in-town destinations), which will usually be three times more expensive than the reasonable meter rate. Walking beyond the tourist area will usually help in finding an honest driver. If the driver has 'forgotten' to put the meter on, just say, 'Meter, kha/khap'.

Friendly strangers Be wary of smartly dressed men who approach you asking where you're from and where you're going. Their opening gambit is usually followed with: 'Ah, my son/daughter is studying at university in (your city)' – they seem to have an encyclopaedic knowledge of major universities. As the tourist authorities here pointed out, this sort of behaviour is out of character for Thais and should be treated with suspicion.

Taxes & Refunds

➡ Thailand has a 7% value-added tax (VAT) on many goods and services. Midrange and top-end hotels and restaurants might also add a 10% service tax. When the two are combined this becomes the 17% king hit known as 'plus plus', or '++'.

➡ You can get a refund on VAT paid on shopping, though not on food or hotels, as you leave the country (p46).

Telephone

Domestic & International Calling

➡ Inside Thailand you must dial the area code no matter where you are. In effect, that means all numbers are nine digits; in Bangkok they begin with ☑02, then a seven-digit number. The only time you drop the initial ☑0 is when you're calling from outside Thailand. Calling the provinces will involve a three-digit code beginning with ☑0, then a six-digit number.

➡ To direct-dial an international number from a private phone, you can first dial ☑001, then the country code. However, you wouldn't do that, because ☑001 is the most expensive way to call internationally and numerous other prefixes give you cheaper rates. These include ☑007, ☑008 and ☑009, depending on which phone you're calling from. If you buy a local SIM card, which we recommend, the network provider will tell you which prefix to use; read the fine print.

USEFUL NUMBERS

Thailand country code ☑66

Bangkok city code ☑02

Mobile numbers ☑08

Operator-assisted international calls ☑100

Free local directory assistance call ☑1133

Internet Phone & Phonecards

➜ The cheapest way to call internationally is via the internet, and many internet cafes in Bangkok are set up for phone calls. Some have Skype loaded and (assuming there's a working headset) you can use that for just the regular per-hour internet fee.

➜ CAT offers the PhoneNet card, which comes in denominations of 200B, 300B, 500B and 1000B and allows you to call overseas via VoIP (Voice over Internet Protocol) for less than regular rates. You can call from any phone (landline, your mobile etc). Quality is good and rates represent excellent value; refills are available. Cards are available from any CAT office or online at www.thaitelephone. com, from which you get the necessary codes and numbers immediately. See www.thai telephone.com/EN/RateTable for rates.

Mobile Phones

➜ If you have a GSM phone you will probably be able to use it on roaming in Thailand. If you have endless cash, or you only want to send text messages, you might be happy to do that. Otherwise, think about buying a local SIM card.

➜ If your phone is locked, head down to MBK Center to get it unlocked or to shop for a new or cheap used phone (they start at less than 2000B).

➜ Buying a prepaid SIM is about as difficult as finding a 7-Eleven store. The market is supercompetitive and deals vary so check websites first, but expect to get a SIM for as little as 49B. More expensive SIMs might come with pre-loaded talk time; if not, recharge cards are sold at the same stores and range from 300B to 500B. Domestic per-

minute rates start at less than 50 satang. The network will have a promotional code (eg 🖉006 instead of 🖉001) for calling internationally, which affords big discounts on the standard international rates.

➜ The main networks:

AIS (1 2 Call) (www.ais. co.th/12call/th)

DTAC (www.dtac.co.th)

TrueMove (www.truemove. com)

Time

➜ Thailand is seven hours ahead of GMT/UTC. Thus, noon in Bangkok is 9pm the previous night in Los Angeles, midnight the same day in New York, 5am in London, 6am in Paris, 1pm in Perth and 3pm in Sydney. Times are an hour later in countries or regions that are on Daylight Saving Time (DST). Thailand does not use daylight saving.

➜ The official year in Thailand is reckoned from the Western calendar year 543 BC, the beginning of the Buddhist Era (BE), so that AD 2014 is 2557 BE, AD 2015 is 2558 BE etc. All dates in this book refer to the Western calendar.

Toilets

➜ If you don't want to pee against a tree like the túk-túk drivers, you can stop at any shopping centre, hotel or fast-food restaurant for facilities. Shopping centres typically charge 3B to 5B for a visit.

➜ In older buildings and wát you'll still find squat toilets, but in modern Bangkok expect to be greeted by a throne.

➜ Toilet paper is rarely provided, so carry an emergency stash. Even in places where sit-down toilets are installed,

the septic system may not be designed to take toilet paper. In such cases there will be a waste basket where you're supposed to place used toilet paper and feminine hygiene products. Many toilets also come with a small spray hose – Thailand's version of the bidet.

Tourist Information

Bangkok has two organisations that handle tourism matters: the Tourism Authority of Thailand (TAT) for countrywide information, and Bangkok Information Center for city-specific information. Also be aware that travel agents in the train station and near tourist centres co-opt 'T.A.T.' and 'Information' as part of their name to lure in commissions. These places are not officially sanctioned information services, but just agencies registered with the TAT. So how can you tell the difference? Apparently it's all in the full stops – 'T.A.T.' means agency; 'TAT' is official.

Bangkok Information Center (Map p252; 🖉0 2225 7612-4; www.bangkoktour ist.com; 17/1 Th Phra Athit; ⊙9am-7pm Mon-Fri, to 5pm Sat & Sun; 🚢Tha Phra Athit, Banglamphu) City-specific tourism office provides maps, brochures and directions. Kiosks and booths are found around town; look for the green-on-white symbol of a mahout on an elephant.

Tourism Authority of Thailand (TAT; 🖉1672; www. tourismthailand.org) Head office (Map p270; 🖉0 2250 5500; 1600 Th Phetchaburi Tat Mai; ⊙8.30am-4.30pm; Ⓜ Phet-chaburi exit 2); Banglamphu (Map p254; 🖉0 2283 1500; cnr Th Ratchadamnoen Nok & Th Chakrapatdipong; ⊙8.30am-4.30pm; 🚢Tha Phan Fah); Suvarnabhumi International

Airport (☏0 2134 0040t; 2nd fl, btwn Gates 2 & 5, Suvarnabhumi International Airport; ⊙24hr)

Travellers with Disabilities

➜ Bangkok presents one large, ongoing obstacle course for the mobility-impaired, with its high kerbs, uneven pavements and nonstop traffic. Many of the city's streets must be crossed via pedestrian bridges flanked with steep stairways, while buses and boats don't stop long enough to accommodate even the mildly disabled. Except for some BTS and MRT stations, ramps or other access points for wheelchairs are rare.

➜ A few of the top-end hotels make consistent design efforts to provide disabled access. Other deluxe hotels with high employee-to-guest ratios are usually good about providing staff help where building design fails. For the rest, you're pretty much left to your own resources.

➜ The following companies and websites might be useful:
Asia Pacific Development Centre on Disability (www.apcdfoundation.org)
Society for Accessible Travel & Hospitality (SATH; www.sath.org)
Wheelchair Holidays @ Thailand (www.wheelchair tours.com)

Visas

➜ Thailand's **Ministry of Foreign Affairs** (www.mfa.go.th) oversees immigration and visa issues. In the past five years there have been new rules nearly every year regarding visas and extensions; the best online monitor is **Thaivisa** (www.thaivisa.com).

➜ Citizens of 41 countries (including most European countries, Australia, New Zealand and the USA) can enter Thailand at no charge. These citizens are issued a 30-day visa if they arrive by air or 15 days by land.

Visa Extensions

➜ If you need more time in the country, apply for a 60-day tourist visa prior to arrival at a Thai embassy or consulate abroad. For business or study purposes, you can obtain 90-day nonimmigrant visas but you'll need extra documentation. Officially, on arrival you must prove you have sufficient funds for your stay and proof of onward travel, but visitors are rarely asked about this.

➜ If you overstay your visa the penalty is 500B per day, with a 20,000B limit; fines can be paid at any official exit point or at the **Bangkok Immigration Office** (☏0 2141 9889; Bldg B, Government Centre, Soi 7, Th Chaeng Watthana; ⊙8.30am-

noon & 1-4.30pm Mon-Fri; ⍟Mo Chit & access by taxi). Dress in your Sunday best when doing official business in Thailand and do all visa business yourself (don't hire a third party). For all types of visa extensions, bring along two passport-sized photos and one copy each of the photo and visa pages of your passport.

➜ You can extend your stay, for the normal fee of 1900B, at the immigration office. Those issued with a standard stay of 15 or 30 days can extend their stay for seven to 10 days (depending on the immigration office) if the extension is handled before the visa expires. The 60-day tourist visa can be extended by up to 30 days at the discretion of Thai immigration authorities.

Women Travellers

➜ Everyday incidents of sexual harassment are much less common in Thailand than in India, Indonesia or Malaysia, and this might lull women familiar with those countries into thinking that Thailand is safer than it is. If you're a woman travelling alone it's worth pairing up with other travellers when moving around at night or, at the least, avoiding quiet areas.

➜ Whether it's tampons or any other product for women, you'll have no trouble finding it in Bangkok.

Language

Thailand's, and therefore Bangkok's, official language is effectively the dialect spoken and written in central Thailand, which has successfully become the lingua franca of all Thai and non-Thai ethnic groups in the kingdom.

In Thai the meaning of a single syllable may be altered by means of different tones. In standard Thai there are five: low tone, mid tone, falling tone, high tone and rising tone. The range of all five tones is relative to each speaker's vocal range, so there is no fixed 'pitch' intrinsic to the language.

➡ **low tone** – 'Flat' like the mid tone, but pronounced at the relative bottom of one's vocal range. It is low, level and has no inflection, eg bàht (baht – the Thai currency).

➡ **mid tone** – Pronounced 'flat', at the relative middle of the speaker's vocal range, eg dee (good). No tone mark is used.

➡ **falling tone** – Starting high and falling sharply, this tone is similar to the change in pitch in English when you are emphasising a word, or calling someone's name from afar, eg mâi (no/not).

➡ **high tone** – Usually the most difficult for non-Thai speakers. It's pronounced near the relative top of the vocal range, as level as possible, eg máh (horse).

➡ **rising tone** – Starting low and gradually rising, sounds like the inflection used by English speakers to imply a question – 'Yes?', eg sǎhm (three).

WANT MORE?

For in-depth language information and handy phrases, check out Lonely Planet's *Thai Phrasebook*. You'll find it at **shop.lonelyplanet.com**, or you can buy Lonely Planet's iPhone phrasebooks at the Apple App Store.

The Thai government has instituted the Royal Thai General Transcription System (RTGS) as a standard method of writing Thai using the Roman alphabet. It's used in official documents, road signs and on maps. However, local variations crop up on signs, menus etc. Generally, names in this book follow the most common practice.

In our coloured pronunciation guides, the hyphens indicate syllable breaks within words, and some syllables are further divided with a dot to help you pronounce compound vowels, eg mêu·a·rai (when).

The vowel a is pronounced as in 'about', aa as the 'a' in 'bad', ah as the 'a' in 'father', ai as in 'aisle', air as in 'flair' (without the 'r'), eu as the 'er' in 'her' (without the 'r'), ew as in 'new' (with rounded lips), oh as the 'o' in 'toe', or as in 'torn' (without the 'r') and ow as in 'now'.

Most consonants correspond to their English counterparts. The exceptions are b (a hard 'p' sound, almost like a 'b', eg in 'hip-bag') đ (a hard 't' sound, like a sharp 'd', eg in 'mid-tone'); ng (as in 'singing'; in Thai it can occur at the start of a word) and r (as in 'run' but flapped; in everyday speech it's often pronounced like 'l'). If you read our coloured pronunciation guides as if they were English, you shouldn't have problems being understood.

BASICS

The social structure of Thai society demands different registers of speech depending on who you're talking to. To make things simple we've chosen the correct form of speech appropriate to the context of each phrase.

When being polite, the speaker ends his or her sentence with kráp (for men) or kâ (for women). It is the gender of the speaker that is being expressed here; it is also the common way to answer 'yes' to a question or show agreement.

In this chapter the masculine and feminine forms of phrases are indicated where relevant with 'm/f'.

Hello.	สวัสดี	sà-wàt-dee
Goodbye.	ลาก่อน	lah gòrn
Yes.	ใช่	châi
No.	ไม่	mâi
Please.	ขอ	kŏr
Thank you.	ขอบคุณ	kòrp kun
You're welcome.	ยินดี	yin dee
Excuse me.	ขออภัย	kŏr à-pai
Sorry.	ขอโทษ	kŏr tôht

How are you?
สบายดีไหม sà-bai dee măi

Fine. And you?
สบายดีครับ/ค่ะ sà-bai dee kráp/
แล้วคุณล่ะ kâ láa·ou kun lâ (m/f)

What's your name?
คุณชื่ออะไร kun chêu à-rai

My name is ...
ผม/ดิฉันชื่อ... pŏm/di-chăn chêu ... (m/f)

Do you speak English?
คุณพูดภาษา kun pôot pah-săh
อังกฤษได้ไหม ang-grìt dâi măi

I don't understand.
ผม/ดิฉันไม่เข้าใจ pŏm/di-chăn mâi kôw jai (m/f)

ACCOMMODATION

Where's a ...?	...อยู่ที่ไหน	...yoo tee năi
campsite	ค่ายพักแรม	kâi pák raam
guesthouse	บ้านพัก	bâhn pák
hotel	โรงแรม	rohng raam
youth hostel	บ้าน	bâhn
	เยาวชน	yow-wá-chon
Do you have	มีห้อง ...	mee hôrng ...
a ... room?	ไหม	măi
single	เดี่ยว	dèe·o
double	เตียงคู่	đee·ang kôo
twin	สองเตียง	sŏrng đee·ang

air-con	แอร์	aa
bathroom	ห้องน้ำ	hôrng nám
laundry	ห้องซักผ้า	hôrng sák pâh
mosquito net	มุ้ง	múng
window	หน้าต่าง	nâh đàhng

SIGNS

ทางเข้า	**Entrance**
ทางออก	**Exit**
เปิด	**Open**
ปิด	**Closed**
ห้าม	**Prohibited**
ห้องสุขา	**Toilets**
ชาย	**Men**
หญิง	**Women**

DIRECTIONS

Where's ...?
... อยู่ที่ไหน ... yòo têe năi

What's the address?
ที่อยู่คืออะไร têe yòo keu à-rai

Could you please write it down?
เขียนลงให้ได้ไหม kĕe·an long hâi dâi măi

Can you show me (on the map)?
ให้ดู (ในแผนที่) hâi doo (nai păan têe)
ได้ไหม dâi măi

Turn left/right.
เลี้ยวซ้าย/ขวา lée·o sái/kwăh

It's ...	อยู่ ...	yòo ...
behind	ที่หลัง	têe lăng
in front of	ตรงหน้า	đrong nâh
near	ใกล้ๆ	glâi glâi
next to	ข้างๆ	kâhng kâhng
straight ahead	ตรงไป	đrong bai

EATING & DRINKING

I'd like (the menu), please.
ขอ (รายการ kŏr (rai gahn
อาหาร) หน่อย ah-hăhn) nòy

What would you recommend?
คุณแนะนำอะไรบ้าง kun náa-nam à-rai bâhng

That was delicious!
อร่อยมาก à-ròy mâhk

Cheers!
ไชโย chai-yoh

Please bring the bill.
ขอบิลหน่อย kŏr bin nòy

I don't eat ...	ผม/ดิฉัน	pŏm/dì-chăn
	ไม่กิน ...	mâi gin ... (m/f)
eggs	ไข่	kài
fish	ปลา	ƀlah
red meat	เนื้อแดง	néu·a daang
nuts	ถั่ว	tòo·a

Key Words

bottle	ขวด	kòo·at
bowl	ชาม	chahm
breakfast	อาหารเช้า	ah-hăhn chów
cafe	ร้านกาแฟ	ráhn gah-faa
chopsticks	ไม้ตะเกียบ	mái đà-gèe·ap
cold	เย็น	yen
cup	ถ้วย	tôo·ay
dessert	ของหวาน	kŏrng wăhn
dinner	อาหารเย็น	ah-hăhn yen
drink list	รายการ	rai gahn
	เครื่องดื่ม	krêu·ang dèum
fork	ส้อม	sôrm
glass	แก้ว	gâa·ou
hot	ร้อน	rórn
knife	มีด	mêet
lunch	อาหาร	ah-hăhn
	กลางวัน	glahng wan
market	ตลาด	đà-làht
plate	จาน	jahn
restaurant	ร้านอาหาร	ráhn ah-hăhn
spicy	เผ็ด	pèt
spoon	ช้อน	chórn
vegetarian	คนกินเจ	kon gin jair
with/without	มี/ไม่มี	mee/mâi mee

Meat & Fish

beef	เนื้อ	néu·a
chicken	ไก่	gài
crab	ปู	ƀoo
duck	เป็ด	ƀèt
fish	ปลา	ƀlah
meat	เนื้อ	néu·a

pork	หมู	mŏo
seafood	อาหารทะเล	ah-hăhn tá-lair
squid	ปลาหมึก	ƀlah mèuk

Fruit & Vegetables

banana	กล้วย	glôo·ay
beans	ถั่ว	tòo·a
coconut	มะพร้าว	má-prów
eggplant	มะเขือ	má-kěu·a
fruit	ผลไม้	pŏn-lá-mái
guava	ฝรั่ง	fa-ràng
lime	มะนาว	má-now
mango	มะม่วง	má-môo·ang
mangosteen	มังคุด	mang-kút
mushrooms	เห็ด	hèt
nuts	ถั่ว	tòo·a
papaya	มะละกอ	má-lá-gor
potatoes	มันฝรั่ง	man fa-ràng
rambutan	เงาะ	ngó
tamarind	มะขาม	má-kăhm
tomatoes	มะเขือเทศ	má-kěu·a têt
vegetables	ผัก	pàk
watermelon	แตงโม	đaang moh

Other

chilli	พริก	prík
egg	ไข่	kài
fish sauce	น้ำปลา	nám ƀlah
noodles	เส้น	sên
oil	น้ำมัน	nám man
pepper	พริกไทย	prík tai
rice	ข้าว	kôw
salad	ผักสด	pàk sòt
salt	เกลือ	gleu·a

QUESTION WORDS

What?	อะไร	à-rai
When?	เมื่อไร	mêu·a-rai
Where?	ที่ไหน	têe năi
Who?	ใคร	krai

soup	น้ำซุป	nám súp
soy sauce	น้ำซีอิ๊ว	nám see-éw
sugar	น้ำตาล	nám đahn
tofu	เต้าหู้	đôw hôo

Drinks

beer	เบียร์	bee·a
coffee	กาแฟ	gah-faa
milk	นมจืด	nom jèut
orange juice	น้ำส้ม	nám sôm
soy milk	น้ำเต้าหู้	nám đôw hôo
sugar-cane juice	น้ำอ้อย	nám ôy
tea	ชา	chah
water	น้ำดื่ม	nám dèum

EMERGENCIES

| Help! | ช่วยด้วย | chôo·ay dôo·ay |
| Go away! | ไปให้พ้น | ไbai hâi pón |

Call a doctor!
เรียกหมอหน่อย　　rêe·ak mŏr nòy

Call the police!
เรียกตำรวจหน่อย　rêe·ak đam·ròo·at nòy

I'm ill.
ผม/ดิฉันป่วย　　pŏm/di·chăn ปbòo·ay (m/f)

I'm lost.
ผม/ดิฉัน　　　　pŏm/di·chăn
หลงทาง　　　　lŏng tahng (m/f)

Where are the toilets?
ห้องน้ำอยู่ที่ไหน　hôrng nám yòo têe năi

SHOPPING & SERVICES

I'd like to buy ...
อยากจะซื้อ ...　yàhk jà séu ...

How much is it?
เท่าไร　　　　　　tôw-rai

That's too expensive.
แพงไป　　　　　paang ไbai

Can you lower the price?
ลดราคาได้ไหม　　lót rah-kah dâi măi

There's a mistake in the bill.
บิลใบนี้ผิด　　　bin bai née pit ná
นะครับ/ค่ะ　　　kráp/kâ (m/f)

TIME & DATES

What time is it?
กี่โมงแล้ว　　gèe mohng láa·ou

morning	เช้า	chów
afternoon	บ่าย	bài
evening	เย็น	yen
yesterday	เมื่อวาน	mêu·a wahn
today	วันนี้	wan née
tomorrow	พรุ่งนี้	prûng née

Monday	วันจันทร์	wan jan
Tuesday	วันอังคาร	wan ang-kahn
Wednesday	วันพุธ	wan pút
Thursday	วันพฤหัสฯ	wan pá·réu·hàt
Friday	วันศุกร	wan sùk
Saturday	วันเสาร์	wan sŏw
Sunday	วันอาทิตย์	wan ah-tít

TRANSPORT

Public Transport

bicycle rickshaw	สามล้อ	săhm lór
boat	เรือ	reu·a
bus	รถเมล์	rót mair
car	รถเก๋ง	rót gĕng
motorcycle	มอร์เตอร์ไซค์	mor-đeu-sai
taxi	รับจ้าง	ráp jâhng
plane	เครื่องบิน	krêu·ang bin
train	รถไฟ	rót fai
túk-túk	ตุ๊ก ๆ	đúk đúk

When's	รถเมล์คัน ...	rót mair kan ...
the ... bus?	มาเมื่อไร	mah mêu·a rai
first	แรก	râak
last	สุดท้าย	sùt tái

A ... ticket,	ขอตั๋ว ...	kŏr đŏo·a ...
please.		
one-way	เที่ยวเดียว	têe·o dee·o
return	ไปกลับ	ไbai glàp

NUMBERS

1	หนึ่ง	nèung
2	สอง	sŏrng
3	สาม	săhm
4	สี่	sèe
5	ห้า	hâh
6	หก	hòk
7	เจ็ด	jèt
8	แปด	bàat
9	เก้า	gôw
10	สิบ	sìp
11	สิบเอ็ด	sìp-èt
20	ยี่สิบ	yêe-sìp
21	ยี่สิบเอ็ด	yêe-sìp-èt
30	สามสิบ	săhm-sìp
40	สี่สิบ	sèe-sìp
50	ห้าสิบ	hâh-sìp
60	หกสิบ	hòk-sìp
70	เจ็ดสิบ	jèt-sìp
80	แปดสิบ	bàat-sìp
90	เก้าสิบ	gôw-sìp
100	หนึ่งร้อย	nèung róy
1000	หนึ่งพัน	nèung pan
1,000,000	หนึ่งล้าน	nèung láhn

I'd like a/an ... seat.	ต้องการ ที่นั่ง ...	đôrng gahn têe nâng ...
aisle	ติดทางเดิน	đìt tahng deun
window	ติดหน้าต่าง	đìt nâh đàhng

| ticket window | ช่องขายตั๋ว | chôrng kǎi đǒo·a |
| timetable | ตารางเวลา | đah-rahng wair-lah |

What time does it get to (Chiang Mai)?

ถึง (เชียงใหม่)	tĕung (chee·ang mài)
กี่โมง	gèe mohng

Does it stop at (Saraburi)?

รถจอดที่ (สระบุรี) ไหม	rót jòrt têe (sà-rà-bù-ree) mǎi

I'd like to get off at (Saraburi).

ขอลงที่(สระบุรี)	kŏr long têe (sà-rà-bù-ree)

Driving & Cycling

I'd like to hire a/an ...	อยากจะ เช่า ...	yàhk jà chôw ...
4WD	รถโฟร์วีล	rót foh ween
car	รถเก๋ง	rót gěng
motorbike	รถ มอร์เตอร์ไซค์	rót mor-đeu-sai

I'd like ...	ต้องการ ...	đôrng gahn ...
my bicycle repaired	ซ่อมรถ จักรยาน	sôrm rót jàk-gà-yahn
to hire a bicycle	เช่ารถ จักรยาน	chôw rót jàk-gà-yahn

Is this the road to (Ban Bung Wai)?

ทางนี้ไป (บ้านบุ่งหวาย) ไหม	tahng née bai (bâhn bùng wǎi) mǎi

Where's a petrol station?

ปั๊มน้ำมันอยู่ที่ไหน	bâm nám man yòo têe nǎi

How long can I park here?

จอดที่นี้ได้นานเท่าไร	jòrt têe née dâi nahn tôw-rai

I need a mechanic.

ต้องการช่างรถ	đôrng gahn châhng rót

I have a flat tyre.

ยางแบน	yahng baan

I've run out of petrol.

หมดน้ำมัน	mòt nám man

Behind the Scenes

SEND US YOUR FEEDBACK

We love to hear from travellers – your comments keep us on our toes and help make our books better. Our well-travelled team reads every word on what you loved or loathed about this book. Although we cannot reply individually to your submissions, we always guarantee that your feedback goes straight to the appropriate authors, in time for the next edition. Each person who sends us information is thanked in the next edition – and the most useful submissions are rewarded with a selection of digital PDF chapters.

Visit **lonelyplanet.com/contact** to submit your updates and suggestions or to ask for help. Our award-winning website also features inspirational travel stories, news and discussions.

Note: We may edit, reproduce and incorporate your comments in Lonely Planet products such as guidebooks, websites and digital products, so let us know if you don't want your comments reproduced or your name acknowledged. For a copy of our privacy policy visit lonelyplanet.com/privacy.

OUR READERS

Many thanks to the travellers who used the last edition and wrote to us with helpful hints, useful advice and interesting anecdotes:

Maarten de Jong, Janine Kaestner, Debbie Liang, Philippe May, David Ochel, Lucia Piccioli, Gita Pitter, Anke Schneider, Edwin Schuurman, Anne-Marie Schuurman-Kleijberg

AUTHOR THANKS

Austin Bush

A huge shout out to LPers for life Ilaria Walker and Bruce Evans, super carto Diana Von Holdt and new LPer Sarah Reid, as well as to the kind folks on the ground in Bangkok.

ACKNOWLEDGMENTS

Illustrations pp60-1 and pp64-5 by Michael Weldon. Cover photograph: Wat Benchamabophit, Bangkok, Naxerdam/Getty Images.

THIS BOOK

This 11th edition of Lonely Planet's *Bangkok* guidebook was researched and written by Austin Bush, who also wrote the previous edition. The Bangkok Today chapter was written by Dr Thitinan Pongsudhirak, Director of the Institute of Security and International Studies, Chulalongkorn University. The Sex Industry in Thailand chapter was written by China Williams and repurposed by Austin Bush. This guidebook was commissioned in Lonely Planet's Melbourne office, and produced by the following:

Commissioning Editors
Glenn van der Knijff, Ilaria Walker

Destination Editor
Sarah Reid

Product Editor
Kate James

Assisting Editors Katie Connolly, Trent Holden, Kellie Langdon, Ali Lemer

Senior Cartographer
Diana Von Holdt

Assisting Cartographer
Alison Lyall

Book Designer
Wibowo Rusli

Language Content
Branislava Vladisavljevic

Cover researcher
Naomi Parker

Thanks to Imogen Bannister, Bruce Evans, Claire Naylor, Karyn Noble, Martine Power, Angela Tinson

See also separate subindexes for:

✕ EATING P245

🍷 DRINKING & NIGHTLIFE P246

☆ ENTERTAINMENT P247

🔒 SHOPPING P247

🏃 SPORTS & ACTIVITIES P248

🛏 SLEEPING P248

Index

Sights 000
Map Pages 000
Photo Pages 000

Bangkok Maps

Map Legend

Sights
- Beach
- Buddhist
- Castle
- Christian
- Hindu
- Islamic
- Jewish
- Monument
- Museum/Gallery
- Ruin
- Winery/Vineyard
- Zoo
- Other Sight

Eating
- Eating

Drinking & Nightlife
- Drinking & Nightlife
- Cafe

Entertainment
- Entertainment

Shopping
- Shopping

Sports & Activities
- Diving/Snorkelling
- Canoeing/Kayaking
- Skiing
- Surfing
- Swimming/Pool
- Walking
- Windsurfing
- Other Sports & Activities

Sleeping
- Sleeping
- Camping

Information
- Bank
- Embassy/Consulate
- Hospital/Medical
- Internet
- Police
- Post Office
- Telephone
- Toilet
- Tourist Information
- Other Information

Transport
- Airport
- Border Crossing
- Bus
- Cable Car/Funicular
- Cycling
- Ferry
- Monorail
- Parking
- S-Bahn
- Taxi
- Train/Railway
- Tram
- Tube Station
- U-Bahn
- Underground Train Station
- Other Transport

Routes
- Tollway
- Freeway
- Primary
- Secondary
- Tertiary
- Lane
- Unsealed Road
- Plaza/Mall
- Steps
- Tunnel
- Pedestrian Overpass
- Walking Tour
- Walking Tour Detour
- Path

Boundaries
- International
- State/Province
- Disputed
- Regional/Suburb
- Marine Park
- Cliff
- Wall

Geographic
- Hut/Shelter
- Lighthouse
- Lookout
- Mountain/Volcano
- Oasis
- Park
- Pass
- Picnic Area
- Waterfall

Hydrography
- River/Creek
- Intermittent River
- Swamp/Mangrove
- Reef
- Canal
- Water
- Dry/Salt/Intermittent Lake
- Glacier

Areas
- Beach/Desert
- Cemetery (Christian)
- Cemetery (Other)
- Park/Forest
- Sportsground
- Sight (Building)
- Top Sight (Building)

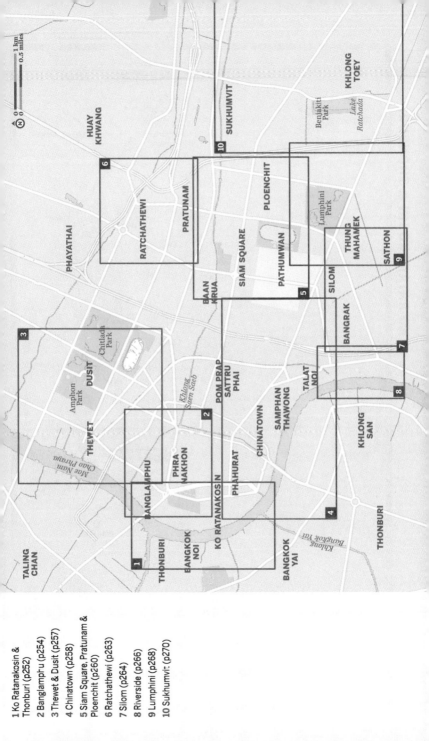

N

0 _____ 500 m
0 _____ 0.25 miles

A **B** **C** **D**

1

Tha Saphan
Phra Pin Klao

Th Phra Athit

Saphan Somdet
Phra Pin Klao

See map
p254

Bangkok
Noi

🏛 9

Khlong Bangkok Noi

Bangkok
Information
Center ℹ

Th Somdet Phra Pin Klao

BANGLAMPHU

🏛 Bangkok
Noi Train
Station

Th Ratchini

🏛 7

2

Siriraj
Hospital

14 🏛

Th Na Phra That

24 ⭐

8 🏛

Tha Wang
Lang (Siriraj) 🏛

Th Phrannok

Tha
Phra
Chan

15 ◉

3

Soi Sala
Ton Chan

4 ◉
26

Th Maha Rat

27

10
⊕

Sanam
Luang

Th Ratchadamnoen Nai

Khlong Lawt

Th Atsadang

Tha
Maharaj

19 ⊗

13 🏛

Tha Wat
Rakhang 🏛

Commuter
Long-tail Boat

⊗ 20

Th Na Phra Lan

ℹ 5

Th Lak Meuang

4

Tha Chang 🏛
18

🏛 16

12

Mae Nam Chao Phraya

Th Maha Rat

Th Sanam Chai

Th Ratchini

🏛 3
**Wat Phra Kaew
& Grand Palace**

KO RATANAKOSIN

5

Khlong Mon

Th Arun Amarin

Saranrom
Royal
Garden

11 🏛

Th Charoen Krung

See map
p258

Tha Thai Wang

2 25

Wat Pho

Tha Tien 🏛

22 ⊗

6

THONBURI

Th Arun Amarin

Tha Wat Arun 🏛

23
36
34

29
21
33
17
35

Soi Pratu
Nokyung

Soi Pen Phat

Soi Pansuk

🏛 6

30
28

Th Maha Rat

Th Ratchini

1 🏛
Wat Arun

31
32

7

Th Wang Doem

Khlong
Bangkok Yai

Th Saphan Phut

Th Saphan Phut

Tha Pak Talat
(Atsadang) 🏛

Khlong Lawt

KO RATANAKOSIN & THONBURI

Key on p256

BANGLAMPHU

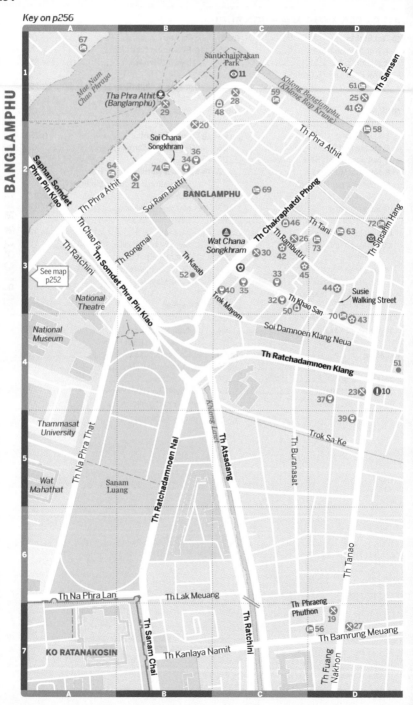

Santichaiprakan Park

Mae Nam Chao Phraya

Tha Phra Athit (Banglamphu)

Soi Chana Songkhram

BANGLAMPHU

Soi Ram Buttri

Saphan Somdet Phra Pin Klao

Th Phra Athit

Th Chao Fa

Th Rongmai

Th Somdet Phra Pin Klao

Th Ratchini

See map p252

National Theatre

National Museum

Wat Chana Songkhram

Th Kasab

Trok Mayom

Th Chakraphatdi Phong

Th Tani

Th Rambuttri

Th Sipsahm Hang

Th Khao San

Susie Walking Street

Soi Damnoen Klang Neua

Th Ratchadamnoen Klang

Thammasat University

Th Na Phra That

Sanam Luang

Wat Mahathat

Th Ratchadamnoen Nai

Khlong Lawt

Th Atsadang

Th Buranasat

Trok Sa-Ke

Th Tanao

Th Na Phra Lan

Th Lak Meuang

Th Phraeng Phuthon

Th Sanam Chai

Th Ratchini

Th Kanlaya Namit

KO RATANAKOSIN

Th Bamrung Meuang

Th Fuang Nakhon

Soi 1

Th Samsen

Khlong Banglamphu (Khlong Rop Krung)

Th Phra Athit

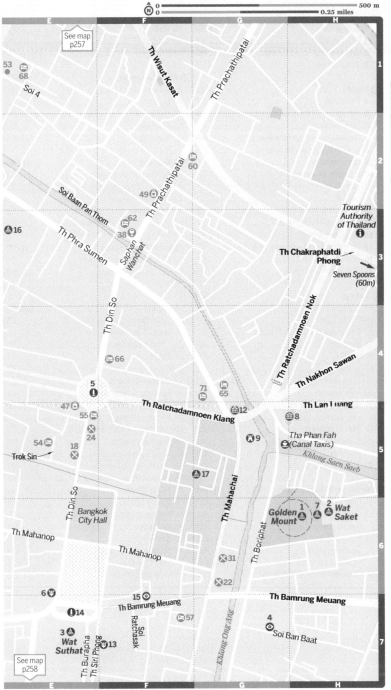

0 — 500 m
0 — 0.25 miles

See map p257

Th Wisut Kasat

Th Prachathipatai

53
68
Soi 4

60

Th Prachathipatai

49

Soi Baan Pan Thom

62
38

16

Th Phra Sumen

Saphan Wanchat

Tourism Authority of Thailand

Th Chakraphatdi Phong

Seven Spoons (60m)

Th Din So

Th Ratchadamnoen Nok

66

71
65

Th Ratchadamnoen Klang

Th Nakhon Sawan

5

47
55
24

Th Lan Luang

12

8

9

Tha Phan Fah (Canal Taxis)

Khlong Saen Saeb

54
18

Trok Sin

17

Th Mahachai

Golden Mount
1
7
2 **Wat Saket**

Bangkok City Hall

Th Din So

Th Mahanop

Th Mahanop

Th Boriphat

31

22

6

14

15

Th Bamrung Meuang

Th Bamrung Meuang

3 **Wat Suthat**

Th Burapha
Th Siri Phong
13

Th Ratchasak

57

Soi Ban Baat
4

Khlong Ong Ang

See map p258

BANGLAMPHU *Map on p254*

⊚ Top Sights	(p79)
1 Golden Mount	H6
2 Wat Saket	H6
3 Wat Suthat	E7

⊚ Sights	(p78)
4 Ban Baat	G7
5 Democracy Monument	E4
6 Dhevasathan	E6
7 Golden Mount & Wat Saket	H6
8 King Prajadhipok Museum	H5
9 Mahakan Fort	G5
10 October 14 Memorial	D4
11 Phra Sumen Fort & Santichaiprakan Park	C1
12 Queen's Gallery	G5
13 Saan Jao Phitsanu	F7
14 Sao Ching-Cha	E7
15 Th Bamrung Meuang Religious Shops	F7
16 Wat Bowonniwet	E3
17 Wat Ratchanatdaram	G5

⊗ Eating	(p81)
18 Arawy Vegetarian Food	E5
19 Chote Chitr	D7
20 Escapade Burgers & Shakes	B2
21 Hemlock	B2
22 Jay Fai	G6
23 Kimleng	D4
24 Krua Apsorn	E5
25 May Kaidee's	D1
26 Phen Thai Food	C3
27 Poj Spa Kar	D7
28 Roti-Mataba	C1
29 Sheepshank	B1
30 Shoshana	C3
31 Thip Samai	G6

⊙ Drinking & Nightlife	(p84)
32 Center Khao Sarn	C3
33 Club	C3
34 Gecko Bar	B2
35 Hippie de Bar	C3
36 Madame Musur	B2
Mulligans	(see 43)
37 Phra Nakorn Bar & Gallery	D4

38 Rolling Bar	F3
39 Taksura	D5
40 Triple-d	C3

⊛ Entertainment	(p86)
41 Ad Here the 13th	D1
42 Barlamphu	C3
43 Brick Bar	D4
44 Molly Bar	D3
45 Suk Sabai	C3

⊜ Shopping	(p86)
46 Nittaya Curry Shop	C3
47 RimKhobFah Bookstore	E5
48 Taekee Taekon	C1
49 Thai Nakon	F2
50 Thanon Khao San Market	C3

⊕ Sports & Activities	(p87)
51 Grasshopper Adventures	D4
52 Sor Vorapin Gym	B3
53 Velo Thailand	E1

⊜ Sleeping	(p180)
54 Baan Dinso	E5
55 Baan Dinso @ Ratchadamnoen	E5
56 Bhuthorn	D7
57 Chern	F7
58 Diamond House	D2
59 Fortville Guesthouse	C1
60 Hotel Dé Moc	G2
61 Khaosan Immjai	D1
62 Lamphu Treehouse	F3
63 NapPark Hostel	D3
64 New Siam Riverside	A2
65 Old Bangkok Inn	G4
66 Pannee Residence	F4
67 Praya Palazzo	A1
68 Rajata Hotel	E1
69 Rambuttri Village Inn	C2
70 Rikka Inn	D4
71 Sourire	G4
72 Suneta Hostel Khaosan	D3
73 Villa Cha-Cha	D3
74 Wild Orchid Villa	B2

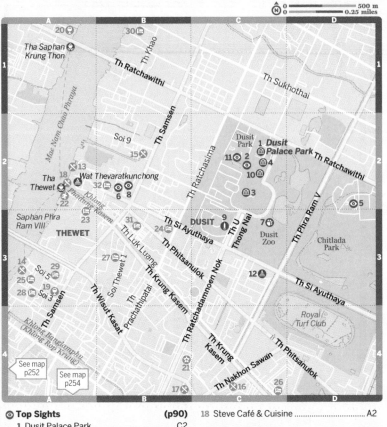

CHINATOWN

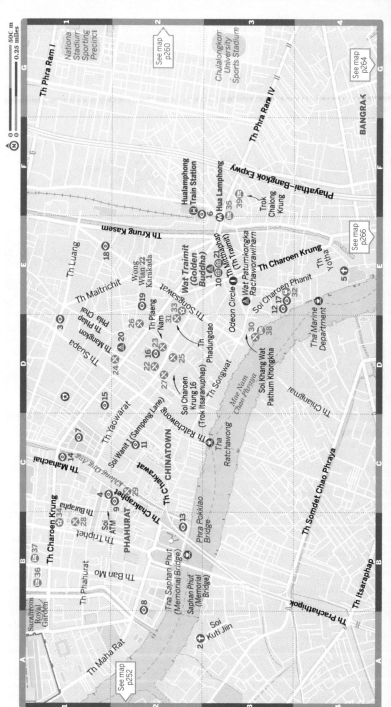

See map p260

See map p264

See map p266

See map p252

National Stadium Sporting Precinct

Chulalongkorn University Sports Stadium

BANGRAK

Th Phra Ram I

Th Phra Ram IV

Phayathai–Bangkok Expwy

Hualamphong Train Station

Hua Lamphong

Th Krung Kasem

Th Luang

Th Maitrichit

Wong Wian 22 Karakada

Wat Traimit (Golden Buddha)

Th Mithaphap

Th Songswat

Odeon Circle

Th Traimit

Wat Patumkongka Rachaworawiharn

Th Charoen Krung

Sol Charoen Phanit

Th Yotha

Th Phlap Phla Chai

Th Maikon

Th Plaeng Nam

Th Phadungdao

Th Suapa

Th Mangkon

Soi Charoen Krung 16 (Trok Itsaranuphap)

Th Songwat

Tha Marine Department

Th Chiangmai

Mae Nam Chao Phraya

Th Yaowarat

Soi Want 1 (Sampeng Lane)

Khlong Ong Ang

Th Ratchawong

Soi Khang Wat Pathum Khongkha

Th Chakkrawat

CHINATOWN

Tha Ratchawong

Th Somdet Chao Phraya

Th Chakraphet

PHAHURAT

Th Mahachai

Th Charoen Krung

Th Burapha

Soi ATM

Th Triphet

Th Ban Mo

Phra Pokklao Bridge

Tha Saphan Phut (Memorial Bridge)

Saphan Phut (Memorial Bridge)

Th Maha Rat

Saranrom Royal Garden

Th Phahurat

Soi Kuti Jiin

Th Prachathipok

Th Itsaraphap

Trok Chalong Krung

CHINATOWN

SIAM SQUARE, PRATUNAM & PLOENCHIT

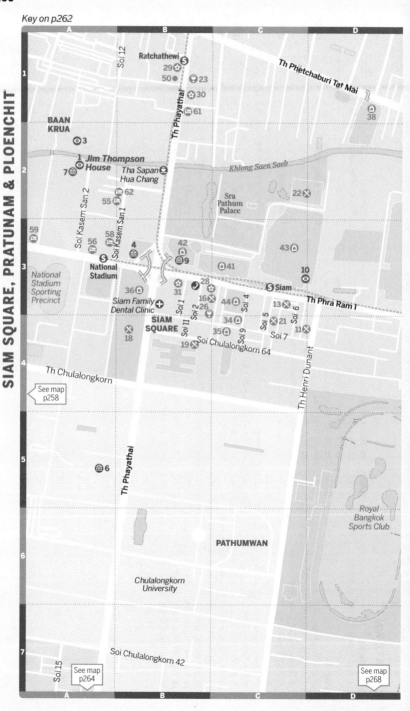

Soi 12

Ratchathewi Ⓢ
29
50 ●   🍴 23
🍴 30
🍴 61

1

Th Phayathai

**BAAN
KRUA**
◉ 3

1 🏛 **Jim Thompson
House**
7 🏛
Tha Sapan Ⓢ
Hua Chang

Khlong Saen Saeb

2

🏬 62
55 🏬

Sra
Pathum
Palace

22 ✕

59 🏬

56 🏬
58 🏬

Soi Kasem San 2
Soi Kasem San 1

4
🏛

42 ☆
🏛 9

41 🔒

43 🔒

10 ◉

3

**National
Stadium** Ⓢ

*National
Stadium
Sporting
Precinct*

36 🔒

Siam Family ✚
Dental Clinic

**SIAM
SQUARE**

31 ☆
28 ☆
16 ✕
26 🍴
44 ✕

Soi 4

Siam Ⓢ

Th Phra Ram I

13 ✕
21 ✕
11 ✕

Soi 1
Soi 2
Soi 11

34 ✕
35 🔒

Soi 9

Soi 5
Soi 7

Soi 6

18 ✕

19 ☆
Soi Chulalongkorn 64

Th Henri Dunant

4

Th Chulalongkorn

See map
p258

🏛 6

5

Th Phayathai

*Royal
Bangkok
Sports Club*

PATHUMWAN

6

*Chulalongkorn
University*

7

Soi 15

Soi Chulalongkorn 42

See map
p264

See map
p268

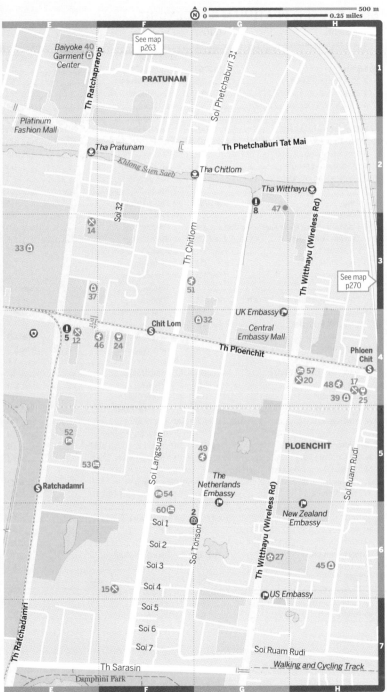

0   500 m
0   0.25 miles

See map p263

PRATUNAM

Soi Phetchaburi 31

Th Ratchaprarop

Platform Fashion Mall

Baiyoke 40
Garment Center

Tha Pratunam

Khlong Saen Saeb

Th Phetchaburi Tat Mai

Tha Chitlom

Tha Witthayu

8   47

33

Soi 32

Th Chitlom

Th Witthayu (Wireless Rd)

14

37

51

See map p270

5   12

46   24

Chit Lom

32

Th Ploenchit

UK Embassy

Central Embassy Mall

Phloen Chit

57
20

48   17
39   25

52

53

Ratchadamri

Soi Langsuan

49

PLOENCHIT

Soi Ruam Rudi

54

60
Soi 1

2

Soi Tonson

The Netherlands Embassy

New Zealand Embassy

Th Witthayu (Wireless Rd)

Soi 2

Soi 3

27

45

15

Soi 4

US Embassy

Th Ratchadamri

Soi 5

Soi 6

Soi 7

Th Sarasin

Lumphini Park

Soi Ruam Rudi

Walking and Cycling Track

SIAM SQUARE, PRATUNAM & PLOENCHIT Map on p260

RATCHATHEWI

0 — 380 m
0 — 0.2 miles

Minivans to Aranya Prathet (for Cambodian border) & Mae Klong (for Amphawa)

Minivans to Pak Chong & Khao Yai National Park

Minivans to Chanthaburi, Kanchanaburi, Phetchaburi & Suvarnabhumi International Airport

Minivans to Nakhon Pathom & Southern Bus Terminal

Victory Monument

Minivans to Ayuthaya & Ban Phe (for Ko Samet)

Th Ratchawithi

Th Ratchawithi

Th Din Daeng

Asoke - Ratchadapisek Expwy

Th Phayathai

Th Rang Nam

Th Ratchaprarop

RATCHATHEWI

Suan Pakkad Palace Museum

Phaya Thai

Th Si Ayuthaya

Soi Ratchataphan (Soi Mo Leng)

Sol 17

Ratchaprarop

Makkasan Train Station

Th Makkasan

PRATUNAM

See map p260

SILON

See map p268

See map p258

See map p266

500 m
0.25 miles

Lumphini Park

Th Phra Rarr. IV

Si Lom

Si Lom

Th Sala Daeng

Soi Sala Daeng

Th Sala Daeng

Irish Consulate

Th Thaniya

Soi 4

Th Convent

BNH

Th Sathon Nyua (North)

Soi 7 (Soi Phra Phinit)

Bangkok Christian Hospital

Th Silom

Soi Patpong 2

Soi Patpong 1

Soi Phiphat 2

Soi 3

Th Sathon Tai (South)

Th Narathiwat Ratchanakharin (Chong Nonsi)

Soi Than Tawan

Soi 5 (Soi Lalai Sap)

Soi 7

Chong Nonsi

Th Sathon Tai (South)

Soi 10

Soi 9 (Suksavithaya)

Th Sap

Th Surawong

Soi 12

Th Decho

Soi 16

Soi 18

Soi 13 (Trok Yaithi)

Th Pan

Th Naret

Th Silom

Myanmar Embassy

Soi 20 (Soi Pradit)

Th Pramuan

Soi 26

Soi 19

Th Mahesak

Th Surasak

St Louis
Hospital

Surasak
⦿ 41
🚇 50

Th Sathon Neua (North)

⦿ Sights (p120)
1 H Gallery	C4
2 Kathmandu Photo Gallery	C3
3 MR Kukrit Pramoj House	F4
4 Neilson Hays Library	C2
Number 1 Gallery	(see 6)
5 Sri Mariamman Temple	B3
6 Tang Gallery	A3
Thavibu Gallery	(see 6)

⊗ Eating (p124)
7 Bonita Cafe & Social Club	B4
8 Chennai Kitchen	B3
9 Daimasu	E1
10 D'Sens	G1
11 Eat Me	F3
FooDie	(see 47)
12 Indigo	F2
13 Jay So	F3
14 Kalapapruek	B4
15 Krua 'Aroy-Aroy'	B3
16 Le Du	D3
17 Mizu's Kitchen	E1
18 Ran Nam Tao Hu Yong Her	D3
19 Soi 10 Food Centres	D2
20 Somboon Seafood	D2
21 Somtam Convent	F2
22 Sushi Tsukiji	F1
23 Taling Pling	B3

⦿ Drinking & Nightlife (p128)
24 Balcony	F1
25 Barley	D2
26 Bearbie	F1
27 DJ Station	G1
28 G Bangkok	F1
29 Ku Dé Ta	E4
30 Maggie Choo's	A3
31 Tapas Room	F2
32 Telephone Pub	F1

⊕ Entertainment (p130)
33 Duangthawee Plaza	E1
34 Patpong	E1

⦿ Shopping (p130)
35 House of Chao	C2
36 Jim Thompson	F1
37 Jim Thompson Factory Outlet	D1
38 July	G2
Patpong Night Market	(see 34)
39 Soi Lalai Sap	E2
40 Tamnan Mingmuang	F1

⦿ Sports & Activities (p132)
41 Blue Elephant Thai Cooking School	G1
42 Health Land	A3
43 Ruen-Nuad Massage Studio	F3
44 Silom Thai Cooking School	C3

⦿ Sleeping (p186)
45 Bangkok Christian Guest House	F2
46 Café Ice Residence	E3
47 Glow Trinity Silom	E3
48 HQ Hostel	E2
49 Le Méridien Bangkok	E1
50 Littlest Guesthouse	B5
51 Lub*d	C2
52 LUXX	C2
53 Mile Map Hostel	B3
54 Rose Hotel	E1
55 Saphaipae	A3
56 Siam Heritage	E1
57 Silom Art Hostel	C3
58 Smile Society	E2
59 W Bangkok	E4

RIVERSIDE

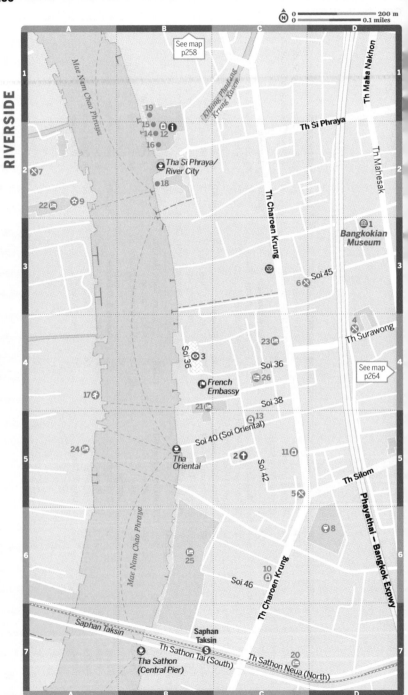

See map p258

See map p264

N 0 _____ 200 m
0 _____ 0.1 miles

Mae Nam Chao Phraya

Khlong Phadung Krung Kasem

Th Si Phraya

Th Maha Nakhon

Th Maha Nakhon

Th Mahesak

19
15 12
14
16

Tha Si Phraya/
River City

18

Th Charoen Krung

Bangkokian
Museum 1

6 Soi 45

22 9

7

4
Th Surawong

23

Soi 36 3

Soi 36

French
Embassy 26

Soi 38

17

21

13

Tha
Oriental 2

11

Soi 40 (Soi Oriental)

24

Soi 42

5

Th Silom

8

25

10

Soi 46

Th Charoen Krung

Phayathai – Bangkok Expwy

Mae Nam Chao Phraya

Saphan Taksin

Saphan
Taksin

Th Sathon Tai (South)

Tha Sathon
(Central Pier)

20

Th Sathon Neua (North)

RIVERSIDE

LUMPHINI

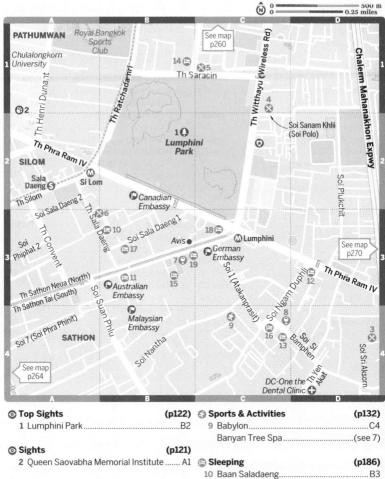

SUKHUMVIT *Map on p270*

SUKHUMVIT

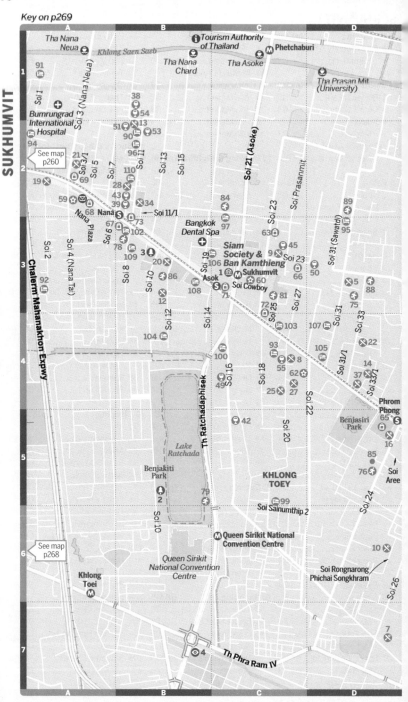

THE HALF HUNTER

John Sherwood

Anne Barrow was hauling her tightly-trousered form over Channel View's high window-sill when Jim Marsden first saw her. At seventeen, he reacted predictably. But when he slithered in after the pretty little housebreaker, his run-of-the-mill boy-meets-girl intentions ran into trouble. For green-eyed Anne no sooner filled Jim with a mixture of sympathy and suspicion than she vanished, leaving him to cope with angry parents, ice-skating beatniks, and an unsolved murder. The hunt was on; but which was Jim – the hunter or the hunted?

This witty thriller marks one of the most blissful débuts in the Penguin crime list for a long time.

'You will simply have to read it . . . . This is our answer to the American suspense school' – Maurice Richardson in the *Observer*

'I found it absolutely fresh and its youth and gaiety delightful. What an enormous difference a little genuine wit makes to a lighthearted tale' – Margery Allingham

NOT FOR SALE IN THE U.S.A.

RAYMOND CHANDLER

'He is not just one more detective writer – he is a craftsman so brilliant, he has an imagination so wholly original that no consideration of modern American literature ought, I think, to exclude him' – Elizabeth Bowen in the *Tatler*

The following books by Raymond Chandler are also available in Penguins:

THE BIG SLEEP

'A book to be read at a sitting' – *Sunday Times*

FAREWELL, MY LOVELY

'The dialogue crackles, the killer kills, the action covers a great deal of ground and hard knocks at terrific speed' – *Spectator*

THE HIGH WINDOW

'Very tough, very tense, enormously lively' – *Observer*

THE LADY IN THE LAKE

'It is most efficiently written: the story travels at exhilarating speed. It is a brilliant who-dun-it' – Desmond MacCarthy in the *Sunday Times*

THE LITTLE SISTER

'Raymond Chandler's powerful books should be read and judged, not as escape literature but as works of art' – W. H. Auden

THE LONG GOOD-BYE

'Chandler is the most brilliant author now writing this kind of story' – Somerset Maugham

PLAYBACK

His last great thriller 'carries the genuine Chandler label' – *Guardian*

For a complete list of books available please write to Penguin Books whose address can be found on the back of the title page

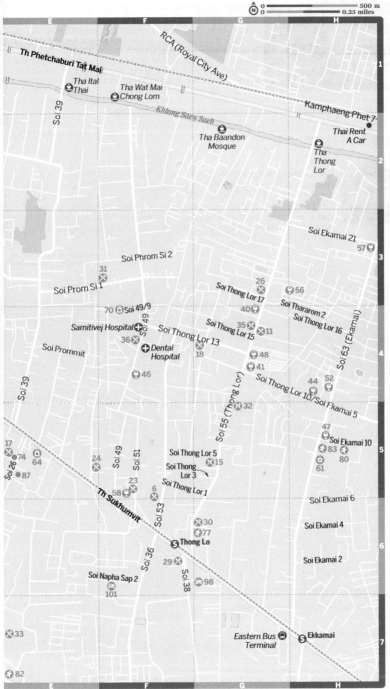

Our Story

A beat-up old car, a few dollars in the pocket and a sense of adventure. In 1972 that's all Tony and Maureen Wheeler needed for the trip of a lifetime – across Europe and Asia overland to Australia. It took several months, and at the end – broke but inspired – they sat at their kitchen table writing and stapling together their first travel guide, *Across Asia on the Cheap*. Within a week they'd sold 1500 copies. Lonely Planet was born.

Today, Lonely Planet has offices in Franklin, London, Melbourne, Oakland, Beijing and Delhi, with more than 600 staff and writers. We share Tony's belief that 'a great guidebook should do three things: inform, educate and amuse'.

Our Writer

Austin Bush

Coordinating Author Austin Bush came to Thailand in 1999 as part of a language study program hosted by Chiang Mai University. The lure of city life, employment and spicy food eventually led Austin to Bangkok. City life, employment and spicy food have managed to keep him there ever since. Austin is a native of Oregon, and a writer and photographer who often focuses on food; samples of his work can be seen at www.austinbushphotography.com.

Read more about Austin at:
lonelyplanet.com/members/austinbush

Published by Lonely Planet Publications Pty Ltd
ABN 36 005 607 983
11th edition – Sep 2014
ISBN 9781742208848
© Lonely Planet 2014   Photographs © as indicated 2014
10 9 8 7 6 5 4 3 2 1
Printed in China